BEYOND TOCQUEVILLE

Civil Society: Historical and Contemporary Perspectives

BRIAN O'CONNELL
Civil Society: The Underpinnings of American Democracy

PHILLIP H. ROUND
*By Nature and by Custom Cursed: Translatlantic Civil Discourse
and New England Cultural Production, 1620–1660*

BOB EDWARDS, MICHAEL W. FOLEY, AND MARIO DIANI, EDITORS
Beyond Tocqueville: Civil Society and the Social Capital Debate in Comparative Perspective

KEN THOMSON
From Neighborhood to Nation: The Democratic Foundations of Civil Society

BEYOND
TOCQUEVILLE

Civil Society and the Social Capital

Debate in Comparative Perspective

Edited by Bob Edwards,
Michael W. Foley, and Mario Diani

Tufts University

PUBLISHED BY UNIVERSITY PRESS OF NEW ENGLAND
HANOVER AND LONDON

Tufts University

Published by University Press of New England, Hanover, NH 03755

© 2001 by the Trustees of Tufts University

The chapters herein by Keith Whittington; Sheri Berman; John A. Booth and Patricia Bayer Richard; Kent Portney and Jeffrey M. Berry; Charles H. Heying; Lane Kenworthy; Dietlind Stolle and Thomas R. Rochon; Carla M. Eastis; Mark R. Warren; Debra C. Minkoff; Jackie Smith; Kenneth Newton; Andrew Greeley; James Youniss, Jeffrey A. McLellan, and Miranda Yates; and Richard L. Wood were previously published in Volume 42, Number 1 (1998), and Volume 40, Number 5 (1997), of the *American Behavioral Scientist*, entitled "Civil Society and Social Capital in Comparative Perspective" and "Social Capital, Civil Society and Contemporary Democracy," respectively. Copyright 1997, 1998 by Sage Publications, Inc. All rights reserved. They are republished here by permission of Sage Publications.

Full publication information appears on the opening page of each chapter.

LIBRARY OF CONGRESS CATALOGING-IN-PUBLICATION DATA

Beyond Tocqueville : civil society and the social capital debate in comparative perspective / edited by Bob Edwards, Michael W. Foley, Mario Diani.

   p.   cm. — (Civil society)

Includes bibliographical references.

   ISBN 1–58465–125–3 (pbk.)

   1. Civil society.   2. Social networks.   3. Social structure. I. Edwards, Bob, 1958–   II. Foley, Michael W.   III. Diani, Mario, 1957– IV. Series.

JC337.B48 2001

306—dc21   00–012463

Contents

Preface

BOB EDWARDS AND MICHAEL W. FOLEY

This volume addresses a set of questions that have emerged as a result of the provocative work of Robert Putnam on the sources of a vibrant civic life in contemporary democracies. While we have no illusions that we have provided conclusive answers to those questions, it is our hope that the volume will provide readers with both theoretical and empirical bases for evaluating current claims about the virtues of "civil society" and "social capital" in fostering civic engagement and healthy democracy. At the same time, we have attempted to structure the volume so that readers gain both a broad introduction to the terms of the contemporary debate and an understanding of the salient issues.

Our own efforts to come to terms with the contemporary debate about civil society grew out of some of the final meetings of a long-standing social-movements reading group in Washington, D.C., organized over the years by John McCarthy. An upcoming discussion of Robert Putnam's *Making Democracy Work* and "Bowling Alone" provoked a long discussion between Foley and Edwards on just what it was that was alternately appealing and dissatisfying about Robert Putnam's vision of the promise and plight of "civic community." We were particularly troubled by the neo-Tocquevillean elements of Putnam's argument, which placed so much weight on the socializing effects of traditional secondary associations.

Our dissatisfactions led to the first essay in our now six-year collaboration, "The Paradox of Civil Society," published in the *Journal of Democracy* in 1996. In it we began to develop a critique that was at that stage less focused on the emerging concept of "social capital" than on the uses to which many writers were putting the notion of "civil society." As we sought to widen the circle of our dialog by co-editing two issues of *American Behavioral Scientist*, our attention, like that of many researchers, turned more and more to the concept of social capital. In the hands of political scientists and economists inspired by Putnam's work, we thought, a rather promising concept was increasingly being used as little more than a new label for the old "political culture" variables of the public opinion survey tradition. At the same time, we could see little connection between the sort of microsociology embodied in the notion of social capital—however defined—and large-scale effects like economic growth or "vibrant democracy." Nor were we fully convinced that the sheer density of secondary associations in a society by itself had any predictable effect on political or economic outcomes. We sought contributors, accordingly, who could think critically about the theoretical claims of the emerging social capital literature and offer the results of empirical investigations into the role of associations of various sorts in contemporary societies. Most of the chapters published here are revised versions of articles previously published in the two volumes of *ABS* that emerged from that quest. Thanks to Sara Miller McCane, publisher of *ABS*, for permission to reprint those articles here.

As we continued to engage the ongoing debate, our thinking about what social capital actually was moved away from a more cultural interpretation toward a structural, networked conception distinct from "cultural capital." Given our mutual interest in social movements and an increasingly networked conceptualization of social capital, we joined forces with Mario Diani, who played a key role in recruiting the contributors from the U.K. and pushing our thinking with respect to social networks. We have drafted a new introduction, drawing on some of our earlier work, and adapted, with Mario's incisive editing and elaboration, an article originally published by Michael Foley and Bob Edwards in the *Journal of Public Policy* to serve as our conclusion. We thank Prof. Richard Rose, editor of that journal, for permission to reprint that article here.

How We Organized the Volume, and Might Have Done It Differently

When confronted with the task of organizing the range of material, we found we could group the chapters in a number of ways. We have organized them as attempts to grapple with four broad issues. The first part examines relations between civil society and the state, highlighting ways in which society organizes itself *independently of the state* or *over against the state*, but argues that states shape their societies as profoundly as the reverse. The second part takes up the political economy of civil society in order to begin to redress the scant attention paid to the impact of momentous economic changes that, potentially at least, profoundly affect citizens' attitudes toward their government and the larger society. The third part addresses relationships between associational membership and political attitudes and behaviors associated with participation in specific kinds of groups, with particular focus on the ways that explicitly political or contentious groups produce social capital. Finally, the last part turns to the broader, theoretical questions: What is social capital? What difference does it make? Each part begins with its own brief introduction.

We are confident that others reading this book, and especially those considering its use in university courses, will see other ways chapters could have been grouped and may well assign them to be read out of the sequence presented here. Chapters by Mario Diani, Debra Minkoff, Jackie Smith, Mark Warren, and Richard Wood could comprise a coherent section on *social movements*. Similarly, one could build a unit on *urban political economy, politics, and policy* with chapters by Heying, Maloney, Smith and Stoker, Portney and Berry, Warren, and Wood. Chapters by Whittington, Rose, and Booth and Richard all examine *emerging democracies*, as those by Greeley, Wood, Warren and Youniss, McLellan and Yates in complementary ways address the role of *religious associations*.

Acknowledgments

We have acquired many debts in the course of the work that led to this volume. The intellectual one owed to John McCarthy is perhaps the most subterranean of these and deserves mention. John's appreciation of the subtle, yet powerful, role meso-level patterns of social organization and uneven access to social infrastructures play in either facilitating or constraining citizen action inspired much of the thinking that has shaped this volume. To Jim Youniss, for encouraging our first proposal to *American Behavioral Scientist*; to Sara Miller McCune, *ABS*'s publisher, who took the project in hand on our first round; to Laura Lawrie, whose able editorial direction saw us through two volumes; to Ken Newton, for encouraging us to forge ahead with an edited volume based on the earlier collections. Mario Diani joined the project after extending a generous invitation to Bob Edwards to participate in a small conference on social capital at the University of Strathclyde. We owe a debt to the participants in that conference for their willingness to add their voices to the discussion captured here. Richard Rose deserves special thanks for his encouragement to publish Michael Foley and Bob Edwards's "final thoughts" on social capital in the *Journal of Public Policy* under his editorship. (A version of that article, expanded and edited by Mario Diani, appears as the conclusion to the present volume.) At different junctures along the way this research was supported by grants from the East Carolina University Faculty Senate, the Thomas W. Rivers Endowment, and the Sociology Department at East Carolina University for underwriting five years of related long-distance calling, postage, copying, overnight shipping, and travel. We also acknowledge the generous assistance of the Committee for Faculty Research Grant-in-Aid of The Catholic University of America for help in covering the costs of indexing.

We owe special thanks to our contributors, who were distinguished for their enthusiasm for the project in each of its stages, their patience under Bob's editorial scalpel, and the promptness with which they returned first one revised version, then another. Among our academic debts, finally, we would like to thank Robert Putnam for producing a body of work capable of provoking the kind of fruitful and relevant debate reflected in this volume and elsewhere since the early 1990s.

Civil Society and Social Capital

A Primer

BOB EDWARDS AND MICHAEL W. FOLEY

Recent debate about the role of civil society in democratic governance around the world and the "decline of social capital" in the United States has raised a variety of theoretical and empirical questions about the character of contemporary societies and the social and institutional bases for sound and dynamic democracies. This debate has reached a wide audience in North America and Europe not limited to academia. The predominant refrain in the debate, following Alexis de Tocqueville's 160-year-old analysis of democracy in America, attaches tremendous significance to the role of voluntary associations in society. Participation in such groups is said to produce social capital, sometimes linked to high levels of social trust. Social capital in turn is conceived as a crucial national resource for promoting collective action for the common good.

The concept of social capital has gained increasing popularity among political sociologists and political scientists since being introduced by Pierre Bourdieu and James Coleman in the 1980s.[1] Robert Putnam's work on Italy (1993a) and his provocative claim that social capital is somehow in decline in the United States (1995a, 1995b) stimulated a flurry of research and writing, including efforts to apply the notion of social capital in disciplines as disparate as criminology, epidemiology, and economics, not to mention sociology and political science. The World Bank has recently institutionalized the concept in its evaluation criteria by requiring social capital assessments for current and future projects. In the United States, major foundations like Ford and the Pew Charitable Trusts have implemented funding criteria related to social capital.

While the concepts of civil society and social capital have raised important questions about the dynamics of social life, the sources of citizen involvement in political life, and the role of trust in facilitating social action, both notions have proven difficult to define and apply in a coherent manner. At the same time, and as a result of their very success, these terms have been stretched conceptually, at the risk of hampering, rather than facilitating, our understanding of the social and political processes they were meant to illuminate. Without pretending to definitively resolve these concerns, this volume is intended to help clarify the issues at stake and illustrate the rich empirical work that has followed on the debate.

The Many Civil Societies

The notion of civil society owes its birth to the influential formulation of Scottish Enlightenment figure Adam Ferguson (1995). In Ferguson's usage, "civil society" represented the realm of "civilization" and rising standards of living based on specialization or the "division of labor." While a civil society thus offered all the advantages of modernity, it also risked social division, as the diverse interests of the individuals who made it up and their devotion to the pleasures and refinements of civilization threw into doubt their willingness to unite in common cause in defense of their liberties. As they became more "civilized," Ferguson worried, people were becoming less decidedly "citizens." The German philosopher G. W. F. Hegel (1945) took up these same questions, likewise seeking to reconcile the increasing division of labor and diversity of interests of modern society with the republican ideal of a unified citizenry. Civil society is thus juxtaposed to the state, but Hegel, at least, finds the solution to the problems posed by Ferguson in a modern and enlightened state. For the early-twentieth-century Italian Marxist Antonio Gramsci (1971), by contrast, the conflict at the heart of civil society provides the arena in which subordinate classes may contest the dominance of the ruling class crystallized in the state.

Consciously or unconsciously, twentieth-century variants of the notion of civil society take up this Gramscian understanding, utilizing the notion less as an analytical tool than as a polemical one and posing "civil society" as an alternative to the existing political and economic order. Whether as "society against the state" in the Polish and Latin American conceptions of the 1970s, or as a sphere of social autonomy and democratization from below among the German Greens and the French "Second Left"during the same era, the concept served to juxtapose a sphere of voluntary, purposive association to the forces of chaos, oppression, or atomization of the time. Competing concepts of civil society thus almost invariably bear the marks of the political struggles within which they were born. Considerable overlap in the sorts of social actors identified as central to "civil society" among these conceptions gives the notion an air of universality—suggesting that, if only we could come to agreement about just who and what is included under its umbrella, we could achieve a comprehensive theory of state-society relations. Yet, the real purchase of the notion of civil society today is polemical and normative and tied closely to the debates that currently shape it.[2]

In each of the cases mentioned above, "civil society" crystallized projects of social autonomy over against the dominant power(s) of that time and place. In the Poland of the 1970s, civil society was more a wish than a reality until the explosive growth of the Solidarity movement in 1980–81. Prior to Solidarity's emergence, the context of political opportunities in Eastern Europe under the Brezhnev Doctrine constrained the possibilities for action and convinced thinkers like Adam Michnik and Vaclav Havel that only by carving out spheres of authentic and autonomous action in "civil society" could dissidents construct a third way between reform of the Communist regime from above and open revolt from below. After 1981, events in Poland outstripped theory, and what started as simply an assertion of social autonomy in the face of Communist power quickly became a highly charged and dangerous (if ultimately successful) political movement (Pelczynski 1988). Latin American conceptualizations reflected both the struggle against the military dictatorships of the 1970s and 1980s and a widespread conviction that conventional party politics had failed these societies. Latin American activists and thinkers thus framed civil society not only as "society against a repressive state" but as society in place of the parties (Garreton 1989; Fals Borda 1992). The leftist orientation of many antigovernment activists led to an identification of civil society with the so-called "popular sector"—including a wide variety of lower-class and leftist groupings under this umbrella, but generally excluding even those sectors of the business and professional classes that eventually joined in the opposition.

In Western Europe during the 1970s and 1980s, proponents of civil society developed their thinking against the backdrop of the neocorporatist arrangements that had incorporated organized labor and business into institutionalized patterns of governance, but afforded little access for other constituencies. Civil society was conceptualized in opposition to the status quo of this neocorporatist political settlement. By establishing "action spaces" within civil society in which to create new social and cultural organizations and institutions, representatives of environmentalist, feminist, and peace movements (among others) sought to embody alternative ways of achieving collective goods and a conceptualization of democracy that was at least implicitly critical of traditional forms of representation (Melucci 1989; Dalton and Keuchler 1990; Edwards 1995, ch. 2). Similar notions, without explicit appeal to the term "civil society," made inroads in the United States beginning with the "new left" of the 1960s (Brienes 1982) and continuing with advocates of local citizen organizing (Boyte

1980). They were subsequently applied more generally to an array of historical and contemporary social movements (Evans and Boyte 1986).

Explicit usages of the term "civil society" in the U.S. context often appeared to have been imported, each school of thought tending to emphasize those aspects of the concept that best suited its particular ideological or theoretical purposes.[3] The apparent crisis of the "welfare state" in the 1970s contributed to a search for a new paradigm in the United States, as elsewhere, but the initial results were neoliberal remedies based on slapdash deregulation and the confidence that open, market economies would eventually "lift all boats."[4] Academic and think tank economists, central banks and international lending institutions led by the World Bank and the International Monetary Fund, and U.S. government agencies from the Reagan through the Clinton administration promoted economic liberalization and the unfettered play of market forces as the most efficient means of providing public goods. The uneasy fit between these prescriptions and the notion of civil society, with its implicit critique of purely market-driven approaches, is evident in the World Bank's tardy attempt to incorporate the organizations of civil society into discussions of economic restructuring and state reform in the developing world. And what the Bank meant by civil society was, more often than not, the new professionalized service and advocacy groups (NGOs) rather than unions, community organizations, or the traditional nonprofit sector. The eventual emergence of the term *civil society* in the United States, similarly, seemed often to reflect a belated effort to appropriate the energies of groups deemed both "civic-minded" and capable of replacing governmental efforts with private charity—not those likely to demand that government do more of what it had once promised to do and do it better.

As an analytical concept, the contemporary notion of civil society and the sectoral models to which it is attached thus suffer from acute definitional fuzziness. At least two related factors underlie this lack of clarity. First and most important, the definitional confusion stems from variations across the many civil societies that have been the implicit empirical basis for the varying conceptualizations of the term thanks to its origins in specific polemical and normative contexts. At the same time, paradoxically, the notion's precision suffers from the sheer historical and even transnational sweep of its application and the consequent temptation, despite the variation referred to above, to treat civil society and the "sectors" ("state" and "market") to which it is juxtaposed as ideal types (Foley and Edwards 1996; Edwards and Foley 1998).

Despite this lack of clarity, the notion of civil society has the merit of calling attention to neglected dimensions of modern societies. While conceived largely in response to the perceived failures of the twentieth-century state, the rediscovery of civil society—whether in the United

States or abroad, by the left or the right—also springs from a rejection of the dominant economism of modern social thought. In this respect, every variant of the civil society argument critiques the ways that predominant economic models, whether Marxist or neoclassical, unduly limit the kinds of social organization that "count" to those that fit clearly within either "the market" or "the state." By directing analytical attention toward forms of social organizations, collective actors, and forms of action excluded by prevailing economistic perspectives, such efforts have considerable heuristic value. However, when pushed too far, all such sectoral models lead quickly into efforts to specify the definitional boundaries between sectors, and to debates over which groups fit what sector and to what extent. Such efforts yield largely descriptive accounts or appeal to arbitrary classification schemes and come at the expense of empirical inquiry into how the related social processes actually work.

Given the diversity of perspectives and conceptions associated with the notion of civil society, it would be difficult to claim that the concept represents a distinctive "paradigm" for social scientific inquiry. The polemical and normative turn of many of these conceptions, moreover, means that often we are dealing more with what Seligman calls an "ethically obtainable ideal" of civil society (1992:26) than with an analytical concept capable of guiding empirical inquiry by grounding a coherent body of testable hypotheses. The best-known version of these conceptions in the U.S. setting, for instance, that of neo-Tocquevilleans like Robert Putnam, and the one most apparent in the essays that follow, is notably silent on some of the key attributes of civil society under other conceptions. Nevertheless, it is important to situate that understanding in the larger tradition, if only to provoke consideration of alternative conceptualizations more capable of addressing the evident lacunae in contemporary American accounts. The essays that make up this volume take up various of the claims of the civil society argument, particularly those tied to the concept of "social capital."

"Civil society" plays three broad roles in these various accounts. Foremost in recent debate is the neo-Tocquevillean emphasis on its *socialization* function: the associations of civil society are thought to play a major role, if not *the* major role, in building citizenship skills and attitudes crucial for motivating citizens to use these skills.

Many proponents would add, however, that civil society carries out a wide variety of *public and quasi-public functions*. The associations of civil society aid efforts or directly act to heal the sick, counsel the afflicted, support the penniless, educate both young and old, foster and disseminate culture, and generally provide many of the necessities and adornments of a modern society. It does this best, some argue, when left to itself; but others insist that it could not or would not do it as well or as extensively without the encouragement and support of government. The wide literature on the "third sector" or "voluntary sector" focuses on precisely those organizations that tend to take on such quasi-public functions (see, for example, Salamon 1995; Van Til 1988; Wuthnow 1991).

A distinctive tradition, more in tune with the European and Latin American uses of the notion of civil society, stresses the *representative or contestatory functions* of social organizations outside the state. Civil society gives identity and voice to the distinct interests and diverse points of view characteristic of a modern society; it stimulates public debate and presses government for action on a thousand and one matters of public interest. Because of the special circumstances in which the notion of civil society emerged for Eastern European and Latin American writers, many of these stress the oppositional character of this role, seeing in civil society a bulwark against the state wherever state purposes seem to threaten the plurality and autonomy that civil society is thought to enshrine.

Those approaches which lay stress on the public and quasi-public functions that civil society plays often take for granted its ability to produce "civic engagement" and public-spiritedness. Others, including many of the neo-Tocquevilleans, recognizing the conflictive and divisive tendencies of certain sorts of groups, privilege only those groups thought to produce such virtuous attitudes and behavior. But, more important, and whether from the left or the right, proponents of a vigorous civil society point to the ability of civil society to realize public ends independently of state power and direction. Whether the emphasis is on "the voluntary spirit" or "social autonomy," the idea is that private initiative and organization enjoy certain advantages over state action and can obviate some of the worst abuses and failures of state power. The implicit criticism of prevailing representative institutions is rarely articulated. At the same time, there is considerable disagreement over the role of private enterprise in such activities. While the European left sees civil society as every bit as much an antidote to corporate power as to the overreaching state of the twentieth century, American conservatives propose to stimulate the privatization of public functions and the active engagement of business within civil society. Liberal voices (and most of the empirical research) emphasize the continuing role of the state in stimulating, supporting, and funding private initiatives.[5]

Neo-Tocquevillean liberals and conservative proponents of civil society tend to ignore or actively exclude from consideration those sorts of organizations and activities that are associated with advocacy and political action, considering them divisive or simply beside the point. Both the oppositionist conception of civil society developed in Eastern Europe and Latin America and the European-inspired conceptions associated with the "new pluralism" (Keane 1988a, 1988b), on the other hand, put particular stress on the representative, contestatory, or political function of civil society. Civil society organizes itself not just to perform vital public functions independently of the state (and corporate power) but to defend social autonomy and promote policy change and, in the extreme, regime change. In this view, whether a politicized civil society is considered a substitute for the party system or a complement to it, it is charged with giving expression to societal identities and representing societies' interests and points of view. Again, there is considerable difference between those conceptions which imagine civil society united against the state and those which stress the irreducible pluralism of modern civil societies; but both approaches endorse a politically activated, even combative, civil society. Political activity, moreover, is here conceived of as group action more than individual level electoral participation or civic engagement, and there is consequently no necessary bias against socially homogenous groups based on class, occupational, ethnic, religious, or other social distinctions, as there is in the neo-Tocquevillean and conservative versions.

Robert Putnam's original formulation, in *Making Democracy Work*, identified a strong civil society with high levels of civic engagement, suggesting a correspondence between structural features of society—the density of face-to-face associations cutting across social cleavages more than anything else—and a certain kind of political or civic culture (1993a). This approach, which clearly reflects a view of associations as primarily socializing agents, has been particularly attractive to writers in the civic republican tradition, who argue that the health of democracy depends crucially on certain moral commitments among the citizenry and that these have their roots in traditions of community-mindedness and public-spiritedness that are endangered in an individualist and consumerist culture.

This "civic culture" argument has deep roots in American political science. "Generalized social trust" (trust in people in general), trust in government and public officials, tolerance, and optimism are all seen, in many versions of the argument, as integral components of social capital linked directly to its beneficial impact on participation and on civic engagement and democracy in general (Brehm and Rahn 1997; Muller and Seligson 1994; Stolle and Rochon, this volume). This list of ingredients, however, along with a common preference for broadly "inclusive" groups, stems from the empirical democratic theory of the 1950s, whose explicit fear was that an effervescent and contentious civil society would undermine democracy in the face of the "threat of Communism." The theory of the "civic culture" epitomized by Gabriel Almond and Sidney Verba's five-nation comparative study of the same name (1963) argued that the participatory impulse had to be tempered by a large dose of what Almond and Verba called "subject orientation," that is, a willingness to be led and to abide by the decisions of the authorities. Bred of the Cold War and a

profound mistrust of popular mobilization outside the most narrow channels of then conventional political behavior, the theory highlighted virtues
such as generalized social trust and trust in government as key ingredients
in "stable democracies," with the emphasis decidedly on stability. While
Putnam's work betrays elements of this older approach, he has been more
inclined to argue that associational life ("a vigorous civil society," in contemporary parlance) itself has a significant impact on political culture, and
thus on civic engagement, via its impact on social capital and not the other
way around.

Theories of Social Capital

Three relatively distinct tributaries of social capital theorizing are evident
in recent literature (Wall, Ferrazzi, and Schryer 1998). That associated
with the work of Pierre Bourdieu (1986) stresses unequal access to resources via the possession of more or less durable relationships. Where
Bourdieu builds his notion of social capital on essentially Durkheimian
microfoundations, James Coleman (1988, 1993) incorporates a similar
understanding of social capital into a theory grounded in rational choice
theory. Where Bourdieu's macrosociology owes its greatest debt to Marx,
Coleman remains within the functionalist tradition of Durkheim and Par-
sons. Work by political scientists and others following the lead of Robert
Putnam (1993, 1995a, 1995b, 1996), finally, presents a vision of social capital more congruent with the Weberian assumptions of the political culture
argument in American political science, in which exogenously generated
attitudes and norms such as trust and reciprocity stand alongside social
networks as ingredients enabling a society to undertake collective action.[6]
Bourdieu and Coleman's conceptions of social capital take the analogy with
financial capital seriously, seeing it as instrumental in the flow of goods and
services to individuals and groups. Putnam, by contrast, has popularized a
notion of social capital that ties it to the production of collective goods
such as civic engagement or a spirit of cooperation available to a community or nation at large.

Bourdieu defines social capital as "the aggregate of the actual or potential resources which are linked to possession of a durable network of more
or less institutionalized relationships of mutual acquaintance and recognition—or in other words, to membership in a group—which provides each
of its members with the backing of the collectivity-owned capital, a
'credential' which entitles them to credit, in the various senses of the word"
(1986:248–49). For Bourdieu, social capital is one of three forms of capital
(economic, cultural, and social) that taken together, "explain the structure
and dynamics of differentiated societies" (Bourdieu and Wacquant

1992:119). Differential access to capital, not merely an individual's pursuit of self-interest, shapes both economic and social worlds in Bourdieu's sociology. Similarly, the fundamental structures that produce and reproduce access to social capital are not, for Bourdieu, self-regulating markets but networks of connections, which themselves are "the product of an endless effort at institution." Bourdieu's emphasis on "institution rites," "the alchemy of consecration" and gift-giving at the heart of the transformation of "contingent relations, such as those of neighborhood, the workplace, or even kinship, into relationships that are at once necessary and elective, implying durable obligations subjectively felt" (Bourdieu 1986:249–50), underlines the Durkheimian roots of this conception.

If the mechanisms for the construction of social capital in Bourdieu's account may appear elusive to some readers, his understanding of how we might measure and weigh social capital has a clarity and coherence not found in Coleman and Putnam. For Bourdieu, "the volume of the social capital possessed by a given agent . . . depends on the size of the network of connections he can effectively mobilize and on the volume of the capital (economic, cultural or symbolic) possessed in his own right by each of those to whom he is connected" (249).

Perhaps the most influential formulation of the concept of social capital, nevertheless, is that of sociologist James Coleman. Coleman defines social capital as "a variety of entities having two characteristics in common: They all consist of some aspect of a social structure, and they facilitate certain actions of individuals who are within the structure. . . . Unlike other forms of capital, social capital inheres in the structure of relations between persons and among persons. It is lodged neither in individuals nor in physical implements of production" (Coleman 1990:302). The forms of social capital identified in Coleman's most extended treatment of the subject include "obligations and expectations," "information potential," "norms and effective sanctions" (grouped together because, as Coleman notes, norms are a "powerful, but sometimes fragile, form of social capital"), "authority relations," "appropriable social organization," and "intentional organization"—understood as "direct investment in social capital" (Coleman 1990:306–13).

Coleman has been criticized by some commentators for the relative incoherence of this laundry list (Portes 1998). The relationships that Coleman draws attention to, moreover, are conceived of in instrumental terms, as elements in the rational calculations of self-interested agents, and not, as in Bourdieu, as constitutive of individual identities and strategies. As Charles Tilly remarks, "Coleman feinted repeatedly toward relational accounts of norms, commitments, and similar phenomena but pulled his punches as they approached the target. Although his verbal accounts mentioned many agents, monitors, and authorities who influenced individual actions, his mathematical formulations tellingly portrayed a single actor's computations rather than interactions among persons" (1998:19).

Nevertheless, like Bourdieu, Coleman highlights the sense in which concrete social relationships can give individuals access to crucial resources not otherwise available despite ample endowments of human or financial capital. He underlines the limited fungibility of social capital: "a given form of social capital that is valuable in facilitating certain actions may be useless or even harmful for others" (1990:302). Moreover, he insists that social capital is embedded in relations, not borne by individuals wherever they might go. Finally, he insists that such subjective attributes as trust, expectations, and norms are endogenous to specific social relations. Indeed, the "trust" that figures prominently in Coleman's account is not the "generalized social trust" of the political science literature, but a feature of the specific context in which specified individuals or classes of individuals can be trusted. Thus, social capital is conceived as "social-structural resources" available only in and through relationships and social structures.

Robert Putnam's initial interpretation, in *Making Democracy Work* (1993a) and "Bowling Alone" (1995a), gave a distinctively Weberian and Tocquevillean reading, consonant with a long tradition in American political science, to Coleman's concept. Putnam defined social capital as "features of social life—networks, norms, and trust—that enable participants to act together more effectively to pursue shared objectives" (1995a:664–65). For Putnam, associations, particularly those featuring face-to-face, horizontal relations among individuals, generate trust, norms of reciprocity, and a capacity for civic engagement, which are essential to the functioning of a modern democracy. In the absence of a strong associational life, citizens would lack the skills and inclinations necessary to work together on economic and political projects. Neither informal networks nor large, national-level membership groups could substitute for the powerful effects thought to emanate from the face-to-face associations characteristic, Putnam argued, of vibrant democracies (Putnam 1993a, 1995a). A handful of aggregate indicators, readily available in existing survey data sets, thus come to stand in for Coleman's (and Bourdieu's) context-specific notion of social capital: "generalized social trust," membership in organizations, and norms such as reciprocity, cooperation, and tolerance.

Putnam's argument has been attacked for neglecting the "dark" side of social capital (Portes and Landolt 1996), avoiding politics and political structure (Foley and Edwards 1996, 1997; Tarrow 1996) and underemphasizing the role of large-scale economic changes in undermining civic engagement in the United States and elsewhere (Skocpol 1996a). At the same time, his conceptual framework has been criticized for incoherence, in particular for failing to specify under what conditions face-to-face interaction can be thought to generate the desirable civic traits of the argument (Foley and Edwards 1998; Edwards and Foley 1998). Jackman and Miller's careful reanalysis of Putnam's Italian data, moreover, undermines the notion that a coherent "civic culture" can be discerned behind the differences in performance Putnam found among Italy's regional governments (1996a).

Despite these criticisms, and despite Putnam's own turn to a more social structural notion of social capital, Putnam's initial formulation was tremendously influential in the spate of empirical work that appeared in the wake of "Bowling Alone." This work, particularly among political scientists and economists, focuses on the relationships among associations, trust, and other attitudes and norms, on the one hand, and between one or more of these variables and social, economic, and political outcomes, on the other. At the same time, network analysts in particular, and sociologists and applied social scientists more generally, have adopted versions of the social capital concept more in keeping with the social structural versions enunciated by Coleman and Bourdieu, in that they emphasize the role of individual and organizational social ties in predicting individual advancement or collective action.

Social Capital in Recent Empirical Research

Analysts of education have been examining the connections between social capital and schooling (for example, Teachman, Paash, and Carver 1996, 1997) ever since sociologist James Coleman introduced the concept to American readers as a way to capture variations in family-school-community relations thought to affect school performance and individual academic achievement (Coleman 1988, 1994). Recently, the concept of social capital has taken hold in scholarly research communities as diverse as criminology, epidemiology, international development, and economics, as well as sociology and political science.

Two of the editors of this volume recently reviewed much of this literature from researchers across a variety of disciplines (Foley and Edwards 1999). In the majority of these analyses, social capital is treated as an independent variable affecting such outcomes as civic engagement, national-level economic growth, volunteering, dropping out of school, mortality rates, returns to human capital, fertility, local economic development, neighborhood stability, housing quality and levels of crime, government-community relations, juvenile delinquency, and organizational effectiveness. In other studies, social capital is treated as a dependent or intervening variable, with particular emphasis on the sorts of voluntary organizations said to produce it, but including work on the impact, in producing and/or shaping it, of schools and youth programs, varying types of network linkages within and between micro enterprise programs, housing mobility resulting from desegregation policies, spatial design of communities or the "architecture of engagement," political context, government policy, economic restructuring, and even national elections.

Even a cursory review of recent empirical literature utilizing the concept of social capital reveals striking differences across disciplines both in how the term is understood and in how it is employed. Among political scientists and the handful of economists and psychologists who have busied themselves with the concept, social capital refers mainly to attitudes, as measured by survey responses to items on social trust, norms of reciprocity and tolerance, and, occasionally, trust in institutions. Though social organization of all sorts is considered a form of social capital in Coleman's work, political scientists and economists tend to see "associational membership" more as a source of social capital than as another form of it. "Civic engagement," measured as voting, contacting public officials, or, occasionally, membership in groups, is most often seen as an outcome of high levels of social capital, though sometimes these variables, too, are used as indicators of social capital. Most of this literature rests on, and sometimes tests, the hypothesis that social capital or associational density has a direct impact on economic performance and the health of democracy, following Putnam's lead (1993).

Sociologists, including applied sociologists working in international or community development, tend by contrast to conceptualize social capital as primarily a social structural variable, using it to describe social networks, organizations, or linkages between individuals and/or organizations. Even where it is conceived partly in subjective terms (i.e., as norms and values), it may be understood as social structures, as when Flora, Sharp, Flora, and Newlon identify their "entrepreneurial social infrastructure" as a "format for the mobilization of social capital" that effectively creates and directs energies for rural community economic development (1997). In such studies, comparisons among nations are difficult if not impossible, because the level at which social capital is presumed to operate is tied to mainly local social structures. The emphasis, following Coleman, is decidedly on the role of social capital in enhancing the flow of goods and services to specified individuals or groups.

A recent theoretical development within this literature distinguishes what might be called "within group" social capital from "between group" social capital. Drawing expressly on Durkheim, Michael Woolcock suggests we attend to both "integration" (at the group level) and "linkage" (between groups, or between groups and influential others) (1998). Briggs suggests a similar dyad, "social support and social leverage" (1998). Lang and Hornburg offer "social glue and social bridges" (1998), while Warren, Brenner, and Saegert suggest "bonding social capital" and "bridging social capital" (1999). All such efforts should be seen as extensions of the insight that the value of social capital at any given level depends on the larger context, including the insertion of the individual or group in question into networks of relations at higher levels of social organization (Edwards and Foley 1997, 1998; Foley and Edwards 1999).

Organization of the Volume

The articles collected below take up a wide range of questions raised in the recent debate. We have organized them as attempts to grapple with four broad issues. Part I addresses the theme of Civil Society and Political Context. The civil society argument focuses on the ways in which society organizes itself *independently of the state* or *over against the state*. But states arguably shape their societies as profoundly as the reverse. They provide the constitutional, legal, political, and even moral framework within which social organizations arise and operate. This is what Michael Walzer calls "the paradox of the civil society argument"—that a democratic civil society seems to require a democratic state, and a strong civil society seems to require a strong and responsive state (1992:102–103). What, then, are the relations between political context and civil society? Under what circumstances can civil society contribute to a healthy democracy, and under what circumstances do specifically political institutions and processes come to the forefront, for good or ill? The first set of articles addresses these questions by looking at the very different settings of antebellum Kansas, Weimar Germany, Central America at the end of the 1980s, and post-Soviet Russia. In addition, two further articles consider how local government may decisively enhance opportunities for citizen participation with and without the aid of voluntary associations.

Part II, The Political Economy of Our Discontent, takes up the political economy of the current turn to civil society: Much of the debate on the "decline of social capital" in the United States has focused on declining rates of membership in traditional civic organizations, declining voting rates, and the increasing rancor of politics. Ignored in these discussions are momentous economic changes that, potentially at least, profoundly affect citizen attitudes toward their government and the larger society. The long, steady decline of real incomes for the majority of American families that characterized most of the last three decades, coupled with the wrenching effects of globalization for many working and middle-class Americans, surely must be taken into account in considering the evidence of declining levels of social trust and civic engagement in recent years. Two articles in this collection take up this challenge, looking at the ways in which changing economic relations at the local level affect social solidarity in a classic "company town" and civic philanthropy in Atlanta. Two more articles look at the ways in which changing economic incentives, including some sparked by governmental initiatives, may contribute to cooperation and new alliances in diverse settings.

In Part III, Civil Society and Civic Engagement, our authors address the exact relationship between associational membership and people's civic and political attitudes and behaviors. The neo-Tocquevillean argument has often been presented as if all associations were alike in their impact on attitudes and behaviors, including civic engagement. Robert Putnam, on the other hand, has often stressed the special role of broadly inclusive, face-to-face civic associations. But why would voluntary associations in general, or Putnam's civic associations in particular, have a special capacity to produce social capital or civic engagement? The third section takes up these questions, examining, first, what sorts of groups are associated with what sorts of attitudes and behaviors among their members, then looking closely at more explicitly political associations. The four final articles in the section take up the challenge of much contemporary thinking about civil society, which implicitly or explicitly excludes, as divisive, advocacy and social movement organizations and is more concerned with a Washington lobbying presence than with building social capital among members. In general, they present a variety of ways in which just such groups may contribute positively to building citizen engagement.

Finally, Part IV, Social Capital Reconsidered, turns to the broader, theoretical questions, What is social capital? What difference does it make? As we have seen, the notion of social capital has become a central one in recent discussions of the importance of civil society for healthy democracies. Nevertheless, debate continues about the meaning and usefulness of the concept. From varying points of view, each of the authors in our final section reviews recent usages and attempts to refine a concept of social capital that will bear scrutiny theoretically while providing useful guidelines for empirical inquiry. In the concluding essay, the editors attempt to reconstruct the notion of social capital in a way that might prove most fruitful for future empirical research.

I

Civil Society and Political Context

Editors' Introduction

Growing disillusionment with the political process in the United States—from critiques of "big government" and the welfare state on the right to concerns about the "buying of the Congress" and the apathy of the electorate on the left—have contributed to a widespread perception that the solution to the problems our society faces is to be found, not in government or political parties, but in the private sector and civil society. Political figures as diverse as Pat Schroeder, Sam Nunn, and, until recently, Bill Bradley, have retired from public office to escape partisan divisions and seek new common ground in an expanding civil society movement. The expectation, best captured in Robert Putnam's revival of Alexis de Tocqueville's observations on the contributions of associational life to the health of democracies, is that social and cultural factors, rather than political or economic ones, are keys to strong democracy and effective governance. A strong and vibrant civil society characterized by a social infrastructure of dense networks of face-to-face relationships that cross-cut existing social cleavages such as race, ethnicity, class, sexual orientation, and gender will underpin strong and responsive democratic governance.

According to the neo-Tocquevillean argument, a chief benefit of participation in "secondary associations" is their capacity to foster norms of reciprocity, citizenship, and social trust and provide networks of social relations that can be mobilized to pursue shared goals for the common good. In other words, civil associations are the major sources of social capital in the neo-Tocquevillean view. Thus, the apparent disengagement from civic associations over the last several decades has depleted American reserves of social capital and is chief culprit for the much lamented deterioration of public life.

The American debate thus adds a distinctive note to the notion of civil society that re-emerged in Europe and Latin America two decades ago, where civil society was seen as primarily a bulwark and a rallying point against an overweening and often repressive state. But even in the United

States, the neo-Tocquevillean argument has not gone uncontested. While neo-Tocquevilleans argue that a strong democratic state depend upon a strong civil society, others insist that the character and strength of civil society depend upon the character of the political institutions in which it works. In other words, the role that organized groups in civil society will play depends crucially on the larger political setting. As Michael Walzer puts it, "there is no escape from power and coercion, no possibility of choosing, like the old anarchists, civil society alone." What Walzer calls "the paradox of the civil society argument" is that a democratic civil society seems to require a democratic state, and a strong civil society seems to require a strong and responsive state (1992:102–103).

The first two essays in this section examine the relationship between political institutions and civil society in two historical cases that have profoundly shaped thinking about contemporary democracy: the formation of Antebellum democracy in America and the collapse of the Weimar Republic and the rise of the Nazis in interwar Germany. Keith Whittington reconsiders Tocqueville's classic analysis and the American scene that inspired it, noting both the importance of civil associations for developing vital citizenship skills and the problems inherent in civil society, particularly an exclusionary tendency in voluntary associations and the conflict inherent in civil society. Sheri Berman argues that the nature of civil societies is shaped significantly by nation-specific attributes of a broader political context and in particular by the degree of institutionalization of the political system. Weimar Germany did not lack civil society organizations of all kinds. Its democracy was endangered, however, by the ability of political groups of various hues to take over such organizations and provoke a polarization that the political institutions were not equipped to handle.

Where the state is not responsive, its institutions nondemocratic, or its democracy ill-designed to recognize and respond to citizens' demands, the character of collective action will be decidedly different than under a strong and responsive democratic system. Citizens will find their efforts to organize for civil ends frustrated by state policy, sometimes met with repression, at other times simply ignored. Increasingly aggressive forms of civil association will spring up, and more and more ordinary citizens will be driven into either active militancy against the state or self-protective apathy. The breakdown of the tutelary democracies and authoritarian states of Latin America in the 1970s and 1980s attests to what more than one observer has euphemistically called "the dangers of excluding reformists from power." In such settings, all of civil life may become polarized, as Samuel Huntington pointed out long ago (though the solutions he chose proved elusive); and even Putnam's choral societies and bowling leagues—even nuns and bishops!—may become "subversives," enemies of the state.

The next two essays in this section directly address these issues in the emerging democracies of Cental America and post-Soviet Russia. Richard Booth and Patricia Bayer Richard investigate the relationship between civil society and the state in the urban centers of the Central American nations. Their findings demonstrate the extent to which political context—specifically, variable levels of state-sponsored repression—affects the development and character of civil society. Contrary to a strong neo-Toquevillean argument, they conclude that state behavior may shape civil society rather than the other way around. Richard Rose examines the significance of social capital in contemporary Russia. Drawing on over 1,900 face-to-face interviews, Rose explores how Russians accomplish a variety of everyday tasks in a context of organizational and governmental failure. He critiques strictly cultural or social-psychological conceptions of social capital and develops a situational and network-oriented view complementary to that expressed by the editors in the concluding chapter of this volume.

The last two essays examine avenues of citizen participation in contemporary urban government in the United States and Britain. Both emphasize the effectiveness of political contexts that formally and substantively incorporate citizen participation into the local governing process. In a study of five American cities Kent Portney and Jeffrey Berry take on the neo-Toquevillean argument that a strong, local civil society will lead to a more effective and responsive local government. Rather, they find that strong, local, democratic structures such as the neighborhood associations of Birmingham, Alabama, Dayton, Ohio, Portland, Oregon, and St. Paul, Minnesota, are more effective avenues of minority political incorporation than, for example, citywide issue organizations, service/self-help groups, or crime watches. Maloney, Smith, and Stoker use their study of contemporary Birmingham, England, to examine how patterns of civic engagement have changed since the 1970s, stressing the importance of conceptualizing social capital as a context-dependent resource that inheres in relations between actors in a variety of locations. After critiquing neo-Tocquevillean analysts for neglecting the role of changing political context in influencing associational activity and social capital, they argue for a top-down approach in which purposive government initiatives can have the positive effect of enhancing and creating social capital.

Revisiting Tocqueville's America

Society, Politics, and Association in the Nineteenth Century

KEITH WHITTINGTON

Alexis de Tocqueville's (1969) study of Jacksonian America has recently inspired a range of social scientists to reemphasize the importance of civil society in "making democracy work." Dense networks of social interaction are said to foster trust and social capital. Bowling together increases our willingness to rely on others generally and to participate in collective endeavors. A robust civil society increases political participation, makes for a happy citizenry, and helps secure government effectiveness (Putnam 1993a, 1993b, 1995a; Walzer 1992; Taylor 1990; Edwards and Foley 2001). For such neo-Tocquevilleans, civil society becomes the key variable for explaining the success of democratic government. Robert Putnam's (1993a) fascinating account of modern Italy is specifically designed to hold constant both policies pursued and government institutions employed, in order to determine the effects of different civic cultures. He found that an active civil society correlates with better institutional performance. A strong society makes for a strong state. For Italy, it would appear, institutions do not matter; cultural traditions do.

But all of this raises some difficulties. Is it necessarily true that expanded civic engagement will support democracy? Tocqueville himself was more ambivalent about the relationship between civil society and democracy. As Adam Seligman (1992:x) writes, "The idea of civil society thus embodies for many an ethical ideal of the social order, one that, if not overcomes, at least harmonizes, the conflicting demands of individual interest and social good." Recourse to civil society as the keystone of democratic vibrancy is

Revised from an article of the same title in *American Behavioral Scientist* 42, no. 1 (1998): 21–32. I thank Michael Foley and Tracey Storey for their helpful suggestions.

of uncertain benefit if interests are not so easily synthesized. Civil society may be as much a threat to democratic institutions as a support. Reconsideration of Tocqueville's analysis, and of nineteenth-century America, suggests using some caution before embracing civil society. A well-functioning democracy depends not only on social relations, but also on political institutions and on a constitutional order that structures the relationship between them. The point is not a fundamentalist one, whether recent analysts of political culture have gotten Tocqueville right. Although Tocqueville serves as the inspiration for the present civil society revival, little turns on whether current scholars are faithful interpreters of Tocqueville. A return to Tocqueville, however, does provide a convenient starting point for reconsidering the relationship between politics and society and the place of social capital within democratic theory.

Democracy and Society

For at least one strand of the social capital movement, a strong civil society reinforces a strong state (Putnam 1993a:182). Tocqueville's analysis, however, was less state-centered and less certain about the relationship between state and society. Indeed, Tocqueville was struck by America's flourishing civil society in part because of its connection to America's weak state. "Democracy" could work even if the state did not. For Tocqueville, democracy is a social condition and not just a form of government (Aron 1968). To the French aristocrat, it seemed all too obvious that the declining social prestige and resources of the nobility precipitated and accompanied their loss of political power. The most distinctive feature of the age of democracy was "equality of condition." Tocqueville's reporting on conditions in the United States is not always reliable. His time in America was brief, and he relied heavily on his informers among the beleaguered Federalist and Whig elite (Rodgers 1988). As a consequence, he seriously overstated the egalitarianism to be found in Jacksonian America (Pessen 1985; Wilentz 1988). There remained substantial economic inequality and social segregation in the cities of the antebellum United States. But Tocqueville was not only concerned with the relative distribution of wealth. The relevant comparison was with feudalism, in which political and social power was grounded in birth and arms. By contrast, in a democratic society "the work of the mind had become a source of power and wealth," and America had "opened a thousand new roads to fortune and gave any obscure adventurer the chance of wealth and power" (Tocqueville 1969a:11). The rigid and hierarchical world of feudalism had given way to a fluid and complex world of democratic capitalism. If it was not really true that the noble and the commoner were about to "touch" on the social scale, Tocqueville, among others, was convinced that the vast distances separating the two under feudalism had been bridged and were no longer so meaningful (11). Distinctions in a democratic society worked on a different logic than they did in the *ancien regime* (Huston 1993).

This emphasis on society has significant implications for Tocqueville's analysis of democracy in America and the relation between society and government. Voluntary associations were necessary for the successful resolution of common problems, according to Tocqueville, because other possible providers of public services were missing or exceedingly weak in American society (Tocqueville 1969a:514). In Europe, the nobility had both the resources and the social obligation to solve problems on behalf of the local community. In the alternative, relatively elaborate government bureaucracies were available in Europe to engage in public projects. By contrast, Tocqueville detected no powerful individuals capable of shouldering public burdens in the egalitarian United States. In addition, the weak governmental structures of the United States were hardly capable of providing more than a handful of basic public services. Even public affairs that relied on influence, rather than financial resources, were beyond the reach of the weak American state and individuals. There were no nobles to set an example for the masses, so moral exhortation had to come from the masses themselves. Voluntary associations emerged from this context of weakness and compensated for the underdeveloped political and social institutions of a democratic society. Social capital, in this sense, was compensatory for deficiencies in a democratic society, arising from otherwise unmet social needs. If such needs could be met by other means, they would be. Putnam's contention that government policy is more effective when unrelated voluntary associations flourish bears little resemblance to Tocqueville's analysis of either democratic society or democratic politics. Tocqueville's voluntary associations multiply as a consequence of a democratic social condition and state weakness, regardless of how policies are determined or government officials selected. By contrast, Putnam hopes to discover a link between a strong civil society and a strong state, though Putnam's analysis also has little to say about the political mechanisms for translating popular desires into government policy (Tarrow 1996).

Tocqueville's analysis of voluntary associations also raises some difficult questions for the ready acceptance of civil society as the foundation for democratic politics, for he thought voluntary associations posed a threat to political institutions. The neo-Tocquevilleans have correctly emphasized Tocqueville's belief that civil society serves a crucial political function, but they have underemphasized the problems that such an arrangement can create for the state and the democratic values it protects. Given that democracy allowed widespread participation in politics, political skills likewise had to be widespread. Social activities ranging from children's games to social clubs helped spread those skills among Americans, who were constantly "campaigning" for the support of their fellows and practicing self-governance in a variety of pursuits (Tocqueville 1969a:189). The training ground of civil society provided not only such important individual skills, but also the social trust of particular concern to the social capital debate. In social activities, individuals learned the limits of both their own capabilities and their interdependence with their fellow citizens. Individuals became aware of their social interests and learned to rely on others to help them pursue those interests (510, 520–22). Social engagement helped overcome the individualism that Tocqueville thought was endemic to democratic equality, while teaching the mores necessary for maintaining a healthy society and polity.

The associations formed in democratic society carried risks for democratic politics, however. Voluntary associations were competitors with the state for the loyalty of the citizenry. Such associations challenged the effectiveness of government, since they performed many public functions that might otherwise be exercised by the state. More fundamentally, private associations challenged the moral authority of government (191–93). For Tocqueville, civil society was constitutive of the citizenry (Siedentop 1979). Associations helped to socialize individuals, teaching them both how to behave and how to think. On the one hand, such socialization was clearly necessary in any polity. On the other hand, Tocqueville was wary of the fact that voluntary associations served a crucial political function and yet were outside the control of the state. Feudalism had at least integrated a variety of social and political institutions into a coherent and mutually reinforcing whole. American democracy cut civil society loose from civil government, inviting potential conflict between them, often to the detriment of the state (see also, Migdal 1988). The problem was even greater than one of lack of coordination. Since the ultimate touchstone of political legitimacy in a democracy was the faithful representation of the will of the people, then government officials were particularly vulnerable to being undermined by voluntary associations that could make their own claims to popular representation. Tocqueville warned that private associations could "form something like a separate nation within the nation . . . with all the moral prestige" derived from the representation of their members (1969a:190). As modern analysts have observed in the American context, "interest groups" gain leverage over elected officials precisely because of the former's representative authority (see esp., Hansen 1991). Civil society was not merely a foundation for democratic governance; it was also a potentially disruptive force, subversive of regime legitimacy (Foley and Edwards 1996). Democratic governance risked deteriorating into mere anarchy. Social institutions were both a tool and a threat to democracy. A well-functioning democracy required more than a strong society. It also required a good constitutional order to structure and integrate social and political institutions. Ultimately, that constitutional task requires that we move beyond Tocqueville.

Constitutionalism and Society

Nineteenth-century America offers illustrations of several related concerns about the relationship between civil society and democracy. Tocqueville's America may have created social capital, but the use of that capital was not always to the benefit of the polity. Ultimately, our assessment of social capital in any given setting depends less on our commitment to democracy than on the specifics of the social situation and our conception of what kind of democracy we want. Just as society may be useful for making political institutions work effectively, the state may be essential to maintaining social order. Four examples of this dynamic are considered here: the exclusionary possibilities of social capital, the relationship between social demand and state institutions, the integration of political institutions into the socialization process, and the problems of state capacity.

Nineteenth-century churches and social clubs illustrate that the very voluntary associations that create social capital also tend to be exclusionary in their membership, presenting difficulties for a democratic politics. James Coleman defines social capital as consisting of "some aspect of a social structure" and facilitating "actions of individuals who are within the structure" (Coleman 1990:302). Like other forms of wealth, social capital is valuable in part because of its scarcity and exclusivity. Those within a given association have access to it, but nonmembers are excluded from its benefits. Max Weber found it to be characteristic of "American democracy that it did *not* constitute a formless sand heap of individuals, but rather a buzzing complex of strictly exclusive, yet voluntary associations" (Weber 1958:310). Both the voluntary and exclusive nature of such associations came into play in Weber's analysis of American churches. The size of the United States and the mobility and anonymity of Americans made the development of new business relations difficult. The trust upon which developed capitalism depends was difficult to form when individuals were not already known. Americans had addressed this problem through their churches, Weber argued. "Admission to the congregation is recognized as an absolute guarantee of the moral qualities of a gentleman, especially of those qualities required in business matters" (305). Knowing the church affiliation of a potential business partner provided an indication of creditworthiness. In order for the system to work, however, membership had to be voluntary and churches had to serve as gatekeepers. The social capital of trust depended on the ability to exclude the untrustworthy (see also, Greif

1989). Likewise, associations tended to be mutually reinforcing, for access to the "right" contacts depended in turn on membership in the "right" churches and clubs. The "power elite" of an earlier literature grew out of just such an interlocking network of social connections that gave advantage to a few but necessarily excluded the many (Mills 1959). Such networks allow individuals to extend their trust beyond a few close relatives and neighbors to those who would otherwise be unknown and presumptively untrustworthy. Trust grows within an associational society, but along particular and exclusionary lines.

The exclusion problem suggests the possibility that social capital can be an antidemocratic force in the polity, and potentially a disruptive one. The anti-Masonic movement of the early nineteenth century arose out of concerns over the elitist threat of the secret society. The Masons flourished in the founding era, and a large number of prominent politicians were included in their number. As an elite social club, the Masons provided opportunities of association that helped unify the social and political elite and provided some organizing structure in a politics where parties had not yet developed. As Ronald Formisano (1983:199) concluded, "Masonic activity, like church activity, was a way of aiding a political career." Led by an up-and-coming but marginalized class of moralists, the anti-Masonic movement of the 1820s and early 1830s mobilized large numbers of new political participants in populist revolt against elite government and secret societies. For the members of evangelical churches that formed the leadership of the anti-Masonic movement, it was their exclusion from the established networks of social influence that indicated the breakdown of democratic politics (Formisano 1983; Benson 1964). The instability of political authority in a democracy has fed a recurrent tendency in American politics to re-establish political identity through the defensive fear of exclusion and the offensive exclusion of others. Coercion and repression have been repeatedly marshaled against a constantly moving threat of subversion from cohesive and successful, but potentially invisible, groups ranging from the Masons to the Communists, the "slave power" to the "unassimilable" Chinese (Rogin 1987). Civic associations fostered social capital that could be converted to economic and political success, but they also fostered resentment that could lead to political turbulence and distrust.

Civil society not only allows state institutions to function more effectively, as Putnam found, but it also places demands on the state, redirecting the mechanisms of government to serve private ends (Olson 1982). Such a transmission of social demands to the state can be a crucial element of democratic politics, of course. But the extent to which the state should be responsive to social demands, and the nature of the demands to which the state should reasonably respond, as the tariff and temperance politics considered below illustrate, are prior constitutional questions that must be answered before the health of a democracy can be evaluated. Putnam, like other neo-Tocquevilleans, appears largely to assume away the problem of social demand. In his study of Italian democracy, Putnam takes his set of examined policies as given. His concern is with how policies are implemented, not with why they are pursued in the first place. No effort is made to discover whether state institutions are pursuing policies actually desired by the populace. But civil associations are likely to be as concerned with what the government does as with how it does it—and the goals that such associations might develop for society may well be unhealthy ones (see also, Berman, this volume; Berman 1997). More generally, Putnam's emphasis on the ability of voluntary associations to build social trust seems to minimize the possibility of social conflict. If we would bowl together more often, we would learn to trust our neighbors and be less suspicious of government officials. Distrust of government and wariness of others, in this reading, become a matter of mere cynicism rather than political judgment. The Jacksonians would have been surprised. Antebellum Americans suffered not from a lack of civic association, but from a conflict of goals among social and political groups. Sometimes those conflicts arose from the direct self-interest of various factions within society. At other times, however, political conflict arose not from competing interests, but from competing visions of the public good derived from and reinforced by unrelated voluntary associations.

Two of Tocqueville's primary examples of voluntary associations illustrate these possibilities. Protective tariffs were a subject of great controversy during the Frenchman's visit to America, and he reported on the meeting of the 1831 anti-tariff convention as an example of association for self-interested political ends. Although Tocqueville thought political associations were a necessary check against majority tyranny in a democracy, he looked upon such meetings with "alarm" and suggested that the convention served as the catalyst for the "open revolt" of state nullification the following year.[1] Such "factions" organizing in support of their own self-interest constantly brought the nation to the verge of "anarchy," as the government's policies and legitimacy were under continuous assault (Tocqueville 1969a:193). The temperance movement served as another prime example of the kinds of voluntary associations that he saw proliferating in democratic America. This movement, however, was more closely identified with advocating one, contestable vision of the public good than with pursuing the self-interest of a mere faction within society. In egalitarian America, social influence required numbers. Like-minded advocates of temperance united together in order to serve as a more visible example to their less sober neighbors (Tocqueville 1969a:189, 516). Temperance associations often found such forms of persuasion inadequate, however, leading them to place demands on the state to back up their moral vision with force. Associations dedicated to temperance in alcohol consumption, the prohibition of gambling, respect for the Sabbath, and other forms of social control were widespread. Moreover, reformers grew out of other social groupings, developing their ideas and mobilizing their support from specific class, ethnic, and religious foundations. Such associations cut across some cleavages, while reinforcing others (Smith-Rosenberg 1986).

Politics involves not only the implementation of policy, but also the determination of which policies to pursue and whether certain kinds of policies should be pursued at all. American politics has been riven by clashing visions of the public good, one category of which is the scope of the state itself in resolving such conflicts. Social reform movements sparked pitched battles not only between those who favored the goals of the reformers and those who did not, but also between "anti-coercion" reformers and those who favored government involvement (Johnson 1978; Tyrrell, 1979; Norton 1986). There is no question that substantial social and human capital was built through such activism, as individuals were drawn into politics and identified allies whom they grew to trust and support. The politics of social control was also deeply divisive, however, pitting churches, classes, and neighborhoods against one another over the proper use of the state and the goals of society. The growth and activism of both the evangelical churches and the conservative elites are exemplary of the production of social capital, but whether we view either side or the course of their conflict as good for antebellum democracy depends a great deal on our answer to prior constitutional questions about the appropriate role of the state in society and our conception of the public good. Social goals do not emerge innocently from a harmonious civil society, but must also be constructed through political conflict. In this context, the constitutional question is even prior to the policy question, but the social capital literature begs them both.

A third consideration arising from the interaction of state and society concerns the institutions that give purpose to social life. For Tocqueville, the state must also play a socializing role. Laws and political institutions did not simply establish a neutral arena for competing social interests, but were themselves purposive and sought to shape the polity. The relative weakness of traditional social structures in a democracy made the socializing function of state institutions particularly important. The state itself must impart such values as respect for tradition and community, which might otherwise be missing among democratic individuals. But the division between state and society that existed in democracies risked the possibility that government and social institutions would advocate different or even contradictory goals. A democratic state was less likely to work in coordination with society to define social values and more likely to be a competitor for the hearts and minds of the citizenry. Well-designed political institutions were crucial to sustaining democratic values. Tocqueville himself singled out the American legal system as exemplary of the type of governing structure that was necessary to making democracy work. Lawyers served as a kind of democratic aristocracy, preserving the "habits of order" and a "taste for formalism" that were critical to any society but were threatened by the natural tendencies of democratic society (Tocqueville 1969:264). Similarly, the Anglo-American jury system helped socialize average citizens in the ways of the law. More to the point, juries taught individuals respect for order, the idea of right, and the recognition of duty (Lerner 1968:274). Interestingly, Tocqueville singled out the judiciary not because of its relative isolation from the people, but because he was struck by the degree to which the people penetrated even into the operations of the courts. The primary value of the American judicial system for Tocqueville was its effect on the national *mores*, the extent to which it reshaped individual citizens even as they participated in the implementation of the laws. In the case of the judiciary, the appropriate habits of the heart for a democratic citizenry did not depend on a reinvigorated civil society. Rather, democracy required the direct intervention of political institutions in the development of individual character in order to instill in citizens a proper sense of social purpose and to serve as a corrective to defects in democratic society. Somewhat differently, the mass political parties that were developed during the Jacksonian period can also serve as vehicles for integrating individual citizens into the broader political order. In building successful electoral coalitions, the parties reached across pre-existing social divisions while wedding their membership to the success of the existing political system (see also, Berman this volume).

A final example focusing on the dispute over the introduction of slavery into the territories suggests the important role political institutions play in safeguarding democracy within a society. In contrast to the assumptions of the neo-Tocquevilleans, society is rife with conflicts. The social interaction that forms social capital may well intensify rather than ameliorate those conflicts as individuals identify fellow partisans and become more committed and aggressive in their pursuit of favored goals. When this happens, the structure and strength of government are crucial to containing those conflicts. As noted above, social fault lines may be widened as activists seek to enlist the resources of the state on their own side. Ambiguity about the government's purpose can invite the efforts of those who seek to exploit government for their own purposes. State weakness can raise another difficulty, however. The state may invite social conflict through its own weakness and its apparent unwillingness to intervene to alter social dynamics. Social pressures may erupt because political institutions are not properly designed to relieve or contain them. The following example of "Bleeding Kansas" illustrates the potential dangers of the perverse use of social capital in the absence of well-functioning political institutions.

Conflicts over slavery and race were a persistent problem in nineteenth-century America, and such conflicts intensified through the years leading up to secession and civil war. The federal government had been erected, in part, through an uneasy compromise on slavery (Finkelman 1987; Graber 2001). The North gained the benefits of union with the hope that slavery would gradually die off after the international slave trade was ended. The South gained the benefits of union, including aid in recapturing fugitive slaves, with the expectation that domestic slavery could not be abridged without the consent of the slaveholding states. Social divisions were simply replicated in the new political institutions. As the nineteenth century progressed, Congress and the political parties reached a delicate equilibrium on the slavery issue. Southern representation in the Senate and the Electoral College blocked antislavery legislation and discouraged presidential competition based on slavery politics. As both antislavery advocates and slaveholders hardened their positions in the antebellum period, national politicians sought to avoid or compromise the issue. "Popular sovereignty" in the western territories reflected this political impasse. Fearful of upsetting the regional balance in the Senate and unwilling to take a firm stand on the disposition of the territories, Congress delegated to the territorial governments the responsibility to determine whether the territory, and ultimately the new state, would permit slavery within its boundaries.

This "solution" broke down when put to the test in the Kansas territory in the mid-1850s. "Popular sovereignty" required some mechanism for local determination of the slavery issue, but the embryonic territorial government was incapable of settling the issue itself. Whoever was able to draft a proposed state constitution would likely be able to determine the future of slavery within Kansas. Given the balance of power in the national legislature, the determination of whether Kansas would enter the union as a free or slave state held significant implications for the future of national slave policy. Given the intensity and hostility of the various activists on the issue, there was little chance of a social compromise. The delegation of responsibility to the territorial government had the consequence of setting off a mad race by each side to populate the territory with its partisans in order to swing local elections, while adding ideological fuel to the already volatile conditions of territorial settlement and uncertain land claims. "Kansas clubs" were organized across the nation to send immigrants and materiel to the territory. Within Kansas, armed militias were formed to defend towns and raid others. The result was the sectional division of the territory into two hostile camps, widespread election fraud as "raids" of activists crossed the borders from neighboring states to cast votes, armed conflict as each side tried to drive the other from the territory or settle disputes with deadly force, and ultimately the formation of rival territorial governments and constitutions. Before order was restored, two years of conflict had resulted in 200 deaths and encouraged the rise of a more militant brand of political activism, exemplified in the career of John Brown as an abolitionist revolutionary (Potter 1976; Stampp 1990). The Kansas example illustrates in extreme form the importance of well-functioning state institutions for channeling social conflict. Social capital can be used in many ways, often in ways that are inconsistent with social order or democratic aspirations. Well-functioning state institutions are necessary to contain social conflict and turn aside the "natural" tendencies of civil society (see also, Skocpol and Finegold 1982). In Kansas, weak political institutions exercised little effective control and invited a contest of rival voluntary associations for command of the territory. Ironically, the crisis in Kansas emerged out of a misguided effort to maximize democracy under the name of "popular sovereignty," by emphasizing society in a period of institutional flux and political stalemate. Conflicts within society itself, however, could not be resolved without effective political institutions.

Conclusion

These examples do not suggest that civil society does not matter for democracy or that social capital does not have its uses. They do indicate, however, that civil society must be placed within a political and institutional context. Once we move beyond the relatively innocuous components of Putnam's civil society—bowling leagues, choral groups, and bird-watching societies—to voluntary associations concerned with political mobilization and the transmission of citizen demands to the government—such as religious groups, ethnic organizations, and business associations—then the formation of social capital begins to raise difficult questions about social conflict and political ends. The proper functioning of democracy depends on a particular interaction of society and political institutions, and not simply on the maintenance of societal activity per se. The evaluation of the benefits of civil society in any given context depends, in turn, on a prior assessment of the political ends embraced by a particular community. Social capital is an important instrument for achieving social goals, but concentrating on the formation of social capital begs the question of the ends for which that capital is to be used. Without equal attention to political institutions, social capital may well be directed against other members of society. Without attention to the constitutional order, social groups may well place demands on state institutions that are undesirable or unsustainable. Given the possibility of social conflict, distrust of government and of others can be a reasonable political choice, and not simply the product of a weak society. Reconsideration of Tocqueville's America suggests that institutions do in fact matter for democracy, both in shaping cultural traditions and in constraining them.

Civil Society and Political Institutionalization

SHERI BERMAN

In recent years totalitarian regimes have collapsed and new democracies have proliferated, while old democracies seem to have lost their momentum, optimism, and vigor. Social scientists, accordingly, have devoted increasing attention to explaining what causes democratization in the first place, as well as what makes democracies vibrant and successful over the long term. Where a generation ago most scholars tackling these questions stressed economic, political, or institutional factors, today societal and cultural variables are in vogue. Tocqueville is the theorist of the decade, having emphasized the crucial role played by "habits, opinions . . . in a word, mores" in shaping democracy in America (Tocqueville 1969b:308). Neo-Tocquevilleans such as Robert Putnam (Putnam 1993a, 1993b, 1995a, 1996) argue that civil society is crucial to "making democracy work" while authors like Francis Fukuyama (1995a) and Benjamin Barber (1995), who differ on everything else, agree that civil society plays a key role in driving political, social, and even economic outcomes.

Societal and cultural factors are indeed worth studying. By looking at them in isolation from their broader context, however, neo-Tocquevilleans leave crucial questions unanswered and fundamentally misinterpret some of the most important dynamics of political development. In particular, many authors fail to recognize that under certain circumstances a robust civil society may not produce beneficial effects, but rather may signal—and hasten—a democratic regime's degeneration. To know whether the activity of civil society will have positive or negative consequences for democratic development, we need to marry an analysis of societal and cultural factors to the study of political institutions—something that recent neo-Tocquevilleans (unlike the master himself) have ignored.[1]

Revised from an article of the same title in *American Behavioral Scientist* 40, no. 5 (1997): 562–74.

To some extent, social science history may be repeating itself here, as the current boom in civil society parallels another movement, several decades ago, in which "mass society" theorists tried to explain Europe's slide into barbarism during interwar years. Then as now, political development was held to be a function of societal and cultural factors; then as now, Tocqueville was seen as the guiding light of political analysis. Since "mass society" and contemporary neo-Tocquevillean analyses share many of the same diagnoses and fears, it is worth examining them in conjunction.

Mass Society and Neo-Tocquevillean Theories

A crucial goal of the postwar mass society theorists was to "specify the social conditions that sustain liberal democratic institutions. The sources of strength and weakness in democratic political systems," these scholars argued, should be "sought in . . . social structure." Their central argument was that "insofar as a society is a mass society, it will be vulnerable to political movements destructive of liberal democratic institutions" (Kornhauser 1960:7). They defined a mass society, in turn, as one where "an aggregate of individuals are related to each other only by way of their relation to a common authority, especially the state. That is, individuals are not related to one another in a variety of independent groups" (Kornhauser 1960: 32–33, 228). Mass society theorists could be found on all parts of the political spectrum: Jose Ortega y Gasset (1932), Erich Fromm (1941), William Kornhauser (1960), and Hannah Arendt (1973) were all proponents of some version of this theory.[2]

For many of these scholars, civil society was a crucial antidote to the political viruses to which mass society was vulnerable. Kornhauser, for example, selected as the epigraph to his classic *The Politics of Mass Society* Tocqueville's warning that "If men are to remain civilized or to become so, the art of associating together must grow and improve in the same ratio in which the equality of conditions is increased" (Kornhauser 1960:32). Participation in civil society associations, it was argued, could help counter the alienation engendered by modernity. Ripped from their traditional moorings by liberalism and capitalism, Western publics found themselves bereft and rootless, searching for ways of belonging—and hence open to the blandishments of totalitarian movements. Civil society could help counter these trends by providing citizens with an alternative set of linkages and communal bonds. Furthermore, where modernity released individuals from the constraints placed upon them by traditional social ties and mores, civil society activity helped keep them in check and maintain order. "Without a multiplicity of independent and often conflicting forms of association people lack the resources to restrain their own behavior as well as that of others. Social atomization engenders strong feelings of alienation and anxiety, and therefore the disposition to engage in extreme forms of behavior to escape from these tensions" (Arendt 1973:316–17). Finally, mass society theorists argued that participation in civil society associations created cross-cutting cleavages, fostered the skills necessary for democratic governance, and perhaps most importantly helped to generate a "consciousness of common interest" among the disparate individuals composing western societies.

Today's neo-Tocquevilleans, although differing in certain respects, share with mass society theorists the fundamental belief that the key to successful democracy lies in societal and cultural factors. Both schools also view the vibrancy of associational life as a crucial measurement and predictor of the health of democracy. Robert Putnam, for example, argues that

> [c]ivil associations contribute to the effectiveness and stability of democratic government . . . both because of their "internal" effects on individual members and because of their "external" effects on the wider polity. Internally, associations instill in their members habits of cooperation, solidarity, and public spiritedness. . . .Externally . . . a dense network of secondary associations . . .[enhances the articulation and aggregation of interests and] contributes to effective social collaboration. (1993a:89–90)

As did mass society theorists, contemporary neo-Tocqeuevillians praise associational life for its effects on the way individuals relate to each other and their society; in particular, they see participation in the organizations of civil society as producing the patterns of individual behavior and social interaction necessary for healthy democratic governance. Associational life helps "foster sturdy norms of generalized reciprocity and encourage[s] the emergence of social trust" (Putnam 1995a:67). These norms and values, in turn, help resolve dilemmas of collective action and smooth economic and political negotiations (see also, Coleman 1990). In addition, associations "broaden the participants' sense of self, developing the 'I' into the 'We'" (Putnam 1995a:67). They thus foster what Tocqueville termed "self-interest properly understood," as well as a wider sense of community and social purpose. Vibrant civil society, in short, creates the cultural and societal building blocks of successful democracy—which is why signs of civil society's decay (such as a decline in group bowling) should be cause for worry.[3]

The Problems with Mass Society and Neo-Tocquevillean Analyses

Since mass society and contemporary neo-Tocquevillean analyses share so many similarities, it is not surprising that they share key weaknesses as well. Most important, both fail to recognize that civil society can often serve to weaken rather than strengthen a democratic regime. Because they are unable to differentiate between the positive and negative consequences of a vibrant associational life, both theoretical schools are thus unable to predict or account for situations where civil society activity produces inauspicious patterns of individual behavior and social interaction. To correct this critical flaw and move debate forward, however, we must first understand what these theories get right.

Mass society and contemporary neo-Tocquevillean scholars are correct in arguing that individuals in modern societies often feel atomized and ineffectual, and in noting that these feelings can be overcome through participation in civil society organizations. They are also correct in arguing that such organizations can facilitate collective endeavors and create critical social skills and connections. They err, however, in assuming that collective endeavors and activist skills are good things *in and of themselves*, without regard to the purposes to which they will be directed. There is no intrinsic reason why civil society activity should bolster an existing political system; under certain circumstances, in fact, civil society organizations may help dissatisfied individuals come together to air and share their grievances, mobilizing them for subversive political activity. Indeed, without a stable associational infrastructure, opponents of a regime would find it impossible to form a "consensus on the causes of dissatisfaction, on the solution to the situation and on plans for coordinating actions" (Couch 1968:318).[4]

Sure enough, research during the 1960s and 1970s—spurred in part by mass society theorizing—found that the rise of radical and antidemocratic movements during the interwar and postwar eras was not the work of unattached, isolated individuals but rather of those who actively participated in civil society organizations. As one scholar noted: "Intermediate structures . . . serve to facilitate mass movements by offering means of mobilization and communication and providing motivation and legitimation (Parkin 1968:12–14). The individuals most likely to be affected by these factors are the most highly integrated, not the least, as argued by mass theory" (Halebsky 1976:87). Poujadism in France, extreme right wing activity in the United States, and Naziism in Germany were all supported by a vibrant associational infrastructure (Berman 1997; Gusfield 1962; Hagtvet 1980; Pinard 1971; Wolfinger 1964). Mass society and contemporary neo-Tocquevillean theorists are also correct in pointing out that a well-functioning democracy (and, indeed, any type of stable political regime) requires a "sense of common interest" and a commitment to a national community. But they err in assuming that civil society alone can produce these outcomes. Indeed, civil society activity often serves to fragment rather than unite a society, accentuating and deepening already existing cleavages. Perhaps the most dramatic example of this dynamic came in interwar Germany where, in contrast to the assertions of mass society theorists, civil society flourished but exacerbated rather than alleviated the country's painful divisions. Socialists, Catholics, and bourgeois Protestants each joined their own choral societies and bird-watching clubs, and, however civic-minded and "horizontally organized" these associations may have been, they served to hive their memberships off from each other and contribute to the formation of what one observer called "ferociously jealous 'small republics'" (Fritzsche 1990; see also, Berman 1997). Civil society activity alone was not able to overcome the social cleavages or provide the political cohesion that would have been necessary to weather the crises that beset Germany after 1914. The Weimar example is buttressed by research on a wide variety of cases, which should make us skeptical about the ability of associational ties to create attachments to a wider national community or set of institutions and structures (Halebsky 1976, ch. 4). Some scholars have argued that just the opposite is in fact the case, emphasizing the danger that a vibrant civil society may split into "warring factions (a possibility that theorists since Hegel have worried about) or degenerat[e] into congeries of rent-seeking 'special interests'" (Foley and Edwards 1996:39).[5] The formation of a rich associational infrastructure has been a crucial factor in the development and perpetuation of "subcultures" in varied settings across the globe.

A crucial question to ask, therefore, is why civil society often produces, in the words of one scholar, "unsocial" instead of "social" capital (Levi 1996). Why are the social skills and relationships generated by civil society activity sometimes placed in the service of nondemocratic rather than democratic goals? Why does participation in associational life sometimes serve to fragment rather than integrate a society?

One suggested answer directs us to look at the internal characteristics of civil society organizations themselves. An early and underappreciated statement of this viewpoint is found in Harry Eckstein's "A Theory of Stable Democracy" (1961). Eckstein argues that "a government will tend to be stable if its authority pattern is congruent with the other authority patterns of the society of which it is a part" (1961:234). Since democracy requires a mixture of behavior patterns (i.e., democratic, constitutional, and authoritarian), he claims, countries where civil society organizations and social relations reflect and foster such mores will tend to have stable and effective systems of democratic governance. "If a society has a vigorous associational life, but if the associations themselves are highly undemocratic," Eckstein notes, "then, upon my theory, democracy should not be stable, and upon Kornhauser's, it should" (1961:282). Putnam echoes this conclusion in *Making Democracy Work*, arguing that only where civil society is organized around "horizontal bonds of mutual solidarity" rather than "vertical bonds of dependency and exploitation" will it produce trust and cooperation (esp. 144–45 and 174–75).

Yet, however reasonable this criterion may sound in the abstract, in practice it is extremely problematic and serves primarily as an arbitrary way for neo-Tocquevilleans to praise the groups they favor and denigrate those they do not. For example, in his study of Italy, Putnam argues that organizations such as the Church and the Mafia should not be considered "true" components of civil society since they are "vertically" organized (Greeley, this volume; Edwards and Foley, this volume).

Yet participation in religious life and associations is one of the civil society activities most often praised in the United States, dating back to Tocqueville himself! Why the Church should foster different attitudes and patterns of behavior in Italy than it does in the United States is unclear. Such examples abound. The Boy Scouts are a hierarchically organized group, yet they seem to be placed by most neo-Tocquevilleans squarely in the civil society camp while militias and other nationalist organizations—which civil society proponents generally ignore or distance themselves from—do not appear to be much more vertically organized than other types of civil society associations. They clearly do foster, moreover, precisely the sense of solidarity and trust, as well as a willingness to engage in collective endeavors, that neo-Tocquevilleans celebrate; the problem is that the skills and relationships fostered by such organizations are used in the service of goals of which most of us would not approve. Finally, the sociability of the "capital" generated by civil society organizations is not set in concrete. Even the most seemingly harmless and "civil" organizations can, under certain circumstances, be turned to antidemocratic purposes. The Nazis, for example, were able to use choral societies and bird-watching clubs in their infiltration and eventual takeover of German society (Berman 1997).

It is not that the internal characteristics of organizations have no bearing at all on the behavior and attitude of their members; they probably do have some (Stolle and Rochon, this volume; Eastis, this volume). A more important factor to examine in determining when civil society activity will bolster or weaken a democratic regime, however, is the political context within which that activity unfolds. We need to shift our focus back, in other words, from looking at how social context shapes the performance of political institutions to looking at the crucial role played by political institutionalization in shaping the character of civil society and its impact on political development. The most important difference between civil and uncivil polities and well-functioning and problematic democracies, I contend, is not to be found in an analysis of societal and cultural factors, but rather in an examination of political institutions.

The Importance of Political Institutionalization

At the same time that mass society scholars were grappling with the question of why modern, industrial societies succumbed to the lure of fascism, other social scientists were trying to explain why some countries were having trouble achieving modernity and industrialization in the first place. By the 1960s the high hopes accompanying postwar decolonization and Third World independence movements were rapidly fading. Attempts at political modernization and development had not catapulted new countries into the First World, but instead left many of them mired in economic stagnation and political instability. Samuel Huntington's *Political Order in Changing Societies* urged us to explain this state of affairs not by looking to economic or societal variables, as most scholars were doing, but rather by focusing on political ones. Huntington argued that the fundamental difference between developed and developing societies lay not in their levels of wealth, health, or education, but rather in their level of political institutionalization. Developing countries were characterized by a "lag in the development of political institutions behind social and economic change" (1968:5); above all else they were being held back by "a shortage of political community and of effective, authoritative, legitimate government" (1968:2). The solution to underdevelopment, in this view, lay in creating political institutions capable of dealing with the challenges confronting developing societies.

Like mass society and contemporary neo-Tocquevillean theorists, Huntington sought to understand what lay behind political stability, a sense of community, and a citizenry willing and able to compromise and cooperate to achieve collective goals—in short, to understand what lay behind "civic" polities. He found the answer, however, in political institutions instead of civil society:

> The degree of community in a complex society thus, in a rough sense, depends on the strength and scope of its political institutions. The institutions are the behavioral manifestation of the moral consensus and mutual interest. The isolated family, clan, tribe, or village may achieve community with relatively little conscious effort. . . .As societies become larger in membership, more complicated in structure and more diverse in activities, the achievement or maintenance of a high level of community becomes increasingly dependent upon political institutions. . . .[Indeed], without strong political institutions, society lacks the means to define and to realize its common interests. The capacity to create political institutions is the capacity to create public interests. (1968:10, 24)

In this view, the more complex and diverse a society, the greater the need for strong political institutions capable of bringing together people with a wide variety of interests and associational affiliations and mobilizing them in the service of societal, rather than individual, goals. Civicness could not be created by civil society alone because this sphere remained too tied to the varied and particularistic interests of citizens; only strong political institutions worked in the service of society as a whole rather than its individual components. For similar reasons the trust necessary to hold together modern societies required strong political institutions capable of overcoming the diverse and often competing interests of individual citizens and focusing on the achievement of long-term rather than short-term goals—of representing and implementing, in other words, the public rather than merely private interests: "[T]hose societies deficient in stable and effective government are also deficient in mutual trust among their citizens, in national and public loyalties, and in organizational skills and capacity. Their political cultures are often said to be marked by suspicion, jealousy, and latent or actual hostility toward everyone who is not a member of the family, the village, or perhaps the tribe" (Huntington 1968:28).

This type of analysis cut against the grain of much of the existing literature on development, and Huntington attributed resistance to his conclusions to a reluctance to "give up the image of social harmony without political action. This was Rousseau's dream. It remains the dream of statesmen and soldiers who imagine that they can induce community in their societies without engaging in the labor of politics" (Huntington 1969:9–10). He was correct, and the attitudes he described have continued to distort analysis of these questions, particularly among scholars prone to extrapolate from America's unique history. Blessed in the century after its founding with a high level of social harmony and equality, economic abundance, and a lack of external threats, the United States was able to modernize without the assistance of a strong centralizing government or political institutions. This created an abiding belief in a natural harmony of interests, as well as a view that political stability emerges naturally from economic development and social modernization, without the need for strong political institutions. Both pluralist and mass society analyses, for example, are premised on the "assumption that there is a natural harmony of interests which sustains the social and political system"; to the extent this is true, strong governmental and political institutions are not only unnecessary but also potentially a threat to freedom (Gusfield 1962:26–27). Unfortunately, history offers few examples of such harmony. Even in Europe industrialization and modernization forced a centralization of government authority and a strengthening of political institutions; only the United States managed to develop successfully while maintaining a political framework suited to dealing with the conflicts and problems of sixteenth- and seventeenth-century England.

In *Political Order*, Huntington focused on the developing world because it was there that the political gap seemed greatest: the challenges facing such societies were extremely high, while the level of political institutional-ization was very low. Yet in theory such a gap could appear anywhere: if the level of social conflict and the problems confronting a society grew and its political institutions did not evolve to be able to deal with these changes, political frustration and even instability would follow. In this situation, strengthening civil society might exacerbate rather than alleviate prob-lems. Civil society activity will not be able to create the sense of national community or commitment to the public interest that such a polity needs; by bringing together dissatisfied individuals, moreover, associational activ-ity might actually deepen societal cleavages and serve as a base from which oppositional movements can be launched. The definition of an uncivic pol-ity for Huntington, in fact, is one in which citizens are highly active and mobilized, while political institutions are weak and unresponsive.

Here, it seems to me, lies the answer to the question of when civil soci-ety activity produces social and when it produces unsocial capital: it de-pends heavily upon the political context. If a country's political institutions are capable of channeling and redressing grievances, then associationism will probably buttress political stability and democracy by placing its re-sources and beneficial effects in the service of the status quo. This is the pattern Tocqueville described.

If, on the other hand, political institutions are weak and/or the existing political regime is perceived to be ineffectual and illegitimate, then civil so-ciety activity may become an alternative to politics for dissatisfied citizens, increasingly absorbing their energies and satisfying their basic needs. In such situations, associationism will probably undermine political stability and have negative consequences for democracy by deepening cleavages, furthering dissatisfaction, and providing rich soil for oppositional move-ments to grow in. A flourishing civil society under these circumstances sig-nals governmental and institutional failure and bodes ill for political stabil-ity and democracy.

This latter pattern seems to fit a large number of cases, with provocative implications. The weakening of communist regimes in Eastern Europe, for example, was hastened by a rise in civil society activity there in the 1980s; parts of the contemporary Arab world are witnessing a remarkable growth in Islamist civil society activity that feeds on the citizenry's frustration with the region's unrepresentative and unresponsive authoritarian governments. In such situations civil society may not necessarily promote liberal democ-racy, as the neo-Tocquevilleans would predict it, but rather corrode the foundations of the current political order and provide an organizational base from which it can be challenged. From this perspective, the fact that a militant Islamist movement, for example, provides its supporters with religious classes, professional associations, and medical services tells us little about what might happen should the movement ever gain power; it tells us much more about the political failure and gloomy prospects of the nation's existing regime.

Unfortunately, one need not look so far abroad to find examples of this dynamic, one that may only be exacerbated by the policy advice contemporary neo-Tocquevilleans offer: to foster local associational life as the key to reinvigorating American democracy. If a population increasingly perceives its government and its political institutions to be inefficient and unresponsive, diverting public energies and interest into secondary associations may only worsen the problem, fragment society, and weaken political cohesion further. There are, unfortunately, all too many examples of this dynamic in our own country. Many have remarked on the increasing tendency for middle- and upper-class Americans to opt out of the public sector and provide everything from their own police forces to their own schools:

> Many associations—gated suburbs and business improvement districts . . . are driven in some respects by self-concerned fear. They represent a secession of a smaller, more privileged community from the larger one. The recently arrested Viper militia in Arizona fits Tocqueville's description of a classic American association: a small group of like-minded neighbors gathering together for a common purpose. . . . Tocqueville would not be surprised to learn that America also leads the world in militia movements. (*Time* 1996)

Militia movements, business improvement districts, and home schooling societies all arise out of dissatisfaction with how the public institutions are doing their jobs; all of them should be seen as signs of sickness rather than signs of health.

Conclusion

In the years since Tocqueville visited the United States, American society has changed dramatically. Tocqueville's America was characterized by extreme social equality, a relatively simple economic structure, and disengagement from the larger world. This picture had already changed dramatically by the end of the nineteenth century, and ongoing processes of industrialization, immigration, and world engagement almost obliterated the image entirely. By the 1960s America was once again poised for dramatic change, with the civil rights movement and the Vietnam war highlighting significant social cleavages. Interestingly, it is from this period onward that most contemporary neo-Tocquevilleans date the beginning of democracy's problems in America.[6] Rather than blaming this primarily on a decline in civil society activity (or the rise of television), however, we should probably consider the main culprit to be the inability of political institutions to respond to the new challenges confronting American society. As Huntington argued years ago, if the social conflicts and problems facing a society grow but their political institutions prove unable to adapt, the result may be political instability and even degeneration. This "political gap" (as Huntington would call it) has only expanded as the collapse of communism has deprived the American government of some of the legitimacy and purpose provided by the Cold War, while globalization has at least to some degree eviscerated the power of governments and political institutions everywhere.

Instead of focusing on civil society, therefore, people concerned about democracy in America might do better to focus on making government more responsive to citizen needs and strengthening those political institutions that have fallen into a state of disrepair. One obvious place to start might be with our political parties—institutions long vilified in American life, but ones that *can* provide a crucial link between citizens and government and that are a necessary component of a well-functioning democracy. Parties can not only bring together a wide variety of citizens in the service of the public good, they can also provide perhaps the most powerful institutionalized linkage between the private and public sectors. Furthermore, political parties themselves are a crucial source of civil society activity.[7] Another place to start might be the system of campaign finance, which so obviously corrupts the nation's political system and undermines public confidence in its fairness and purity. Whatever one's opinion on where the reforms should begin, however, one can say with confidence that unless the decline of American political institutions is not reversed, then the problems and conflicts confronting our society are not likely to be adequately addressed, no matter how many bird-watching clubs and benevolent associations we all join. Fostering voluntarism, in other words, despite being politically palatable because nonpartisan and requiring little effort or expenditure on the part of government, will not alone solve the problems facing advanced, industrial democracies. Instead, concerned citizens, elites, and politicians should focus on trying to find ways of helping our political institutions cope with the problems of the contemporary era.

Civil Society and Political Context
in Central America

JOHN A. BOOTH AND PATRICIA BAYER RICHARD

Robert Putnam draws upon de Tocqueville to argue eloquently that civil society—citizen participation in formal organizations—contributes to the success of democracy. In his study of Italy (1993a), Putnam offers evidence that citizens' engagement in diverse groups contributes to more effective governmental performance. Drawing upon Coleman (1988), he argues that membership in groups creates "social capital"—"networks, norms, and social trust that facilitate coordination and cooperation for mutual benefit" (Putnam 1995a:67).

In Italy, Putnam finds that regions with a more vibrant associational life, and thus greater social capital, have more successful regional governments. In a widely cited later article, he expresses fear for the fate of democracy in the United States, as "bowling alone" rather than together erodes social capital (1995a). He also speculates that democracy could be advanced in developing countries by building civil society and social capital.

We believe, along with Blair (1994:8–10), that civil society contributes to the development of new democracies by mediating between citizen and state, articulating citizen interests to government, inculcating democratic norms, and constraining government by stimulating citizen activity. Many other scholars have similarly argued that citizen involvement in organizations contributes directly or indirectly to political participation (Conway 1991; Nagel 1987; Rosenstone and Hansen 1993; Verba and Nie 1972; Verba, Nie, and Kim 1978), democratic values (Booth and Richard 1996),

Revised from article of the same title in *American Behavioral Scientist* 42, no.1 (1998): 33–46. The authors thank Micahel W. Foley for his helpful suggestions on an earlier version of this chapter.

democratization (Blaney and Pasha 1993; Booth and Richard 1998; Bratton 1986; Cohen and Rogers 1992; Diamond 1992), and economic development (Carroll 1992; Clark 1991; Esman and Uphoff 1984; Hirschman 1984). Here we test some of these ideas in six Central American nations.

Theory

Although widely cited, Putnam's influential theory and research have also attracted criticism, helpfully summarized by this volume's editors Bob Edwards and Michael W. Foley in their introductory chapter. Tarrow faults Putnam for errors in historical inference and interpretations of Italian history (1996). In particular, Tarrow suggests that rather than civil society having shaped government performance, as Putnam argues, the opposite probably occurred: the state (along with political institutions such as parties) stimulated high levels of associational activity. In their chapters in this volume, Charles Heying, Michael Schulman, and Cynthia Anderson make a similar argument about organizations in U.S. communities. They contend that an evolving political or socioeconomic context shapes groups and how they form social capital. Tarrow and others (see also Heying, this volume; Nowland-Forman 1998; Portney and Berry this volume; and Youniss, McLellan, and Yates, this volume) thus challenge Putnam's causal reasoning and fundamentally question how political context influences civil society.

Scholars have criticized Putnam for misreading Tocqueville's interpretation of civil society (Foley and Edwards 1997, 1998; Warren, this volume; Whittington, this volume). Foley and Edwards, for example, maintain that Putnam misinterprets Tocqueville's view of civil society, which he believed arose from rather than caused democracy (1997, 1998). As Keith Whittington shows in his chapter in this volume, de Tocqueville also saw civil society as generating political conflict rather than reinforcing civility. Foley and Edwards elaborate on Tocqueville and posit two, quite distinct, faces for civil society: "Civil Society I" resembles Putnam's interpretation and emphasizes the "ability of associational life . . . and the habits of association . . . to foster patterns of civility in the actions of citizens" (1996:39). In contrast, their "Civil Society II" refers to "action that is independent of the state [and] capable . . . of energizing resistance to a tyrannical regime" (1996:39).

Foley and Edwards further find that Putnam overlooks Tocqueville's critical insistence that civil society can be strong only where political association is truly free (1996:44). Like Tarrow, they argue that political context—the environmental conditions of citizen participation and association—strongly shapes civil society. "[T]he political variable includes the prevailing 'political settlement' that governs who plays, the rules of the game, and acceptable outcomes" (1996:47). This argument has particular power in such cases as El Salvador, where intense political repression in the 1970s profoundly shaped civil associations by forcing them into the conflictive and antityrannical (Type II) mode (Foley 1996). Others, including Sherri Berman, Dietlind Stolle and Thomas Rochon, and Carla Eastis in their chapters in this volume, further demonstrate that different kinds of organizations promote very different types of social capital, some of which may be antidemocratic and promote incivility.

Putnam has been challenged for inadequate theorizing about and specification of civil society and social capital (Kenworthy, this volume; Newton, this volume; Wood, this volume). In particular, we believe that he failed to explicate sufficiently how civil society actually impinges upon government. Putnam holds that, as citizens participate in groups, networks of civic interaction develop that promote norms of reciprocity and encourage social trust. These networks "pervasively influence public life" insofar as they "facilitate coordination and communication," reduce incentives for "opportunism," and enhance "the participants' 'taste' for collective benefits" (1995:67).

Putnam thus views "social capital" as linking group activism and regime performance. Social capital includes interpersonal trust, networks, and norms that aid in mutual cooperation. But the mechanisms or processes by which civil society generates social capital remain elusive. Moreover, he fails to explain how group involvement affects citizen behavior or attitudes in ways that might shape government performance and enhance the democratic prospect.[1]

We seek to clarify how associational activity might affect the relationship of citizens to the state. In his approach to social capital in this volume, Ken Newton clearly specifies (and in doing so is more helpful than Putnam) what social capital consists of and suggests how it may influence institutions. Thus we turn to specific social capital links between group activism and state performance, contending that associational activism may foster attitudes and behaviors that actually influence regimes.[2] We call these attitudes and behaviors "political capital." Political capital consists of civic norms that support democratic governance (support for democratic liberties) and conventional political participation. Such attitudes limit or motivate regime actions while citizen participation conveys interests, preferences, and demands to the regime.[3] Both have been shown to have an impact upon government performance (Booth & Richard 1998).

Bearing in mind such concerns, we test here the relationships between civil society and the development of social and political capital within the political context of contemporary Central America. We consider empirically the extent to which associational activity contributes to elements of social capital (interpersonal trust and political information) and to political capital (democratic norms and citizen participation). We also set this within the political context by specifically exploring the effect of repression upon the formation of social and political capital. States employ repression to constrain and direct citizen behavior. We have found that repression affects democratic norms and participation (Booth and Richard 1996).

Hypotheses

This discussion suggests four basic hypotheses. Hypotheses 1 and 2 postulate that political repression will depress civil society and the formation of social and political capital. Hypotheses 3 and 4 state that activism within civil society will increase social and political capital.

> Hypothesis 1: Higher levels of national political repression will inhibit civil society (associational activism).
>
> Hypothesis 2: Higher levels of national political repression will inhibit the formation of social and political capital.
>
> Hypothesis 3: Higher levels of activism within civil society will contribute to higher levels of social capital.
>
> Hypothesis 4: Higher levels of civil society activism will contribute to higher levels of political capital.

The nations of contemporary Central America provide a valuable setting in which to study civil society and the formation of social and political capital. The entire Mesoamerican isthmus underwent roller-coaster economic changes beginning in the 1960s and a period of sociopolitical turmoil during the 1970s and 1980s. A full-blown revolution and then a counterrevolutionary civil war occurred in Nicaragua. There were protracted national revolts in Guatemala and El Salvador, and the United States invaded Panama in 1989. This turbulence subsided in the 1990s as all the nations of the region moved toward formal democracy (Booth and Walker 1999; Bulmer-Thomas 1987; Seligson and Booth 1995; Williams 1994).

Given Central America's protracted tumult and its very recent return to political stability, what is the status of civil society in these fledgling liberal democratic regimes? Do organizations through their influence upon citizens contribute to the formation of social and political capital? Might civil society thus promote the consolidation of democracy through increasing political civility? What effect does repression have on civil society and social/political capital formation?

Data

To test the hypotheses, we analyze public opinion surveys [4] administered in the early 1990s among comparable cross-sections of the urban citizens of six Central American nations—Costa Rica, El Salvador, Guatemala, Honduras, Nicaragua, and Panama.[5] Items included in these surveys focused upon support for democratic norms, other political attitudes and values, and political participation. The political participation and democratic norms items have been widely validated and field tested in various cultural settings (Muller et al. 1987; M. A. Seligson and Gómez 1989; Booth and M. A. Seligson 1984; M. A. Seligson and Booth 1993).

Civil Society Measures

To develop our indices of civil society we examined responses to queries about activity in several types of organizations among our respondents (see notes to table 1). Factor analysis revealed two clusters of civil society variables: formal group activism (in unions, civic associations, cooperatives, and professional groups) and communal activism (community-level groups and collective local problem-solving efforts). Communal activism, for example, includes participating in school, church, and community development groups, as well as working together on local betterment projects. Table 1 presents the mean levels of civil society activity for the urban populations of the six Central American nations, divided into two groups based upon lower and higher levels of system repressiveness. The results reveal marked differences among the nations in the levels of group activism and lesser differences in communal activism.

Social Capital Measures

We have two indicators of social capital, each based upon multiple items: political knowledge and interpersonal trust (see table 1 for details on item construction and for variable means).

Political Capital Measures

We developed four political capital variables: First, a factor analysis of eight political participation items identified three citizen activity factors that have been developed into indexes of voting behavior (registering to

TABLE 1. Civil Society, Social Capital, and Political Capital Scores, by Country

Variables	Lower repression countries			Higher repression countries			Significance
	Honduras	Costa Rica	Panama	Guatemala	El Salvador	Nicaragua	
Civil Society							
Group activism[a]	1.05	.47	.84	.66	.33	.43	***
Communal activism[b]	1.04	1.01	1.03	1.31	1.24	1.17	***
Social Capital							
Information level[c]	1.43	.83	1.37	.62	1.25	1.03	***
Interpersonal trust[d]	.87	.82	1.12	.74	.78	.74	***
Political Capital							
Democratic norms[e]	6.98	6.77	7.33	5.51	5.57	6.42	***
Voting behavior[f]	1.86	1.91	1.72	1.51	1.39	1.62	***
Contacting public officials[g]	.77	.56	.56	.41	.32	.17	***
Campaign activism[h]	1.08	.87	.84	.25	.17	.47	***

Significance levels: * < .05; ** < .01; *** < .001.

[a] At least sometimes attend union, civic association, cooperative or professional association; yes = 1, no = 0 for each; range = 0–4.
[b] Involvement in 5 community self-help group activities; 1 = yes, 0 = no for each; range = 0–5.
[c] Index of political information based upon correctly naming U.S. Secretary of State, Russian President, and number of seats in national legislature; range 0–3.
[d] Index of interpersonal trust (based on 3 trust orientation items); range 0–3; higher value = greater trust in others.
[e] Overall support for democratic liberties (mean of 14 items expressing support for participatory rights); range 1–10.
[f] Registered to vote plus voted in last election; yes = 1, no = 0 for each; range 0–2.
[g] Ever contacted president, legislative deputy, city council member, or national government agency; yes = 1, no = 0; range = 0–4.
[h] Attempted to persuade others how to vote or worked on campaign in last or prior election; 1 = yes, 0 = no for each; range = 0–3.

vote and voting), contacting various types of public officials, and campaign activism (attempting to persuade others how to vote—see table 1).[6] Table 1 presents the means of each index.

Second, a measure of citizen commitment to democratic norms was developed based on the two major approaches to measuring democratic political culture, one associated with the civic culture/polyarchy concept and the other with political tolerance.[7] The former focuses on the general willingness to extend rights of political participation to others, while the latter focuses on citizens' willingness to grant political rights to disliked groups. Our fourteen items measured support for democratic liberties based on both approaches. We constructed an overall democratic norms measure that is the arithmetic mean of respondents' scores for all fourteen items. Table 1 breaks down the samples' mean scores on democratic norms.

Demographic and Contextual Measures

Demographic traits of citizens and contextual characteristics of nations also influence citizens' behavior and attitudes and thus have the potential to affect the relationships we are examining. In parts of the analysis we therefore employ, as control variables, measures of respondent sex, living standard, and education, as well as the social system traits of economic development level and level of regime repressiveness.

We treat repression as a polity-level constraint upon individuals. Our index of political repression by the regime contains historical and current components: We include a historical component in our index (estimated intensity of regime repression over the decade before each national survey) because we assume that the impact upon individuals of past repression will decay gradually, even after actual repression levels have declined. However, since the immediate context matters as well, we also estimate the regime repression level within each nation at the survey date. The two scores for each country are averaged. The resulting measure provides a repression score for each country that is assigned to each respondent.[8]

Analysis

Table 1 presents data on mean levels of civil society activism, social capital, and political capital for urban Central America, with the countries grouped by overall level of repression. Formal group activism tends to be greater in the less repressive nations of Central America than in the more repressive ones. This supports hypothesis 1. Contrary to prediction, however, communal activism reflects an opposite tendency, with higher activity levels in the more repressive countries. This is an interesting anomaly which we explore further below. Table 1 also reveals that, as hypothesis 2 predicts, levels of both social and political capital are greater where repression is lower. These findings amply support contentions of Foley and Edwards (1996), Tarrow (1996), and several contributors to this volume (Berman, Heying, Maloney, Smith, and Stoker) about the importance of political context for civil society, and by extension for social and political capital.

We use multiple regression techniques to test our remaining hypotheses. We examine first the basic questions expressed in hypotheses 3 and 4—whether greater civil society (group and communal) activism elevates levels of social and political capital, leaving aside for the moment possible demographic and contextual influences.

Table 2 presents the results of a multiple regression analysis of civil society activity on social and political capital. As hypothesized, formal group activism appears to contribute strongly to political information and interpersonal trust. Communal activism, however, contributes positively to trust (contrary to prediction) but negatively to political information levels. We suspect that national- and international-level political knowledge are either irrelevant or counterproductive for community activism.

The negligible impact of associational activity on interpersonal trust strikes us as quite important because it contradicts one of Putnam's main predictions. Table 2 shows that the combined explanatory power (variance explained) of both forms of associational activity for interpersonal trust is less than 1 percent (R^2 = .008). That civil society has such a small impact on trust places seriously in doubt, for Central America at least, Putnam's central notion that civil society builds the social capital of interpersonal trust in ways sufficiently important to affect regime performance.

Turning to the political capital, table 2 confirms the hypothesis that formal group civil society will be positively and significantly associated with democratic norms and with the participation variables. In sharp contrast, the hypothesized effects for communal activism find mixed support, with a statistically significant, positive link only to contacting public officials, a significant negative link to democratic norms and campaigning, and no effect on voting.[9] Overall explained variance is small for voting (1.3%) but three to six times that for the other political capital variables.

The results so far are somewhat confounding. They provide very little support for Putnam's theory (hypothesis 3) about social capital except to affirm that formal group activity contributes to political information levels. The results concerning our proposed political capital variables are mixed. Formal group activity increases political capital, as hypothesis 4 predicts, but the effects of communal activism run counter to prediction on three of four variables.

TABLE 2. The Impact of Civil Society Activism on Social Capital and Political Capital

	Social capital		Political capital			
	Political information	Interpersonal trust	Democratic norms	Voting	Campaigning	Contacting
Group activism	.253***	.054***	.192***	.117***	.198***	.191***
Communal Activism	-.097***	.059**	-.091***	-.011	-.066***	.164***
R^2	.250	.008	.037	.013	.038	.078
Standard Error	1.025	.937	1.953	.613	.919	.821
F	127.57	15.14	68.16	23.77	69.47	148.21
Probability of F	.0000	.0000	.0000	.0000	.0000	.0000
(N)		(3849)			(3526)	

Significance levels: * < .05; ** < .01; *** < .001.

This finding, and those of Carla Eastis and of Dietlind Stolle and Thomas Rochon elsewhere in this volume, raise intriguing questions: Why does communal-level civil society correlate with increased trust and contacting, but with diminished democratic norms, campaigning, and political information? Does communal civil society activism in Central America somehow generate confrontational, alienated, or even antidemocratic forms of political capital?

To improve our understanding, we introduce demographic and contextual factors that may intervene between civil society activism and political and social capital. Specifically, we consider levels of economic development and political repression, since both appear very important in Central America (Booth and Richard 1996). We also include the demographic traits of sex, education, and living standard, which almost certainly affect group behavior, political participation, and attitudes to some degree. Table 3 provides evidence about civil society activity's impact upon social and political capital, controlling for key contextual and demographic variables.

Table 3 clearly reflects the power of one key contextual variable. Regime repression, in particular, significantly lowers social capital (information and trust) and even more sharply reduces political capital (democratic norms, voting, contacting, and campaigning). This strongly confirms hypothesis 2's prediction that political context (here repression) will affect the formation of social and political capital. Thus, not only does intense repression drive Central Americans into communal activity and away from other formal group participation, it reduces all forms of social and political capital. Here is compelling evidence that governmental repression dramatically constrains the ability of group activism to shape the behaviors, attitudes, and networks critical to civil society theory. Repression thus has profound implications for the potential impact of civil society's impact on the state.

We also expected gross domestic product per capita to correlate positively with social and political capital, but table 3 demonstrates that, other factors controlled, it does not.[10]

Table 3 also reveals which demographic variables affect social and political capital. The most interesting findings relate to sex. Respondent's sex does not affect interpersonal trust, but women have significantly less political information and political capital than men (even controlling for civil society activism, education, and living standards). This phenomenon presents an intriguing puzzle for which civil society theory per se has no persuasive solution. Why do women have less social and political capital than men, even controlling for their associational activity and socioeconomic status? We suspect that gendered expectations about political roles account for much of this difference.[11]

Turning to the independent effect of the civil society variables upon social and political capital, table 3 presents a clearer picture, if one that reveals

TABLE 3. The Impact of Civil Society Activism on Social Capital and Political Capital, with Demographic and Contextual Controls

	Social capital			Political capital		
	Political information	Interpersonal trust	Democratic norms	Voting	Campaigning	Contacting
Group activism	.080***	.022	.095***	.051**	.118***	.158***
Communal activism	-.009	.077***	-.013	.048**	.013	.192***
Standard of living [a]	.202***	.082***	.072***	.031	-.059**	-.018
Educational Attainment[b]	.307***	.034	.126***	.034	.084***	.043*
Sex (M = 1, F = 2)	-.200***	.026	-.035*	-.069***	-.121***	-.058***
Repression level[c]	-.037*	-.054**	-.289***	-.240***	-.350***	-.112***
GDP per capita[d]	-.232***	-.016	-.095***	-.016	-.057**	.007
R^2	.284	.023	.146	.079	.152	.094
Standard error	.896	.929	1.831	.591	.862	.823
F	219.09	13.12	90.89	45.54	95.82	55.16
Probability of F	.0000	.0000	.0000	.0000	.0000	.0000
(N)	(3867)			(3738)		

Significance levels: * < .05; ** < .01; *** < .001.

[a] Living standard measures family wealth based upon owning color televisions, refrigerators, washing machines, telephones, and automobiles; range 0–15.

[b] Years of formal education completed.

[c] Index of systemic repression level for decade prior to and time of survey; range = 1–5; higher score = greater repression (Booth and Richard, 1996).

[d] Gross domestic product per capita, 1990 (UNDP, 1993, T. 1).

differentiated links between the two types of civil society and social capital. Formal group activism retains a positive effect on political information, but its contribution to interpersonal trust disappears entirely with controls introduced. Communal activism's effect, on the other hand, has no impact on information but enhances interpersonal trust.

The introduction of contextual and demographic controls to assess the independent effect of formal group activism upon political capital (table 3) changes little from the findings in table 2. The positive independent association of group activism with each of the political capital variables remains, although somewhat weaker. On the other hand we find that communal activism's anomalously negative links to political capital (table 2) have vanished (table 3). Community-level activism now increases voting and contacting as predicted by hypothesis 2, while the significant, negative betas for democratic norms and campaigning have disappeared.

In sum, table 3 clarifies linkages between Central Americans' civil society activity and both social capital (hypothesis 3) and political capital (hypothesis 4). Controlling for demographics, repression, and development levels, formal group activism increases political information levels but not interpersonal trust, while communal activism does the reverse. We may understand these opposed relationships by reflecting on the differences in the kinds of civil society activity. Formal groups link members to politics, making political information more accessible to participants. Working at the local level with others builds a confidence in the others involved. Overall, though, the minuscule contribution of civil society to explained variation in interpersonal trust in Central America calls into question Putnam's claim that trust forms the crucial link among citizens who can influence the performance of the state. The analysis, however, makes evident that formal group activism independently elevates all political capital variables, while communal activism increases two of four, voting and contacting. Thus associational activism increases political capital more robustly and consistently than it does social capital.

The independent and powerfully depressing effect of repression upon social and political capital demonstrated in table 3 also stands out sharply. This finding underlines the importance of considering relevant political contextual factors like repression when evaluating civil society comparatively, especially in situations of rapid political change. This makes sense because repression's purpose is to curtail citizen activity, organization, and demands upon government. Repression thus directly affects the likelihood that citizens will develop or join formal associations and pushes citizens toward safer, less formally organized communal activism. By doing so repression impedes the consequent development of social and political capital.

Conclusion

Our findings vindicate the addition of the concept of political capital (be-haviors and attitudes that impinge directly upon the state and its perfor-mance) to theory about civil society and its contributions to democracy. Our political capital variables register as more robust products of civil so-ciety than the two social capital variables we operationalized based on Putnam's writings. This strongly argues that the scholars seeking to assess the importance of civil society, whether for democratization or other as-pects of regime performance, should incorporate into their analyses citi-zen attitudes and behaviors that can affect the state—what we call political capital.

Our findings also demonstrate how powerfully the political context, in particular political repression, affects the formation and nature of civil so-ciety in Central America. They support the contention of Tarrow (1996), Foley and Edwards (1997, 1998), Heying (this volume), Nowland-Forman (1998), Portney and Berry (this volume), and Youniss, McLellan, and Yates (this volume) that the causal or, at least, sequential connection may move from state behavior to civil society development, not the reverse.[12]

Government repression discourages formal group activity but encour-ages citizens to engage in community-level activity (or leaves them only this forum). This probably occurs because repressive states view the local venues and the narrowly specific demands typical of community activism as less threatening than the objectives and actions of higher-order formal groups. For citizens in repressive nations, working with neighbors to repair a bridge or to collect funds to buy books for a village school's library, for in-stance, seem much less likely to attract the wrath of security forces than would joining in a labor union. We suspect that repressive states, whether wittingly or unwittingly, make the community arena a relatively safer place for participation by making formal organizations seem more dangerous, causing citizens to adjust their activities accordingly. Indeed, our findings suggest that the national climate of freedom or repression may well have greater impact than civil society on the formation of social and political capital.

When Government Fails

Social Capital in an Antimodern Russia

RICHARD ROSE

Networks for the production of goods and services are an inevitable feature of all societies. In premodern societies social capital often involves informal associations of individuals; in a modern society it often takes the form of large, impersonal, bureaucratic organizations such as commercial airlines, social security agencies, and universities. But what is the role of social capital networks in an "antimodern" society permeated by governmental failure, in which formal organizations do not operate impersonally, predictably, and in accord with the rule of law? Do individuals retreat into informal networks to substitute for discredited formal organizations? Is this paralleled by social failure, that is, individuals displaying "amoral familism" and refusing to cooperate? (cf. Banfield 1958). Or do informal networks penetrate formal organizations, seeking to correct for their shortcomings or reinforcing antimodern features by sustaining favoritism and bribery?

Understanding societies distant from Weber's ideal-type modern society or Putnam's (1993) civic democracy is necessary if theories of social capital are to be sufficiently robust to apply in many parts of the world where the rule of law and impersonal, efficient, bureaucratic organizations are not dominant, and social capital networks may be invoked against an antimodern state. This article addresses the significance of social capital in Russia today.

To describe post-Communist societies as "in transition" focuses on the

This paper is part of a project on Coping with Organizations: Networks of Russian Social Capital, Leverhulme Trust Grant F/273/X. It makes use of data collected as part of the World Bank Social Capital Initiative, supported by a grant from Danish government development funds. An earlier version of this argument appeared in *Social Capital: A Multicultural Perspective*, edited by Partha Dasgupta and Ismail Serageldin, World Bank, Washington D.C., 1999.

TABLE 1. Comparing Modern and Antimodern Societies

	Modern	Antimodern
Operation	Complex	Complex
Signals	Prices, laws	Rules, politics, bribes, personal contacts
Openness	Transparent	Translucent, opaque
Lawful	Yes	Rigidity modified by waivers
Cause and effect	Calculable	Uncertain
Output	Efficient	Inefficient
Effectiveness	Yes	Usually, but not always

Source: As discussed in Rose (1999).

goal rather than on the point of origin. However, the contemporary state remains greatly influenced by the antimodern Soviet legacy, as are the social networks of Russians, which are a response to the distinctive mobilizing efforts of the Soviet Union in its Stalinist heyday (cf. Linz 1975). A totalitarian society is full of organizations seeking to mobilize compliance with the regime's dictates. If anything, it is over-organized, using bureaucratic commands and ideological coercion in efforts to make people do what the regime wants. But it is simultaneously under-bureaucratized, in that the rule of law does not apply, and the system encourages people to create informal networks as protection against the state and to circumvent or subvert its commands. The result is a "dual society" in which informal and formal networks are in opposition.

Russia appears to be a modern society in terms of its physical and human capital. Nearly everyone in the labor force has at least a secondary education, three-quarters of the population is urban, and telecommunication and transport link a population dispersed across eleven time zones. But attempts at total mobilization by the Communist party-state drove individuals to seek refuge in private and unofficial networks. Russians created "second economies" and "second polities" (Grossman 1977; Gitelman 1984:241) to insulate themselves from intrusive organizations and to exploit formal organizations. These networks were not destroyed by the collapse of the Soviet Union; to a substantial degree, Russians continue to rely on unmodern networks to get by amid the turbulence of transformation. However, the persistence of such networks is a formidable barrier to Russia's transition from an antimodern to a modern society (cf. Rose 1993).

Contrasting Approaches to Social Capital Networks

Social capital is here defined as the stock of formal or informal social networks that individuals use to produce or allocate goods and services. In common with other definitions, this emphasizes that social capital is about recurring relationships between individuals.

Networks Both Informal and Formal

Face-to-face relationships create *informal* networks among a limited number of individuals bound together by kinship, friendship, or propinquity. Informal networks are institutions in the sociological sense of having patterned and recurring interaction. But they are not formal organizations, because they lack legal recognition, full-time officials, and written rules. The characteristic output of informal networks is a small-scale do-it-yourself service such as help with child care or with repairing a house or barn. Reliance on informal networks belongs to the world of Tocqueville, that is, pre-industrial society. When he wrote *Democracy in America* in the 1830s, the United States was a rural society in which face-to-face relationships were dominant; more than 90 percent of the population lived in communities of fewer than 2,500 people.

Formal organizations that are pervasive in modern societies are rule-bound and bureaucratic, having a legal status and secure revenue from the market or the state. A formal organization can have individual members—for example, a professional association of doctors—or its members can be organizations, as in an association of hospitals. However, the links between individuals and organizations are often mediated many times, as with the relation between the managers of a joint stock firm and its nominal owners. Formal organizations are a necessary part of a *modern* society, which requires impersonal bureaucratic organizations of state and market that can routinely produce complex goods such as automobiles, and services such as university education (cf. Woolcock 1998:169ff.). In a study of corporatism, Schmitter goes so far as to argue, "Organizations are becoming citizens alongside, if not in the place of, individuals" (1995:310).

There are many links between informal and formal organizations, both horizontal (a family books a holiday through a travel organization) and vertical (individuals can have informal relations within their union branch, which is affiliated with the district and regional levels and a distant national headquarters). However, a formal organization cannot behave as individuals interacting informally do, for its employees are officials of a rule-bound formal organization. An informal network has fewer resources and rules but more flexibility and, in the literal sense, more sympathy with those it embraces.

The relationship between informal networks and formal organizations is contingent. Informal networks can have positive consequences within formal organizations, and especially in the interstices between formal organizations, as in Edmund Burke's hypothesis that soldiers fight for their platoon rather than for a bureaucratic military organization. But in the antimodern Soviet Union, informal and formal networks often contradicted each other. Uncertainties arising from the behavior of formal organizations encouraged the formation of informal horizontal networks that individuals used to insulate themselves from exploitative organizations. When individuals were caught up in the activities of formal organizations, they could de-bureaucratize the relationship by relying on personal contacts, barter, or bribes to get what they wanted (see Ledeneva 1998). Mutual cooperation was based on the morality of face-to-face groups, which Max Weber characterized as *Binnenmoral*; the complement was "outsider morals" (*Aussenmoral*), which justified a group's exploitation of formal organizations of the state. Russia today continues to suffer from a missing middle: organizations linking informal grassroots networks and modern organizations. The gap is sometimes filled by antimodern enterprises run by ex-nomenklatura officials or by *Mafiya* organizations (cf. Shlapentokh 1989:4ff.; Hedlund and Sundström 1996).

Three Approaches

The political economy approach of James S. Coleman defines social capital in *situational and instrumental* terms (1990:302). Individuals use networks in order to produce a tangible flow of goods and services, such as minding another person's child or finding a job. The type of network needed varies from one situation to another. To claim a pension involves interaction with officials in a large bureaucratic organization, whereas organizing a church social event depends on personal networks. Empirically, situational theories of social capital predict: an individual relies on a heterogeneous set of social capital networks. The type of network invoked depends on how things get done in a given situation. An important implication of the variability of networks from one situation to another is that social capital cannot be reduced to a static quantity single unit possessed by individuals, and even less can it be aggregated from various individual attributes into a summary statistic characterizing a whole society.

A second approach treats social capital as a set of *social psychological or cultural beliefs and norms:* in Inglehart's phrase, "a culture of trust and tolerance in which extensive networks of voluntary associations emerge" (1997:188). People who trust each other interact to form associations in situations ranging from choirs and sports groups to the workplace and thereby become more trusting.[1] In Inglehart's view, "social capital [that is, trust] plays a crucial role in both political and economic cooperation." From this perspective, networks result from people trusting each other rather than trust emerging as a byproduct of association. Social capital not only spills over from one situation to another, it also spills up, creating the large-scale representative institutions such as political parties important in *Making Democracy Work* (Putnam 1993a). This leads to the empirical prediction: There is consistency in networks chosen by an individual from one situation to another. An individual's quantum of social capital can thus be measured by a disposition to trust other people and institutions of society. Research then focuses on why some people are more trusting than others. This is a long way from the bottom line concern with the production of goods and services central to Coleman's political economy approach.

Fukuyama's study of "social virtues and the creation of prosperity" has a Durkheimian emphasis on culture as the source of trust and cooperation (1995a:26ff.). Fukuyama cites cross-cultural differences in social capital networks to explain cross-national differences in forms of economic organization, specifically, a predisposition toward firms based on family and kinship in societies such as France, as against those societies in which there are strong ties to impersonal corporations, for example Japan. Empirically, cultural theories predict homogeneity in social capital between individuals within a society, and consistency from one situation to another.

The Situational Character of Social Capital

Even in an antimodern society there is no escape from becoming involved with organizations to obtain education, health care, housing, and employment. What do Russians do? If social capital networks are culturally determined, a single anecdote from the society might suffice. If social capital were based on individual trust, then assessing the disposition of individuals on this score would be sufficient to understand networks. But we can only determine the validity of these arguments after examining the kinds of networks that individuals are disposed to invoke in a multiplicity of different situations.

The social capital data analyzed here come from a questionnaire specially designed to identify the networks that Russians turn to in everyday situations. It was used to interview 1,904 adult Russians face-to-face in a multistage randomly stratified sample covering the whole of the Russian Federation, urban and rural, with 191 widely dispersed primary sampling units. Fieldwork by VCIOM (the Russian Centre for Public Opinion Research) took place between 6 March and 13 April 1998 (for sample details, see Rose 1998:72ff.). The questionnaire drew on the experience of six previous New Russia Barometer surveys conducted since January 1992.

The first criterion in selecting situations to ask about was that they affect a majority of households rather than being minority interests such as bowling or singing in a choir. The situations included getting food, housing, protection from crime on the streets and at home, income security, health, and governance. Additional questions were asked about situations involving a substantial portion of the population: care and education of children for the 44 percent with children; employment-related networks for those in the labor force; and getting paid a pension for those in retirement (for details, WWW.socialcapital.ac.uk).

Second, to determine the extent to which Russians rely on formal organizations as in a modern society, the questionnaire dealt with situations in which they are major sources for the delivery of goods and services, such as hospital treatment, education, and employment. This avoids the anthropological fallacy of treating every relation as "outside" modern structures; it also avoids the formalist fallacy of assuming that government organizations actually do what citizens want them to do. Asking about the delivery of goods and services that the respondent, family members, or friends and neighbors use provides evidence with greater face validity than questions about trust in distant national institutions for which television and press are the primary media of information.[2]

Third, each situation focused on the production of a particular good or service, such as house repair, or on allocation or misallocation—for example, securing university admission for a youth whose grades did not entitle him or her to a place. The phrasing of the questions left open whether an individual relied on a modern organization to produce what was required or would turn to an alternative network.

Alternative Tactics for Getting Things Done

In the ideal-type modern society, people do not need a repertoire of tactics for dealing with formal organizations. Bureaucratic organizations predictably deliver goods and services to individuals as citizens and customers. To invoke Weber, modern organizations operate like a vending machine: a person inserts an entitlement or money and the expected good or service is delivered. In a modern society we do not think it unusual if electricity is supplied without interruption and regularly billed, an airline ticket booked by phone is ready to pick up at the airport, or a pension is paid routinely each month. Even if people use informal networks to get some things done, in a modern society this is not interpreted as evidence of governmental failure.

But what if modern organizations do not work in the ideal-type way? Given the centrality of money incomes in a modern society, the inability of organizations to pay wages or a pension indicates the extent of organizational failure in Russia. The social capital survey found that fewer than two in five Russians routinely receive the wage or pension to which they are entitled. Wages are more likely to be paid late to employees of such public sector organizations as the military, education, and state enterprises than to employees in the private sector. Moreover, pensions, a state responsibility that is easy to routinize in a modern society, are even more likely to be paid late than wages.

Confronted with organizational failure, individuals have a choice of alternatives. Informal networks can substitute for the failure of modern bureaucratic organizations. Additional tactics include trying to personalize relations with impersonal bureaucrats; using connections or bribery in an attempt to get bureaucrats to violate rules; or fatalistically accepting that nothing can be done. In each module of the questionnaire, respondents were asked what they would expect to do or advise a friend to do to get something done in a familiar situation. For each situation, a multiplicity of tactics was offered, including the government organization working as it ought to. The answers show which network or networks Russians rely on and the extent to which tactics vary with the situation (for examples, see table 2; for full details, see Rose 1998).[3]

In almost every situation, a majority of Russians did not expect to obtain what they wanted with vending machine efficiency. Food shops are the only set of organizations that a majority of Russians expect to work as they are supposed to; 74 percent of respondents go to food shops regularly and think that prices are actually charged as marked. While in a modern society this appears obvious, in Russia it is a novelty, for, in the command economy, food stores allocated goods by a combination of queuing, the black market, and arbitrary fiat. Only two-fifths have confidence in the police providing protection from house burglars, and only a third rely on social security offices to pay entitlements.

In a modern society, the mega-network of the *market* offers those with sufficient income an alternative to government failure. In Russia, choosing what you want from competing shops is a novelty. The great majority of Russians have sufficient money to pick and choose their food in the marketplace, and stores now regularly have ample stocks of food to sell. However, when costs are higher, the proportion able to turn to the market falls precipitously. Less than one in three expect to have enough financial resources to consider buying a house, and only one in six reckons he or she could secure a bank loan.

Individuals can exit from modern organizations by *substituting production by a nonmonetized informal network*. Four-fifths of Russian households, including a large majority of city dwellers, continue to grow some food for themselves (cf. Rose and Tikhomirov 1993). While only one in four Russians has any savings and a big majority of the unemployed do not receive a state unemployment benefit, most Russians can draw on informal networks of social capital for cash. A total of 66 percent report that they could

TABLE 2. Alternative Tactics for Getting Things Done

	% Involved
MODERN ORGANIZATIONS WORK	
Public sector allocates by law	
Police will help protect house from burglary	43
Social security office will pay entitlement if you claim	35
Market allocates to paying customers	
Buy a flat if it is needed	30
Can borrow a week's wage from bank	16
INFORMAL ALTERNATIVES	
Nonmonetized production	
Growing food	81
Can borrow a week's wage from a friend	66
PERSONALIZE	
Beg or cajole officials controlling allocation	
Keep demanding action at social security office to get paid	32
Beg officials to admit person to hospital	22
ANTIMODERN	
Reallocate in contravention of the rules	
Use connections to get a subsidized flat	24
Pay cash to doctor on the side	23
PASSIVE, SOCIALLY EXCLUDED	
Nothing I can do to:	
Get into hospital quickly	16
Get pension paid on time (pensioners only)	24

Source: Nationwide New Russia Barometer Survey VII (Rose 1998). Number of respondents: 1,904.

borrow a week's wages or pension from a friend or relative. In a developing society such informal networks can be described as premodern. However, in the Russian context they are evidence of de-modernization, a means of avoiding the consequences of the failure of bureaucratic organizations. Even though such activities do not turn up in national income accounts, they are nonetheless real to those who rely on them.

When a formal organization does not deliver and an individual cannot substitute the market or an informal network, these networks can be invoked to de-bureaucratize dealings with an organization to make it produce goods and services. A person can try to *personalize* his or her relationship, begging or cajoling officials to provide what is wanted. Since the great majority of Russians do not expect to get paid an unemployment benefit when they file a claim, a common tactic is to pester officials until it is paid. This is not a retreat into a premodern informal network so much as it is a stressful attempt to compensate for the inefficiencies of bureaucratic organizations by stepping back into a premodern relationship in which individuals pleaded for benefits.

The behavior of organizations in Soviet times encouraged Russians to adopt antimodern tactics. The social capital survey found that 68 percent thought that to get anything done by a public agency in Soviet times you had to know people in the Party. It was even more widely assumed that you had to have connections, a network of friends and friends of friends or even friends of friends of friends. In the words of the folk saying, "Better a hundred friends than a hundred roubles." The Russian concept of *blat* usually refers to using connections to misallocate benefits by getting an official to "bend" or break rules (cf. Berliner 1957;182ff.; Ledeneva 1998:37ff.). *Connections*, that is, asking for favors on the basis of being part of a "circle" (*svoim*) or network is also found today. For example, 24 percent endorse connections as the way to get a government-subsidized flat.

The introduction of the market has increased opportunities for paying cash rather than invoking connections to break rules to produce benefits. Taxation provides an excellent example, for the capacity to collect taxes is a defining characteristic of the modern state. Russia has yet to meet this requirement; there are estimates that half of anticipated state revenue is not collected—and some that is collected is "levied" rather than paid by modern means. The great majority of Russians see taxation in antimodern terms. Among employed persons, only 41 percent say that taxes are deducted when their employer pays wages. A majority, 56 percent, say that there is no need to pay taxes if you don't want to do so, for the government will never find out, and 77 percent believe that a cash payment to a tax official would enable a person to evade payment of taxes claimed. Altogether, five-sixths of Russians think that taxes can be evaded; they differ only as to whether taxes can be completely ignored or a "tip" to a tax official is needed to avoid legal obligations.

The assumption that everybody is doing it, whatever "it" is, ignores the fact that networks are exclusive as well as inclusive, and resources for getting things done are not equally distributed throughout a society. As a measure of *social exclusion* (Room 1995), the Russian social capital survey regularly offered the alternative statement: Nothing can be done. The replies showed that a large majority of Russians are not socially excluded, that is, they are able to draw on some form of social capital when problems arise in everyday situations (fig. 1). Depending on the situation, 73 percent to more than 90 percent have some sort of network for getting things done.

Measures of Social Exclusion if Organization Fails

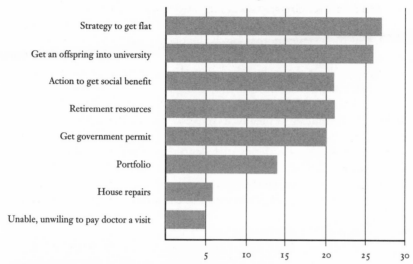

 % saying nothing can be done to obtain service or good
Source: New Russia Barometer Survey VII (1998). Fieldwork by VCIOM
Number of respondents: 1,904

The minority who feel helpless is a large one when wages are not paid, an indication that the enterprise itself is short of money, and cajoling or bribery will be of no avail.

Government failure is not a sign that nothing works within a society but that formal organizations do not work as in a modern society. When a formal organization fails to operate routinely, most Russians have social capital networks to get things done. The appropriateness of networks often varies with the situation. There is far more scope for informal cooperation in house repair than in hospital treatment; more scope for using bribery or connections to obtain a flat; and growing vegetables is a straightforward method to produce food. In every situation, more than one network is applicable—and Russians differ in their choice. Whatever the situation, some people will rely on the public bureaucracy to deliver goods and services, while others rely on informal do-it-yourself cooperation, personal cajoling of bureaucrats, or antimodern bending or breaking of rules, and if the situation makes it feasible, some turn to the market.

Redundancy in the Face of Uncertainty

Uncertainty is the bane of an antimodern society. The presence of formal organizations is evidence that goods and services can be produced, but intermittent organizational failure is a warning that they cannot be relied on to work. In such circumstances it is rational for individuals to rely on *redundancy*, maintaining links with more networks than are normally necessary so that if one fails another can be invoked. Even if redundancy is inefficient, it can be effective, ensuring that by one means or another something will get done. In this way pathological government organizations transfer significant costs to individuals.

Job search is a classic example of redundancy, since people can look for work by a multiplicity of means. Economic transformation has made Russians insecure; more than three-fifths of those employed worry about losing their job. Yet these anxieties are balanced by confidence in being able to find another job; almost two-thirds think they could do so. Redundancy contributes to this confidence. Four-fifths have some idea of what they would do to find a job, and a majority can call on at least two different networks in a job search. The alternatives, and the frequency with which they are named, are:

Informal networks: Ask friends, 50 percent, family, 11 percent.

Market networks: Approach employers directly, 33 percent; read help wanted advertisements, 23 percent; move to another city, 3 percent.

Public organization: Go to an employment bureau, 19 percent.

Antimodern: Offer a payment to the manager, 1 percent.

Excluded: Don't know, 20 percent.

Most unemployed Russians are able to proceed on a trial-and-error basis, trying at least two different networks in searching for a job.

Access to multiple networks is what works best, as this enables individuals to pursue different strategies until what is wanted gets done (Simon 1997:421ff.). Health care illustrates a similar use of networks, since what is needed changes radically with the physical intensity of discomfort. In the past year, 42 percent of Russians had no need to invoke any health care network, since they had not felt ill. Of those who did feel ill at some point in time, a third did not think it necessary to visit a doctor, staying home and treating their aches with a home remedy. If medical treatment was required, seven-eighths say they would rely on state services, a clinic near their home or connected with their place of work. Only 5 percent said they would use connections to get a doctor, and 3 percent would pay for private treatment. Only one in eight of those who went to a doctor for treatment said that they had to make a side payment for this notionally free service.

However, when dissatisfaction with health care rises, few Russians accept the bureaucratic rule: Wait your turn. When asked what a person with a painful disease should do if a hospital says that treatment will not be available for some months, only one in six says nothing can be done. The most frequently cited tactic for queue jumping is antimodern; using connections to get hospital treatment promptly is endorsed by 44 percent and offering a tip to officials by 23 percent. The proportion ready to buy a "free" service under the table is greater than the fifth who would turn to the market to buy private treatment legally. A begging personal appeal to officials that involves no expenses was endorsed by 22 percent. It can be tried at no expense. The tactics endorsed are not mutually exclusive: a person in pain could proceed sequentially, first begging a hospital to speed things up, then turning to connections, and, if that did not work, offering a cash payment. Only if all three tactics failed would a person be left with the stark choice of waiting in pain or borrowing the cash to pay for expensive private treatment.

The great majority of Russians have a portfolio of social capital networks combining different types of resources. The commonest portfolio appears to be defensive; a person tries a modern organization and, if this fails to produce satisfaction, falls back on informal social networks as a substitute. The portfolio is defensive inasmuch as it is a form of retreat or insulation from modern society. An enterprising person can combine modern market and antimodern networks, getting some things done by buying them in the market, while achieving other goals by buying services of officials in government agencies or using connections. The use of connections is likely to be much influenced by coincidence: the occupations of relatives, neighbors, schoolmates who have gone diverse ways, and so forth. While nearly everyone will have connections in some situations, people cannot expect to live by connections alone.

In an antimodern society, vulnerability is greatest when an individual relies solely on public organizations, since these cannot be depended on to deliver. When organizations fail, the vulnerable are effectively pushed into the ranks of the socially excluded. However, social exclusion is situation-specific rather than a pervasive characteristic of some Russians. Across eight different situations, only 1 percent of Russians say that nothing can be done in a majority of situations. Moreover, when Russians are asked how much control they have over their lives, on a scale with 1 representing no control at all and 10 a great deal, the mean reply is almost exactly in the middle, 5.2. Only 7 percent place themselves at the bottom, feeling without any control of their lives.

Implications for Theory and Practice

Many Sovietologists have argued the uniqueness of Russia. However, commonalities across cultures are assumed by theories of socialist and market economies and by theories of democratization and undemocratic rule. The spread of the Communist system from Moscow made it relevant to upwards of 400 million people in Europe. Substantial elements of Marxism such as collectivist agriculture have appeared in 33 countries across Africa, Central America, and Asia. If China is included, the total population that has been or remains subject to Communist one-party rule and a nonmarket economy rises to 1.5 billion (cf. World Bank 1996).

The significance of totalitarianism for the formation of networks is underscored by Shi's picture of how Chinese people get things done, based on a survey in Beijing just before the Tiananmen Square massacre (1997:53, 268). Nine-tenths did not passively accept the directives of the Communist regime. Instead, people formed networks to allocate goods and services to themselves. The networks were not used to change laws, which was neither possible nor necessary, for most Chinese laws are vague (316). Individuals influenced the implementation of central directives by using *guanxi* networks, tactics familiar to students of the Soviet system (69, 121ff.). While all undemocratic regimes offer more incentives to retreat or subvert formal organizations than do established democracies, a totalitarian or "post"-totalitarian legacy of mobilizational coercion encourages more antimodern behavior than does a "normal" dictatorship (Rose and Shin 2000).

There is no single "silver bullet" formula making it possible to sum up all forms of social capital into a single index number. To use "trust in people" as a proxy indicator for social capital ignores the possibility that trust in other people may be a consequence rather than a cause of trustworthy organizations (Dasgupta 1988). Moreover, confronted with untrustworthy organizations, individuals may learn to distrust most people they know (Mishler and Rose, 2001).

Nor can organizational memberships be used as a proxy for social capital networks. The social capital survey found few Russians belonging to any kind of voluntary association. In reply to direct questions, fewer than 5 percent said they belong to a sports, music, or arts club or to a housing or neighborhood association or a political party (Rose 1998: 60). Altogether, 91 percent are not members of any of the face-to-face organizations described as building blocks of a civic democracy. Furthermore, national leaders of organizations may not be trusted to represent their members. While 53 percent of Russian employees reported being members of a trade union, fewer than half (that is, 22 percent of all workers) trusted their local union leader to look after their interests, and fewer than 11 percent trusted national union officials to look after their interests.

Paradoxically, it can be easier to measure social exclusion from networks. But individuals should not be labeled as excluded or included on the basis of a single indirect indicator such as income or education (Rose

2000), nor is exclusion usually cumulative from one situation to another. While most Russians are "outside the loop" in some situations, an overwhelming majority are inside the loop (that is, having a network they can turn too) in most situations. In addition to being situational, exclusion from effective networks may be a phase in the life cycle, for example, young people not yet having a steady job or elderly widows living alone with few interpersonal connections. Insofar as this is the case, the incidence of exclusion shows an egalitarian distribution, since every citizen is similarly at risk at a given stage of the life cycle.

Organizational failure in Russia often reflects the combination of too many bureaucratic rules and too little adherence to bureaucratic norms. A surfeit of rules imposes delays and unresponsiveness, as different public agencies must be consulted. Individuals then have to invest an unreasonable amount of time in pleading and pushing to compensate for organizational inefficiencies. If bureaucrats offer to waive obstructive regulation in return for a bribe, this delivers a service—but in an antimodern way. The result is popular ambivalence about the rule of law. A total of 71 percent of Russians say that the national government is a long way from the idea of a law-governed state *(pravovoye gosudarstvo)*. But if this were to come about, it would not be entirely welcome, for 62 percent think that laws are often very hard on ordinary people, and 73 percent endorse the belief that harsh Russian laws can be softened by their non-enforcement.

The classic Schumpeterian solution to the failure of government is to throw the rascals out at a general election and give the opposition a chance to show what it can do. In the Russian Federation there have been three elections of a Duma and two presidential elections. But what is to be done if a sequence of elections simply results in the "circulation of rascals," as one unpopular government is replaced by another that appears no better (cf. Rose et al. 1998: ch. 10)? Where antimodern practices are rampant, the immediate need is not to change the values and attitudes of the mass of the population; it is to change the way the country is governed. If post-Communist governors want people to rely less on informal or antimodern social capital, they should attack the failings of government organizations that encourage individuals to use social capital against an antimodern state.

Mobilizing Minority Communities

Social Capital and Participation

in Urban Neighborhoods

KENT E. PORTNEY AND JEFFREY M. BERRY

An unusually strong consensus has emerged among academics as to the problem: Americans are disengaged from civic life. Increasingly we live in splendid isolation, relating to friends but paying little attention to our community (Barber 1984; Putnam, 1995a). We no longer live in Tocqueville's America but in a society where the town square has been replaced by the mall, cable television, and the Internet. Yet Americans claim they want to be more involved in working together with their neighbors on civic problems; that they want to have more of a voice in the political process; and that we ought to have smaller government and more voluntarism by rank-and-file citizens. These sentiments are easily articulated to pollsters; actually taking the time to work with one's neighbors is another thing entirely.

Although there is widespread agreement as to the indictment, there is not much consensus as to the underlying causes. There is even less agreement as to the cure. Whatever the causes and potential solutions, it is clear that a central issue in determining the public's involvement in community life is how the opportunities to participate are structured. If people want to participate but are failing to do so, it may well be that they do not find avenues for participation accessible or inviting. In this essay we ask what kinds of political organizations are most effective in mobilizing minorities in city politics. We look at people of minority status because the debate about

Revised from an article of the same title in *American Behavioral Scientist* 40, no. 5 (1997): 632–44.

social capital and civic engagement is largely a debate that concentrates on white, middle-class America. Virtually none of the debate, and as far as we can find, no empirical analysis, considers whether poor people, people of minority racial or ethnic status, and people in inner cities have also experienced the trends in civic engagement. Indeed, there is an assumption that, whatever the state of engagement is in general, it must be worse for African Americans and for Hispanics, who are certainly thought to be less connected, less civically engaged, and less well-equipped to compete in mainstream political processes.

We emphasize neighborhoods because neighborhoods are where the bonds of community are built. They are the wellsprings of social capital. People's sense of community, their sense of belonging to a neighborhood, caring about the people who live there, and believing that people who live there care about them, are critical attitudes that can nurture or discourage participation.

Drawing on data gathered from five American cities, we examine the impact of structures of strong democracy on community building. By "structures of strong democracy" we mean institutions that give all residents an opportunity to participate at all stages of the policymaking process, and that give citizens the authority to determine the final outcomes of the policy matters considered in this participatory process. By "community building" we mean those beliefs and types of political behavior that contribute to positive attitudes by residents about their neighborhood and encourage a willingness to work cooperatively on its behalf.

If our goal is to understand civic engagement, civil society, and the creation of social capital, neighborhood associations seem to be an ideal focus. They offer citizens an opportunity to discuss community problems with other neighbors. They are forums where city officials come to respond to the questions and demands of ordinary citizens. Successful neighborhood associations should promote cooperation, encourage voluntarism, and enhance feelings of community.

Five American Cities

To further explore these issues of participation, race, and community, we conducted research in five cities—Birmingham, Dayton, Portland (Ore.), St. Paul, and San Antonio—where participatory democracy is taken seriously. Elsewhere we explain how these cities were chosen, but in general terms they were selected because they were thought to have the most impressive citizen participation systems in the country (Berry, Portney, and Thomson 1993).

Four of these cities have citywide systems of neighborhood associations. In each and every neighborhood there is a neighborhood association that has substantial authority over the community and is run cooperatively by residents. Although they are purely voluntary associations very much like the types of organizations touted by Kenneth Newton in this volume, these neighborhood associations have real powers and are not merely planning or advisory boards. Their strongest authority lies in the area of zoning and land use. In the city of St. Paul, for example, a resident wanting a zoning permit or a variance must go to his or her neighborhood association rather than to city hall. For all intents and purposes, there is no appealing a zoning decision made by one of the city's neighborhood associations. This applies to businessmen and developers as well as homeowners. Thus project proposals for new businesses or housing must gain the support of the neighborhood association before they can be carried out.

Birmingham, Dayton, and Portland are variations on the same theme. In San Antonio, there is a different model of citizen participation. An Alinsky-style advocacy group, COPS (Communities Organized for Public Service), has been an effective representative of San Antonio's Hispanic community. As discussed by Mark Warren in this volume, COPS has organized residents in the solidly Hispanic section of town along the parish boundaries of the Catholic Church (see also Wood, this volume). Drawing hundreds and sometimes thousands of supporters into its confrontations and meetings with city officials, COPS has empowered San Antonio's Hispanics. It is widely considered to be one of the most powerful, if not the most powerful, community group in the country. The rest of San Antonio, however, is not organized nearly as well. There is no set of city-sponsored neighborhood associations, and, where neighborhoods are organized, it is entirely at the initiative of residents.

City administrators and elected officials respect the neighborhood associations in the citywide systems because of the authority they have within the structure of city government. In San Antonio, respect comes from the ability of COPS to make city officials' lives miserable when the government comes into conflict with the organization. The neighborhood associations are broadly and enthusiastically supported by residents. Participation usually involves a time-consuming and demanding task, such as attending the monthly meeting, serving on a committee, or communicating with city officials on behalf of the neighborhood association. Even those who don't participate in the neighborhood associations regard them positively. Eighty-eight and a half percent of those interviewed in the cities believe that no other organization better represents their community than their neighborhood association, and 62.9 percent believe that the neighborhood association would offer them the opportunity to be involved on a major issue.

Race and Neighborhoods

Neighborhood associations are one way of trying to build community. These are organizations that encourage neighbors to come together and to talk to each other about their community and the problems that it faces. In face-to-face meetings, men and women can learn from each other, reason with one another, and search for common interests. Ideally, bonds of friendship and community are forged as neighbors look for solutions to the issues before them. Political participation becomes an educative device rather than an occasionally exercised civic obligation.

The city governments pay for community organizers, office space, and communications (such as newsletters or newspaper inserts) from the neighborhood associations to all their constituents. On a per neighborhood basis, the amounts of money are decidedly modest. Despite this financial support, the neighborhood associations are independent of city hall; they are not bound to support those in office because they receive city funds. The financial and administrative support is critical because it is very difficult for residents in any neighborhood to build a stable, ongoing organization that has the capacity to react immediately to issues affecting their community.

Within the five cities, there is substantial diversity in terms of their racial and ethnic makeup. Birmingham is 55.6 percent black and Dayton 36.9 percent black. Portland (7.6 percent) and St. Paul (4.9 percent) have considerably smaller black populations. None of these four cities has a significant number of Hispanic residents. San Antonio is 53.7 percent Hispanic and 7.3 percent black. The surveys we took indicated that race wasn't a dominant issue in any of the cities at the time of the research. Race, however, is not far beneath the surface in these cities either. In San Antonio, issues often divide Anglos and Hispanics. In Birmingham, the relatively new majority status of the African-American population was a cause of some uneasiness on the part of the city's white minority. In Dayton, white flight is a continuing concern, and, in Dayton and St. Paul, racial quotas in city hiring were an issue during the time of our fieldwork.

Surveys of about 1,100 residents in each of the five cities were completed in 1986–87. Around the same time, fieldwork was conducted in each of the cities and elite interviews were done with city councilors, administrators, interest group leaders, and activists in the neighborhood associations. What is unusual about these data is that we are able to identify the neighborhood that respondents reside in, thus allowing a comparative analysis of neighborhoods within and between cities. The surveys were, in fact, stratified by neighborhood so that the number of interviews in each neighborhood is proportionate to its population within the city.

Questions in the surveys cover a wide variety of topics intended to measure the attitudes and behavior relevant to the neighborhood associations and to city government and politics. To assess the relationship between the citizen participation systems, neighborhood, and race, we can draw on a number of relevant questions from the interviews. First we look at participation and mobilization. What is the relationship between the racial composition of neighborhoods and the racial composition of activists in the neighborhood associations? Is there a racial bias in the patterns of participation? Second we ask about neighborhood and sense of community. Do neighborhood associations designed around principles of strong democracy build community more successfully than other kinds of political organizations?

Participation and Mobilization

One of the central elements underlying the idea of strong democracy is what we call face-to-face political participation—communal activities that seem capable of helping to rebuild American democracy. In this paper, we focus on four specific types of activity, including some of the most frequently practiced forms of face-to-face activity in American cities. We concentrate on participation in the neighborhood associations, in independent issue-based citizens organizations, in neighborhood crime watch organizations, and in social, civic, self-help, and service organizations. In any major U.S. city, significant numbers of residents are likely to be active in these kinds of organizations.

We have shown elsewhere that the neighborhood associations do not increase the overall number of people who participate in city politics. They are successful, however, in increasing the frequency with which residents take part in face-to-face political activities (Berry, Portney, and Thomson 1993:71–98). But compared to other forms of participation, how well do the citywide systems of neighborhood associations engage people who reside in racially diverse or predominantly African American neighborhoods?

To examine this question we compare citizen involvement in different kinds of voluntary organizations, distinguishing between neighborhood associations, issue-based citizens groups, crime watch organizations, and social, service, or self-help organizations. Each of these kinds of organizations provides theoretical opportunities for citizens to be civically engaged. But do they all offer similar opportunities in practice? Are there perhaps subtle or implicit cues that encourage or discourage people of various backgrounds from participating? If there are differences in participation across types of organizations, how do neighborhood associations compare?

Equally important, we ask whether each of these kinds of organizations is capable of helping to build a sense of community. There are theoretical reasons to suggest that neighborhood associations may be better able to accomplish this. To the extent that a "sense of community" implies the development of a common sense of community purpose, participation must involve some process whereby people's disagreements can be discussed and where citizens can work to reach common ground. Neighborhood associations promise greater ability to build community mainly because they tend by their nature to be the only type of organization among those examined here that provide face-to-face opportunities for people to be in the presence of other people with whom they might disagree on important social and political issues. Issue-groups, crime watch organizations, and self-help or service organizations, while providing opportunities for civic engagement, are not generally thought of as providing abundant opportunity for being confronted by contrary views. Indeed, issue-based groups attract people who are, by their nature, all in agreement with the positions of the groups. Thus, neighborhood associations are the most likely kind of organization to provide opportunities for "democratic talk," a characteristic thought to be necessary in building strong democracy (Barber 1984).

To begin addressing these kinds of questions, we break participation rates down according to the racial composition of the neighborhood and the socioeconomic status of the respondent. Using neighborhood statistics data from the 1980 census, we group together respondents from our surveys who live in neighborhoods with African American populations of 0 to 20 percent (predominantly white), between 21 and 50 percent (racially diverse), or over 50 percent (predominantly black). Respondents' socioeconomic status (SES) is determined by a simple composite measure, based on the respondent's total family income and personal educational attainment.[1]

Table 1 presents these participation rates. Although participation in neighborhood associations appears to follow the standard socioeconomic model of political participation to a greater degree than other forms of participation, it is not characterized by any sort of bias against people who live in racially diverse or predominantly black neighborhoods. Indeed, the participation rate of low-SES residents of predominantly African American neighborhoods is almost twice that of low-SES residents of neighborhoods with a low minority population. The same general pattern is evident for people at each socioeconomic level. This pattern stands in stark contrast to the findings for independent issue-based citizen organizations. Although citizen group participation among residents of low–minority population neighborhoods is comparable to that for neighborhood associations, these independent organizations do not seem to be as effective at reaching residents of racially diverse or predominantly black neighborhoods.

When the participation rates are broken down by the race of the respondent (as is done in table 2) instead of socioeconomic status, the patterns lead to similar conclusions. Participation among African Americans in neighborhood associations is consistently higher than in issue-based organizations regardless of the racial composition of the neighborhood. African Americans and whites participate in social, service, and self-help organizations at relatively high rates, but only in predominantly non–African American neighborhoods. In predominantly black neighborhoods, only neighborhood associations stand out as providing clearly superior opportunities for African Americans to become civically engaged.

We also analyzed how well neighborhood associations conduct their outreach activities, especially in racially diverse and predominantly black neighborhoods. To do this we asked respondents: "In the past two years,

TABLE 1. Participation in Face-to-Face Activities by Socioeconomic Status

	Percent African American in neighborhood			
Percent who participate	*0–20%*	*21–50%*	*51% or more*	*χ^2 significance[a]*
In neighborhood associations				
Low SES	15.2	26.3	31.3	.007
Middle SES	24.2	41.9	41.0	.001
High SES	34.3	53.3	58.3	.083
χ^2 significance[b]	.000	.267	.163	
In issue-based citizen groups				
Low SES	27.2	10.5	21.9	.209
Middle SES	27.4	12.9	19.2	.079
High SES	32.4	0.0	16.7	.016
χ^2 significance[b]	.237	.356	.883	
In crime-watch organizations				
Low SES	12.0	26.3	26.6	.005
Middle SES	12.2	16.1	24.4	.016
High SES	4.6	26.7	8.3	.001
χ^2 significance[b]	.000	.598	.397	
In social, service, or self-help organizations				
Low SES	45.6	36.8	20.3	.000
Middle SES	36.2	29.0	15.4	.001
High SES	28.7	20.0	16.7	.516
χ^2 significance[b]	.000	.562	.742	

[a] χ^2 is based on the cross-tabulation between racial composition of respondents' neighborhoods and type of participation for each level of respondents' socioeconomic status.

[b] χ^2 is based on the cross-tabulation between respondents' socioeconomic status and type of participation for each category of respondents' neighborhood racial composition.

TABLE 2. Participation in Face-to-Face Activities by Race

| | Percent African American in neighborhood | | | |
Percent who participate	0–20%	21–50%	51% or more	χ^2 significance[a]
In neighborhood associations				
African Americans	31.3	38.9	45.9	.331
Whites	23.9	40.0	17.4	.069
χ^2 significance[b]	.341	.937	.012	
In issue-based citizen groups				
African Americans	18.1	0.0	18.4	.137
Whites	29.9	14.3	30.4	.138
χ^2 significance[b]	.175	.092	.198	
In crime-watch organizations				
African Americans	18.8	38.9	20.4	.192
Whites	9.2	14.3	17.4	.263
χ^2 significance[b]	.070	.042	.744	
In social, service, or self-help organizations				
African Americans	31.3	22.2	15.3	.137
Whites	37.3	31.4	34.8	.782
χ^2 significance[b]	.506	.481	.032	

[a] χ^2 is based on the cross-tabulation between racial composition of respondents' neighborhoods and type of participation for each category of respondents' race.

[b] χ^2 is based on the cross-tabulation between respondents' race and type of participation for each category of respondents' neighborhood racial composition.

has anyone personally contacted you to ask you to take part in [neighborhood association] activities?" Table 3 presents the percentage of people answering affirmatively, broken down by the racial composition of the neighborhood, respondents' race, and socioeconomic status. The results suggest that neighborhood associations' outreach is usually more effective in contacting people in racially mixed and predominantly black neighborhoods than in low–minority population ones. This tends to be true regardless of the race or socioeconomic status of the respondent. It may well be that neighborhood associations in these cities experience relatively high participation rates in racially mixed and black neighborhoods because of their relatively effective outreach there.

We further investigated the question of whether independent organizations or city-sponsored organizations are better at mobilizing citizens, by taking a detailed look at San Antonio. Some argue that city-sponsored public involvement programs are a poor model for citizen advocacy. Organizations sponsored by the city will be too limited in what they can do, and this will quickly become apparent to residents, thus dampening their

TABLE 3. Outreach of Neighborhood Associations by Socioeconomic Status and Race

Percent contacted by their neighborhood association	Percent African American in neighborhood			
	0–20%	21–50%	51% or more	χ^2 significance[a]
Low SES	22.5	42.9	31.0	.091
Middle SES	26.8	33.3	51.3	.000
High SES	35.5	36.8	53.8	.404
χ^2 significance[b]	.001	.823	.021	
African Americans	32.3	40.0	43.6	.521
whites	28.1	34.1	25.0	.657
χ^2 significance[b]	.612	.728	.091	

[a] χ^2 is based on the cross-tabulation between racial composition of respondents' neighborhoods and contact by neighborhood association for each level of respondents' socioeconomic status or category of race.

[b] χ^2 is based on the cross-tabulation between respondents' race or socioeconomic status and contact by neighborhood association for each category of respondents' neighborhood racial composition.

enthusiasm and their participation in them. Saul Alinsky described the War on Poverty as "political pornography," and he labeled leaders of community action agencies "stooges" for city hall (1965:41, 43). Piven and Cloward (1979) argue that the social structure will take protest activity and channel it into safe—and ultimately ineffectual—paths. The question of whether to be part of the system or to stand aside from it is particularly important for poor, minority neighborhoods. Does participation in a city-sponsored system mean co-optation and dilution of the demands made on city hall for those who have the greatest needs?

In San Antonio there is no question that COPS is highly effective in getting government to respond to the needs of the residents in the predominantly Hispanic area of the city (Sekul 1983). As a vehicle for involving people in the political process, however, COPS fares poorly. An index of political activity used to compare respondents in the five cities, along with ten other cities that we used as a statistical baseline, places San Antonio at the very bottom. In the COPS section of town, the participation rate is very low. (It's difficult to make a comparison between Hispanics in the COPS part of San Antonio and Hispanics in other parts of the city because residents in the COPS area are significantly poorer.)

In fairness to COPS, since its constituency is relatively low in income and some COPS area residents are recent immigrants, the organization's task of mobilizing people is more difficult than in many of the neighborhoods in this study's other core cities. Yet in comparison to neighborhood associations in low-income black neighborhoods in the four cities with citizen participation programs, COPS still does worse in terms of participation rates. We think that some of this difference is explained by greater elite domination in COPS as compared to typical neighborhood associations. There is much more of a role for rank-and-file citizens in the neighborhood associations in the other four cities than there is for residents of the COPS neighborhoods.

Overall, if judged solely on the basis of how well they mobilize people in racially diverse and predominantly black neighborhoods, the neighborhood associations appear to stand out as being the most effective among the four forms of face-to-face participation. But, of course, we are also interested in some of the consequences of participation for attitudes about the community.

Community

Despite the repeated calls for programs that build community, the exact mechanisms by which a sense of community can be nurtured are hazy at best. Building community usually has been a secondary objective of programs with larger purposes, and government has been held more accountable for those other goals than it has for its progress in strengthening citizens' sense of community. Still, for some theorists, the path to community is clear. Rousseau (1968), for example, saw participation as a means to educate citizens and, by doing so, to transform them. A more contemporary participatory theorist, Benjamin Barber, argues similarly that participation enhances a community by giving it "a moral force that nonparticipatory rulership rarely achieves" (1984:8). Communitarians are the most evangelical about the power of community to transform people. Michael Sandel laments the lack of shared values in modern communities and claims that America produces citizens who are "strangers" to each other (1984:3).

Measuring sense of community is difficult because it is an elusive concept, seemingly encompassing all that is positive about neighborhood life. Robert Booth Fowler notes that there are literally hundreds of definitions of community in the academic literature (1991:3). Given the ambiguity of the term, it seemed wisest to use a general question, allowing survey respondents to react at an instinctive level about whether they felt a sense of community in their neighborhood. All interviewees were asked: "Some people say they feel like they have a sense of community with the people in their neighborhood. Others don't feel that way. How about you? Would you say that you feel a strong sense of community with others in your neighborhood, very little sense of community, or something in between?"

Despite the variety in the way the concept is treated by social scientists and philosophers, there are two fundamental concerns that seem to be at the core of this idea. The first is the belief that there is an identifiable community and that one feels a sense of belonging to it (Crenson 1983). The second is a sense of *common purpose*. People may believe that they and their neighbors share goals and that there is a willingness to work together to achieve them (Fowler 1991:3). The wording of the question used in these surveys should tap either or both of these sentiments.

In table 4 responses are once again broken down by the racial makeup of neighborhoods and by the type of organizations respondents participate in. The figures indicate the percentage of respondents who said they feel a "strong sense of community." Two findings stand out. First, the neighborhood associations appear superior to other types of organizations in nurturing a strong sense of community. In all three racial composition groupings, neighborhood associations achieve the highest response rate for those who indicate they have a strong sense of community.

The second pattern is that in the neighborhoods that have a majority of African American residents, respondents' sense of community tends to be higher across the board. The one exception to this is that for social and service organizations there is no significant difference between the largely black neighborhoods and those with greater racial diversity. This pattern is not an unexpected finding. It seems logical that members of a group that has minority status in the broader society might feel more a part of a neighborhood where they are in the majority. Our earlier analysis also showed that sense of community does not vary by class. Poor, middle-class, and wealthy residents are indistinguishable in their feelings of attachment with their neighborhoods (Berry, Portney, and Thomson 1993:238).

Looking once again at San Antonio alone, the results are not as encouraging (see table 5). In terms of sense of community, there is little difference

TABLE 4. Sense of Community by Type of Participation and Racial Composition of the Neighborhood

Percent with a "strong" sense of community	Percent African American in neighborhood			
	0–20%	21–50%	51% or more	χ^2 significance[a]
Neighborhood associations	53.9	54.5	75.0	.025
Issue-based citizen groups	32.2	33.3	60.7	.010
Crime watch organizations	39.4	38.5	72.4	.006
Social, service, and self-help organizations	34.5	41.2	41.7	.671
None of the above	23.7	34.2	33.6	.044
χ^2 significance[b]	.000	.131	.000	

[a] χ^2 is based on the cross-tabulation between racial composition of respondents' neighborhoods and sense of community for each type of participation.

[b] χ^2 is based on the cross-tabulation between type of participation and sense of community for each category of respondents' neighborhood racial composition.

TABLE 5. Sense of Community for Hispanics in San Antonio

Percent with a "strong" sense of community	Hispanics who live in:		Tucson and El Paso	χ^2 significance[a]
	San Antonio			
	Non-COPS areas	COPS areas		
All socioeconomic status	33.5	29.3	34.3	.252
Low and middle SES	32.7	28.9	32.0	.231

[a] χ^2 significance is based on the cross-tabulation between area of residence and sense of community for each socioeconomic status group.

between those who live in the COPS areas of San Antonio, those who live in other parts of San Antonio, and those who live in two cities (Tucson and El Paso) matched with San Antonio on the basis of similar SES characteristics.

If sense of community is an essential building block for creating a participatory democracy and transforming the way people behave in the political process, then the cities with citywide systems of neighborhood associations have a valuable resource. These neighborhood associations are more effective than other types of organizations in nurturing feelings of identity and shared purpose with one's neighbors.

Conclusion

Political theorists have long argued that participatory democracy will lead to more citizen involvement in community life. If people talk to each other and work with each other to solve problems, this will lead to a community where people care about each other. Individuals will discover common purposes and develop stronger ties to their neighborhoods and cities. If America is becoming more individualistic and less community-oriented, then participatory democracy would appear to be an appealing solution. But does it work? More specifically for our purposes here, are structures of strong democracy of particular help to minority groups as they compete in urban political systems?

It appears so. Although neighborhood associations do not increase the overall number of people who participate in city politics, minority participation rates tend to increase as their percentage of the neighborhood population increases. It seems clear that neighborhood associations are comfortable places for residents in racially mixed and predominantly African American areas. Furthermore, in comparison to other kinds of organizations, participation in the neighborhood associations is more strongly associated with a high sense of community.

The neighborhood associations in Birmingham, Dayton, Portland, and St. Paul are not just another kind of political organization. Although they are independent of government because they are run by volunteers, they are also an official part of city government. They have meaningful and autonomous powers, and city officials have strong incentives to be responsive to the neighborhood associations' requests and preferences. Neighborhood residents understand that these organizations have clout within city government. In stark contrast to these successful citywide systems is San Antonio, where only one section of town is organized. On a host of attitudinal and behavioral measures, both Hispanics and whites in San Antonio demonstrate less support and less involvement in the governmental process.

Poor black neighborhoods are often stereotyped as communities where social and political institutions have badly deteriorated and where antisocial behavior is all too prevalent (Wilson 1987). In the cities we studied, poor black neighborhoods and black neighborhoods at all economic levels demonstrate a relatively high degree of political participation in neighborhood associations. These neighborhood associations are effective in cultivating among African Americans attitudes that are supportive of the community. In neighborhoods with significant numbers of black residents, strong democratic structures work.

Social Capital and the City

WILLIAM MALONEY, GRAHAM SMITH,

AND GERRY STOKER

The growing interest in social capital has caused urban political scientists to attend to features of the civic infrastructure of cities that are often neglected. Such study may explain why political activity (and more broadly social and economic activity) displays greater vitality and appears to be more effective in some localities than in others. Much of the research on social capital has been dominated by the work of Putnam, who emphasizes the positive impact of individual social capital on the performance of political institutions, the development of effective and democratic governance, and important policy outcomes in areas such as education, health, crime, welfare, and economic growth.

Putnam's approach is limited on a number of counts. First, its individual-level analysis neglects the variety of *locations* in which social capital is generated, accessed, and inhibited. Social capital is a property of relations between *corporate actors* as well as persons (Coleman 1988:98). We should study not only the relationship between individuals, but also that between associations and institutions.

Second, in taking a bottom-up perspective, Putnam perceives the state to be an exogenous factor (Tarrow 1996:395), neglecting the role played by political structures and institutions in shaping the *context of associational activity* and hence in creating social capital. The governing bodies of an area are affected by social capital but also influence social capital. Political institutions play a significant role in helping to sustain civic vibrancy and probably in stimulating its growth as well. Public authorities are deeply

The research reported in this chapter is supported by the U.K. Economic and Social Science Council Cities Programme (award number L130251052) and draws on an earlier article, Maloney et al. (2000).

implicated in the shape and activities of voluntary associations,[1] whether it be in terms of the institutions created to encourage engagement and participation, the form of grants and service-level agreements, or the nature of capacity building programs. The political system does not determine civil society; rather, there is an interpenetration of state and civil society.

Third, given this interpenetration, Putnam's claim that it is possible to read off the implications for governance from knowledge about associational activity and stocks of social capital becomes deeply problematic. Knowledge of civic organizations and a generic understanding of their civic vibrancy expressed through their numbers and their access to information and networks does not enable us to make immediate comment on the quality of governance in a given locality. Nor does the identification of a certain set of values and attitudes held by individuals in a community provide a sufficient basis for ascertaining the performance of governance arrangements.

An analysis of associational life in Birmingham, U.K., highlights the importance of investigating social capital as a relational concept that can be applied to a variety of locations. In particular we focus on the relationships between voluntary associations and between voluntary associations and the local authority. What becomes clear is that there is an uneven distribution of social capital and that different actors have differential access to social capital resources. Social capital is context specific (Edwards and Foley 1998; Foley, Edwards, and Diani, this volume). Only by being sensitive to the different locations in which social capital is created or inhibited is it possible to judge its impact on governance.

Patterns of Civic Engagement in Birmingham

Putnam has recently argued that in general terms civic organization has declined in the United States: the *Bowling Alone* phenomenon. There are many who question Putnam's civic deficit thesis: but in the case of Britain, Hall concludes that "levels of social capital, at least on most indicators, have not declined significantly in recent decades" (Hall 1998:32). He further argues that there is strong evidence that government policies "have made a major contribution to sustaining the kind of associations that augment the level of social capital in Britain" (Hall 1998:21).

The national-level policy environment has been well disposed toward associational activity, but so too have local initiatives. Indeed, it has been argued that the late 1970s and 1980s saw a general opening out of local authorities and a strengthening of the diversity and capacity of local group politics (Stoker 1988; Stoker and Wilson 1991). There is much general evidence to support the view that the 1990s has seen the continuation of such local trends with increased support for local voluntary associations and more avenues for engagement with local authorities (Young 2000; Lowndes et al. 1998).

An analysis of levels of associational activity in Birmingham provides an excellent opportunity to pursue the debate and move from a general level of evidence to a particular illustration of trends in an individual city. In his study of Birmingham in the late 1960s and early 1970s, Newton (1976) recorded 4,264 groups. We carried out a similar mapping exercise of voluntary and community activity in Birmingham in 1998, and this is compared with Newton's findings (using his original classification system) in table 1.

While both sets of data are very much partial analyses and an underestimation of activity, there nevertheless appears to be an increase of at least a third in the number of voluntary associations in Birmingham over the last three decades. If we were to disregard sports clubs, where the figure for 1998 is a substantial underestimate, then there is at least a doubling in the number of groups: in 1970 there were 2,120 nonsport voluntary associations; in 1998 this figure was up to 4,397. While we don't want to make a direct correlation between numbers of groups and levels of social capital, this simple analysis of associational activity across three decades suggests that the "civic decline" thesis is misplaced. Also it is suggestive that we

TABLE 1. Comparison of Number of Voluntary Associations in Birmingham in 1970 and 1998[a]

Type of association	Number in 1970	Number in 1980
Sports	2,144	1,192[b]
Social Welfare	666	1,319
Cultural	388	507
Trade Associations	176	71
Professional	165	112
Social	142	398
Churches	138	848
Forces	122	114
Youth	76	268
Technical & Scientific	76	41
Educational	66	475
Trade Unions	55	52
Health	50	309
Not Classified		75
Total	4,264	5,781

[a] For 1998 sources see Maloney et al. 2000.

[b] This figure is a substantial underestimate. There are no specialist sports lists available and no recent systematic analysis of sports associations in Birmingham by the relevant local administrative bodies.

need to be sensitive to the wider political context within which associations operate.

Many of the shifts in the numbers of associations across different fields of operation reflect changes in the political environment of the last thirty years or so (Stoker 1997; Taylor 1997). For example, as local government powers and functions have been progressively eroded in such traditional service delivery areas as housing, existing or new voluntary and community organizations have taken over some of these responsibilities and developed new areas of work. This in turn has opened up new opportunities for arms-length providers. In other areas, there has been a shift to more of an enabling role rather than direct provision of social services. The doubling of the number of groups in the social welfare category reflects the impact of such trends. This category includes not only social care providers but also associations within the areas of community economic and social development, housing, employment and training, as well as civic advocacy groups. The growth in education groups reflects a rise in parent-teacher associations, nurseries, play schemes, and after-school clubs. A similar trend can be observed in the youth sector, as well as in health, where we see dramatic rises in numbers.

Local government has also moved into new policy fields such as economic development, environmental protection, and crime prevention and has done so in cooperation with a range of "third force" organizations (Stoker and Young 1993). The impact of these trends is reflected in the growth in the social welfare, social, and health categories. Again, while Newton did not record environmental associations as a separate category, our analysis recorded forty-four groups.

Shifts in the type of voluntary associations over time suggests that the changing political environment, and specifically the changing role played by local authorities, has had a significant impact on voluntary activity, and inevitably on the creation of social capital. On the other hand, the steady state of trade unions and declines in professional and trade associations probably reflect wider shifts in the economic and industrial base of Birmingham. Finally, the category of churches has expanded rapidly. This can be accounted for by the emergence of new Christian denominations and the rise of other faith-based associations in Birmingham's expanding ethnic minority communities.

A postal survey of voluntary and community organizations in Birmingham in November 1998 provides more details of the relationships between voluntary associations and between associations and the local authority.[2] The belief that a new range of associations has emerged is supported by the finding that two-thirds of our sample of groups were established after 1970. More than that, our data on the current dynamics of Birmingham's voluntary sector reveal evidence to suggest not only that there are more groups but also that they are more politically active, better connected, and generally positive about associational life in Birmingham.

In the early 1970s, Newton found a relatively quiet world of connections between established groups and officialdom, underwritten by close contacts and grant provision arrangements that enabled useful social care and other public service objectives to be achieved. Most groups remained politically inactive—only about 30 percent of all voluntary organizations in Birmingham had asked about a decision or contacted the local authority or another public body in the city in the previous year. The active groups tended to work with the permanent officials in departments rather than with councilors or other political figures. When asked about the operation of the local political system, the secretaries of the active groups reported a general view that they were paid sufficient attention (60 percent of the sample) and that their dealings with both councilors and officers were helpful. General interview material confirmed for Newton that groups were "well satisfied with their relationships with public bodies and officials in the city." Some interests, such as those of Birmingham's already substantial ethnic minority communities, were largely sidelined.

In 1998, we see a relatively healthy picture of civic life in Birmingham. Many associations are involved in extensive networks of organizations both inside and outside the geographical boundaries of Birmingham. Some 85 percent of respondents claimed to have "contact with other voluntary and community groups in Birmingham" and 54 percent say that they have "contact with other voluntary and community groups outside Birmingham." Over half the sample (56 percent) indicated that they have regular contact with officers and/or councilors in the city council. The importance and variety of information networks is also apparent (see table 2). Although the single most important source of information for many groups is their own members and users, almost 70 percent of associations in Birmingham place a high premium on contact with other associations and public authorities, pointing to the importance to civic activity in the city of networking and information exchange. Information flows and networks are typically seen as an important element of social capital (Coleman 1988).

TABLE 2. Main Sources of Information for Voluntary Associations in Birmingham

Sources	Percent very important	Percent important	Percent fairly important
Members of own group	51.4	24.8	7.8
Birmingham City Council	27.6	23.5	17.6
Other public body	17.8	25.3	17.8
Other local voluntary association	25.1	28.2	19.6
National organization	26.1	24.3	17.3

There is also evidence of the impact of financial support from the City Council. Just under a third of the sample (31 percent) have a grant from Birmingham City Council as a main source of funding. Some 22.5 percent of groups report that they are involved in a service-level agreement with the Council. Newton found that in 1971 the City Council was spending £1 million of grant funding and support for service provision by voluntary organizations. The figure for 1998 was £17 million. Between 1970–71 and 1997–98 prices went up by 8.6 times, so in real terms there has been roughly a doubling of grant funding provided to the voluntary sector.[3]

Trust in the City

If information flows and networks are one element of social capital, trust is typically seen as another. In examining responses to a series of questions about their relationship with other associations and the City Council, some interesting insights into social capital in the city emerge.

Against a backdrop of high trust levels between voluntary associations (some 70 percent of organizations agree that they trust other voluntary groups in Birmingham), the drop in the perception of the trustworthiness of relations between voluntary organizations and the City Council is marked: 44 percent of voluntary groups in Birmingham agreed that there is a high level of trust. About half that number (21 percent) disagreed with the statement. This drop in trust may be of some concern given that the overwhelming majority of the sample (90 percent) agrees that trust between Birmingham City Council and voluntary and community groups is essential.

Although these findings raise some interesting questions for social capital analysts, overall frequencies tell us nothing about the *type* and *activities* of voluntary associations that are more likely to trust the City Council. If

TABLE 3. Trust in the City

Trust	Percent agree or strongly agree	Percent neither agree nor disagree	Percent disagree or strongly disagree
Our organization trusts other voluntary and community groups in the city. (N = 357)	70	44	90
There is a high level of trust between our organization and the City Council. (N = 355)	27	35	10
Trust between the City Council and voluntary and community groups is essential for a healthy city. (N = 357)	3	21	0

TABLE 4. Who Trusts?

There is a high level of trust between our organization and the city council.	Percent agree or strongly agree	Percent disagree or strongly disagree
All organizations	44	21
Regularly involved in council forums		
Yes	51	19
No	30	25
Regular contact with councilors/officers		
Yes	57	19
No	24	24
City Council grant is very important		
Yes	66	13
Annual income above £50,000		
Yes	54	18
No	37	24

trust is an indicator of social capital, where is it more likely to be found? Are there specific characteristics of organizations and their activities that make them more likely to be perceived as trustworthy? Table 4 begins to unpack some of the characteristics of voluntary associations that are more and less trusted.

A number of characteristics emerge quite strongly. In particular, the level of trust is consistently higher for organizations regularly involved in City Council consultation forums, have regular contact with councilors or officers, declare that a City Council grant is a very important source of income, and have an annual income of over £50,000. So, for example, between 21 and 23 percent more organizations state that there is a high level of trust between them and the City Council if they are regularly involved in forums or have regular contact with Council officials. Those organizations that feel there is a high level of trust between them and the City Council are those that have some form of regular contact with, or significant financial support from, the Council and that have a relatively large turnover. An annual income of above £50,000 is indicative of an association that has the capacity to employ staff and thus is more likely to have the necessary resources to engage consistently with the local authority.

Also noteworthy is that those organizations that have a City Council grant as a "very important source of income" exhibit the highest level of trust of all the types of respondents (66 percent). This finding raises some interesting questions for those such as Misztal, who argues that trust can not "be purchased or bribed, since, as an old-age truth—immortalized by

King Lear—illustrates, any attempt to 'buy' trust can only destroy it" (Misztal 1996:21). It seems that Birmingham City Council's attempts to "buy" trust have not been so disastrous.

Understanding the Political Context of Associational Activity

A basic analysis of the survey data from Birmingham offers interesting insights into social capital in cities. First, there is a distributional quality to social capital—certain groups may be excluded from accessing social capital in different locations. The important finding here is that trust and information flows are related to levels of contact. Second, the results suggest that social capital can be actively generated and promoted by local public authorities through the use of consultation forums, outreach work, capacity building, funding regimes, etc. However, other findings may undermine this second conclusion, or at least require it to be amended.

One of the structures that Coleman highlights as generally facilitating social capital is "closure of social networks," by which they become unavailable to those defined as outsiders. Such closure creates the conditions for (a) the emergence of effective sanctions that can monitor and guide behavior and (b) trustworthiness of social structures that allows the proliferation of obligations and expectations (Coleman 1988:105–107). In cities, such closure is achieved for voluntary organizations through access to forums and relationships with councilors and officers and funding regimes. As our results show, regular contact is related to higher levels of trust and better information flows. Organizations that regularly engage with the City Council tend to recognize that their own relationships with the Council are more trusting and engender good information flows.

This is reinforced by the responses to another statement put to voluntary organizations. Only 8 percent of groups in Birmingham *disagreed* with the statement that "the City Council favors certain voluntary and community groups." The social capital generated through closure is recognized by voluntary organizations. Local authorities simply do not have the resources or even the will to engage with all groups in the city. If this is the case, it becomes clear that, in urban areas, social capital is "neither brokered equitably nor distributed evenly" (Foley and Edwards 1998:2).

What these findings point to is a need for those interested in social capital to understand the nature of the relationship between local authorities and voluntary associations. One way of thinking about this is to introduce the concept of the *political opportunity structure* (POS), borrowed from analysts of political protest and collective action (Kriesi 1995; Tarrow 1994; McAdam, et al. 1996). Understanding the nature of the urban POS facilitates the development of a more contextual analysis of the creation, inhibition, and appropriation of social capital. It enables us to explore three issues in greater depth. First, it encourages an awareness of the various sites and locations for the creation and use of social capital especially with respect to the relationships between voluntary organizations and government. Second, it directs attention to the distributive dimension of social capital. The deployment of a POS analysis aids the process of understanding the way social capital is distributed and recognizes the possibility that "some may be organized 'in' and others 'out' by the same set of developments" (Hall 1998:34). Finally, the introduction of the POS concept supports an understanding of the link between social capital and governance. While utilizing the POS as an explanatory concept, we need to recognize that it does not *determine* associational activity and the creation of and access to social capital, but it may well be a *substantial influence*.

In his classic study of protest behavior in American cities, Eisinger found that the incidence of protest was "related to the nature of a city's political opportunity structure." The POS refers to the "openings, weak spots, barriers and resources of the political system itself" (Eisinger 1973). Tarrow defines the POS as "consistent—but not necessarily formal or permanent—dimensions of the political environment that provide incentives for people to undertake collective action by affecting their expectations of success or failure." The POS is generally seen as being predicated on at least three broad sets of properties of a political system: (1) formal institutional structure; (2) informal procedures and prevailing strategies; and (3) the political context in which relations between governmental actors and voluntary associations take place (Kriesi 1995).

The degree of formal access to political decision-making processes will be a function of a number of factors, such as the degree of decentralization, the degree of coherence in public administration, and the capacity of upper-tier authorities to impose conditions or requirements for involvement of voluntary and community associations.[4] So, for example, Birmingham City Council's recently introduced devolution initiative, Local Involvement Local Action (LILA), provides more formal avenues for participation and engagement, particularly for local and neighborhood associations. Equally, engagement will be affected by the existence of departmental "fiefdoms" and "clientelism" or by central government initiatives, such as the Single Regeneration Budget or New Deal for Communities, which stress the need to develop formal partnerships with the voluntary sector.

Looking beyond the formal structure of the POS, we need to take into account the informal manner in which these arrangements are applied. From a social capital perspective, such informal elements are crucial to the generation of trust and norms of reciprocity. Kriesi usefully distinguishes between two broad strategies that "emerge from the political process and

guide the actions of authorities": "exclusive (repressive, confrontative, po-
larizing)" and "integrative (facultative, cooperative, assimilative)" (Kriesi
1995:173–74). Exclusive approaches to voluntary associations can often be
traced to factors such as the professionalization and specialization of functional areas (e.g., planning and social work) or to the ideological outlook of
the dominant political party. Here there is often "closure of social networks" (Coleman 1988:105). Closure facilitates social capital for participants with shared ideological or professional backgrounds, but makes these
social capital resources unavailable for "outsider" voluntary and community associations.

Associational engagement is further affected by the nature of political
alignments and conflict among political elites and by the presence and absence of allies. So for example, the distribution of power within and
between local political parties is obviously an important factor affecting
engagement—electoral instability is just one situation that may induce political elites to compete for support from voluntary associations (Tarrow
1994:88). Additionally, the configuration of power between senior officers
and different departments will create cleavages and divisions that can be
exploited by voluntary associations. Conflicts within the government
structure and a concern for support in the external community can, by the
law of "anticipated reactions," create opportunities and openings for voluntary associations. This political context within political authorities
shapes both formal and informal dimensions of the POS.

Political Opportunity Structure and Social Capital

By combining the different formal structures, informal strategies, and political context, we can begin to see how the POS changes over time and affects the ability of voluntary associations to engage with public authorities. The POS can extend from "full exclusion" through to "substantive
integration"—from a completely closed authority to one in which associations are involved in the creation and implementation of local policy.
However, it needs to be reinforced that not every association faces or perceives the same POS and that the POS may differ across different policy
issues. Different associations may face a different POS even around the
same policy issue. A particular POS may discriminate against certain types
of associations.

Changes in the nature of the POS will affect the ability of associations to
access and generate social capital resources. In the face of governmental
intransigence, full exclusion may generate the conditions for mass
community-level creation of social capital, but not at the level of inter-
change between associations and government (Berman, this volume). The

assumption is simply that any form of inclusion or integration creates the *potential* for social capital at the interface between citizens and the state. The deeper and more developed that relationship, the stronger the potential is likely to be.

Again though, we need to be careful about generalizations. Fuller access to and integration into decision-making processes may discourage collective action on the part of associations (Tarrow 1997:86). Social capital may be generated among and between political elites and community leaders but may not flow down to the grassroots and the wider community. Access to, and creation of, social capital can thus be dependent on the "brokerage" role played by community leaders and representatives. How far is it possible for community representatives to be integrated into new elite networks and simultaneously continue their role in their former associational networks (Diani, this volume)? In order to access and generate social capital, brokers have both "representation" and "gate-keeping" roles (Gould and Fernandez 1989). In the latter role, brokers are the conduit through which information flows back to their associations and relations of trust are developed. Brokers can use their position for positive and negative ends— to facilitate the flow of information and the development of trustworthy relationships, or to block such developments.

The analysis of the POS—as adapted and amended here—provides a potentially useful contextual approach for examining the interface between government and associations. It does not enable us to read off the prospects for the creation of social capital, but it does provide a framework in which those prospects can be explored.

The Politics of Race in Birmingham: POS in Transition[5]

The politics of race in Birmingham demonstrates the significant impact of institutional design on associational life and social capital. Race relations in Birmingham have been a particularly sensitive political issue over several decades. Birmingham is one of the most ethnically diverse populations in the U.K.—according to the last census (1991), almost 20 percent of the population is from black or south-Asian ethnic groups. The institutions that govern the engagement of ethnic minority associations with Birmingham City Council are in transition and provide a clear example of how changes in the POS affect the ability of different ethnic minority associations to access and generate social capital.

In the 1960s and early 1970s, Newton found that interviews with council members "revealed a fairly widespread ignorance about the basic facts of the city's colored population mixed in a large minority of cases, with an unmistakable degree of racism and bigotry" (Newton 1976:208). No formal structures existed to engage ethnic minority associations: "the issue has been gently shunted onto a political siding" (Newton 1976:222).

The 1980s saw a period of political mobilization on the part of ethnic minority communities. Where there had been only one black councilor prior to 1979, by 1993 there were 20 ethnic minority councilors out of a total of 119. Solomos and Back offer an account of this process of mobilization, which was particularly centered on the Labour Party whose primary constituency was the ethnically diverse inner city wards (Solomos and Back 1995). After a period of urban unrest (culminating in the Handsworth Riot in September 1985), the City Council was under pressure to develop mechanisms to engage the more politically active ethnic minority communities and their associations. The Labour Party, in particular, felt the need to respond to ethnic minorities in order to sustain its voting base. The growth of ethnic minority representation in Birmingham provides an important example of excluded groups accessing social capital and mobilizing in response to poor institutional design and the relatively closed POS of the 1970s and early 1980s.

In 1988, the City Council proposed the development of an innovative democratic framework for the engagement of ethnic minority associations—the creation and evolution of a number of self-organized ethnic and faith-based Umbrella Groups (UGs). By 1993 there were nine UGs. In 1990 the Standing Consultative Forum (SCF) was established as a single body through which the UGs could collectively represent the views of ethnic minority communities. It was formally constituted in 1992 with three representatives from each UG. However, the UGs saw little meaningful commitment to the development of race equality and threatened to withdraw their support (Solomos and Back 1995:195). In response, the City Council created new community development posts in each UG—officers who would be jointly managed by the City Council's Race Relations Unit and the executive of the UGs.

Within a decade, ethnic minority associations had moved from a situation of full exclusion and were edging toward substantive integration (Birmingham City Council 1994). As the POS changed, so did the opportunities for accessing and generating social capital. The composition of the SCF and the ability of community development officers to work across communities and access City Council resources allowed the emergence of relations of trust and cooperation. Social capital was being accessed to achieve collaborative outcomes.

However, by 1998 the whole SCF-UG arrangement was under review and it was clear that the Council's preferred outcome was the creation of a new multi-agency and multi-sector Race Action Partnership (RAP) with a completely different mechanism for engaging ethnic minority communities. In comparison to the previous Race Relations Unit, which had supported and nurtured the development of the SCF-UG framework, the creation of the Equalities Division in 1997 saw the emergence of a less integrative attitude. The fiscal situation had tightened and the SCF and UGs were seen as unrepresentative and unable to play the brokerage role originally envisaged by the City Council.

The proposal for RAP entails the creation of a series of "issue-based race equality forums" on, for example, housing, social protection, educational attainment, health, and access to the labor market. Each forum would elect community auditors who would be the ethnic minority community representatives on the RAP Board. Community development officers would work across the issues and support the community auditors, rather than a specific ethnic minority community. At the same time, the City Council is also promoting Local Involvement Local Action (LILA), a decentralization initiative. The City Council argues that the emergence of these new opportunities to engage reduces the need for the SCF-UG structure (Birmingham City Council 1999:5-7).

What is clear is that the emerging governance of race equality will restructure opportunities for engagement and thus for access to and generation of social capital. The Equalities Division stresses that issue-based forums will allow the evolution of cross-community collaboration. However, the UGs are concerned that representatives of their communities and associations are going to find it difficult to cover all the relevant issues. Questions have also been raised as to the accountability of the new community auditors and their ability to act as social capital brokers. Whether the new arrangements will have the potential of the SCF-UG arrangement to develop substantive integration and to access and generate social capital between political elites and community representatives remains an open question. As the POS changes so does the location and potential of social capital generation.

Conclusion

Social capital is an important and potentially powerful explanatory concept for urban political science. Dimensions of social capital such as networks and information channels, the trustworthiness of relations between actors and institutions, and norms and effective sanctions are of fundamental importance in shaping political, social, and economic life. However, social capital research that focuses solely on the density of associational activity or the democratic attitudes and values of individuals as cultural variables reduces considerably the explanatory power of the concept. Social capital should be understood as context dependent, and as a resource that inheres in the relations between actors in a variety of locations.

The empirical material presented in this paper illustrates the importance of developing a top-down and contextual approach within social capital research. The level of interpenetration of public authorities and voluntary associations needs to be recognized. Our survey material highlights the high level of contact between the two sectors, the importance of information flows between public authorities and associations, and the high level of financial and other informal support given to voluntary and community associations. Research on social capital should not only focus on the effect of civic activity on government performance, but also the effect of government-associational relationships on social capital. A top-down perspective needs to supplement the more usual bottom-up approach championed by Putnam.

A more contextual approach is warranted in order to understand the ways in which the nature of the POS affects access to, and creation of, social capital. So, for example, differential levels of trust exist between voluntary associations and the Birmingham City Council that are partly explained by participation in Council forums and contact with councilors and/or officers. Again, the case study of the transitions of the race equality POS in Birmingham illustrates how formal structures, informal relations, and the political context within the local authority affect the ability of different associations to engage with political elites. Changes in the POS affect the activities of voluntary associations and their ability to access and generate social capital. Where local authorities develop new partnerships, they are not only creating opportunities for developing new forms of relationships with other local actors, but will also affect previous social capital relationships with associations.

Collaborative relationships can develop at different locations and levels. Purposive top-down initiatives can have a positive effect in the enhancement and creation of social capital. However, empirical research is likely to reveal contradictory images. In some circumstances poor government and poor institutional design may actually aid the generation of social capital, while in others (and probably more frequently) they may destroy it. Put starkly, institutional design and the political opportunity structure are critical variables in social capital analysis.

II

The Political Economy

of Our Discontent

Editors' Introduction

As we have seen, concern that the quality of civic life is somehow endangered is widespread. Cultural conservatives are apt to blame liberalism, moral decay, or the ravages of a "sin-sick society"; economic conservatives are more likely to blame litigious personal injury lawyers, the proliferation of "frivolous" rights, or simply big government run amok. Liberals and conservatives alike worry about the "incivility" of contemporary politics. More central to the concerns of this volume, neo-Tocquevilleans point to what they consider to be a precipitous decline in civic engagement since the 1960s. They argue that declining membership in traditional secondary associations like the League of Women Voters, the Boy and Girl Scouts, or the Rotary Club signals a decline in the social capital that undergirds a vibrant and healthy democracy and thus has eroded the capacity of American society to rise to the challenges that confront it.

Such accounts of the "decline of social capital" and the sources of citizen disenchantment in the United States, however, are striking in their silence about two of the most far-reaching changes in late-twentieth-century life, namely the twin phenomena of economic globalization and the retreat of governments from responsibility for social welfare. A global "race to the bottom" in search of heightened profit margins has shifted jobs to low-wage manufacturing platforms in the developing world and put pressure on governments everywhere to cut spending and minimize their economic interventions. The resulting fiscal and political constraints on the capacity of government at all levels has joined with a ferocious globalizing economy to overturn communities and shatter the expectations of millions over the last twenty years. This twin trend simply cannot be ignored as we attempt to understand the sense of malaise that afflicts civic life and public discourse in the United States and elsewhere. In the face of increasing disparities in income and life opportunities, it is only natural that civil society as we have known it should contract and social capital be withdrawn from circulation and rechanneled in new ways.

The three chapters in this section all stand the neo-Toquevillean framework on its head by arguing that social capital, and the character of civil society itself, are more likely to be shaped by broader economic and political trends than the other way around. The first two essays take up the economic issue while the third examines the role of the government in shaping outcomes.

Charles Heying and Michael Schulman and Cynthia Anderson examine how economic restructuring during the twentieth century has affected the production of social capital in Atlanta, Georgia, and Kannapolis, North Carolina, respectively. Heying directs our attention to the changing role of business elites in the voluntary sector. He shows that as company interests in Atlanta shifted from a local to a national, then a transnational focus, so, too, did the commitments of business elites. The result has been decreasing support for local community organizations and a growing sense of crisis in the nonprofit sector.

Schulman and Anderson examine how economic restructuring has eroded the traditional "paternalist" social capital that characterized social relations between Cannon Mills, Inc., and its associated textile-mill community. At the same time, the changing socioeconomic context has also created an opening that was exploited by successive union organizing campaigns to reshape social relations in Kannapolis and produce worker-based horizontal social capital that partially replaced the hierarchical, company-based social capital.

The last chapter questions the neo-Toquevillian argument that associational life produces social trust, which in turn enables cooperative economic behavior and effective governance. Lane Kenworthy illustrates how government policy initiatives can institutionalize an incentive structure that facilitates cooperation independent of social trust or other features of the neo-Tocquevillean argument. His cross-national analysis shows that economic incentive structures, often created in governmental efforts to manage economic conflicts, can promote cooperation even in hostile environments. Where neo-Toquevillians like Robert Putnam argue that associational life fosters economic prosperity by encouraging trust and cooperation, Kenworthy contends that the forms of cooperation that are most economically beneficial stem from institutional incentives rather than from such informal and indirect mechanisms.

Civic Elites and Corporate Delocalization

An Alternative Explanation for Declining Civic Engagement

CHARLES H. HEYING

With a tour de force of articles and lecture-circuit appearances, Robert Putnam has become one of academe's most widely quoted social commentators.
At conferences and in classrooms, speakers and scholars alike thoughtfully
reflect on "America's declining social capital" (1995a:65). Putnam's message
is compelling: America's once vibrant civic networks, social norms, and
public trust are eroding, placing this country on a downward slide from historic levels of civic participation. The cohort of citizens who grew up in the
Depression, joined the PTAs, and spent afternoons with their kids in scouts
and evenings bowling in leagues is now in its senior years when civic engagement begins its natural decline. As they move from the scene, that
younger cohort of active citizens, who were expected to pick up the civic
and political slack, has not materialized. In the aggregate, Putnam argues,
American's willingness to build community by joining, volunteering, and
participating is in decline. And Putnam knows the reason why—TV—or
more specifically, too much time spent watching it. The generation of kids
who grew up with television participates less in community-building activities because its time is monopolized by TV and its attitudes are corrupted
by the pervasive cynicism of the media. The results, suggests Putnam, are
likely to be disastrous for our democratic polity.

Putnam's (1995b) argument is seductive, and he marshals an impressive body of evidence to support it. In lawyerly fashion, he dismisses some
of the usual suspects: time pressure, mobility, changing social roles, race,
co-optation by the welfare state, and instead fixes blame on the combined

Revised from an article of the same title in *American Behavioral Scientist* 40, no.5 (1997):
657–68.

impact of generational effects and television. But, he admits, his case is not airtight. "I have a prime suspect that I am prepared to indict, but the evidence is not yet strong enough to convict" (1995b:665). It's an opening that doubters have subsequently exploited (for a review of the social capital debate see Foley and Edwards 1999; Edwards and Foley, [this volume]).

Elsewhere I have argued that Putnam's correlation of cohort effects (TV generation) with decline in civic engagement is a classic case of false attribution; mistaking one of the more visible and pervasive expressions of social transformation for the whole (ARNOVA-L listserv discussion, Nov. 13–Dec. 9, 1995). Entertainment habits are only one of many elements in the economy, technology, and social order that have undergone revolutionary change with the shift from a national, industrial, goods-making economy to a global, informational, service-producing economy. Accompanying and reifying these transformations have been the decline of central cities and growth of suburban and edge cities, the entry of women into the workforce, altered patterns of family size, permanence, structure, and behavior, changes in national demography and in household mobility, and shifts in modalities of transport and communication.

In developing this argument, I suggested that Putnam's treatment of social transformation variables was inadequate because he dismisses them on a case-by-case basis rather than considering their comprehensive impacts. For example, Putnam's use of indicators showing working women and suburbanites to be personally more trusting and engaged does not remove the social phenomenon they represent from the list of causal factors for the so-called decline in social capital. Suburbanization does not just affect suburbanites, it impacts the whole urban system. Similarly, the entry of women into the work force does not just affect women, it impacts the whole occupational system. And these two factors (plus innumerable others) create interactive, recursive, and cascading effects on women, men, and social systems.

I continue to find compelling the case for social transformation having abetted the decline of social capital. In this paper, I further develop this thesis. In doing so, I do not attempt to navigate the global domain of these structural changes; instead, I sketch a thesis of more limited scope, but one that illustrates at the micro level the working out of the macro phenomenon previously described. The focus of my project is the local community and the impact of macro transformations on the patterns of and incentives for local elite engagement. I argue that economic transformations have considerably diminished the ability of local communities to be mobilized by a cohesive local elite leadership with historic ties to the community. I present evidence demonstrating declining rates of social engagement of elites at the community level and connect this logically to the economic delocalization of corporations. In making this argument I do not, to paraphrase

Putnam (1995b), have sufficient evidence to convict. Rather, my intention is to offer an alternative explanation for declining social capital that is at least as plausible as Putnam's and to draw attention to a phenomenon that is more complex than Putnam suggests.

Civic Elites in Atlanta: 1931, 1961, 1991

My case is primarily developed using data from my longitudinal study of elite networks in Atlanta, Georgia (Heying 1995). In this study, I examine the structure of urban leadership at three points in time, 1931, 1961, and 1991, by identifying patterns of overlapping membership across governing boards of (a) business corporations (b) nonprofit institutions, and (c) government boards and commissions. By examining these patterns of overlapping directorships in connection with the occupational and demographic profiles of those individuals who were most central to the networks formed by these linkages, I test various hypotheses about the nature and character of civic leadership.

Data and Methods

For the Atlanta study, I developed a comprehensive database of board memberships of organizations in three sectors. Using *Standard and Poor's Register of Corporations Directors and Executives* (1931, 1961, 1991), I identified all board members of Atlanta metropolitan business corporations for the three periods. From archival sources such as annual reports, I identified board members of the largest nonprofit organizations in the community. For the three years, I obtained board member lists for 88 percent of the 153 nonprofit organizations selected for inclusion in the study. Finally, from public records and other sources, I was able to identify 98 percent of the members of all public councils and commissions in existence in Atlanta and Fulton County at each point in time. In all, the database included nearly 7,000 board members, filling over 9,000 positions, on over 1,000 boards.

To analyze the data, I employed a body of techniques called social network analysis. Relationships, connections, or flows are the defining elements of network analysis. Relationships are determined for entire networks and for individual nodes. The density of the network as a whole is determined by the aggregate number of shortest distance paths it takes to connect all nodes. High levels of network connectedness indicate high levels of social cohesion. Centrality is the most common measure of individual node connectedness. Centrality is determined by comparing the direct and indirect connectedness of individual nodes to that of all other individual nodes in the network (Wellman and Berkowitz 1988).

Social network analysis is especially appropriate for understanding structural characteristics such as social cohesion because it uncovers emergent structural properties by directly examining patterns of relationship. This compares favorably to traditional social science techniques where an understanding of structural properties (social networks, social cohesion) is deduced by proxy through the aggregation of individual attributes such as attitudes and behaviors (Wellman and Berkowitz 1988).

In the Atlanta study, emergent structural properties were discovered by examining the connections established by those who sat on multiple boards. Direct connections were made between individuals when they sat on the same board. Indirect connections were made when two individuals, who did not share a common board, both shared boards with a common third individual. Because of the large number of individuals included in the study and because sources for biographical data were usually limited to the most important local elites, I focused my analysis on the top seventy individuals at each point in time. The top seventy individuals were those with the highest individual network centrality scores.

Results

By examining the organizational affiliations of the top seventy elites, I discovered that, for all three periods, the central core of civic leadership in Atlanta was consistently dominated by the highest ranking executives from: locally owned bank, insurance, and credit companies; region-serving utility companies headquartered in Atlanta; large retail merchandisers such as department stores; elected officials, especially those with land-based business interests; locally owned real estate and land development firms; prominent Atlanta-based manufacturing companies; local newspaper and broadcast companies; and established Atlanta law firms. Also included among the elite at all points in time was a core group of women, primarily wealthy arts patrons, and at least one president of an established local university.

These general findings are easier to understand if specific examples are provided. A description of the top ten elite leaders in 1961 is illustrative. James D. Robinson, Jr., the highest ranking individual in 1961, was chair of First National Bank, the largest bank in Atlanta. Ivan Allen, Jr., the number two individual, was vice chair of Ivan Allen Company, the largest office supply company in Atlanta. Charles E. Thwaite, Jr., the third-ranking individual, was chair of Trust Co. of Georgia, the second largest bank. Gordon Jones, fourth ranked, was president of Fulton National Bank, the third largest bank. Ben S. Gilmer, the fifth ranked, was president of Southern Bell Telephone and Telegraph, the largest employer in Atlanta. John A. Sibley, ranked sixth, was the chair of the executive committee of Trust Co. of Georgia and a partner in King and Spalding, one of the oldest and most prestigious Atlanta law firms. Russell Bellman, ranked seventh, was the co-founder of Haverty Furniture Co., the regions largest home furnishings chain store. John Joseph McDonough, the number eight elite, was the president of Georgia Power Co., whose revenues were the fifth largest in Atlanta in 1961. Ranked ninth was Richard Rich, president of Rich's, Inc., the region's leading department store. The tenth ranked individual was Fred J. Turner, the recently retired president of Southern Bell Telephone and Telegraph. This list of occupational affiliations for 1961 is not unique. The top ten lists for 1931 and 1991 are remarkably similar, with many of the same industries (often the same company) of equal size and rank represented.

Critical to the purpose of the present discussion is the finding that the business leaders who were central to these elite networks were affiliated with corporations that were overwhelmingly home-grown. On average over the three periods, 90 percent of the top seventy elites were affiliated with Atlanta-based businesses. It is also important to note that over one-third of all the top seventy elite leaders for the three periods were affiliated with only two institutional groups: (a) bank, life insurance, and credit institutions, and (b) regional utility companies.

The finding that the elite leaders were overwhelmingly drawn from home-grown industries is critical because it is logically connected to a separate finding of the study that the overall cohesiveness of the local elite network reached a high point in 1961. Measures of network density that indicate the overall social cohesiveness of the network show that network density in 1961 was 45 percent greater than in 1931, and 100 percent greater than in 1991. This critical finding is supported by other useful indicators of social cohesion such as the number and centrality of those who sit on multiple boards across business, nonprofit, and public sectors. By these measures, 1961 is again the peak year of social cohesiveness among elites. The mean centrality of those individuals who interlock across three sectors is higher in 1961 than either of the other years. Also, the total number of those who interlock across three sectors is two to three times higher in 1961 than in 1931 and 1991. The presence of multiple-sector interlockers is important because it is an indication that these individuals have wider civic connections and a broader civic outlook than those whose board interlocks are limited to one or two domains.

The year 1961 is also unusual in the level of integration of the business and government sector. This finding is not unique to my study of Atlanta elites but has been chronicled by other urban scholars (Abbott 1981; Stone 1989). In my Atlanta study, the integration of business and government sectors is evident in the number and centrality of elected officials in the top seventy as well as in the character of their linkages in the network. In 1961, Atlanta's mayor-elect, Ivan Allen, Jr., is one of the city's most well-connected business leaders. Ivan Allen, Jr. is one of five elected officials in elite ranks in 1961; this compares to two elected officials in 1931 and none in 1991.

In summary, the higher level of network density in 1961, the greater number and centrality of three-sector interlockers, and the increased civic integration of elected officials, all taken together, suggest that there is merit to the argument that the postwar period is remarkable for the social cohesion of its elite leaders.

Discussion

The important question, then, is why network cohesiveness reached its peak in the 1960s, why it was greater at that point than an earlier era, and why it has since declined. The explanation seems to reside in the nature of the local economy and its leadership during each historical period. In 1931, the Atlanta corporate sector was dominated by large numbers of small businesses whose markets were limited by transportation constraints. Similarly, both the nonprofit and government sectors were underdeveloped. By 1961, local corporations had consolidated their organizational structures, reducing their numbers by 73 percent, and, with improvements in transportation and communication, had extended their reach within the regional markets they dominated (Heying 1995). The postwar period was also an important one for home-grown banks and utilities, who uniquely benefited from the place synergies of the postwar building boom and whose local markets were protected from external competition by federal and state regulation. Finally, business consolidation in the postwar period was supported by the growth and increasing professionalism of local government, which responded to new opportunities created by the infusion of federal dollars for urban renewal and transportation (Stone 1989).

The nature of Atlanta's elite leadership was also different in the postwar era. To a certain extent, the difference was generational as these children of the Depression reached their mid-fifties and consolidated their displacement of an older generation of leaders (White and Crimmins 1980). Data from my study (Heying 1995) show Atlanta's elite leaders in 1961 to be more home-grown and more like one another than at any of the other two periods. In 1931 only 41 percent of the top seventy elites were born in Georgia; by 1961 the number of elites born in Georgia had risen to 71 percent, but by 1991 the number had again declined to 49 percent. Atlanta elites in 1961 also lived closer to one another. When I tallied the number of elite leaders living within two zip code areas at each point in time, I found that in 1931, 51 percent of the top seventy lived in the Little Five Points area or the Ansley Park/Inman Circle area. By 1961, however, the new elite havens, Buckhead and Nancy Creek, attracted 74 percent of the top civic leaders. By 1991, the same two areas attracted only 59 percent of the top seventy. Finally, elites in 1961 shared educational backgrounds to a greater extent than elites at other periods. At all points in time, law was the most common profession; however, in 1931 and 1991, only 24 percent and 50 percent respectively of the top seventy elites had law degrees. In 1961, the number of elites with law degrees was 79 percent.

What has happened in Atlanta since the 1960s that might explain the declines in social cohesion among elites? I would argue that the explanation lies in the economic transformations that have taken place since that time. What follows is some suggestive evidence from the Atlanta study to support this contention. Between 1961 and 1991, regional merchandisers such as Rich's department store lost considerable standing within the network of Atlanta elites. In 1961, regional merchandisers were the third ranked occupational group; by 1991 this group had dropped to eleventh in terms of number and centrality of elites. While this change may simply be an anomaly of the study, it is also possible that it points to larger structural changes in the economy. In the years between 1961 and 1991, downtown merchandisers followed the population to the rapidly growing suburbs, were directly challenged by national chains, and in cases such as Rich's, were absorbed in mergers with national firms. I would argue that the impact of competition and national mergers on merchandisers was to lessen their ties to place and their importance to the place-specific benefits of local engagement.

Other evidence from the study is suggestive of the critical role of local attachment. I found that, at all three points in time, managers of large branch plants and corporations who had moved their headquarters to Atlanta were not accorded a role within the elite structure that their importance to the economy should have merited. For example, in 1931, two major auto manufacturers had branch plants in suburban Atlanta, but no executives from these facilities appear in the top seventy. Likewise, since the mid-1940s, Lockheed, one of the nation's largest defense contractors, has been a major Atlanta employer, but no executives from this division are found among the top seventy in either 1961 or 1991. By 1991, United Parcel Service (UPS) had relocated its corporate headquarters to Atlanta, yet no executives from UPS are in the top seventy. Local leaders (Paul B. Kelman, personal communication, 19 May 1993) suggested that UPS did not get involved locally because Atlanta was simply a cost-efficient transportation hub and not a corporate hometown.

Corporate Delocalization: Evidence from Other Cities

In terms of its impact on community civic engagement, the implications for corporate delocalization are considerable. Delocalized corporations with inadequate self-interest in extracting place-dependent value may reduce their civic commitment and philanthropic largesse or direct it elsewhere, resulting in the demise of the local civic structure. The distancing of corporate elites from localities is likely to have a cascading effect on the ability of place-based and donation-dependent nonprofit organizations to carry out their philanthropic missions. Evidence has emerged in scholarly journals and the national press about the consequences of corporate disengagement. In a study of the Chicago area United Way, Kirsten Gronbjerg and her coauthors (Gronbjerg, Harmon, Olkkonen, Raza 1996) identify regional economic restructuring, the increasing dominance of multinational corporations, and corporate downsizing as important contributing factors for the decline of 13 percent from 1992 to 1995 in the overall United Way campaign in the Chicago region. Gronbjerg et al. (1996) note that merged firms not only reduce their local commitments but increasingly give strategically; that is , they rationalize their giving to make it more supportive of private corporate goals. A recent study of corporate giving by the Conference Board provides additional evidence of this move toward "strategic philanthropy" (Tillman 1998).

Rob Gurwitt (1991) describes the impact of corporate delocalization on the medium-sized city of Shreveport, Louisiana. The process began in 1965, when Houston-based Pennzoil successfully took over Shreveport's largest home-town company, United Gas. This was the first of numerous takeovers by out-of-state corporations that transformed the city from a white-collar headquarters town to a blue-collar town dominated by branch plants and absentee owners. As headquarters have been abandoned and home-town companies transformed, local elite leadership has been decimated. Regarding the impacts of this economic transformation, Gurwitt notes that "the whole process is having a profound impact on political and civic life. That is because local owners and leading businessmen are not just players on the economic scene; they also tend to be key figures in civic and political affairs. They give money for concert halls and museums, lend their names to fund-raising drives, work to build the critical mass necessary to get major projects off the ground" (54).

The impact of the buyout of locally-owned banks was cited by Carolyn Teich Adams (1991) as one of the causes for Philadephia's fiscal decline and its inability to breach its racial and economic cleavages. Adams notes that leadership in the 1950s was exercised through "an alliance of civic-minded bankers, lawyers, and business people" who were influential in major policy areas (1991:38). Concerning the possibility of a resurgence of elite leadership, she states that, "in a city so balkanized as Philadelphia in the 1990's, it is hard to imagine business reasserting its vaunted influence of the 1950's, particularly since so many CEOs are transients sent into the city to manage branch offices of companies whose headquarters are elsewhere. Their stake in city politics is simply not as great as that of corporate heads 40 years ago" (39).

Articles examining the community impact of corporate delocalization have appeared in the national press. The *Chicago Tribune* (Leroux and Grossman 1996) and the *New York Times* (Rimer 1996) have both run multiple-part series. The *New York Times* series focused on Dayton, Ohio, a city of home-grown corporations, with National Cash Register (NCR) at its core, that entered the 1970s with confidence. By the mid-1980s, all had changed. Dayton's manufacturing employment had been slashed by a third; union membership went from 70,000 in 1975 to 50,000 in 1996. The crowning blow came in 1991 when AT&T acquired NCR in a hostile takeover with disastrous consequences. By 1996, Dayton was a community with only a few home-town companies and considerable uncertainty about its future. While employment has seemed to recover, replacement jobs have been lower paying, less secure, and less place-bound. Many have stayed to fill these new positions, but others have sought opportunities elsewhere.

The consequences for Dayton's civic sector have reportedly been profound: declining club and church membership, United Way campaign goals unmet, and overworked parents too exhausted to volunteer. And those families who relocated have become rootless Americans, more inwardly focused and less connected to community—an outcome supported by scholarly research on mobility and community attachment (Kasarda and Janowitz 1974; Sampson 1988).

Delocalization of Banks and Utilities

The suggestive findings from my study of Atlanta elites (Heying 1995), supported by evidence from other community studies, leads to informed speculation about the potential effects of changes now unfolding in the banking and utility industries. Changes in these industries are likely significantly to impact communities because their corporate leaders have been the backbone of local elite leadership. The last year of my data collection in Atlanta, 1991, was coincidentally a watershed period for the beginning of large national and international bank mergers. Since 1991, numerous Atlanta-based banks have merged into national corporations that, in several cases, are now headquartered outside of Atlanta (e.g., NationsBank).

Bank mergers are the external manifestations of a long-term trend in banking that has freed capital from its local, land-based dependency. Local bank officers have traditionally been the most central actors in the civic coalition, and it seems likely that bank mergers will decrease their incentives to play prominent roles in local development. Rather than doing the hard work of creating benefits in a specific place, merged banks may prefer to invest in locations where serendipitous place synergies are already creating surplus value. If this is the case, the incentives for local participation are greatly diminished, and this could radically alter the local social order.

A similar story of delocalization is beginning to unfold for regional telephone and electric utility companies that have, until recently, been confined to noncompetitive markets and been untouched by mergers. Deregulation of local telephone monopolies resulting from the passage of the Telecommunications Act of 1996, marks the passage of one of the last vestiges of place-based connections in the telecommunications industry. The opening of local telecommunications markets, combined with the integration of media and entertainment into a blended network unbounded by connection to place, is likely to diminish the incentives for corporate leadership from the media and telecommunications industries to focus on local issues.

Deregulation of local electrical utilities may not be far off, and electrical utilities are gearing up for nationwide competition in electrical rates. Strategic mergers and buyouts are proceeding apace. For example, in 1996, Houston-based Enron Corporation offered $3.2 billion for Portland General Electric (PGE), a home-grown utility that serves a regional market. Enron, an energy broker with annual revenues over $14 billion, is a company with global reach and a corporate strategy to dominate international energy markets. With its foothold in Oregon, Enron hoped to gain access to cheap hydroelectric power and interstate transmission lines that link California to the Northwest power grid (Walth and Barnett 1996). Enron worked skillfully to win favor in Portland, where it promised a $20 million contribution to PGE Foundation to help fund civic projects (Francis 1996). While Oregon's Public Utility Commission finally approved Enron's offer, its purchase of PGE quickly fell victim to changing corporate strategy. In 1999, Enron signed an agreement to sell the utility to Reno-based Sierra Pacific Resources (Leeson 1999).

Enron's buyout of PGE created a new source of funds for Portland philanthropy, but foundation grants will provide only a temporary boost for community projects. In the long run, the sale and resale of PGE has set the stage for the disconnection of the utility from the community it serves. The new owners will be headquartered elsewhere, and community leadership roles, once filled by local corporate owners, will be relegated to professional community relations officers with minimal leverage with distant corporate leaders.

Conclusion

In this paper, I have used the term *delocalization* to refer to the economic transformations that are changing the nature of local economies. Delocalization is preferred over other terms because it does not imply that control is simply shifting from one location to another, instead it suggests the elimination of place as an important variable in the new economy. In presenting evidence from my study of Atlanta elites and supportive evidence from other community studies, I have attempted to demonstrate the connection between the structure of the local economy and the structure of its elite leadership. I have argued that a decline in the cohesiveness of local elite networks is connected to the delocalization of elite interests. In addition, I have offered some informed speculation about how recent economic transformations, in particular national mergers of community-based banks and deregulation of telecommunications and electric utilities, are likely to lead to a further deterioration of elite cohesiveness and elite community leadership. Finally, I have argued that this civic withdrawal will have cascading consequences on the philanthropic sector of the community and that these effects, combined with increasing mobility and anxiousness in the workforce, could reach quite deeply into the community and its ability to sustain a dynamic associational life. This study of the microecology of community leadership, like that of Schulman and Anderson which follows, is intended to provide a glimpse at a more complex and theoretically rich explanation of the decline in social capital. Ironically, this explanation is quite compatible with the generational effects Putnam (1995b) has described. Unfortunately, Putnam has too eagerly dismissed the complex impacts of social and economic transformation in his determination to link the decline of social capital in America to the causal "smoking gun" of television.

The Dark Side of the Force

Economic Restructuring and Social Capital in a Company Town

MICHAEL D. SCHULMAN AND CYNTHIA ANDERSON

From its development in the poststructural theories of Pierre Bourdieu (1986) and the rational choice perspective of James Coleman (1988), the concept of social capital has become a major force in the sociological universe. While social capital is a broad term that has assumed a variety of different meanings and definitions, it is not an undifferentiated glob of positive individual-level social relationships. There are different types and forms of social capital associated with different sets of social relations and institutional environments. Communities can have horizontal, hierarchical, or no social capital. Horizontal social capital involves the social ties and reciprocities that bind together into networks individuals who occupy similar social locations. Hierarchical social capital refers to the networks that bind together individuals who occupy different social locations. The absence of social capital is indicated by social fragmentation and isolation (Flora and Flora 1993).

In this chapter, we call attention to the "dark side" of social capital, recognizing that reserves of social capital are unevenly distributed and differentially accessible depending on the social location of the groups and individuals who attempt to appropriate it. Dominant classes may use their power to make strategic conversions of one type of capital to another to further solidify their class position (Bourdieu 1986). Social capital can negatively impact certain groups through downward leveling pressures and group conformity (Portes and Landolt 1996). The value of a particular form of social capital for facilitating group or individual social

Revised version of paper originally published in *Rural Sociology* 64, no.3 (1999): 351–72. Support for this research came from USDA/CSRS NRI Rural Development Grant 0166485 to North Carolina State University and from the North Carolina Agricultural Research Service.

action varies according to social, spatial, historical, and geographic location (Edwards and Foley 1998). Social capital can be deployed for both positive and negative ends, and a given form of social capital confers costs as well as benefits (Woolcock 1998). As an embedded set of social relations, social capital should be influenced by changes in the organization of work, community, labor market, firm, and commodity system contexts. In other words, social capital connects the face-to-face relationships and common experiences of people with structural social processes involving class, power, and domination.

We use a case study of a Southern textile community to show how a specific form of social capital, which we label paternalist social capital, has a dark side that is embedded in the local context of power and domination and to illustrate how this form of social capital is transformed in the process of restructuring. The firm studied was a traditional paternalistic employer. The associated community was a stereotypical mill town dominated politically and economically by the firm. Transformations in the organization of the textile industry and the firm changed social and economic relations in the mills and the community. Family ownership was replaced by corporate ownership. New owners attempted to maintain the outward vestiges of paternalistic social capital while instituting major changes in the workplace and the community. Mergers, unionization efforts, changes in the racial composition of the labor force, and expansion of the regional labor market have led to the decline of the paternalist form of social capital.

The Paternalist Form of Social Capital

Paternalism is a form of traditional authority. It involves hierarchical differentiation between classes, concentration of power, and the identification of the subordinate class with members of the dominant class (Newby 1975). Key aspects of paternalism in Southern textile communities include company control of land, buildings, goods, and services in the mill villages as well as an ideology that overlies the relations between workers and mill owners.

Because it draws attention to the particular forms of power relations, to norms and values, and to the interconnections among dominant and subordinate groups, paternalism is a useful concept for analyzing the embeddedness of social and economic relations in Southern mill communities. The danger is that a focus on paternalism has a tendency to produce either undersocialized or oversocialized interpretations of mill/community relationships (Simpson 1981). Undersocialized interpretations emphasize the mill community as a near-total institution dominating all aspects of social life. Oversocialized interpretations emphasize the cultural values of the workers and their indoctrination with the values of mill owners (Jackman 1994). We argue that paternalism in Southern textile mill towns can be reconceptualized as a locally and historically specific form of social capital.

We follow Bourdieu's emphasis that capital is a generalized resource that can assume monetary and nonmonetary, tangible and intangible forms, and we add the emphasis on embeddedness from the new economic sociology (Portes 1995). Paternalist social capital is a combination of hierarchical and horizontal social capital based on the interpenetration of workplace and community social relations. For paternalist social capital, norms of beneficence, deference, and patron-client relationships permeate both the workplace and community. Hierarchical social capital outweighs horizontal social capital. Social relations of identity are not counterbalanced by social relations of autonomy (1998). Horizontal social capital (e.g., network relationships with groups or institutions that are autonomous) is not totally absent, but it is relatively quiescent and can mobilize workers when the norms governing patron-client relations are violated. When workers use horizontal social capital to organize, the power of the state is often used to repress workers and defeat class mobilization. As illustrated by the case study of Kannapolis and Cannon Mills, access to social capital depends on the social location of groups, and the value of social capital depends on who appropriates it (Edwards and Foley 1997).

The Case Study

The case study focuses on Fieldcrest Cannon and the town of Kannapolis, North Carolina. Owned and controlled by members of the Cannon family until the 1980s, the firm was at one time the largest producer of household textiles, and the town of Kannapolis was the largest unincorporated community in North Carolina (Kearns 1995).

The case analysis suggests three key periods in the organization of the firm and the local community. The first period is almost a century long, from the late 1800s to 1982, during which the Cannon family controlled the firm and the community. This is the era of paternalist social capital. Strong hierarchical social capital in the form of patron-client relations between the Cannon family and the workers dominated mill and community. Horizontal social capital was weak, but could be mobilized by workers when the norms governing hierarchical social capital were broken. The second period, 1982 to 1986, is marked by a leveraged buyout of Cannon. The paternalist form of social capital began a period of transition, as many of the vestiges of hierarchical social capital were withdrawn as a consequence of restructuring. Unionization efforts, though unsuccessful, attempted to forge horizontal social capital among both white and black workers (see Anderson and Schulman 1999). The final period, 1986 to the present, is characterized by the merger of Cannon Mills with other firms, by the municipal incorporation of Kannapolis, and by a series of unionization struggles that end in a victory for pro-union workers.

For the case study, we collected primary and secondary data using a variety of techniques. Historical data were used to study the selected firm and the community. Data were obtained from textile trade journals, house publications, books on community history, newspaper clippings, and company reports. Descriptive statistical data were obtained from the Textile and Business Information Systems (TABIS) developed at North Carolina State University, and from Census city and county databases.

Semistructured interviewing was conducted with current and former workers, company managers, community development officials, and social service providers. Informant interviewing resulted in information about the labor process, support for collective action, and relations between the firm and workers. To generalize findings beyond the individual level, informants were asked to report, not just about themselves, but about people like themselves; not just about their personal behavior, but about practices common to their group. This technique generated qualitative, descriptive data that capture individual and community-level variation.

The qualitative interviews were based on a purposive sample. For workers, a snowball sampling method was used to pursue new leads during fieldwork and to take advantage of unexpected potential informants. Respondents from local community and activist groups (e.g., churches, civic clubs, Amalgamated Clothing and Textile Workers Union local office) gave us introductions to friends and neighbors. Additionally, contacts via professors at the North Carolina State University College of Textiles facilitated interviews with industry experts. While not a random sample, informants represent different social locations within the research site. They vary by race, class, gender, and age.

Phase I: The Cannon Family Mills

The textile industry in the U.S. South sprang up during the 1880s following the destruction of the agriculture-slave basis of the Southern economy. Labor was recruited from white yeoman and tenant farmers who were rapidly being proletarianized because of the depression in Southern agriculture. Blacks were considered unfit for industrial labor and were needed as workers in the cotton sharecropping/debt peonage system (Williamson 1984). Landless and impoverished white farmers and their families left agriculture to become textile workers in the newly created mill villages.

James William Cannon raised $75,000 and began a small yarn-spinning plant in Concord, North Carolina, in 1894 (Rankin 1987). Machinery and cotton were purchased locally and white sharecroppers were recruited to work as mill hands. To centralize textile production, James Cannon installed cards, looms, and other machinery that allowed raw cotton to be transformed into the final product, sheeting. Housing the entire process under one roof broke the established pattern of segmented production. In contrast to selling the fabric simply as cotton cloth, James Cannon put a name brand on it, reasoning that customers who liked the product would be able to ask for it by name, thereby increasing demand (Rankin 1987). In 1898, he opened another mill to produce terry towels and expanded again in 1908 with the opening of new production facilities.

Along with the expansion of the mill, Cannon purchased a 600-acre parcel of land, previously a cotton plantation, and began developing the community that became Kannapolis. Local historians claim the name is a combination of two Greek words meaning "city of looms" (Rankin 1987). As the primary investor, Cannon controlled the development of the town. From 1905 to 1910, James Cannon bought farmlands and spent thousands of dollars (in the form of donations, loans, and gifts) to build mills, houses, churches, stores, schools, and business buildings. Workers, recruited from nearby farms, lived in white-painted clapboard houses owned by Cannon. The houses surrounded the mill in a circle, facilitating travel to work and close supervision at all times. A large lake was constructed as part of the expansive recreation facilities (Young 1963). Cannon later funded the beginnings of the police department, post office, theater, railway station, and a highway to span the nine miles between Kannapolis and Concord (Kearns 1995). Power was reflected in the spatial organization of the locality. Workers lived in the unincorporated town of Kannapolis, while owners and managers lived in Concord, the county seat.

When James Cannon died in 1921 he controlled twelve mills with over 15,000 employees, more than 600,000 spindles and 10,000 looms, and an estimated $40 million (1920s dollars) in annual sales (Collins 1994; Young 1963). His son, Charles Cannon, took office during a period of decline and industry-wide worker strife (Hall et al. 1987). In 1920, the textile industry declined as markets dwindled. Many Southern mill owners reacted by cutting wages, going on short time, imposing stretch-outs, and closing plants (Zingraff 1991). Workers responded to these changes in reciprocity within the mill "family" by pressuring the United Textile Workers Union to call a region-wide strike in 1921. The strike was quickly defeated when the state militia arrived in Concord and overwhelmed the union.

During the Depression of the 1930s Cannon Mills continued to operate on a limited basis by building warehouses and storing unsold goods. As in the 1920s, mill closings and declines in wages and working conditions precipitated strikes and worker unrest. In 1934, a General Strike organized by the United Textile Workers, involving nearly 400,000 Southern workers, virtually closed the industry. Mill executives and townspeople panicked, and Southern governors responded by dispatching 14,000 troops with machine guns and bayonets. The strike was over after twenty-two days. As Zingraff (1991) reports, the activists were purged from the textile labor force, the unions lost credibility, the workers who remained on the payroll were demoralized, and the inflamed mill owners further rationalized their strategies for production and control over local communities.

The Cannon Family Mills period exemplifies the paternalist form of social capital. Workers provided labor for the family that owned the mills and, in exchange, owners provided for the social and moral welfare of their workers (McLaurin 1971). The family nature of labor, where multiple members of the family were employed by the mill, ensured survival for workers' families and reinforced dependency (Hall et al. 1987). The visibility of the owner reinforced the image and reality of patron-client relationships. Both James and Charles Cannon used to come through the mills and stop to talk with people and shake their hands. Horizontal social capital among workers was relatively weak given their lack of resources and dependency on the firm for both employment and community services. Community social life revolved around the mill: the company sponsored a band, funded the YMCA community center, provided funds for school construction, and supported local churches. The mill sent trucks to haul trash and pump toilets (many houses did not have bathrooms until after World War II) (Kearns 1995). Informants recounted stories about workers being fired (and their families thrown out of mill housing) because they had returned to the community after drinking in a nearby town and been reported by a neighbor or by a supervisor when they returned to work. In sum, Cannon Mills and the community of Kannapolis were one and the same.

The labor unrest and unionization attempts of the 1920s and 1930s demonstrate that reserves of horizontal social capital among workers could be mobilized. Common circumstances and communication in racially homogeneous mill villages provided a basis for bounded solidarity among white workers, especially when employers violated norms of reciprocity by changing hours, wages, or working conditions. How did workers mobilize networks to overcome the spatial isolation and power vacuum of company towns? Historical accounts point to organizers forming "flying squads" of workers going from town to town, giving daily radio talks, and traveling musicians singing of labor organizing (Kearns 1995). However, the Cannon's hierarchical social capital based upon the integration of mill and community (and backed by the power of the state) meant that workers' attempts to develop horizontal social capital were at a severe structural disadvantage.

In the 1940s, at Kannapolis's peak of prosperity, the mill employed more than 25,000 workers (Collins 1994). Kannapolis was the largest unincorporated town in the United States (see *Raleigh News and Observer,* 1 September 1985). Incorporation was opposed by Charles Cannon because it would mean a loss of company control and higher taxes for the firm. Over the next several decades, Cannon continued the paternalist form of social capital. He donated land and funds for the Cabarrus Memorial Hospital. He gave scholarships to children of mill employees and announced at high school graduation classes that Cannon Mills would have a job for every graduate who applied. At Charles A. Cannon Appreciation Day in Kannapolis on 21 May 1967, Charles Cannon is quoted as saying, "I am proud to boast one of the largest, and one of the finest families in this country—all 25,000 of them" (Kearns 1995:202). Described by a community leader informant as a "benevolent dictator," an ex-mill employee told us, Charles Cannon was the "daddy of the town,"a "one horse town with two rear ends."

When Charles Cannon died in 1971, Cannon Mills owned seventeen plants and was the largest employer in the state of North Carolina. Kannapolis, as an unincorporated town, had no mayor, town council, or legal charter. Cannon Mills paid for the community's police and fire services and was responsible for its water and sewage system, trash collection, and street maintenance. The company still owned approximately 1,600 houses that it rented to mill employees as well as all the property within the one-square-mile business district (Collins 1994).

Phase II: Leveraged Buyout by Murdock

The next historical phase is relatively brief, encompassing four short but extremely turbulent years. In 1982, David H. Murdock, a self-made millionaire from California, purchased Cannon Mills and 660 surrounding acres (including the Kannapolis business district) in a $413-million leveraged buyout from eleven Cannon family heirs and other stockholders (Collins 1994). Murdock took control of seventeen plants, the employees' pension fund, downtown real estate, the community water supply, the wastewater treatment plant, the Cannon Country Club, and 1,600 homes (Kearns 1995).

David Murdock's takeover of Cannon Mills caught the community by surprise. As Chairman, CEO, and majority stock holder, Murdock took the company private and proceeded aggressively to alter the way Cannon did business. Plans were announced for a $200-million capital improvement program, primarily for new machinery and technology (Rankin 1987).

During this time, workers and community members experienced the confusion of the dismantling and reconstruction of paternalist social capital. For example, Murdock donated land, cash, and company labor to help Kannapolis build a senior citizens' center, park, and library (Collins 1994). He also instigated new employee health benefits and allowed workers to own the mill houses where they lived (Rankin 1987). Although the average price for mill houses was $20,000 (*Raleigh News and Observer*, 1 September 1985), not all workers were able to purchase their homes. As one interview informant noted, workers living in company houses "hadn't saved a dime . . . and I can't blame them a bit." Typical workers, assuming their needs would be at least minimally taken care of, had no reason or incentive to save the little extra money they earned.

At the same time mill workers were struggling to adjust to changes in home ownership, Murdock was making other changes. Four blocks in downtown Kannapolis were remodeled and leased as factory outlet stores in the hope of drawing tourists from nearby Interstate 85. With teams of industrial engineers to evaluate plant efficiency and revise jobs and salaries, Murdock created significant changes in the workplace, including layoffs (3,000 between 1982 and 1986) and the closing of three mills (Collins 1994).

Many mill workers were not pleased with Murdock's innovations. According to the pastor of one of the local churches, "back when the Cannons owned the mills the attitude was 'The Cannons would take care of us . . .' Most people felt Cannon would not break the trust, that there was a covenant between the workers and Cannon. When the [Murdock] sale went through, it just destroyed that perception of people" (*Charlotte Observer*, 29 Sept. 1985). Reacting to the massive changes within the firm, including steps to increase production and worker control, the Amalgamated Clothing and Textile Workers Union (ACTWU) attempted to organize Cannon employees. The effort culminated in an election in October 1985. The union had failed previously, most recently in 1974 by a 44 to 56 percent vote. Murdock fought the union in a bitter campaign. Using economic, social, symbolic, and cultural capital, Murdock jetted frequently into Kannapolis from California, toured the factories, and shook hands with company employees (Rankin 1987). One female respondent claimed that Murdock appeared on television crying and that the company placed full-page newspaper advertisements discouraging workers from supporting the union. The company had a picture of a padlocked gate posted inside the plants and hired an Atlanta law firm that specialized in anti-union campaigns (*Charlotte Observer*, 29 Sept. 1985). Local merchants threatened to revoke credit for union supporters. As is common under these conditions (Billings 1990), the movement to unionize was defeated in a 27 to 63 percent vote (Collins 1994; Rankin 1987).

The Murdock-era union drive was an attempt by workers to use horizontal social capital to enhance their power. Union organizers went door-to-door, produced programs for cable TV, gave speeches to church groups, and hired a community relations director. But the struggle was embedded in a local community, where various social institutions continued to reinforce company-based hierarchical social capital. Nonetheless, the brief period during Murdock's ownership changed the social relationships between community members and the company. Members of the mill community, many of whom had lost their jobs, became critical of the company and less willing to tolerate unfair practices. Although they did not achieve union certification, the insurgency brought attention and raised awareness of employee rights, strengthening worker solidarity.

Within a few months, another important event in Cannon Mills's history occurred. In January 1986, Murdock sold approximately 75 percent of Cannon Mills to Fieldcrest Mills for $231 million (Collins 1994). The sale did not dissolve Murdock's relationship with the firm and community. He retained the real estate holdings, which included most of the commercial real estate in downtown Kannapolis, worth approximately $100 million. In addition, Murdock "absconded" with around $25 million from the Cannon pension fund. ACTWU sued, and the case was settled out of court in 1989 for a reported $1 million, leaving Murdock with $24 million.

Phase III: Corporate Mergers and Unionization Struggles

The third phase in the history of the firm begins in 1986 when Fieldcrest, a leader in the U.S. textile industry, acquired Cannon in the midst of an industry-wide restructuring. Increased global competition and concentration in retailing were driving mergers among textile firms. Surviving firms pursued long-delayed technological upgrading and worker downsizing to remain viable in the changing commodity system. Fieldcrest Cannon increased its investment in new technology, particularly in spinning and weaving (e.g., shuttle-less looms). In some plants, it instituted rotating twelve-hour shifts in place of the traditional three eight-hour shifts and moved workers from production to hourly salaries. A new high-technology towel factory was opened in the Alabama-Georgia region, while two older plants in Kannapolis were closed. In Kannapolis, warehouses were torn down, jobs and workers were eliminated, just-in-time production systems were instituted, and workers were reorganized into teams. The firm relocated many of its New York corporate managers to Kannapolis and built a computer center to better link it to retailers.

Provoked by job cuts and alleged unfair labor practices, workers in the Kannapolis plants attempted to unionize in 1993. As one interview informant stated, "People had gone three to four years without a raise, conditions were bad." In response, the firm instigated an all out anti-union campaign that included local merchants, churches, and lawyers. Two groups of paid lawyers were brought to town, one for white workers and one for black workers, to convince employees that the union was not in their best interests. Several respondents claimed that local ministers who spoke out against the union during this period received gifts, such as church organs and vans. According to one informant, the firm used racist threats to fracture union support, such as telling whites they would have black supervisors if the union was instated. Nonetheless, the vote was close. The union lost by 199 votes out of more than 6,000 ballots cast. Several respondents claimed that the company used unfair tactics to defeat the union, such as registering and voting in the names of deceased people, posting threats of deportation in Spanish, and drawing artificial lines to keep union organizers away from the plant. The workers' claims proved valid. In 1995, after years of litigation, the National Labor Relations Board (NLRB) charged Fieldcrest Cannon with unfair labor practices. Among other things, the company was found guilty of intimidation, coercion, and harassment of employees (*Raleigh News and Observer*, 6 September 1995). An appeal of the decision by Fieldcrest Cannon was rejected and a new election was held in August 1997. As in 1991, the union was defeated in 1997, this time by 369 votes out of the 4,757 votes counted (*Raleigh News and Observer*, 14 August 1997).

Major transformations in Kannapolis and Cabarrus County occurred concurrently with the changes in mill ownership. In 1985, Kannapolis became incorporated and residents assumed responsibility for local services and taxes. While the town itself still relies heavily on textile employment, the county has attracted new industry, including a major cigarette plant.

In 1970, there were 24,720 workers in textiles in Cabarrus County; by 1995 the number was approximately 6,000 (N.C. Department of Commerce 1997). Workers are likely to commute outside the county to jobs. While some 9,000 people have moved into the county between 1980 and 1990, the number of commuters to Charlotte-Mecklenburg County doubled during the same period. The area's labor market geography, based on commuting-to-work data, show that Cabarrus County is now part of a nine-county area dominated by Charlotte (Tolbert, Beggs, and Boudreaux 1995). Not only did the geography and organization of work change, but the racial composition of the locality also changed during this period. African Americans, the "old" or established minority, comprise approximately one-quarter of the population in the nine-county labor market area. In 1990, Hispanics comprised about ten percent. Interviews with social service providers in Kannapolis estimate that over 3,500 Hispanics reside in the community and that over 500 work in a local poultry plant.

Control over the locality decreased as the firm shifted from local to regional labor markets. Paternalist social capital, which started to disintegrate during Murdock's ownership, continued to decline under Fieldcrest. Workers were replaced with new equipment. Outdated plants were closed while new minorities competed for the entry-level jobs in the plants. Shortly after the 1997 union defeat, Pillowtex, a Texas-based manufacturer of high-end home furnishings, announced that it was acquiring Fieldcrest Cannon to create the third largest U.S. home furnishings textile company (*Charlotte Observer*, 12 Sept. 1997). While Fieldcrest Cannon became a subsidiary of Dallas-based Pillowtex, the newly merged firm made a commitment to maintaining a significant operating presence in Kannapolis. Chuck Hansen, Jr., CEO of Pillowtex stated that the name on the Kannapolis plants would not change: "We're not going to put Pillowtex up there . . . Cannon has so much heritage. That would be an insult to Kannapolis and North Carolina" (*Durham Herald-Sun*, 9 February 1998:B6).

The series of mergers, combined with industry-wide restructuring and local labor market expansion, furthered the deterioration of paternalist social capital. The merger with Pillowtex was announced only one month after the failed 1997 vote and while a complaint filed by UNITE accusing Fieldcrest management of unfair tactics and violating federal court orders and labor laws was pending with the National Labor Relations Board. UNITE began a new union organizing drive coincident with the merger, focusing on increased work demands, job changes, pension benefits, and job security. According to Bruce Raynor, the union's organizing director, Pillowtex management opposed the union but obeyed the labor laws and did not resort to threats. In June 1999, workers voted 2,270 to 2,102 for the union in an election described as the cleanest ever (*New York Times*, 25 June 1999). Pillowtex accepted the union victory and began negotiations in November 1999 resulting in a contract covering 5,000 workers in the plants around Kannapolis and 3,500 workers in other Fieldcrest plants. Workers won modest increases in wages, paid sick days, and pension benefits. UNITE promised to work with the financially troubled Pillowtex to ensure that the plants remain competitive by having productive and motivated workers who have a stake in the future of the company.

Conclusion

The analysis of the three phases of company history illustrates how the local form of paternalist social capital was embedded in workplace and community social relations. Beginning with Cannon, the company developed paternalist social capital based upon hierarchical social capital relations and its domination of the community and workplace. These systems began to dissipate with changes in ownership and the organization of social and production relations. The social relations of the labor market have replaced the traditional paternalist form of social capital in Kannapolis. The restructured flexibility of production, in the active context of a global economy, increased competition, and technological advances that decrease the number of workers yet increase the need for motivated employees ultimately led to a new working relationship between unionized workers and the recently merged Pillowtex/Fieldcrest Cannon textile firm.

The unionization drives of the 1920s, 1930s, 1980s, and 1990s represent attempts by the workers to mobilize bounded solidarity and build horizontal social capital. Those of the 1920s and 1930s were spontaneous uprisings caused in part by changes in the organization of hierarchical social capital. Workers' lack of resources and the repressive power of the state militia combined to suppress both attempts. Although troops did not occupy Kannapolis in the 1980s and 1990s, an army of lawyers and media consultants converged on the town to defeat unionization drives during those years. Pillowtex's acquisition of Fieldcrest in 1997 marked the end of paternalist social capital.

Analyzing Southern textile mill town paternalism as a form of social capital reminds us that forms of social capital are embedded in local social and geographic relations. It also takes the concept of social capital back to its roots in Bourdieu's analysis of the structure of power relations. As evidenced by the case study of Cannon Mills and Kannapolis, locally embedded forms of social capital can be created, accumulated, and destroyed.

Patterns of individual and group action create, maintain, and change social capital. However, different groups have differential access to social capital and other resources. Dominant social classes use their privileged access to cultural, human, social, and financial capital to make strategic conversions of one kind of capital to another in order to solidify their positions. Accordingly, different groups may receive differential benefits from their own and other's social capital. Relationships and norms governing how things are done are grounded in the structure of class and power, reinforced by the overt action of those who benefit from them, and maintained through memory, reputation, and family history. The Cannon/Kannapolis paternalist form of social capital provided positive individual and community benefits including employment, the creation of community organizations, and assistance for households during the ups and downs of the business cycle. However, the undercutting of community diversification, worker organization efforts, and worker empowerment illustrates the dark side of the social capital force.

The tragedy of paternalist social capital was not that it ended, but that it was too prolonged. Workers were "freed" of paternalism at the moment when modernization heightened worker insecurity. It was in the interest of the Cannon family to build and maintain paternalist social capital only as long as this form of workplace/community integration ensured capital accumulation that was on a par with its competitors. The family sold their interest in the firm and the community at the point where national and global competition in textiles were threatening the family's control and the firm's profitability. During the Murdock and Fieldcrest periods, attempts to build industrial unionism, in which horizontal social capital would approach hierarchical capital in importance within the workplace and the community, were defeated. With paternalism's demise, the social networks and horizontal social capital built by union supporters contributed to the 1999 victory. But the razing of hierarchical social capital also relied upon restructured production processes, expanded labor market opportunities, and the reorganization of textile capital. At times in this transition it may appear to a casual observer that workers were "bowling alone" and would never join the union team. However, attention to the historical and institutional processes reveals that the local form of paternalist social capital prevented alternative forms of social capital from emerging.

Social Capital, Cooperation, and Economic Performance

LANE KENWORTHY

Robert Putnam (1993a, 1993b; Helliwell and Putnam 1995) has argued that the same factors he believes contribute to a healthy polity—social capital and civic engagement—are critical to a healthy economy as well. Putnam's argument consists of three propositions: (1) Economic progress and prosperity require cooperation. (2) A key source of cooperative economic behavior is social capital. (3) Social capital, in turn, is a function of civic engagement. I argue that his emphasis on cooperation is entirely salutary, but that social capital and civic engagement are less integral to achieving economic cooperation than Putnam suggests.

Cooperation and Economic Performance

The notion that nonmarket or extramarket forms of cooperation contribute to economic health is reasonably well established theoretically and empirically (Aoki 1988; Dore 1986, 1987; Hicks and Kenworthy 1998; Kenworthy 1995; Porter 1992; Soskice 1991; Streeck 1992). Economists have long recognized that markets fail under certain conditions, but a host of recent research suggests that there are in fact numerous areas in which competition is usefully complemented by economic cooperation. These include, among others, cooperation between the state and interest groups, between firms and their investors and suppliers, between competing firms, between labor and management, and between functional divisions

Revised from an article of the same title in *American Behavioral Scientist* 40, no. 5 (1997): 645–56.

within firms. Comparative analysis strongly suggests that cooperation is a key contributor to successful national economic performance in affluent democracies.

Social Capital and Cooperation

But how does such cooperation arise? Putnam's answer is social capital. By this he primarily means trust. There are various ways to conceptualize trust, and Putnam never clearly defines it. His use of the term, however, is similar to the colloquial understanding of it: confident expectations that others will "do the right thing" even when incentives or constraints do not encourage or compel them to do so. Trust enables economic actors to cooperate in prisoners' dilemma-type circumstances, in which each would benefit from cooperation but each has an incentive not to cooperate. "Fabrics of trust enable the civic community more easily to surmount what economists call 'opportunism,' in which shared interests are unrealized because each individual, acting in wary isolation, has an incentive to defect from collective action" (Putnam 1993a:89).

A classic example is employee training. In many instances firms would be better off by providing training for their workers. But each individual firm knows that if it invests in such training, other firms may "poach" its employees (i.e., entice them to leave by offering slightly better pay), thereby enjoying the benefits of better-skilled employees without bearing the cost. Alas, if all companies act rationally and skimp on training, none will have a highly skilled workforce. Another example involves wage-bargaining strategy in a decentralized labor movement. Aggressive bargaining for each individual union is rational on purely defensive grounds, because if workers in other firms win high wage increases there will likely be high inflation, so it needs a comparable pay hike just to break even. And if it succeeds in getting a high wage raise while other unions do not, it will have higher pay in conjunction with low inflation, which is the best outcome among the various possibilities. Regardless of what it believes other unions will do, therefore, the rational choice for each union is to demand a substantial pay increase. Of course, if every union follows this logic there will indeed be high inflation, which will lessen the value of wage gains and reduce the price competitiveness of the country's firms relative to their global competitors.

Social capital, Putnam suggests, makes cooperative behavior reasonable in spite of such incentives. If I trust that nearby firms will not try to poach my employees, I can feel confident spending time and money to train them. If wage negotiators for each individual union can feel assured that others will bargain moderately, they can request modest pay raises with little fear that their members will see the raise rendered null by high inflation.

The principal empirical evidence on which Putnam draws is the industrial districts of north-central Italy, which feature "networks of collaboration among workers and small entrepreneurs." He also points to the "dense social networks" of East Asian economies such as Japan, South Korea, Taiwan, and China. In these countries, he argues, well-developed trust relationships encourage economic actors to cooperate in a variety of productive efforts that fall outside the scope of market relations (Putnam 1993b: 38; 1993a, ch. 6).

Institutional Incentives and Cooperation

There is little question but that trust can contribute to cooperative economic behavior. Trust lubricates economic relationships, making cooperation more likely. Moreover, both trust and economic cooperation have been linked to successful economic performance in quantitative empirical studies (Helliwell and Putnam 1995; Hicks and Kenworthy 1998; Kenworthy 1995; Knack and Keefer 1997). But is trust the principal reason why economic cooperation occurs?

Cooperation can also be induced by *structuring incentives* in such a way that actors no longer face a prisoners' dilemma-type situation. Institutional arrangements such as long-term relationships and formal organization can encourage cooperation whether trust is high or low. In Germany, for example, industry associations require members to fund and participate in the wide-ranging apprenticeship system, which provides classroom and on-the-job training for more than 400 occupations (Streeck 1992). These associations make firms' investments in worker training rational by forcing other firms to make similar investments. Poaching is not entirely eliminated; but because each company is required to train its own workforce in any case, the threat is greatly reduced. Institutional arrangements also help to overcome the wage-bargaining prisoners' dilemma. Where wage negotiations are conducted by a single national confederation or heavily influenced by a relatively small number of unions, these bodies have a strong incentive to bargain moderately, since much of the cost of excessively high wage gains—higher inflation or unemployment, or reduced international competitiveness—will eventually be borne by those they represent. Union coordination, when combined with coordination on the business side, thus tends to encourage wage restraint. This helps explain why the rate of wage increase has been more moderate in nations such as Austria and Norway than in Italy or the United Kingdom (Crouch 1985; Soskice 1990; Kenworthy 1996).

I have argued in more detail elsewhere (Kenworthy 1995, ch. 6) that there are nine chief types of economic cooperation that can be expected to enhance economic welfare and progress. For each type, there are institutional arrangements utilized in various nations that effectively foster cooperative behavior without relying upon trust. Centralized business confederations help to reduce rent-seeking by individual firms and industries. Coordinated wage bargaining, facilitated by a centralized and/or concentrated union movement, encourages wage restraint. Cooperation between government and interest groups, fostered by coordination within interest groups and among government agencies, generates productive, coherent state policies. Long-term, voice-based relationships between firms and their investors permit long time horizons for management. Long-term, voice-based relationships between purchaser and supplier firms foster heightened communication and greater supplier willingness to invest and raise productivity. Selective incentives and other supports provided by industry associations and/or governments encourage alliances among competing firms, which lead to greater investment in research and development and employee training, permit quicker agreement on standards, and provide assistance with matters such as financing, technology diffusion, design, accounting, and marketing. An employment guarantee by firms generates greater cooperation between labor and management; workers tend to be more willing to share valuable knowledge, accept productivity-enhancing technology, and upgrade skills. Participatory teamwork arrangements, by encouraging employees to monitor their peers to prevent shirking, engender greater work effort. Multidivisional teams that link various departments within firms yield a quicker, more effective transition from research and development to production. Table 1 summarizes these nine forms of cooperative behavior, the resulting economic benefits, and the institution(s) promoting the cooperation.

But isn't trust critical to creating such cooperation-inducing institutions in the first place, as Putnam (1993a) and others (e.g., Fukuyama 1995a; Swank 1996) contend? Sometimes yes, but often no. In many instances these institutions are the (intended or unintended) results of historical struggles and compromises. For example, it is sometimes suggested that large Japanese firms offer workers an employment guarantee because management can trust workers to hold up their part of the bargain by working hard (Fukuyama 1995a). But Japan's lifetime employment system grew out of a compromise solution to a series of bitter labor-management struggles following World War II (Kenney and Florida 1988). Once it was created, the system became self-reinforcing. Management in most firms sticks to it because it heightens employee commitment and because a firm that began to lay off employees would quickly develop a bad reputation, making it difficult to attract strong new recruits. Employees work hard for two reasons:

TABLE 1. Economic Cooperation and Institutional Incentives

Actors cooperating	Economic benefits	Institution(s) promoting cooperation
1. Firms across industries	Reduced rent-seeking	Centralized business federation
2. Unions	Wage restraint	Centralized and/or concentrated labor movement
3. Government and interest groups	Coherent, productive government policy	Unified government and centralized interest group organizations
4. Investors and firms	Extended time horizons for firms	Long-term commitment by investors—a product of investors having large ownership stakes and a means of effectively influencing company decision making
5. Purchaser and supplier firms	Heightened communication, greater supplier willingness to invest and raise productivity	Long-term commitment by purchasers
6. Competing firms	Greater investment in R&D and employee training; quicker agreement on standards; assistance with financing, technology diffusion, design, accounting, marketing, etc.	Industry trade associations and/or government incentives
7. Labor and management	Greater willingness on the part of workers to share valuable knowledge, accept productivity-enhancing technology, and upgrade skills	Long-term commitment by employers (employment guarantee)
8. Workers	Heightened work effort	Participatory work teams
9. Functional departments within firms	Quicker, more effective transition from R&D to production	Multi-divisional teams that link departments along the production chain

They know they will be with the company for a long time, so they have an incentive to improve the company's fortunes. Also, the employment guarantee is not absolute, and there is a strong incentive to avoid having to start over with a new firm because pay is based heavily on seniority.

Centralized union confederations arose in Scandinavia not because of "propensities for group membership and collective organization" (Swank 1996:669), but rather in response to the formation of centralized employer confederations, themselves a product of industry concentration and reliance on external trade (Swenson 1991). Once created, these encompassing organizations found it advantageous to coordinate wage bargaining. Although such arrangements have broken down in some countries at various points, on the whole they have been remarkably resilient (Lange, Wallerstein, and Golden 1995).

In the same way, cooperation between firms and their investors in Germany, Japan, and a number of other nations emerged in response to underdeveloped capital markets, which forced companies to rely heavily on large investors (Zysman 1983). It is also the product of lenient financial regulations, in contrast to the United States where laws have strongly discouraged financial institutions from holding large equity stakes in nonfinancial companies. Again, because long-term investor-firm relationships have virtuous consequences for both parties, once created they tend to be self-reinforcing. Trust can certainly help to foster such relationships, but they can occur even if trust is limited.

Perhaps most telling in this regard, Putnam (1995a, 1996) argues that trust has been declining in the United States over the past generation. But if that is so, and if trust is the key to cooperative economic behavior, how can we account for the fact that American firms have only recently begun to experiment with some important types of cooperation, such as research and development alliances, long-term partnerships with suppliers, employee participation, and multidivisional teams? The answer is simple: Firms have been searching for new ways to compete more effectively, and these are among the strategies some have decided to try (Applebaum and Batt 1994; Byrne 1993a, 1993b; Smith 1995; Waterman 1994). To the extent these efforts generate cooperation and improve performance, they may become self-sustaining. In the process they will likely foster trust, but such trust will be largely a consequence, rather than a cause, of cooperation.

How closely, then, does trust correlate with economic cooperation? Drawing upon the growing literature on cooperative economic behavior, I have assigned scores of 0, .5, or 1—representing weak, moderate, and strong cooperation, respectively—to each of eighteen affluent, democratic OECD countries for each of the nine types of cooperation shown in table 1 in each year over the period 1960–94 (Kenworthy 1998). Factor analysis suggests that these nine forms of cooperation load on two dimensions: a macro-level factor and a firm-level factor (Hicks and Kenworthy 1998). The average scores for these two dimensions for each nation are shown in the appendix table. The best available national-level measure of trust comes from the World Values Survey (World Values Study Group 1994), which asks "Generally speaking, would you say that most people can be trusted, or that you can't be too careful in dealing with people?" In their cross-national study of the effects of social capital on economic growth, Knack and Keefer (1997) measure trust as the percentage of respondents in each country replying "most people can be trusted" to this question. These figures, for 1980 and 1990, are also shown in the appendix. The correlations in table 2 indicate that there is virtually no association between trust and either of the two dimensions of economic cooperation, which suggests further reason for skepticism regarding the importance of the former in generating the latter.

Trust, then, appears to be a helpful but not a necessary precondition for economically beneficial cooperative behavior. Indeed, each of the principal forms of economic cooperation I have outlined can be traced, in most empirical instances, to institutional incentives that make cooperation the rational choice for economic actors. That is good news for a nation such as the United States where trust is, seemingly, comparatively scarce and on the decline. Despite this malady, American firms have managed to cooperate more extensively in various ways—with suppliers, with competitors, with labor—in the past decade than was previously the case.

Given the apparent lack of association between trust and economic cooperation across nations, it seems unlikely that Knack and Keefer's (1997) finding of a positive effect of trust on economic growth in cross-country regressions is due to trust being simply a proxy for cooperation. Indeed, in analyses reported elsewhere, Kenworthy and Hicks (2000) find that when trust and firm-level economic cooperation are entered together in multivariate

TABLE 2. Correlations among Economic Cooperation, Social Capital (Trust), Civic Engagement, and Economic Performance Measures for Eighteen OECD Countries, 1960–98

	(1)	(2)	(3)	(4)	(5)	(6)	(7)
(1) Macro level cooperation							
(2) Firm level cooperation	.61 ***						
(3) Trust	.16	−.04					
(4) Voluntary organizations	−.28	−.52	.52 **				
(5) Voting	.33 **	−.04	−.10	−.14			
(6) Growth of per capita GDP	.26 *	.58 ***	−.15	−.46	.02		
(7) Unemployment	−.60 ***	−.46 ***	−.28 *	−.07	−.25 *	.09	
(8) Inflation	−.34 **	−.16	.18	−.14	.22	.10	.32 *

* *Note:* For country scores, variable definitions, and data sources see the appendix.
* p < .10; ** p < .05; *** p < .01 (one-tailed tests).

growth regressions (macro-level cooperation is not related to growth), both variables are positively signed and statistically significant. (The negative *bivariate* correlation between trust and growth shown in table 1 is thus misleading.) This suggests that Putnam and others may be correct in suggesting that trust is economically beneficial but that its benefits work through channels other than cooperation. It may be, for example, that trust makes certain types of growth-enhancing government policies more palatable. Or it could be that trust contributes to growth by facilitating other types of growth-enhancing cooperation than those I have specified here.

Does Civic Engagement Play a Role?

Putnam's primary focus is on civic engagement—participation in voluntary associations, along with activities such as voting and reading newspapers. He argues that civic engagement builds social capital by fostering personal interaction. Repeated interaction facilitates communication and amplifies information about the trustworthiness of others. It also helps to engender "sturdy norms of generalized reciprocity: I'll do this for you now, in the expectation that down the road you or someone else will return the favor" (Putnam 1993b:36–37; 1993a:173–74). For these reasons, according to Putnam, civic engagement is a key source of economic cooperation and prosperity.

For empirical support, Putnam (1993a, 1993b, Helliwell and Putnam 1995) draws on the stark contrast in civic engagement between regions in northern versus southern Italy. For nearly 1,000 years the former have been characterized by greater civic activism—from mutual aid societies to cooperatives, from choral societies to neighborhood associations—than the latter. It is surely no accident, he argues, that the industrial districts so integral to Italy's recent economic progress are concentrated in those north-central regions of the country that feature the most long-standing and extensive patterns of civic engagement. In Putnam's words:

> Typically singled out as essential for the success of industrial districts, in Italy and beyond, are norms of reciprocity and networks of civic engagement. Networks facilitate flows of information about technological developments, about the creditworthiness of would-be entrepreneurs, about the reliability of individual workers, and so on. Innovation depends on "continual informal interaction in cafes and bars and in the street." Social norms that forestall opportunism are so deeply internalized that the issue of opportunism at the expense of community obligation is said to arise less often here than in areas characterized by vertical and clientelistic networks. What is crucial about these small-firm industrial districts, conclude most observers, is mutual trust,

social cooperation, and a well-developed sense of civic duty—in short, the hallmarks of the civic community. (1993a:161)

I have little quarrel with Putnam's explanation of regional variation in economic performance in Italy. Because the industrial districts of north-central Italy are centered upon multitudes of small firms which interact with one another and with the local labor force in assorted ways, it is reasonable to suspect that social interaction in local sports clubs and choral societies plays an important role in facilitating cooperative economic behavior, and thereby in enhancing economic performance. But how relevant is civic engagement beyond the Italian case? For example, how helpful is civic engagement in accounting for economic performance differences among the affluent industrialized nations?

There is reason for skepticism. Industrial districts, though not unique to northern Italy, are not nearly as prominent in any other affluent nation. Furthermore, if trust is of limited importance in fostering the types of cooperative economic behavior that *are* prominent in some other countries, civic engagement may have little to contribute. Civic engagement cannot help us to understand why Austrian labor unions consistently moderate their wage demands, or why large Japanese firms successfully build long-term relationships with their suppliers, or why German banks forge long-term partnerships with firms of which they are part-owners, or why some American companies such as Procter & Gamble make effective use of self-directed work teams.

Two indicators of civic engagement are available to help us explore this issue. One is the average number of voluntary organizations in which people participate. These data, like those for trust, are from the 1981 and 1991 World Values Surveys (Knack and Keefer 1997). Respondents were asked if they had volunteered for any of the following types of organizations in the past year: social welfare services for elderly, handicapped, or deprived people; religious or church organizations; education, arts, music, or cultural activities; trade unions; political parties or groups; local community action on issues like poverty, employment, housing, and racial equality; Third World development or human rights; conservation, the environment, ecology; professional associations; youth work (e.g., scouts, guides, youth clubs). These figures represent the best available cross-national measure of participation in civic associations. (Indeed, they seem preferable to the measure Putnam uses in *Making Democracy Work*: the number of organizations per capita in a region [Putnam 1993a:91].) The second indicator of civic engagement is average voter participation (as a share of eligible voters) over the period 1945–89 (Lane and Ersson 1990). Although voter turnout seems less clearly linked to trust and economic cooperation, the degree to which citizens are willing to participate in the

electoral process may tell us something about the prominence of civic participation norms that foster trust.

Table 2 shows that the voluntary organizations measure is positively associated with trust, as Putnam would expect, though the same is not true
for voting. There appears to be little or no relationship between civic engagement and economic cooperation itself. Since the small firm-based economic cooperation that characterizes northern Italian industrial districts
is of limited relevance in most other industrialized nations, this is not especially surprising. Table 2 also shows correlations between these indicators
of civic participation and 1960–98 period averages for three major components of economic performance growth of per capita GDP, unemployment, and inflation. They suggest that civic engagement has not contributed to successful national economic performance in recent decades. The
only indication of a beneficial effect is a marginally significant inverse association between volunteering and inflation. Results of regression analyses
(not shown here) that include commonly used control variables, and examine subperiods of years (e.g., 1960–73, 1974–79, 1980–89, 1990–98) separately, suggest the same conclusion.

Conclusion

There is a good deal of merit in Putnam's discussion of the economy. He is
right to emphasize the importance of cooperation as a complement to market competition. And it is certainly true that trust can help to promote
cooperative behavior. But in his exclusive focus on trust as a source of
cooperation, and on civic engagement as a source of trust, Putnam makes
too much of the Italian case. Differences in civic engagement may help to
account for the variation in economic performance trends between northern and southern Italy in recent decades, but they are of no help in explaining such variation across the affluent democracies over that period. This
may be because civic activism is not a precondition for the formation of
trust among economic actors, or because trust itself is not the key to cooperative economic behavior. The argument and evidence I have presented
here suggest both.

APPENDIX
Country Scores for Economic Cooperation, Social Capital (Trust), Civic Engagement, and Economic Performance Measures

	Macro level cooperation	Firm level cooperation	Trust (%)	Voluntary organizations	Voting (%)	Growth of per capita GDP (%)	Unemployment (%)	Inflation (%)
Australia	.208	.057	47.8	1.01	92	2.2	5.5	5.9
Austria	.957	.271	31.8	.76	92	2.8	2.6	4.0
Belgium	.721	.271	30.2	.56	87	2.8	6.7	4.3
Canada	.089	.057	49.6	1.03	75	2.3	7.5	4.8
Denmark	.749	.271	56.0	.97	85	2.5	5.3	6.1
Finland	.862	.396	57.2	.40	78	2.9	5.6	6.4
France	.414	.086	24.8	.42	76	2.6	6.3	5.6
Germany	.807	.414	29.8	.74	85	2.6	4.4	3.3
Ireland	.120	.057	40.2	.85	73	4.2	9.7	7.3
Italy	.414	.457	26.3	.38	88	3.0	8.1	7.9
Japan	.762	.932	40.8	.38	72	4.5	2.1	4.7
Netherlands	.638	.075	46.2	1.11	88	2.3	5.1	4.2
New Zealand	.183	.057			89	1.3	3.2	7.4
Norway	.963	.386	61.2	1.09	81	3.2	2.5	5.9
Sweden	.955	.336	57.1	1.08	86	2.0	3.3	6.1
Switzerland	.551	.271	43.2	.73	59	1.4		3.5
United Kingdom	.135	.075	44.4	.92	77	2.1	5.6	7.0
United States	.069	.111	45.4	1.50	59	1.9	5.9	4.6

Note: Macro level cooperation = average score on cooperation types 1–4 and 7 in Table 1, 1960–94 (Kenworthy 1998). Firm level cooperation = average score on cooperation types 5–6 and 8–9 in Table 1, 1960–94 (Kenworthy 1998). Trust = percentage responding "most people can be trusted," 1980 and 1990 (Knack and Keefer 1997: 1285). Voluntary organizations = average number of voluntary organizations per respondent, 1980 and 1990 (Knack and Keefer 1997: 1285). Voting = average share of eligible voters voting in national elections, 1945–89 (Lane and Ersson 1990). Growth, unemployment, and inflation = averages for 1960–98 (OECD 1997, n.d.).

III

Civil Society and Civic Engagement

Editors' Introduction

Over the last several decades, the character of American public life has changed, leading many observers to debate the long-term consequences of what is often portrayed as the increasingly contested terrain of contemporary politics. How shall we characterize this change? Robert Putnam sees it as a product of the passing of the "long civic generation" raised during the Great Depression and of the traditional civic associations they participated in. These associations bridged social divisions and contributed to a spirit of cooperation and civic engagement essential to a healthy democracy, according to the neo-Tocquevillean argument.

The perspective emerging in the first two sections of this volume suggests another analysis. It looks to changes in political and economic circumstances to explain changes in civil society and the character of public life, not vice versa. Proponents of this view might argue that the celebrated—if racially and gender segregated—"civic America" of the 1950s was a hothouse plant. They see it as the product of New Deal reforms, which politically mitigated long-standing domestic economic and social conflicts, and of the ensuing period of relative political unity and cultural consensus, which was forged by World War II and was extended by postwar prosperity and Cold War disincentives to dissent. From this perspective, we might reasonably view the current state of public life in the United States as a "new pluralism" (Keane 1988b) that has emerged in part because the American polity has become more accessible since the 1960s to a wider array of organized constituencies—African Americans and women not the least among them—many of which were marginalized or actively repressed through much of American history. The supposed "incivility" of contemporary politics stems from the twin emergence of civically and politically engaged issue constituencies that have mobilized enough clout to no longer be ignored, and a continuing countermobilization among those who rue their rise from marginalization. Increased contention in public life may be the price we pay for the increased access and openness of a "neopluralist" polity.

This macro level debate has implications for what sorts of groups in civil society each side values and why. In the neo-Tocquevillean perspective, for civic associations to produce social capital and be truly beneficial to democracy, they must bridge social and political divisions and thus, presumably, be autonomous from political forces, indeed, be politically innocuous, averse to conflict, and relatively apolitical. Traditional civic associations like the League of Women Voters, Scouts, and the Kiwanis Clubs generally fit this description. Their declining importance thus might signal a decline in social capital for the nation. In response to such preoccupations, however, others have argued that over the last thirty years new types of associations have emerged and supplanted the traditional sorts of groups near and dear to neo-Tocquevillean commentators. Possible countertrends might be found in the dramatic growth since the early 1960s of nonprofit and service organizations, grassroots and national social movements, and new forms of recreational and sport-related associations. Nicholas Lemann (1996) notes, for example, the dramatic growth of U.S. Youth Soccer from 127,000 members in the mid-1970s, to 1.2 million ten years later, and 2.4 million by the mid-1990s. Neo-Tocquevillean analysts have dismissed or ignored thousands of community-based nonprofit service organizations, from soccer leagues to grassroots environmental groups. Yet, from the standpoint of building social capital, are organizations like Habitat for Humanity or community theater groups inferior to the bowling leagues and choral societies whose potential is unquestioned by neo-Toquevillean analysts? From the standpoint of civil society and social capital, why wouldn't the women's health movement, support groups, and crisis centers for victims of rape and domestic violence be at least as beneficial as the Daughters of the American Revolution, the Junior League, or the League of Women Voters?

Still other critics of the neo-Tocquevillean argument suggest that the impact of the relatively apolitical organizations favored by their opponents is likely to be minimal. They argue that more directly political sorts of organizations—grassroots and national environmental organizations, peace groups, women's organizations, and activist church groups of all political stripes—are more likely to affect people's civic and political involvement in the ways that Tocqueville's argument postulated. After all, didn't Tocqueville himself call specifically political associations—as distinct from civic ones—the "great free schools of association" in American democracy?

The chapters in this section take up a number of these questions. Do associational memberships per se engender civic engagement and produce social capital? Or do specifically political sorts of organizations have their own distinctive impact on the attitudes and propensities of citizens? Drawing on European and U.S. survey data, Dietlind Stolle and Thomas Rochon show that there are indeed significant differences among types of associations in the attitudes and dispositions of their members—with some counterintuitive twists. Do all groups of the same sort have similar effects? Carla Eastis's comparative case study of two community choral groups explores the degree to which internal variations in organizational style cause them to vary dramatically in their social capital potential.

What do specifically political groups—local, national and transnational—have to contribute to civic life? The last four chapters take on the issue of conflict and politicization and their relationship to social capital. At the local level Mark Warren examines the Industrial Areas Foundation and its Project Quest in San Antonio, Texas, describing IAF's "relational" style of organizing and advocacy and its strategic use of conflict. He questions the neo-Tocquevillean suggestion that genuinely to foster a spirit of "wider cooperation" associations must not be "polarized" or "politicized." Warren argues that some forms of conflict can forge new and enduring forms of cooperation in local polities, making them more rather than less responsive and effective. The chapter by Debra Minkoff focuses on the national level to address the question of how associations not based on what Ken Newton below calls the "thick trust" of face-to-face relations produce social capital beneficial to democracy. In doing so she offers a strong challenge to neo-Tocquevillean dismissals of national social movement organizations and their constituencies over the last thirty years as a viable countertrend to disengagement from traditional voluntary associations. Jackie Smith shows how, even at the level of transnational social movements, organizations may generate social capital by providing an infrastructure that facilitates communication and action, cultivating social movement identities, and developing a global public discourse. In this sense, she argues, we are witnessing the emergence of a transnational civil society. The final chapter in this section by Mario Diani argues that social capital is an outcome of collective action that persistently generates new types of interdependence, new solidarities, and new networks. He develops an argument about the influence of social movements and their potential to effect political and cultural change that is a unifying thread running through the chapters by Warren, Minkoff, and Smith.

Are All Associations Alike?

Member Diversity, Associational Type, and the Creation of Social Capital

DIETLIND STOLLE AND THOMAS R. ROCHON

Social capital refers to the networks, norms and values that link citizens to each other and that enable them to pursue their common objectives more effectively.[1] Although social capital may be fostered by a variety of formal and informal interactions between members of society, the full range of these interactions is not observable. What we can observe is the prevalence of memberships in voluntary organizations in a given society. As a result, associational memberships have become the indicator of choice for examining the rate of formation or destruction of social capital. In associations, people interact as trustors and as trustees, building on mutual experience and knowledge. The consequence is increased cooperation and trust within the group, enabling the collective purposes of the group to be achieved more easily.

In addition, the idea of social capital encompasses the claim that the circle of trust is extended beyond the boundaries of face-to-face interaction, to incorporate people not personally known (Yamagishi and Yamagishi 1994). This is generalized interpersonal trust, a trust that goes beyond the boundaries of kinship and friendship, and even beyond the boundaries of acquaintance. It can be used as a lubricant to make possible a variety of forms of social interaction and cooperation in a community or region. We extend the notion of generalized interpersonal trust to include values such as tolerance and cooperation toward citizens in general. These orientations toward fellow citizens are values and attitudes that belong to what we call

Revised from an article of the same title in *American Behavioral Scientist* 42, no. 1 (1998): 47–65.

public social capital. Public social capital benefits the wider society beyond the boundaries of the group itself.

This chapter is a plausibility probe into the claims of social capital theory. We examine the effects of different types of associations on a range of indicators related to public social capital. Specifically, we examine two hypotheses with regard to the connection of associations to public forms of social capital. First, we explore the impact of the type of associational activity, the purposes to which the organization is dedicated. We expect that associations directed to different purposes will have different effects on the development of public social capital. An association whose raison d'être is to extract rents from the government is less likely to promote a community-based sense of reciprocity than is an association dedicated to improving area schools, even though both associations may generate social capital–promoting interactions between their members. Similarly, political skills and participation in collective life outside of the group one joins are more likely to be fostered in an association concerned with political ideas than in a bowling league. In other words, we expect that while all associations may contribute to public social capital in one way or another, not all associations contribute to social capital in the same ways or to the same degree. Because no one has made the claim that associations are perfect substitutes for each other, we see this hypothesis less as a refutation of the theory of social capital than as an attempt to specify the theory more fully.

Our second hypothesis is that the effect of associations on public social capital will vary depending on the inclusiveness of the particular association. Many claims made about the effect of associational memberships on social capital rely on the formative experience of interactions with other members. If those interactions bring one into contact with a broad sampling of members of society, then the formative experience is likely to be much more pronounced than if the association is itself a narrowly constituted segment of society. In the extreme case, the association may not only be narrowly constituted but may also have as its purpose the denial of equal rights or opportunities to others. In such instances it is reasonable to doubt the effectiveness of associational membership in promoting generalized trust or reciprocity.

Social capital, particularly as described by Putnam (1993a), is a collective resource rather than an individual one. We therefore examine the extent to which the members of different associations in the United States, Germany, and Sweden differ from nonmembers in their level of public social capital. Our unit of analysis is thus not the individual but the association, and our conclusions permit inferences about the effects of various associations on public social capital.

Measuring Social Capital

This chapter does not represent a test of the social capital thesis; we instead take the causal reasoning of the theory as a given. Our purpose in this chapter is to uncover and explain variations in the extent to which different associations conform to the patterns predicted by social capital theory. To this end, we rely on indicators of a wide range of aspects of public social capital.[2]

The first set of indicators covers the theme of participation and engagement, both in politics generally and in the community specifically. Studies have long demonstrated that participation in nonpolitical organizations stimulates political involvement and interest. Both the formal and informal activities of the association impart an understanding of political and economic issues. Associations also open up possibilities for political participation by cultivating among their members the "organizational and communications skills that are relevant for politics and thus can facilitate direct political activity" (Verba, Schlozman, and Brady 1995). Organizing personnel meetings at work, setting up a food pantry at church, or chairing community charity drives are all activities that develop social skills and increase one's sense of political efficacy and competence. We examine the effect of associational membership on political action, engagement in community affairs, interest in politics, and political efficacy.

A second cluster of indicators includes measures of generalized trust and reciprocity within the community. Networks of civic engagement are said to foster norms of generalized reciprocity and encourage the emergence of social trust (Putnam 1995b). These norms of reciprocity are generalized when they go beyond specific personal settings to encompass an abstract preparedness to trust others. Coleman (1990) refers in this context to the formation of so-called credit slips that can be created by doing something for others, trusting that the person will reciprocate. This process establishes expectations (on the side of the one who gave) and obligations (on the side of the one who took). Coleman mentions the case of rotating credit associations, which can only exist when there is a high level of trust between people. An individual's preparedness to create open credit slips requires generalized trust. We therefore expect association members to score high on our measure of "community credit slips," just as they do on generalized trust. We measure generalized trust with survey questions on whether people are trustworthy and helpful. We have also developed an indicator of community credit slips, which measures interaction and borrowing between neighbors.

The third block of indicators includes trust toward public officials and institutions. Much of the scholarly and popular attention given to social

capital in recent years has centered on its potential to redefine the partnership between public and private organizations in the provision of collective
goods. For this reconstituted relationship to work, there must be a high degree of trust not only between citizens but also between citizens and
government. Hence, trust in public officials and institutions is part of the
complex of attitudes and behavior that makes up public social capital. We
measure this type of trust with survey questions on the respondent's trust in
public institutions and confidence in the people who run them.

The fourth set of social capital indicators represents a collection of attitudinal variables important to social capital: tolerance, approval of free
riding, and optimism. Tolerance is similar to generalized trust in that it reflects an attitude toward others that goes beyond the immediate circle of
known people. Like trust, tolerance is a basis for cooperative endeavors; it
facilitates acts of reciprocity. Voluntary associations may contribute to
specific tolerance among members by bringing people into contact with
each other. Generalized tolerance, like generalized trust, implies acceptance of those with whom one has had little or no contact, in addition to
acceptance of those with whom one interacts. We will include two different tolerance scales based on responses to questions on whether the respondent would avoid having as neighbors marginalized people and specific groups of outsiders.

Social capital also implies a willingness to do one's share in collective endeavors. In a setting rich in social capital, one is less likely to expect others
to be free riders and, partly in consequence, one is also less likely to be a
free rider. We hypothesize that members of associations will learn an ethic
that considers it wrong to free ride on governmental policies or public
goods. Our measures include questions on approval of free riding in the
use of public services.

Finally, social capital requires confidence in the continuation of social
and political relationships. Cooperation with others is rational only if one
has a positive outlook for the future and a faith that others are also prepared to engage in reciprocal exchange (Uslaner 1999). Our optimism
scale includes questions about the respondent's outlook on the future.

Do Associations Matter for Public Social Capital?

The breadth of these indicators of social capital suggests the extent of the
creative enthusiasm deployed in this literature. Table 1 provides a sweeping
verification of this enthusiasm for associational membership, based on six
surveys from three countries: Sweden, Germany, and the United States.[3]
These surveys yield a total of 102 associations whose members we examine
on twelve indicators of social capital. We calculated the relationship between

TABLE 1. The Impact of Associational Membership on Social Capital
Indicators: Results From Six Surveys in the United States, Germany and Sweden

Social capital indicators	No. of significant differences/ No. of associations observed	Total percentage
Political contacting	23 / 28	82.1 [a]
Political engagement	35 / 45	77.8
Community & social participation	20 / 28	71.4 [a]
Non-campaign political participation	60 / 87	69.0
Community credit slips	19 / 43	44.2
Generalized trust	31 / 74	41.9
Political efficacy	15 / 43	34.9
Trust in public officials and institutions	18 / 57	31.6
Generalized optimism	3 / 14	21.4 [a]
Tolerance of marginalized people	8 / 45	17.8
Tolerance of outsiders	7 / 45	15.5
Disapproval of free riding	7 / 45	15.5

Source: See endnote 3.

Note: Entries are percentages of associations in all surveys whose members are high in social capital (significant at alpha = .05 level). Controls for age, education, gender, size of community, and (in the United States) race are applied. Each social capital indicator was tested separately for each associational membership/nonmembership comparison.

[a] Total percentage based on results from one survey only.

associational memberships and political participation, political engagement, and the other aspects of public social capital arrayed across the top of the table. Analysis of covariance produces adjusted means on each dependent variable for members and nonmembers in each association. We control for age, education, size of community, and gender, because these are commonly identified as the primary determinants of civic and political engagement.[4] Without these control variables, differences between members and nonmembers in the various dimensions of public social capital might be purely a consequence of these other traits of associational members.

The total percentage column of table 1 tells us the proportion of associations whose members were significantly higher than nonmembers on the particular aspect of social capital. Reading the first row, for example, shows that, in 82.1 percent of all associations in our three countries, members scored significantly higher than nonmembers in political contacting. Members of associations were frequently found to be significantly higher than nonmembers on all indicators of social capital. At the same time, members are substantially more distinctive on some aspects of social capital than others.

Relative to nonmembers, associational members score highest on political participation, participation in community activities, and political engagement (measured by interest and frequency of engaging in political discussion). The smallest differences between members and nonmembers are found in optimism, tolerance, and disapproval of free riding. Political efficacy and trust are also found in heightened degree among members, compared to nonmembers.

The heart of social capital theory, the claims made most consistently and most strongly, is reflected in the two measures in the center columns of table 1: community credit slips and generalized trust. And here, the theory of social capital does well. The proportion of significant relationships between associational membership and community reciprocity/generalized trust is lower than the proportion of significant relationships with political and community participation. This is to be expected. People who are inclined to political activity are drawn to associational life, and many types of associations urge their members to participate in politics. None, however, is likely to openly ask members to exchange favors with their neighbors or to trust others in the society. Seen in that light, the fact that members are significantly higher than nonmembers on these traits in more than 40 percent of our cases is an impressive confirmation of the link between social capital and group memberships.

Variation Between Associations

In the enthusiasm for the effect of associations on social capital, distinctions between the different types, purposes, and forms of associations have tended to be lost. In his book on the importance of civicness in several regions in Italy, Robert Putnam has shown convincingly that the prevalence of horizontal associations creates the basis for effective governance, presumably because of the social capital built by associational membership. Putnam refers back to the work of Tocqueville, who praises various kinds of associations, "religious, moral, serious, futile, very general and very limited, immensely large and very minute," as virtuous organizations, all of which "instill in their members habits of cooperation, solidarity, and public-spiritedness" (Tocqueville as cited in Putnam 1993a:90). Even if all organizations are virtuous, though, they need not be equally virtuous. We can take advantage of the presence of forty-three different types of associations in our data sets to examine the relative concentration of social capital in different associational sectors.

The range of membership profiles can be illustrated by looking at the relationship between community credit slips and membership in twenty Swedish organizations (see figure 1). The horizontal line shows the total sample mean on community credit slips, adjusted for age, gender, education, race, and size of community. Even with this range of controls, members of most associations score substantially above the total sample means; in ten

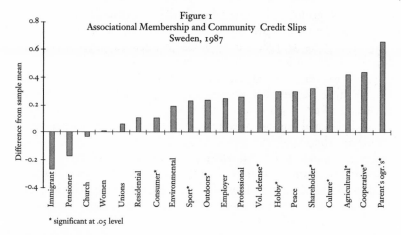

Figure 1
Associational Membership and Community Credit Slips
Sweden, 1987

* significant at .05 level

of them, the difference is significant. Our practice of counting only relationships significant at the .05 level or below is a conservative one, given the small membership samples in many of the associations. Even so, figure 1 shows a pervasive connection between associational membership and community reciprocity.

That said, there is a great deal of variation between associations in the involvement of members in community exchange. The association membership scoring highest on this measure is 33 percent above the lowest. This leads us to ask which associations are most effective in developing these traits. Although we know of no one (other than perhaps Tocqueville himself) who has explicitly said that all associations are equally effective in creating social capital, we have nowhere seen the assembly and testing of hypotheses about which associations are most effective in this regard. The variation in figure 1 motivates our further exploration of the hypothesis that some associations are more effective than others in creating public social capital. We now examine the link between social capital creation and two associational traits: the purposes of the association and the diversity of its membership.

The Impact of Associational Sectors

The surveys available to us ask about membership in forty-three different types of organizations. We have grouped these into seven categories that we call associational sectors.[5] Our first hypothesis is that political, economic, group rights, cultural, community, private interest, and social/leisure organizations will vary in the extent to which their memberships score high on social capital. For example, we expect that members of political, economic, and group rights associations will be more active in their rates of political and community participation, because such groups make demands on their members for political activities. We also expect higher levels of political trust and efficacy among members of political and economic associations. With regard to credit slips with neighbors and to generalized trust, we hypothesize that associational types that emphasize contact between members (such as community organizations, cultural organizations, and personal interest organizations) are more successful in influencing their memberships.

Table 2 displays the rates at which group members proved to be significantly different from nonmembers, in the expected direction and with controls applied, on our dimensions of social capital.[6] The entries in each cell indicate the extent to which members of each associational sector are significantly above the societal norm on our four dimensions of social capital. For example, in all forty (100 percent) political associations from the six surveys, members scored significantly higher on political action than nonmembers. The same was true of 72.2 percent of the thirty-six economic associations in our samples.

Comparisons among the four dimensions of social capital are best seen by reference to the bottom row of table 2, which shows the overall rate at which associational memberships score higher than nonmembers. As expected, we find that membership in all kinds of associational sectors is most closely connected to political action, and matters least with respect to optimism, tolerance, and free ridership.

The "All" column at the right side of table 2 tells us that cultural organizations were particularly likely to have members rich in traits associated with social capital. Group rights and social or leisure organizations, on the other hand, were least likely to stand out with regard to our various indicators of public social capital. These overall rates of social capital concentration within memberships, however, mask a significant degree of specialization between associational sectors in the kinds of social capital found within them.

Members of political, economic, and community groups, for example, are heavily involved in political and community participation. Cultural, personal interest, and community organizations are particularly likely to have members scoring high in generalized trust and in reciprocity with neighbors. Members of cultural, personal interest, and economic groups (but not political groups!) are especially high in political trust and efficacy. These results suggest that while members in all associational sectors contribute to all forms of public social capital, memberships of a particular associational sector are more likely to score high on some dimensions of social capital than on others. This is a reminder that a generalized enthusiasm for the effects of associational membership on social capital must be tempered

TABLE 2. Impact of Associational Membership on Social Capital Indicators, Categorized by Associational Type

Association sector	Political action		Generalized trust/ Community credit slips		Political trust and efficacy		Optimism, tolerance, free ridership		All	
	%	(N)	%	(N)	%	(N)	%	(N)	%	(N)
Political	100.0	(40)	30.0	(20)	15.4	(13)	18.9	(37)	50.0	(110)
Economic	72.2	(36)	40.9	(22)	39.1	(23)	19.0	(21)	47.1	(102)
Group Rights	48.0	(25)	7.7	(13)	27.3	(11)	0.0	(19)	23.5	(68)
Community	75.0	(32)	52.6	(19)	28.6	(14)	10.3	(29)	43.6	(94)
Cultural	69.6	(23)	76.5	(17)	50.0	(14)	35.0	(20)	58.1	(74)
Personal interest	63.0	(27)	57.9	(19)	41.2	(17)	9.5	(21)	44.0	(84)
Social or leisure	60.0	(5)	0.0	(7)	25.0	(8)	50.0	(2)	27.3	(22)
Total	73.4	(188)	42.7	(117)	34.0	(100)	16.1	(149)	44.4	(554)

Source: See endnote 3.

Note: Entries are percentages of associations of each sector whose members are significantly different from nonmembers (significant at alpha = .05 level), controlling for age, education, gender, and size of community, and (in the United States) race. Each social capital indicator was tested separately for each associational membership/non-membership comparison. The (N) in each cell is the number of tests for significance, with each test based on an association-indicator dyad. See endnote 5 for a list of associations in each associational sector.

by a specification of what types of groups we are talking about and what aspects of social capital are being considered.

Associational sectors are defined by group purposes, and group purposes are only one way of categorizing our 102 associations. Let us now consider the relationship between member diversity and social capital.

The Impact of Associational Diversity

Our second hypothesis states that associations whose members bridge major social categories will be more effective in fostering generalized social trust and other components of social capital than will associations whose membership is socially constricted (Putnam 1995b:665). To test this hypothesis, we measured the extent to which association memberships deviate from the population as a whole on six or seven major dimensions of social cleavage. In all three of our countries, we measured the degree of representativeness of association members with respect to education, occupation or occupational prestige, religion and church attendance, partisanship or left-right ideology, age, and gender. In addition to those six dimensions, we also measured racial representativeness in the case of the United States, and representativeness in the proportion of immigrants in the cases of Germany and Sweden. The final diversity score is the sum of the membership deviations from population norms, minus the single dimension on which the association is least representative.[7]

Note that we cannot literally determine the composition of the membership of the group to which the respondent actually belongs. What we can do is to test for diversity within the associational type. When an individual joins a labor union, for example, we believe that person may feel a kinship not only to other members of the same union local but also to all other union members. To the extent this is true, the relevant unit of analysis is the associational-type "labor unions" rather than the specific local affiliate of, say, the Metalworkers' Union in a particular city. However, our assumption about uniformity and solidarity within an associational type is likely to be more valid in some cases than in others. Hobby clubs are almost certainly a less coherent associational type than labor unions. Particular hobby clubs are formed by aficionados of specific hobbies, and these will often be relatively homogeneous. Hobby clubs, in the aggregate, score as very diverse on our measures, but that is not likely to be the case in the specific club to which an individual belongs. Nor do we believe that there is a "hobbyist solidarity" comparable to the solidarity of organized labor. Members of a rare book collector's hobby club, for example, are not likely to feel associational brother- or sisterhood with heavy-metal fan clubs.

The problems of making inferences about the diversity of a local organization from data on diversity in the associational type lead us to the following expectations. If an associational type scores as homogeneous on our measure, the individual organizations will not be substantially more diverse than what we observe. If, on the other hand, an associational type scores as highly diverse on our measure, that does not necessarily indicate diversity within the specific group to which a member belongs. We therefore expect our measure of diversity within associations to take, in effect, two values: "homogeneous" and "indeterminate." This quirk of the measurement must be borne in mind as we examine our results.

Despite these shortcomings, our measure of diversity within associational types does pick up some relatively nuanced differences between different types of groups. Most associational types are composed disproportionately of people from higher education and occupational backgrounds, though this is particularly true of Swedish Shareholder associations, American fraternities and sororities, American arts and educational associations, and peace and professional associations in each country. Most sociable organizations, such as Ordenssällskap in Sweden, Heimat groups in Germany, and fraternal associations in the United States, represent somewhat homogeneous memberships. Similarly, we find that members of pensioners' associations and agricultural associations underrepresent higher levels of education and social class. Political clubs in the United States are representative on many of our dimensions, but their diversity is reduced by an overrepresentation of both liberal and conservative extremes, whereas the middle is underrepresented.

Our diversity measure also reveals some interesting differences between similar associational types in different countries. Unions are generally highly diverse in their memberships, but this is especially true in Sweden because such a large portion of the labor force is organized. For much the same reason, church groups in the US are particularly diverse, but they are not in Germany or Sweden.

Because diversity of membership may be expected to have a particularly strong impact on generalized trust and community credit slips, we have singled out these scales for analysis in figure 2. It groups the fifty-seven associations in our three national surveys into four diversity quartiles, ranging from least diverse to most diverse.[8] Within each quartile, we counted the proportion of associations whose memberships have significantly higher levels of generalized trust and community credit slips, controlling for education, age, gender, and community size. Figure 2 shows that there is a relationship between associational diversity and the extent to which members report generalized trust and involvement in community reciprocity. This relationship is particularly pronounced for groups at the lowest level of diversity (that is, the associations whose diversity we are best able to measure). It is possible that the relatively weak relationship in the

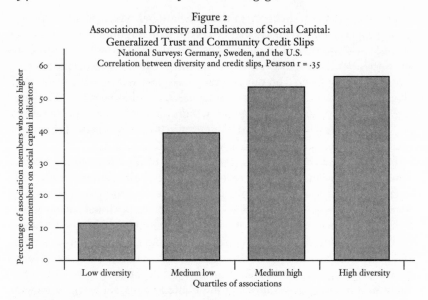

Figure 2
Associational Diversity and Indicators of Social Capital:
Generalized Trust and Community Credit Slips
National Surveys: Germany, Sweden, and the U.S.
Correlation between diversity and credit slips, Pearson r = .35

top three quartiles of associational diversity is due to our inability to measure diversity in the upper ranges. It is also possible that there is a threshold level above which further diversity does not make additional contributions to the membership's trust. Either way, we have shown that the degree of associational diversity is associated with levels of generalized trust and community reciprocity among members. A more nuanced analysis of the effects of group diversity must await a study designed to measure diversity within local associations.

Conclusions

Our inquiry into the connection between associational membership and the attitudes and behaviors that make up public social capital has found that association members are significantly different from nonmembers across a broad range of indicators of social capital. This relationship holds up across all types of associations, from literary societies to political clubs, with a range of statistical controls applied. Although there are differences between types of associations and between countries, these should not obscure the broader pattern, in which we were unable to find a single indicator of social capital that is not positively related to associational membership.[9]

Although the effects of associational membership in producing social capital can only be determined by longitudinal study, our findings help specify the theory in three ways. First, different facets of public social capital are connected to associational membership in varying degrees. Political activities, for example, are strongly related to memberships in voluntary associations of all kinds. Although high levels of generalized trust and community reciprocity are found among the memberships of most associational sectors, tolerance and optimism are not.

Second, different types of social capital are found in different sectors. For example, memberships of cultural associations exhibit a wide range of forms of public social capital. Members of community organizations and personal interest groups show high levels of generalized trust and community reciprocity. Memberships based on personal interest and economic association are particularly high in political trust and efficacy. Members of political associations are the most politically active but are less likely to exhibit high levels of generalized trust, political trust and efficacy, tolerance, optimism, and rejection of free ridership.

Third, the level of diversity in an association has an effect on the connection between social capital and association memberships. We found that the least diverse associations are less likely to have memberships with high levels of generalized trust and community reciprocity. Although we are able to do little more than to certify some associational sectors as "not diverse," our results are supportive of the hypothesis that associational diversity fosters public social capital.

It is worth emphasizing the severity of our tests for links between associations and social capital—a severity that results partly from data constraints and partly from our decisions in the process of doing this research. Although every indicator of social capital examined here has its champions, we know of no one who has suggested that all of them are actually part of social capital. And yet, we have found all of these indicators to be significantly related to associational membership. Those relationships have appeared despite the small samples of members in most associations, making it necessary in some cases for truly heroic differences to appear in the adjusted means before our .05 threshold was crossed. We also found some support for our hypothesis about the effects of diversity within the associational type, despite the necessity of making inferences about local groups based on diversity among the national body of members.

That the social capital theory has withstood these preliminary efforts at subjecting it to cross-national testing suggests that this is certainly an area that will repay further examination. Future studies can overcome issues of measurement with an association-based design that takes specific organizations as the unit of analysis. Such studies should merge contextual variables with individual data, for example, on member diversity, the degree of member activity within the organization, and whether it has a hierarchical or horizontal authority structure (see Stolle 2000). We have demonstrated that the connection between associational membership and social capital is robust across countries and across indicators of social capital. At the same time, we find clear indications of differences between types of associations. These results indicate the need for further specification of the theory of social capital.

Organizational Diversity and the Production of Social Capital

One of These Groups Is Not Like the Other

CARLA M. EASTIS

In recent years, social scientists and pundits have unleashed a flood of commentary and research spurred by the proposition that high levels of social capital and a dynamic civil society are essential to the functioning of democratic institutions. The debate has been lively, and most interesting when it settles on the basics: What is social capital? Where and how is it produced? What sorts of institutions constitute civil society? In this article, I will use an ethnographic approach to illustrate the complexity of a popular topic, namely the production of social capital within voluntary associations. My analytic framework is drawn from two themes that recur in the debate.

The first is that social capital is multidimensional and must be conceptualized as such to have any explanatory value. James Coleman's introduction of the idea emphasized this, identifying social capital as a "variety of entities, with two elements in common: they all consist of some aspect of social structures, and they facilitate certain actions of actors . . . within the structure" (1988:S98). However, as Newton (this volume) points out, many subsequent discussions of social capital confound three entities: norms and values, social networks, and consequences. When the pundits refer to the value of social capital, do they mean the norms of cooperation that my neighbors and I agree upon when forming a neighborhood crime watch? Do they mean the social networks that are broadened when I meet people down the street for the first time? Or do they mean to say that the value of

Revised from an article of the same title in *American Behavioral Scientist* 42, no. 1 (1998): 66–77.

social capital lies in the actual reduction in crime that results from the group's actions, or in the organizational skills that I develop as a member? Often, they seem to mean all three; even more often, they are not explicit about what they mean. The analysis to follow separates these entities, and demonstrates that the forms, and even the presence of different forms, of social capital vary across organizational settings.

The second theme that I will build upon is the assertion that American civil society includes a variety of organizations that are relevant to the debate on social capital. Putnam (1993a, 1995a, 1995b) has focused on small, voluntary associations, arguing that the face-to-face interactions typical of such settings are most likely to support positive democratic outcomes.[1] He acknowledges that even among voluntary associations there is significant diversity. However, he identifies only one dimension, whether ties among participants are more vertical (as in the Mafia or organizations aligned with the Catholic Church) or more horizontal (as in bowling leagues or choral societies). Nevertheless, Putnam's assertion that horizontal ties represent "more productive social capital than vertical ties" provides an excellent beginning to the discussion (1995a:76; see also 1993a, ch. 6). I offer here a more complete conceptualization, informed by organizational theory.

In the first section, I develop a framework to explore how variations in organizational characteristics lead to different social structures and processes that affect the production of social capital. Next, I show how the differences, in terms of structural resources and musical content, between the two choral groups in this study are manifested in specific organizational attributes. The bulk of the paper is devoted to an ethnographic analysis of how organizational characteristics affect the production of three types of social capital: networks, norms and values, and skills for collective action.

An Organizational Perspective

Performing music in a formal group is in some ways a patterned activity. There is a sense of déjà vu in a new setting as the musicians and conductor go through some generic tasks like deciding spatial arrangements at the first rehearsal or coming to attention for warm-ups, for example. Nevertheless, as I knew from years of experience in choirs, orchestras, and bands, the overall "feel" of one group is often very different from the feel of another, despite one's performing the same basic motions in both settings. I sensed that there was something more systematic to this than simply the fact that different people are involved, something that had to do with social structure rather than individuals.

Recognizing that voluntary associations are types of organizations provides a framework for analyzing this experience. Contingency theory, a popular idea in organizational sociology in the 1960s and 1970s, has left us with one very basic insight: there is no one best way to organize. (As primary sources, see Perrow 1967 and Woodward 1980; for an overview, see Perrow 1986:140–46.) In many settings, these researchers found, organizational characteristics (such as the number of levels in a bureaucracy, or the degree of precision in job descriptions) vary systematically. They explained structural variation among the industrial organizations that they studied as an outcome of variation along two dimensions: the flow and quality of raw materials, and the type of technology an organization uses. Raw materials can be anything, iron ore or people, and technology refers simply to the work that the organization performs on the raw materials, whether that is turning metal ores into steel or educating people.

The present work appropriates and adapts the contingency theory argument.[2] Among musical organizations, I maintain that the systematic sources of variation (the analogs to contingency theory's technology and raw materials) are the organization's structural resources and its musical content. Differences along these dimensions cause differences in specific organizational characteristics—size, the average member's level of skill, opportunities for volunteer labor, and patterns of authority in rehearsal—that affect the experience of membership. The qualitative variation of social interactions that results affects the production of social capital in all its forms—networks, norms, and skills.

Sources of Diversity: The Goups Introduced

My data come from four months of participant observation, encompassing an entire "season" from the first rehearsal through a performance. The director of the Collegium at the time of my observations described it as follows:

> The Collegium Musicum is the Department of Music's ensemble for the study and performance of early repertory. It is directed by Steven M., Associate Professor of Music, and specializes in the historically informed performance of early music. The group was founded fifty years ago by composer Paul Hindemith, and was the first musical ensemble in the United States devoted to early music.[3]

The Collegium had twenty members during the time of the study, most of whom had some connection to the university as graduate students, faculty, or staff members. The program for the spring concert was the sacred music of Johannes Ockeghem, a Flemish composer of the fifteenth century.

The Community Chorus is a nonprofit organization, founded by a local radio station in 1963 but financially independent since 1971. "We are people of many backgrounds sharing a common interest—a love of music. Under the direction of David K, our goal is to achieve the highest performance standards possible by a non-auditioning community musical organization."[4] The Community Chorus (hereafter simply "the Chorus") had about eighty members during the time of the study. The program being rehearsed had the theme "Broadway Tonight!" and consisted of medleys and solo pieces from musicals such as *Camelot* and *My Fair Lady*.

There are two critical sources of systematic variation among musical organizations: substantive musical content and structural resources. The substantive difference between the groups is reflected in their choices of repertoire. The Collegium sings early music that many find difficult to understand, as it does not follow the same tonal rules as later classical music. Also, the texts for the music on this particular program were in Latin and French. The Chorus, on the other hand, deals with more contemporary music, in English. These pieces are meant to be emotionally accessible and affecting, and to sound familiar.

The groups also have access to different social structural resources. The network ties that an organization is born with or develops, such as sources of patronage, affiliations with other institutions, and its relationship with the general public through concerts or other public events, place the group in a unique position within the local community. The connections represented by its network position shape access to a number of resources, such as artistic legitimacy, financial support, participants, and audience members.

These general substantive and structural differences lead to significant variation in specific attributes of the two groups. First, there was a noticeable difference in the average level of musical skill displayed by the singers. It would be very unusual for anyone to learn the Collegium's early music repertoire by ear, because it doesn't sound natural or predictable to contemporary listeners. One needs to be able to read music and to have some sight-reading ability. Everyone in the Collegium could do this at a fairly high level. The repertoire of the Chorus, however, was much more familiar in terms of musical conventions and rules and could easily be learned by repetition. It was my assessment that almost half the singers in the Chorus did not read music.

Organizational size is related to both substance and structure. Repertoire and size are closely related for a variety of reasons. Some pieces of music are specifically written to be performed by large or small ensembles. In the performance of classical music, ensembles often will be limited in size in order to maintain historical accuracy.

Also, the size of the groups is indirectly related to organizational requirements. The Chorus has relatively fixed costs; the more members they attract above the break-even point, the larger their financial cushion will grow. It is in the organization's interests to retain as many members as possible. The elite-sponsored Collegium, on the other hand, neither suffers nor benefits financially from changes in size. The conductor is free to restrict membership or to recruit as he sees fit, making these decisions with more reference to repertoire.

Access to different structural resources is most apparent in the groups' different bases of financial support. The Collegium is affiliated with a major university, which allots part of one faculty member's teaching load to the direction of the group. A graduate student member of the group is paid as a teaching assistant to handle much of the administrative work such as making copies, rounding out the Collegium's staffing needs. Also, a separate endowed fund covers those expenses that are not in the regular departmental budget.

The Chorus, though, as a nonprofit membership organization, must attract paying members and concertgoers, as well as occasional donations from benefactors, to cover its expenses. Even though a steady stream of income is produced from these activities, most administrative tasks including fundraising itself must be covered by volunteers. Only the conductor and accompanist are paid for their work.

Producing Social Capital

As a setting for the production of social capital, voluntary associations may be seen as interlocking series of collective action processes. In this section, I will look at three such processes that are a part of any musical ensemble's work and that are shaped by the characteristics noted above, such as size, skill level, and organizational resource base. The recruitment of members illustrates how social *networks* are formed and *used* by voluntary associations. *Norms and values* are produced in the sustained interactions that define the rehearsal experience. And finally, an examination of organizational maintenance processes addresses questions about the development of *skills for collective action*.

Networks: Recruitment Styles

An underexamined empirical question in the social capital debate is: "Do social networks generate the level of trust necessary for civilized social and political life, or is it, on the contrary, the existence of widespread trust that makes the development of social networks possible in the first place?"

(Newton 1997:577). An examination of the ways that organizations recruit members provides some answers.

The first task that a musical organization must accomplish before rehearsing a program for performance is to assemble a group of the right size in one place. One way to be sure that prospective members know something about what they are getting into is to recruit from concert audiences. Both examples below are from programs for the concerts that took place just prior to my field observations.

> The Collegium Musicum is an ensemble of the university Department of Music. Members of the university community who are experienced singers of early music are invited to join the Collegium in the spring semester. Please contact Prof. M if you are interested: xxx-xxxx; e-mail@e-mail.[5]

This ad presents a number of barriers to potential members. The first is the vague reference to "the university community." Assuming one believes oneself to be part of that community, the next important characteristic of the group in this ad is the requirement that one be "experienced." While no formal tests or requirements are stated, neither is one free just to show up and check it out for oneself. A potential member must contact the conductor to find out when and where to appear for rehearsal. Joining this group requires not only initiative but confidence.

In contrast, the Chorus presents its defining characteristic as an enjoyable rehearsal experience.

> The community chorus enjoys lively and instructive rehearsals on Thursday evenings from 7:30 to 10 PM in the Center Church Parish House on XXX Street.
>
> Our first rehearsal in 1996 will be on Thursday, January 11th. Interested choristers are always welcome to attend up to three rehearsals as a guest without obligation.
>
> If you have been looking for a new musical and social experience, call xxx-xxxx, or simply come and join us![6]

There is no indication that the music requires particular experience or skill. Determining whether this group is a good fit for you depends on how much you enjoy it. Note, further, that this appeal to concertgoers provides all the information necessary to just "come and join." There are no barriers to examining the group—a prospective member knows where to go, when to be there, and at least a little bit of what to expect.

The differences in recruitment styles are obvious. Clearly, the Chorus attempts to cast a wider net, which makes sense in terms of both structure and content. A large group is financially desirable, and there is no musical reason to exclude anyone. Their success was apparent: there was a much wider range of ages among the members of the Chorus, and there were many African American and Hispanic members, in contrast to the almost all-white Collegium.

However, the relationship between networks and trust is less obvious. I would argue that, in both cases, those who join are those who already trust in some way. Each organization, in its appeal, has encouraged a type of self-selection by potential members. The Chorus, for example, is clear about its social function. One who is attracted to this description is one who does not mind mixing socializing and rehearsal, and who does not mind interacting with potentially anyone. The Collegium, though, attracts those who have previous experience with this type of setting and some claim to be "university affiliated." These people, walking into the first rehearsal, may reasonably expect to see a group of people like the one they joined the last time they sang early music and a group of people like those they have seen around the university.

Norms and Values: Rehearsal Processes

A second task musical organizations must accomplish is the development of a rehearsal atmosphere that makes good use of limited time. Working relationships among the musicians and between the musicians and the conductor must be created, and some shorthand communications must be agreed upon. The sustained social interactions of the rehearsal process are the setting for the production of norms and values, which determine much of the "feel" of the group. Voluntary associations are presumed to support the development of values and attitudes that "predispose citizens to cooperate, trust, understand, and empathize with each other. . . . [and transform] individuals . . . into members of a community with shared interests, shared assumptions about social relations, and a sense of the common good" (Newton 1997:576). An examination of two specific rehearsal processes will demonstrate that organizations do this with varying degrees of success.

One process important for the development of relationships among participants is the way musicians assess the relative abilities of their peers. In many ensembles, as in these two at the time of the study, some cues about *who* is "good" come from the conductor's choice of soloists and featured performers. However, communication among members about *what* they appreciated in others is revealing, illuminating how peers make judgments about who to praise and why.

In the Collegium, accolades were tied to vocal range, particularly as it related to a section or individual's ability to cover a difficult part. For example:

In one piece, the alto [lowest female] part has a very low note that not all of the altos can hit. In a couple of spots that note is the focus of attention, and it is obvious who is able to sing it. In one rehearsal the successful altos get applause, and one of the men jokes about the testosterone shots paying off. Still, a tenor is assigned to sing along with us to make sure it's covered, and makes a point of saying to me that he hopes I don't mind and that I'm not insulted.

In contrast, among members of the Chorus, the most common exchanges about being "good" were related to sight-reading, the ability to sing the correct pitches and rhythms when reading a piece of music for the first time. Not everyone was presumed to have this skill. Though it was never mentioned as an advantage in the welcoming materials, nor ever commented upon by the conductor, it was mentioned by singers more than once, and in fact first:

> At my first rehearsal with the Chorus other newcomers and I follow the membership officer into the rehearsal hall and find a few empty seats in the next to last row. The membership officer introduces us to the three women in front of us. They ask if we are good sight-readers. I say that I'm not great but getting better. They laugh and say they just have good ears, so they'll be happy to have good readers nearby.

What is noticed and promoted by members as being good and praiseworthy, then, is something beyond what is actually required in a particular setting. Obviously, the low D can be covered by a male singer, and one could learn the Chorus's music simply by repetition.

But by elevating those characteristics that, though not required, make one's task a bit easier, members are socially constructing "talent" as a thing that some people have, as opposed to "skill," which anyone can develop. Near-perfect sight-reading in the Collegium, for example, a skill that is highly developed and frequently practiced by music students, was fairly common and rarely drew attention. In the Chorus, though, most participants are not exposed day after day to the techniques through which one develops this skill. In this setting, sight-reading takes on something of the aura of a talent to be respected, just as having a wide vocal range becomes a basis of divisions in the Collegium.

Another important rehearsal process is the negotiation of shorthand communications between conductor and musicians.[7] The musicians come to know, more or less, what the conductor wants to accomplish when s/he says to do a certain thing. This knowledge can come from the conductor's explicit communication, but more relevant here are processes through which past experience or the characteristics of musicians as a group create a collective understanding.

The rehearsal contexts are partly the result of differences in the substantive content of the two groups. The vast majority of time in rehearsal in the Collegium is spent on experimenting with a variety of abstract rehearsal techniques, treating the difficult-to-learn music as a thing to be understood in itself. The Chorus's rehearsal time is spent learning how to project emotion to an audience through music that is familiar and easily learned.

In the Collegium, musicians were actively involved with and quite aware of the conductor's use of techniques. Sometimes the level of involvement was even greater than the conductor anticipated:

After singing through one piece, Steven [the director] hands out pages on which he has rewritten the music, so that only one part (soprano, alto, tenor, or bass) is visible on each page. We go through it again using these sheets, and it sounds a lot better. He says he knew it would, and asks us why. After some chatter among ourselves we come to the guided consensus that it's easier to see phrases this way and to sing independent musical parts. Some people ask if we can do all the music with part sheets, and there is a brief discussion of the advantages and disadvantages.

During the "chatter among ourselves," when Steven had asked what was different, he seemed to expect people to raise their hands and offer comments in turn. Instead, at least three different conversations broke out among neighbors about how it was different and why it was better. After a moment, Steven regained our attention and we discussed it as a group.

In the Chorus, the conductor's actions were less about "techniques" and more about "direction." Most of his verbal instruction consisted of nontechnical metaphors aimed at getting us to translate the emotional content of the text into actual physical acts.

We spend a great deal of time on the first two notes, on getting good vowels and being expressive to the audience. David sings the lines several times, both the right way and the wrong way, with the wrong way described as "squawking geese sounds" and the right way being "the expressive way." He also has very specific instructions on certain words. To get us to make a note shorter, he doesn't use technical terms like "make that quarter note almost like a dotted eighth." Rather, he says "What does the word stop mean? It means stop, right? So stop on that word."

The level of involvement with rehearsal was much lower in the Chorus. Not everyone in the Chorus felt these were the most productive or most enjoyable ways to rehearse, as was clear from comments during a rehearsal where the regular conductor was out of town unexpectedly and the substitute used less direction and more technical polishing. However, there were no direct challenges or suggestions of alternative techniques when the regular conductor was present. Nor did I ever observe any conversations among musicians that reflected on how we were doing something, except during the substitute's tenure.

In both examples, the values and norms developed during rehearsals cannot be understood outside the organizational context. While in both settings it is important that people "know their place" within the peer hierarchy of talent, the meaning of talent varies. The ability to perform beyond the strict requirements of the organization garners one praise and ongoing recognition, and colors a great many of the personal exchanges that take place during rehearsal. However, the same person may be considered talented in one setting and merely skilled in another, his experience will be very different depending on where he is.

Musicians also know their places with regard to the conductor's authority in teaching music. Of these two settings, the Collegium allows for the development of greater cooperation in regard to how much members trust each other with the musical content of their joint actions. Circumstances in the Collegium are such that, musically, peers are on a more equal footing with each other and with the conductor. They are familiar with the unusual needs of the repertoire, and they can sight-read and figure out how the music is supposed to sound. While the conductor retains ultimate authority and control, if only through the fact that he initiates every rehearsal technique and the musicians can only be reactive, the norm is that everyone is able to contribute to substantive understandings of the project at hand.

Rehearsal processes in the Chorus do not produce a comparable base for cooperation and trust on issues of substantive decisions. While the networks are broader and thus the participants more diverse, which in itself is often noted as a base for the development of trust, people are not as engaged in the rehearsal as a collaborative project.

Skills for Collective Action: Organizational Maintenance

The third and final task I will examine is the need to keep the organization alive. Variations in structural resources have a substantial effect on how organizational maintenance functions are carried out, by whom, and how obvious they are to the average member.

One of the collective benefits that voluntary associations are presumed to provide is the development of organizational skills that are important to active citizenship. Putnam even includes this function as part of the definition of social capital, as the ability to "improve the efficiency of society by facilitating co-ordinated actions" (1993a:167).

It is not often asked explicitly, though, whether networks and norms always have such consequences. Newton points this out, cautioning against confusing "voluntarily produced collective facilities" with other aspects of social capital (1997:575).[8] Clearly, organizational characteristics affect the opportunities one has to practice skills such as speaking publicly and organizing meetings. For example, Verba, Schlozman, and Brady show that involvement in the hierarchical Catholic Church limits one's ability to develop civic skills, compared to the chances a member of a congregationally autonomous denomination has to exercise such skills (1995, ch. 11).

The evidence from the Collegium and the Chorus, moreover, demonstrates that it is possible for a setting to facilitate the development of norms and networks but not leave participants with transferable skills. Variation in structural resources is the key to this aspect of social capital. The Collegium, as an organization with more centralized resources, does not support the development of the civic skills that would allow for smooth collective action in other settings. The Chorus, however, provides many such opportunities.

Since the Collegium's expenses and many other needs are absorbed by the university, the business of maintaining the organization is largely invisible to most participants. When the director thanked the teaching assistant at the final rehearsal for all the work he had done over the semester, many people asked what exactly it was that had needed doing. Members were never asked nor given the opportunity to volunteer to do anything other than put up posters announcing the concert.

In the Chorus, by contrast, fundraising plans are often discussed, and people are frequently reminded to pay their dues and to get involved by volunteering. The discussion of money is a regular part of each rehearsal, as the official announcements from one rehearsal break demonstrate:

> The people who brought refreshments are thanked; we are encouraged to sign up to bring cookies to later rehearsals and reminded to leave a quarter in the coffee can if we take anything tonight. The chorus president shows a picture that a member's son took of the Christmas concert. A soprano tells how much her patients at a dialysis center enjoyed listening to a tape of the Christmas concert (copies of which are still available for $10 each at the back desk). There is a weekly raffle, $1 buys three tickets. The winner gets half of the take, and the other half goes into the treasury.

While discussion of organizational needs is prominent, so is the opportunity to volunteer. The Board of Directors of the Chorus includes twenty members. As elections approach, members are urged to run for the at-large positions. Also, there are no less than six committees (such as publicity, membership, and concert arrangements) through which one can participate in various ongoing or one-time projects.

Conclusion

From the participant's point of view, specific organizational characteristics exert a strong effect on the interactions in which she and her fellow members produce social capital. Even within the narrow category of choral groups, each organization represents a unique mix of networks, norms and values, and collective facilities, each present in different forms and levels if it is present at all.

The Collegium's small size, the high level of musical skill of its participants, and its freedom from organizational maintenance worries create a setting in which singers are more alike than different. Its rehearsal processes provide an opportunity for close cooperation on issues of musical performance. The norms developed in this group support a number of shared understandings of what it means to work together. On the other hand, participants in this group do not have the opportunity to develop organizational skills transferable to other collective action settings. Neither does the Collegium expand the social networks that participants might draw upon for a broader social life beyond the university setting.

The Chorus does develop a broad social network, explicitly creating a setting in which to meet new people "of many backgrounds." Participants may draw upon this network for other social or political purposes. Also, the organizational needs of the Chorus offer participants the chance to develop civic skills for other purposes. However, the bonds among participants are not strengthened by any values that are created in rehearsal in and of itself. The association's core activity is carried out in a way that does little to foster trust in complex issues.[9]

Those who champion the role of voluntary associations in civil society, if they do not acknowledge the complexity of social capital itself and of organizational types, seem to suggest that organizations either produce social capital or they do not. As I have demonstrated, this is not necessarily the case. Is the social capital produced by one group "better" than that produced by another? My intent is not to make such a normative judgement, but rather to show how complex the experience of membership is and how difficult it is to assess completely the effects of voluntary associations on American civil society. Some organizations broaden social networks, participants in others develop strong values that may or may not be supportive of democratic institutions, still other organizations train individuals in civic skills, and, of course, some associations do all or some combination of these. General statements about the consequences for American democracy that are gleaned from examining membership rates in broad categories of voluntary associations are at best simplistic. At worst they distract us from the basis of the debate: What is social capital, anyway?

Power and Conflict in Social Capital

Community Organizing and Urban Policy

MARK R. WARREN

"Invest in Us! Invest in Us!" chanted the six hundred community residents as they marched out of buses arriving from Catholic and Protestant churches across San Antonio.[1] Inside, at the heated city council meeting, the leaders of the organizations known as COPS (Communities Organized for Public Service) and Metro Alliance lobbied San Antonio's mayor and city councilors for the funds to support their job training initiative, Project QUEST. After long negotiations with city officials through the summer, and after assembling $4 million from a variety of federal job training funds, the organizations still lacked the critical funds for day care and other support services from the city budget. When the indoor meeting ended in stalemate, COPS and Metro Alliance leaders invited the mayor and councilors outside to meet their supporters. COPS leader Patricia Ozuna recounts what happened next (author's interview, 20 July 1993; see also Holt, 1991). "Once we were outside, I turned to the mayor and asked him publicly to support QUEST with $2 million, including a specific pledge to find $1.6 million in the city budget. He looked at our people and agreed on the spot. We had a big placard with a pledge for $2 million written on it. Mayor Wolff and six councilors, a majority of the city council, signed the pledge."

Since Project QUEST opened its doors in 1993, it has become a model for job training in urban communities. Most job training under the federal Job Training Partnership Act (JTPA) program provides short-term training for jobs that are often unavailable, while providing no support services. As a result, many people cannot afford to undertake training; and of those

Revised from "Community Building and Political Power," in *American Behavioral Scientist* 42, no. 1 (1998): 78–92.

who do, many leave still lacking sufficient skills for a significant job upgrade. In contrast, QUEST provides training for up to two years, a sufficient time to significantly upgrade skills, and provides living stipends and day care services for trainees. Project QUEST has worked closely with the business community to design appropriate training for jobs that are available and that will pay a "living wage." The program received a highly favorable initial review from M.I.T.'s Sloan School of Management (Osterman and Lautsch 1996), which documented very high wage gains among participants. The Ford Foundation and the John F. Kennedy School of Government awarded QUEST an Innovations in American Government Award in 1995.

Project QUEST's innovative approach comes directly from its ties to COPS and Metro Alliance. These organizations initiated the program, built alliances with the business community and public officials, and supplied the political muscle to acquire funding. Moreover, COPS and Metro Alliance have worked to ensure that the program benefits the urban neighborhoods where they are based. In inner city neighborhoods devastated by the loss of well-paying jobs, such human capital strategies constitute a necessary part of any effort to rebuild urban communities. In San Antonio, QUEST is part of a comprehensive rebuilding effort by these community organizations, which include initiatives in public school reform, affordable housing, infrastructural improvements, public safety, health care, and other areas.

As community builders, COPS, Metro Alliance, and other local affiliates of the Industrial Areas Foundation (IAF) are often cited as examples for developing a more communitarian basis to American politics (for example, Sandel 1996). As the rally for Project QUEST suggests, however, this community-building effort takes a decidedly political turn. The IAF seeks to develop the political capacity of church leaders to reach beyond their neighborhoods in order to influence powerful political and economic institutions. It builds organizations like COPS and Metro Alliance in order to gain the political power necessary to rebuild communities. This approach suggests that the revitalization of American democracy cannot occur through consensual processes within civil society alone, but rather by connecting our civil and political institutions. A critical examination of the IAF's strategy for linking community building to political action, as seen through the case of Project QUEST, can therefore offer important lessons about how to combine conflict and consensus building.

The Industrial Areas Foundation and Its Texas Network

Founded originally by Saul Alinsky in the 1930s, the IAF now represents the nation's largest faith-based community organizing network. Reconstructed after Alinsky's death in 1972 by its new director Ed Chambers, the IAF has built over sixty local affiliates across the country and is rapidly growing. Its potential reach is quite extensive as the IAF claims to incorporate over one million families through its member institutions. The IAF itself has a staff of well over one hundred professional community organizers directed by regional directors (Appleman 1996). The IAF and its organizers provide recruitment and training services under contract to local affiliates, which, in turn, are composed primarily of religious institutions, with schools, labor unions, and other member institutions as well.

Ernesto Cortes, Jr., has built the largest regional IAF network in the Southwest, where he directs a staff of sixty working in twenty local affiliates. In 1973 Cortes founded COPS among Catholic parishes in the largely Hispanic west and south sides of San Antonio. COPS, arguably the most powerful community organization in the country, became the model for the rest of the IAF network. In its twenty-five-year history COPS has directed over $1 billion in resources to its neighborhoods, used for the development of streets and drainage systems, libraries, parks, public health clinics, and a community college. By 1990, COPS worked closely with its sister IAF organization in San Antonio, Metro Alliance, composed of African American, Hispanic, and white congregations. Together the IAF organizations have built affordable housing, initiated community policing programs and developed a multifaceted program of school reform.

Beyond San Antonio, the IAF has operated a state-level network in Texas since the 1980s. The Texas IAF network played a key role in passing indigent health care legislation (Wong 1997) and bringing water services to *colonias*, where thousands of poor immigrants live (Wilson and Menzies 1997). More recently, it has initiated the Alliance Schools project, a statewide compact between the IAF, the state department of education, and over one hundred local schools across Texas to promote parental involvement and innovative schooling (Shirley 1997). Other IAF affiliates around the country have achieved notable success on a range of issues and have begun to operate at the state level in Maryland and California, as well as in the New York metropole.[2]

The campaign for Project QUEST, therefore, occurred in the context of a highly developed IAF regional network. Elsewhere (Warren 2001), I have argued that the effectiveness of the IAF comes from the interaction between professional community organizers and the lay leaders that emerge from congregations. In the Southwest, Cortes has developed the largest and most sophisticated corps of organizers in the IAF. At the same time, social and political conditions in Texas and the southwest generally are quite conducive to the emergence of a broad group of community leaders within the IAF network. In particular, there is a large and relatively homogeneous community of Mexican American Catholics that has provided a strong core of lay leadership and broader support for the Texas IAF network. Meanwhile, a relative vacuum of other community-based organizations or well-rooted party organizations has meant less competition for the IAF.

Social Capital, Civil Society and Political Power

In the context of the fragmentation and atomization of our political life, communitarians and scholars of social capital (Putnam 1993a, 1995a) make an essential point: community must underpin democracy because it provides the relationships of trust and the habits of cooperation essential for members of society to work together to solve our common problems. As our political parties have lost their ties to community-based organizations, they have become candidate-centered vehicles for election (Wattenberg 1990). Meanwhile, despite the development of many advocacy groups since the sixties, few political institutions sustain active participation in cooperative efforts (Walker, 1991; Judis, 1992). Participation in many of these groups consists in membership on a mailing list, while the top officials lobby for the group's cause in Washington. Americans are not well connected to each other or to our political institutions. Consequently, many Americans have become alienated from a political process they see as narrowly self-interested and often corrupt.

Although we need to reestablish a cooperative basis to American politics, the communitarian version of democracy is insufficient because it fails to appreciate politics as the realm of conflict and power as well as collaboration (Foley and Edwards 1997). Strengthening the bonds of one group in civil society may come at the expense of another, once that group enters the political arena. For communities historically excluded from political power, and suffering from social and economic inequality as well, the health of their communities cannot be reclaimed solely by mobilizing their own internal communal resources. They have to exert political power to demand a greater share, if not a restructuring, of societal resources.

The weakness of communitarianism infects the contemporary world of community building. Although a broad movement of citizens to rebuild communities has emerged, few participants see their activity as political (Kettering Foundation 1991). Community development corporations and a wide variety of often church-based community efforts work to involve residents in bettering their neighborhoods and healing the tears in their social fabric (Vidal 1996; Clemetson and Coates 1992). By fostering collaboration, community building efforts have made important gains in combating crime and drug use, involving youth in constructive group activity, cleaning up neighborhoods, and fostering community pride and spirit

(Committee for Economic Development, 1995). Community development corporations (CDCs) have mobilized community resources and brought in public and private funds to build affordable housing and promote economic development. However, as CDCs become focused on developing and later administering housing programs, few have been able to sustain broad popular participation (Vidal, 1992). Like many of our advocacy groups, community-building efforts become dominated by a few staff or key leaders. Relying solely on building consensus with financial institutions and public officials, few develop an independent base of power capable of demanding broader change when resistance occurs (Stoecker 1997). Without an adequate strategy for developing political power, the gains of the community-building movement have remained localized and limited.

The IAF represents an important alternative both to most community-building initiatives and to most forms of political intervention because it attempts to connect community building with political action, addressing both conflict and cooperation. In work reported elsewhere (Warren 2001), I show how IAF organizers unlock the capacities of the social capital embedded in religious institutions. The IAF draws upon the trust that already exists in congregational relations to provide the basis upon which to initiate cooperative action. It taps the moral framework for community concern held by many Jews and Christians to motivate participants and to broaden their conception of self-interest. Rather than elaborate the contributions of religious institutions per se to democratic renewal, this article will focus on the political strategy that IAF organizers bring to the process. The IAF uses a "relational" organizing strategy to deepen the capacity of community networks and to direct them to political collaboration for community betterment. Meanwhile it builds independent organizations that engage political and economic institutions through a nonpartisan strategy combining confrontation with negotiation. The next section of this article will begin to explore the IAF's strategy by discussing its campaign for Project QUEST.

The Campaign for Project QUEST

In January 1990, the Levi Strauss plant on the south side of San Antonio announced it would shut its doors within two months. The plant employed over 1,000 workers, mostly Mexican-Americans, paying them between eight and ten dollars per hour, a decent wage in an area with a low cost of living. Many of these workers lived in the neighborhoods of COPS parishes. COPS, despite its accomplishments in improving services and housing, had long been searching for a way to address the low-wage economy that underlay poverty in its neighborhoods. The plant closing served to symbolize the loss of well-paying jobs and to prompt COPS to take action.

Drawing upon the community leadership it had built up over the years, COPS established a committee to pursue the issue, with veteran COPS leader and school secretary Patricia Ozuna as chair. Meanwhile, the IAF regional director Cortes and his staff had been meeting with labor economists who advocated a human capital approach to economic development. Through discussions among Cortes, COPS's IAF organizer Tom Holler, and COPS leaders like Ozuna, the committee decided to pursue job training as a response to the Levi plant closing.

Consistent with its relational organizing strategy, the committee did not develop a job training program immediately. Instead, it first held a series of house meetings. In summer 1990, COPS asked its network of church leaders to invite friends and neighbors to small group meetings in their homes to discuss their experiences with work and job training. At these meetings, according to Reverend Will Wauters, COPS learned that many community residents had graduated from federally funded job training programs in debt and holding a worthless certificate (author's interview, 20 May 1993). On the other hand, according to Ozuna, "people mentioned the GI bill as a training program that worked because it gave education funds to people to choose their own school" (author's interview, 20 July 1993). The meetings accomplished more than gathering information and ideas. The IAF sought to engage community residents in conversations to find a common ground for action on the problem. During the 1990 meetings, and in another round of house meetings in 1991 that produced a total of three hundred such events, IAF organizers used the forum to identify new participants and recruit them into its developing campaign.

At this point, the IAF broadened these community-based discussions in two important ways. First, within its own network, the IAF sought the participation of Metro Alliance congregations so that the growing effort would be metropolitan-wide and multiracial. It established a joint committee that included approximately forty participants in cooperative action over a two-year period. In addition, Cortes stepped up meetings at the regional IAF level, inviting local leaders to meet with such economists as Vernon Briggs, Ray Marshall, Barry Bluestone, and James Tobin. Second, COPS and Metro Alliance leaders began meeting with local employers. They learned that San Antonio experienced shortages for certain well-paid jobs, like nurses and medical technicians, and that many employers did not think existing job training efforts were very successful.

By the spring of 1991, through discussions within its community and with experts and business representatives, the IAF had developed the basic outlines of its job training initiative. The program would provide long-term training for viable skills; train for jobs that existed and that paid wages sufficient to support a family; provide living stipends, support services, and counseling to trainees; and link funds and training to the needs of the trainee, not the training provider. COPS and Metro Alliance commissioned Bob McPherson, an employment and training expert at the University of Texas, to design Project QUEST in consultation with its congregations (McPherson and Deaton 1992).

The IAF developed a two-part strategy to gain the $5 million in public funds it estimated would be needed to launch the initiative for two years. First, the IAF worked to assemble allies from the business and government community who thought that federal JTPA funds were being ill spent by the local Private Industry Council, controlled by the very proprietary schools that received its grants. The local banker Tom Frost, an earlier opponent of COPS, became a strong ally of the effort, as did officials of the city's Department of Employment and Economic Development and state officials in Governor Ann Richards's office. Frost called a meeting of forty major employers in July 1991 so that COPS and Metro Alliance could make their pitch (T. Frost, author's interview, 22 July 1993). In exchange for tailoring the program to meet employer work requirements, the IAF demanded that businesses provide job commitments. Despite some resistance, employers committed 650 jobs to QUEST graduates.

Second, to pressure city officials to allocate $5 million from the relatively small city budget, the IAF sought to demonstrate a significant amount of public support from its congregations. COPS and Metro Alliance sponsored a series of "accountability nights" for candidates in the spring elections for mayor and city council. They mobilized constituents through their church networks to attend the accountability sessions. Leaders announced the sessions at religious services, handed out leaflets outside churches, and publicized the sessions in church bulletins. IAF conveners for each church had the responsibility of meeting the quota set for the overall congregational turnout. Hundreds of supporters attended each of the sessions devoted to city council candidates. Meanwhile, COPS and Metro Alliance brought 2,000 supporters to a citywide session for the mayoral candidates on April 14th (San Antonio *Express-News*, 14 May 1991).

At the public accountability sessions, most candidates pledged their support to Project QUEST. But in a series of private discussions with newly elected Mayor Nelson Wolff, City Manager Alex Briseno, and long-time COPS ally Councillor Frank Wing, the IAF realized that it was unlikely to get $5 million from the city's limited general revenues. Since the mood of the city's residents restricted officials from raising taxes, such a large demand for QUEST funds would require cuts in other programs, generating political opposition. So COPS and Metro Alliance turned to the state government for some of the funds, using the power of the Texas IAF network to influence state officials.

In the fall of 1990, the Texas IAF network had brought 10,000 supporters to its founding convention in San Antonio, where it asked for support for QUEST from gubernatorial candidate Ann Richards. In the summer of 1991 the IAF sent delegations of leaders from San Antonio and its affiliates in other Texas cities to lobby the newly elected governor for a concrete commitment of funds. Richards, whose election victory came in part from strong support among low-income Mexican Americans and African Americans, agreed to commit the entire $2.5 million in her discretionary Wagner-Peyser job training account that year to Project QUEST.

Meanwhile a corruption scandal erupted in the local Private Industry Council, prompting the reorganization of federal JTPA funds into a new San Antonio Works board. The IAF met with city officials behind the scenes to encourage the appointment of business leaders favorable to QUEST to the new board. The effort paid off. On 3 September, the Works board voted to distribute its uncommitted "bonus funds" worth $2.3 million (later reduced to $2 million) to QUEST (San Antonio *Light*, 4 September 1991).

Neither state nor local JTPA funds, however, could be used for support services such as child care and living stipends for trainees. The IAF needed $2 million in city funds to cover these services. But city officials, already facing a $9 million budget shortfall and an electorate vocal in its opposition to new taxes, were balking even at the reduced price tag. COPS and Metro Alliance offered a further concession, to take $400,000 out of Community Development Block Grant funds that were to be allocated to other projects the IAF organizations had proposed. But they demanded more vociferously the remaining $1.6 million out of city funds. Hence the public rally held at the 3 September city council meeting described in the opening of this article. Even after their public commitment of funds to QUEST at that rally, though, the mayor and councilors still did not vote the funds. The organizations had to confront the mayor again with 1,000 supporters at a 17 November rally. At that rally Governor Richards publicly announced the state's contribution to QUEST, and the banker Frost announced business commitments for 650 jobs (San Antonio *Express-News*, 18 November 1991). It took until March of 1992, after yet another IAF rally, to get the council and mayor to vote the city funds to QUEST. Eventually, Councilor Wing proposed taking the money from a capital reserve account funded by the sale of the local cable television franchise. The money never did come out of general tax revenue (San Antonio *Light*, 22 July 1992; P. Ozuna, author's interview, 20 July 1993).

At this point most community organizations follow one of two directions. They either withdraw from the process and let another agency run the program; or they administer it directly themselves. The IAF took a third way. It set up an independent agency to run QUEST, but it maintained a key role through all phases of project implementation. The IAF reserved one-third of the seats on the QUEST board of directors for its leaders. The IAF offered the political clout that would prove necessary later to acquire continual funding for the program. In exchange, the presence of IAF leaders on the board would help to keep the program in line with the organization's priorities. For example, when QUEST staff suggested taking commitments for jobs that paid below the $7.50 minimum wage, IAF board members forced a retraction (C. Cheever, Jr., author's interview, 21 July 1993).

To ensure that program benefits accrued to its neighborhoods, COPS and Metro Alliance controlled the recruitment process for trainees. At the same time, though, this decision required a major community mobilization effort on the part of the organizations. COPS and Metro Alliance kicked off the QUEST outreach campaign with a rally on 27 September 1992 where 3,000 supporters celebrated with Governor Ann Richards (San Antonio *Express-News*, 28 September 1992). One hundred and forty volunteers subsequently conducted interviews at IAF member churches to recruit candidates, and many followed the later progress of their neighbors through the training program. Businesses, it turned out, strongly supported recruitment by the community-based organizations. Employers felt applicants recruited this way would likely feel more responsibility toward their communities and therefore work harder to make their training a success.

Although Project QUEST attracted some opposition because of its high per-student costs, the program won largely favorable reviews, as noted above. Meanwhile, QUEST has generated broader institutional change, as the community college system, which provides much of the job training, has reformed its curriculum and works more closely with employers. Meanwhile, the state of Texas reorganized its workforce development policies with regard to principles developed by QUEST.

Based upon the success of QUEST, other local affiliates of the Southwest IAF network developed job training initiatives. In Texas, QUEST-like initiatives were successfully launched in Dallas, Fort Worth, El Paso, and the lower Rio Grande valley. Through a strong state and regional network, the IAF has expanded the capacity of local affiliates so that even relatively young organizations like Dallas Area Interfaith can take on complex and costly initiatives. Meanwhile, IAF organizations in San Antonio and the lower Rio Grande valley have proceeded to develop new tax strategies and "living wage campaigns" to encourage high-wage employment in their localities.

Analysis of the IAF's Political Strategy

At the heart of the IAF's political strategy is what it calls "relational organizing," an approach that serves to link more consensual community-building activity with the realities of generating effective political power. Relational organizing involves the deliberate building of relationships for the purpose of finding common ground for political action. Most community and political associations recruit individuals to support an issue campaign. While social movement scholars have appreciated the importance of social networks to political mobilization (Morris 1984), the IAF's approach is different and rather unique. It does not give first place to mobilization of issue campaigns per se. Instead, IAF organizers bring leaders rooted in church communities together first to hold discussions that can lead to issue campaigns. These conversations occur at what the IAF calls "individual meetings" between two participants, at house meetings, and in action committees of local organizations.

Many observers have misunderstood this approach, criticizing community organizing for addressing minor issues such as street lights. Some community organizations never do get beyond campaigning for street lights on neighborhood corners. Communities and their organizations can be isolated and narrow in scope. The relational strategy works best, then, when the institutional context of the organizing network allows for long-term organizing, to build capacity over time. Moreover, more complex and sophisticated campaigns are likely to emerge through discussions among diverse communities and with participants at many different levels. The Southwest IAF conducts its relational organizing in the context of metropolitan-wide organizations networked together at the regional level with ongoing connections to public officials, business leaders and policy experts at the state and national level. Its local affiliates can now address quite large-scale issues of workforce development and public school reform.

The relational strategy helps sustain participation. Consistent with relational organizing, the primary assignment of the IAF community organizer is to recruit and train leaders, who, in turn, formally represent the organization. These efforts produce a continuing source of new leadership for IAF affiliates. In other community-based organizations or political associations, staff members tend to concentrate on program administration or the development of issue campaigns. Over time, many of these groups become dominated by a few key staff or leaders and lose their participatory character. IAF organizers do assert a significant authority in the direction of issue campaigns, and some organizers do come to dominate local affiliates, ignoring the development of community leadership. But when organizers adhere to their primary institutional responsibility for the recruitment and training of leaders, IAF organizations have been able to sustain a broadly participatory character over time.

The relational strategy encourages participants who are community rooted. Most community and political associations recruit individual activists to their efforts without regard to the person's social relationships. By contrast, IAF organizers recruit participants out of church institutions, so they are already immersed in social networks. The IAF then trains these indigenous leaders to develop relationships with each other, relationships directed to cooperative political action. IAF organizations hold leaders accountable for mobilizing their supporters to participate in IAF actions. Leaders are required to demonstrate a following if they want to take on authoritative positions in IAF organizations. In the QUEST campaign, leaders had to organize house meetings among their family and friends; and the organization assigned quotas for the number of supporters to bring to "accountability nights" and other major actions. The political power for the IAF to acquire the public resources for programs like QUEST comes from its ability to mobilize large numbers of supporters through a leadership rooted in community networks.

In order to influence public institutions, the IAF follows a nonpartisan strategy that emphasizes both confrontation and negotiation from an independent organizational base. The IAF is not affiliated with a political party and does not endorse candidates. But it does hold accountability nights to get public commitments from officials. In the spring of 1991 it asked candidates running for local office for commitments to support QUEST and then publicized their responses among its supporters at election time. Through repeated mass mobilization to actions like the rally at city hall for QUEST, the IAF works to hold officials accountable to their organized base.

While the IAF has received much publicity for its more confrontational, public activities, less well known are the continual series of private meetings IAF organizers and leaders hold with institutional representatives. At these meetings, the IAF tries its hand at finding common ground with public officials and business elites, often proving more than willing to negotiate and compromise to forge a winnable deal. In the case of QUEST, the IAF met repeatedly over a two-year period with a wide variety of elected officials, governmental staff at the city and state level, employer representatives and independent experts. With city officials the IAF traded away $400,000 of Community Development Block Grant (CDBG) money allocated to projects it had proposed in order to secure city funding for QUEST. Meanwhile, the IAF forged common ground with Governor Richards, who could use the political capital that might come from a successful job training program to secure her position in competitive state politics.

As important as the contributions of the IAF model are, if this approach is to come to represent a general model for democratic renewal, it must overcome three current limitations. First, addressing the structures of economic, social, and political inequality in the United States is likely to require the kind of redistribution of resources that will end up with some clear losers. IAF organizations do not appear to be afraid of a fight, and they have faced their share of opposition in campaigns. But the relational strategy of the IAF seeks to avoid zero sum conflicts wherever possible. The IAF has worked to avoid taking initiatives in a way that defines a clear group or community that will stand to lose if it succeeds. It has used its state network to mitigate local conflicts. In the case of QUEST, it drew upon state-level resources to avoid painful choices about the spending of local tax money in San Antonio.

Second, democratic renewal will likely require reform of our political institutions, a task that the independent, nonpartisan strategy of the IAF does not directly accomplish. The IAF does hold these institutions accountable to its organized constituency through accountability nights and other public actions. And the QUEST board represents an institutional innovation, as it represents a cooperative arrangement between the business community, public officials, and community-based organizations. But the IAF strategy does not directly alter the main institutions of our political processes, that is, political parties and representative bodies. The gains in public accountability and institutional innovation, important as they are, remain limited to arenas of IAF initiative.

In a similar vein, the increases in political participation generated by the IAF also remain largely within the IAF field of action. One study (Portney and Berry, this volume; Berry, Portney, and Thomson 1993) found that San Antonio, including COPS neighborhoods, ranked very low in its measure of political activity. The city ranked well below fourteen other cities in a composite measure of such activities as contacting officials and participating in a citizen group to solve a community problem. The study did not measure how much COPS might have increased political participation, because it did not measure activity before and after IAF organizing.[3] Nevertheless, the study's findings are consistent with the argument that the IAF's independent strategy keeps its democratic gains limited to its own field of action, at least at this point.

Third, can a strategy that is firmly rooted in local community organizing effectively deal with the national and international processes that affect the health of local communities? QUEST is premised upon the availability of well-paying jobs in San Antonio, jobs for which people can be prepared by two years of training. COPS and Metro Alliance found those positions primarily in health care. With the restructuring of the health care industry, the IAF and Project QUEST again proved adept at discovering new opportunities in other fields, at least for the short run. Ultimately, though, national (and international) economic reform will be necessary to make well-paying jobs available widely to urban residents with moderate skill levels.

The locally rooted, but federated structure of the IAF network does hold promise as a model for national action, as it fits well with the structure of our political institutions. It has already brought community initiatives with strong local roots to the state level in Texas. The IAF has proved capable of exerting political power in Texas by leveraging its base in eleven affiliates. Within a few years, the IAF is likely to have affiliates in seventy or so congressional districts. At that point, Southwest director Ernesto Cortes envisions the IAF taking its first national initiatives.[4] Since the IAF will remain one player in the more complex world of national politics, its network is likely to be able to develop innovative programs and avoid the most divisive issues. Whether the IAF's strategy can handle the level of conflict, as well as build the kind of cooperative alliances necessary to undertake economic restructuring or other fundamental institutional reforms at the national level, remains a challenge for the future.

Conclusion

Both communitarianism and the more dominant model of interest-group political action have much to learn from the IAF's dual strategy of conflict and cooperation. Without deep participatory roots in community life, interest-group politics seem destined to perpetual conflict over relatively narrowly defined issues, while our urban communities stagnate. In that context, the current emphasis on social capital and communitarian approaches to civic engagement provide a welcome antidote. The IAF's relational organizing strategy offers a compelling community-building approach. Rather than mobilizing disconnected individuals around predetermined issues, IAF organizers bring congregational members rooted in religious and community networks together to seek a common ground for action.

Unlike communitarianism, however, the IAF strategy does not deny that conflict, as well as cooperation, constitutes a fundamental part of politics. By avoiding conflict, the communitarian strategy limits the boundaries of community and cooperation to those already in, or to those who can come to forge unity through discussion alone. In a society structured by profound inequalities along race, class, and many other lines, good faith discussion represents only part of the process necessary to rebuild a conception of the common good. In the end, communitarianism does not provide an adequate strategy for overcoming the divisions that prevent broadbased cooperation for the improvement of our common society.

The IAF offers an approach in which conflict becomes a necessary part of the establishment of new forms of cooperation. The IAF has a wellknown slogan, "no permanent allies, no permanent enemies." Many observers have interpreted that slogan in a limited, tactical sense as reflecting a pragmatic approach to politics. While the IAF is tactically pragmatic, the slogan also reflects a deeper strategic approach. The IAF's strategy assumes there are no fundamental, irreconcilable conflicts between groups, and that our political institutions are ultimately open and accessible to all. But the strategy recognizes that confrontation is often required to open up institutions and to push groups or individuals to reformulate their conceptions of self-interest.

In part, the IAF approach resolves conflict by a "quid pro quo" process. For example, in exchange for funding QUEST, the IAF supplies latent political support for elected officials by publicizing their actions among its voting constituents. Public rallies and accountability nights remind officials of the organization's power. Beyond that, however, the relational strategy seeks to open up new political possibilities. Through the QUEST campaign, San Antonio's employers came to understand and help develop a new method of job training that could benefit both themselves and IAF communities. The IAF offers a way for politics to be the realm for the resolution, however peacefully, of conflict that may lead to new, more inclusive conceptions of the common good. In that sense, politics becomes a creative process for community improvement broadly construed.

Producing Social Capital

National Social Movements and Civil Society

DEBRA C. MINKOFF

In the recent debates over the decline in civil society in the United States there is a notable silence about the coterminous expansion of the citizen's advocacy and social movement sector. At the same time that trust is supposedly breaking down all over, Americans have been establishing and maintaining national advocacy groups and social movement organizations at a phenomenal rate (Minkoff 1995; Schlozman and Tierney 1986; Walker 1983).[1] But, because these organizations are less likely to involve face-to-face social relations and more likely to generate societal conflict than consensus, they are not thought to contribute positively to the stability and growth of civil society. Whether or not such groups are—or can be—productive of social capital is still an open question.

My argument is that the growth of a stable sector of national social movement organizations (SMOs) reflects a significant change in how collective identities are constructed and collective action implemented. Local communities and institutions are no longer the sine qua non of mobilization, precisely because identity groups transcend parochial boundaries based on communities of residence, religious or ethnic affiliation, and even perhaps class and race. In some instances the diffuse nature of such social ties limits available social capital and organizational capacities, consequently constraining political effectiveness. However, I want to suggest that national organizations provide an infrastructure for collective action and act as visible proponents of group claims, which produces a kind of symbolic affiliation and social integration. For isolated and marginalized

Revised from an article of the same title in *American Behavioral Scientist* 40, no. 5 (1997): 606–19.

constituencies—the disabled, gay men and lesbians, the poor, and others—this sense of collective identity or "we" may literally be life-saving.

After detailing the recent growth of the U.S. national social movement sector, I consider how civil society frameworks treat national social movement organizations. I then elaborate four reasons why national social movement organizations should be incorporated into our analyses of civil society and social capital. First, they provide trace evidence of denser social networks and social infrastructures of the sort applauded by analysts of civil society. Second, the expansion of the national movement sector contributes to an enduring opportunity structure for activism by marginalized groups. Third, national SMOs serve a critical linkage function for movements with "weak infrastructures" (McCarthy 1987) and have the potential to promote the diffusion of collective identities, providing at least a minimal degree of solidarity and integration for otherwise isolated members of society. And fourth, national SMOs promote public discourse and debate, strengthening the public sphere (Habermas 1974) and the formation of counterpublics (Fraser 1992). In closing, I draw out some implications of this argument for conceptualizing civil society in the United States.

National Organizations in the United States

The climate for social movement activism in the United States has changed dramatically since the 1960s. As protest by African Americans, students, feminists, and others became less prominent, opportunities for putting direct pressure on the government seemed closed. At the same time, a national sector of formal organizations committed to social change was expanding and diversifying (Jenkins 1987; Minkoff 1995). Conventional interest groups and advocacy organizations also became increasingly common, and sometimes even powerful, actors on the political stage (Berry 1979; Schlozman and Tierney 1986; Walker 1983).

The amount and diversity of new organizational activity by social movement actors since 1970 has been unprecedented. Take, for example, the contemporary women's movement: in 1960 there were 40 national membership organizations concerned with women's status in society, most of which provided services (vocational, civic, economic) to their members. In 1971, this number shot up to 127, and then, ten years later, to over 330 organizations, with most groups pursuing advocacy for women. The same period also saw a continued expansion of national organizations representing African Americans and other racial and ethnic minorities. The 40 national civil rights organizations active in 1955 increased to close to 200 in the mid-1980s. Equally significant is that, although the founding of new groups has abated, the number of active organizations has remained relatively stable into the 1990s (Minkoff 1995).

Others have documented similar trends in organization building associated with the poverty advocacy sector (Imig 1996), the peace movement (Lofland 1993), and the gay and lesbian movement (Adam 1987). And yet, observers such as Robert Putnam decry the decline of civil society. Clearly there is a discrepancy that needs further analysis. How and why do current conceptualizations of civil society minimize the role of national social movement organizations? What are the implications of leaving this form of national mobilization out of our understanding of civil society and democratic participation in the United States? These are the questions that take up the remainder of this chapter.

Theorizing the Role of National Mobilization

Most discussions of civil society and social capital emphasize their local dimensions, drawing attention to the sustenance and growth of face-to-face social networks, voluntary associations, and community institutions. Analysts such as Putnam (1993b, 1995a, 1995b) argue that civil society is the main arena for the production of norms of trust and reciprocity that undergird civility, civic participation, and (a liberal vision of) democracy. National social movements, however, presumably lack the same social capital–generating qualities. Even approaches that do incorporate social movements as central actors in civil society (Cohen and Arato 1994; Offe 1985) privilege grassroots, participatory movements over those more reliant on national, professionalized social movement organizations.[2]

One reason some civil society advocates downplay the contribution of social movements relates to the concern with factionalism that informs elite and pluralist theories of state power (Held 1989; Foley and Edwards 1996). Without appropriate, democratic mechanisms for integrating individuals and managing competing interests, the public good will be sacrificed to individual interests. Voluntary associations such as churches, social clubs, choral societies, and other forms of civic engagement are integrative mechanisms that bridge particularistic concerns and involve citizens in networks of social interaction around common activities and presumably shared goals. These forms of participation promote the formation of social capital, which Putnam defines as "features of social organization, such as networks, norms, and trust, that facilitate coordination and cooperation for mutual benefit" (1993b:35).[3]

Horizontal networks of social interaction and the density of associational life foster norms of reciprocity and trust, decrease incentives for opportunistic behavior, and serve as models for subsequent collective action

(Putnam 1993b, 1995a). Participation and membership in secondary groups also "broaden the participants' sense of self, developing the 'I' into the 'we,' or (in the language of rational choice theorists) enhancing the participants' 'taste' for collective benefits" (Putnam 1995a:67). Social movements, however, are often conflict-oriented by design, and tend to be organized around existing social cleavages or (worse yet) generative of new ones. Not only do they lack a central property of civic relationships and social capital—the potential to transcend exclusive social relations and build bridging networks—but they are thought to reinforce them.

A second concern centers on the structure of national SMOs. In contrast with grassroots movements and local organizations that involve intense commitment and interaction with other members of the group, national social movement organizations tend to be centralized and bureaucratic, with a great deal of distance between leaders and members (McCarthy and Zald 1977). In addition, members are linked to the organization and to each other through financial contributions or dues payments. Attendance at meetings is rare, and mobilization amounts to letter-writing campaigns and making donations in response to direct mail solicitations or canvassing efforts (McCarthy 1987; Oliver and Marwell 1992).

This characterization of national SMOs prompts two criticisms from the perspective of civil society advocates. First, these organizations are thought to reproduce hierarchy as a mode of decision making. So, even if they are committed to liberal democratic principles, SMOs are not necessarily participatory institutions (Cohen and Arato 1994; Walzer 1991). They also tend to reproduce existing social inequalities, with white, middle-class members (typically, but not necessarily men) holding leadership positions (Veugelers and Lamont 1991). By implication, such organizations cannot contribute to the development of models of democratic participation and norms of egalitarianism that are central to the vision of civil society advocated by analysts of recent democratic transitions (Cohen and Arato 1994).

A related issue is that, although national SMOs often have massive memberships, member commitment is presumably too weak really to count as such. As Putnam suggests:

> The bond between any two members of the Sierra Club is less like the bond between any two members of a gardening club and more like the bond between any two Red Sox fans (or perhaps any two devoted Honda owners): they root for the same team and they share some of the same interests, but they are unaware of each other's existence. Their ties, in short, are to common symbols, common leaders, and perhaps common ideals, but not to one another. (1995a:71)

Thus, they represent a singular trend—the development of what Putnam terms "tertiary" organizations as distinct from the secondary associations he posits as productive of social capital (1995a, 1995b). This claim—that national social movement organizations do not positively contribute to the development of social capital and are thus not part of the civil domain—is, however, based on a rather limited view of solidary social relations as derived only from direct contact with one's neighbors, co-workers, and associates. As I argue later, mediated or abstract relations that do not entail face-to-face interaction may also provide a basis for solidarity and collective identity, representing an alternative source of social capital.

Community Infrastructures and National SMOs

The first criticism of frameworks that exclude national social movement organizations is that these groups provide trace evidence of the denser networks, grassroots infrastructures, and social capital applauded by advocates of civil society. As Foley and Edwards note, "large groups with national media profiles are simply the most visible promontories in the broader landscape of contemporary social movements" (1996:44). Their point is that grassroots groups both outnumber national organizations and are more active at the local level, developing community infrastructures and social networks.[4] In addition, decades of social movement research have documented that the emergence of national movements requires some degree of internal organization and development of local mobilizing structures.

In almost every case of more recent and visible social movement activity, community-based institutions and organizations were critical. African American churches, colleges, and Southern chapters of the NAACP provided direct routes for mobilization in the early phases of the civil rights movement, delivering their constituents for activism (McAdam 1983; Morris 1984). The contemporary feminist movement benefited from the commitment and activist identities sustained by the National Woman's Party in the "doldrums" of the 1940s and 1950s (Taylor 1989). Cooptable networks provided by traditional women's associations, along with relationships among younger feminists forged in the civil rights and New Left student movements, were also critical (Freeman 1973). A gay/lesbian liberation movement in the 1960s would have been unthinkable without at least some development of a nascent urban community and mobilizing structures such as a gay press, gay bars, and national organizations such as the Mattachine Society and Daughters of Bilitis (D'Emilio 1983). As a final example, the pro-life and New Right movements drew energy and resources from women activists linked together by church-based networks as well as through an extensive network of national organizations such as the Moral

Majority (Klatch 1987; McCarthy 1987). The point is obvious: Without at least a minimal level of self-organization, it is unlikely that social groups will be able to mount the kind of sustained challenges against authorities that we associate with national social movements. And even Putnam concedes that "a grassroots political movement . . . is a social capital-intensive form of political participation" (1995b:665).

The National Social Movement Infrastructure

National social movement organizations, more directly, provide means for accumulating social capital that can be deployed for collective action. In a recent analysis of the relationship between the civil rights and contemporary feminist movements in the United States, I have shown that the expansion of the national social movement sector is one factor that promotes the diffusion of protest across diverse social groups (Minkoff 1997). Associational networks serve as conduits for the spread of protest models, since existing ties among activists provide direct points of contact for the sharing of movement ideas and political socialization (McAdam 1995). The national movement sector also creates a resource and institutional space that enables protest and organization building by a diversity of actors.

Why is this relevant for civil society debates? Protest is a vehicle for making claims that is available to even the most powerless segments of society—those who may not be able to form associations or may be so powerless that their only recourse is to disrupt local routines in the organizations and institutions to which they have access (Piven and Cloward 1977). Protest is important not only because it can put pressure on elites, but also because, in the process of direct political engagement, collective identity and solidarity are formed and strengthened.

McAdam (1988) demonstrates how participants in the Freedom Summer campaign came away from that experience with enduring activist identities that shaped both subsequent levels of political participation and future lifestyle choices. With some qualification, Freedom Summer itself bridged racial and class divisions, if only momentarily, suggesting the potential for cross-cutting ties presented by engagement in progressive social movement activity. The direct action peace movement in the 1980s also brought together a diverse group of activists, especially across age, gender, and religious lines (Epstein 1991). Fantasia clearly illustrates that the "cultures of solidarity" that emerge from workers' strikes bring together striking workers, their families, and members of the broader community and its institutions. Anticipating the kinds of debates discussed here, Fantasia concludes that "cultures of solidarity are potentially durable associational forms" that shape subsequent relationships and "local patterns of life" (1988:238).

What these cases suggest is that involvement in social movements can be a mechanism in the creation of solidarity and the deepening of collective identities that anchor individuals in participatory cultures (W. Gamson 1991). And, as William Gamson points out, "the best long-run guarantor of democratic participation is collective identity that incorporates the idea of people as collective agents of their own destiny, and adopts a practice that encourages them to be active and collaborative" (1991:49; see also, Walzer 1991).

National Organizations and Collective Identity

National organizations also provide a means of integrating isolated individuals who seek some form of collective engagement around trans-local identities and interests. The intentional visibility of national social movement organizations, and their efforts at publicizing the movement's goals and activities, promote a mediated form of collective identity—precisely the kind that Putnam attributes to members of the Sierra Club or Red Sox fans. This form of collective identity is qualitatively different from that generated in direct interaction, but it nonetheless provides a sense of integration into an abstract collectivity, which is a minimal requirement for further involvement in collective affairs.

Not all social movements can draw upon pre-existing infrastructures involving face-to-face interactions of the sort that characterize grassroots participation. John McCarthy (1987), in a comparison of the pro-choice and pro-life movements, introduces the concepts of "infrastructural deficits" and "thin infrastructures" (in contrast to the "thick infrastructures" of the social capital–producing sort). The success of the pro-life movement, according to McCarthy, was its ability to build on the established networks and resources of the Catholic church—which provided leaders, church-based facilities, and an available pool of activists (conservative women who were predominantly homemakers) that could activate phone trees and local mobilization to great effect (see also Luker 1984).

Pro-choice advocates, in contrast, tended to be professional women and health workers who had few such "natural" mobilizing structures available to them (let alone thick ones). Professional associations, which may have represented a logical site for bringing interested individuals together, are rarely empowered by their members to support social movements in any tangible way (McCarthy 1987). The pro-choice movement therefore relied on a distinct vehicle for linking adherents: professional social movement organizations. These organizations deploy "modern technologies of mobilization" such as direct mail, canvassing, publicity, and, increasingly, more advanced information technologies to vet supporters (McCarthy

1987; Oliver and Marwell 1992). Such methods also influenced the rapid growth of the New Right in the 1980s. Thin structures that consist of names and contact information for individuals who might be receptive to the organization's goals represent "very weak communication networks along which resources and information may pass" (McCarthy 1987:59). Such information channels, although weak, are nonetheless a cooptable form of social capital that provides a basis for action (Coleman 1988).

It is exactly this reliance on modern, mediated technologies that holds out the potential for national organizations to serve as a link between isolated members of a movement constituency. If we consider the social locations of many recently mobilized groups, it becomes clear that the traditional bases of collective identity have expanded from the local, community level to encompass collectivities that are linked by both symbolic forms of affiliation and similar social-structural positions. Although the reasons for this shift are beyond the scope of this chapter, structural barriers to mobility have loosened, and economic or ethnic communities are no longer primary sources for forming collective identity. Movements and identities are correspondingly less local and more likely to bridge traditional social cleavages. This extension of the bases for collective identity and group formation implies that contemporary social movements are also more likely to represent social formations with weak infrastructures.

So, let us reconsider Putnam's dismissal of new organizational activity by women, environmental activists, the elderly, as well as lesbians and gay men, the disabled, Native Americans, and peace activists. In each case, some form of institutional infrastructure and deep networks helped generate national activity. At the same time, these groups invested heavily in the formation of national organizations to represent their interests in political and nonpolitical institutions. Putnam is correct that, in these cases, the constituency is tied together by common symbols and shared ideology. That is, their relationship is mediated by the organization with which they affiliate (which may or may not take the form of membership). But, in the absence of the opportunity or resources to establish face-to-face interactions, such symbolic affiliation may be the only available mobilizing structure that can link isolated individuals.

The result is the establishment of "symbolic communities" or communities of affinity in which "group members share . . . an attachment to a particular set of identity symbols" (Cornell 1996:271). Symbolic identities are based on "weak or thin culture," which nonetheless provides the initial self-concept and organization necessary for the further development of group ties (Cornell 1996).[5] Such collective identities are themselves the outcome of negotiation and may represent only partial understandings or agreements about what defines the group (Cohen 1999; J. Gamson 1996). It is important that national organizations act as carriers of these collective definitions and play a role in disseminating them more widely (Friedman and McAdam 1992).[6]

National SMOs and the Public Sphere

Finally, national social movement organizations help shape and expand the public sphere by promoting debate on issues pertinent to the concerns and agendas of their constituents. In so doing, they raise issues about what constitutes the public good, promoting the diffusion of new ideas, publicity, and abstract models of identity (Calhoun 1992). National SMOs are central actors in enlarging the arena of political discourse and at least challenging the limits of democratic participation in polities such as the United States.

The public sphere is a critical part of civil society, including a broad array of institutions such as the media and public meeting places that promote open discussion (Habermas 1974). As Nancy Fraser clarifies, the public sphere is the "space in which citizens deliberate about their common affairs, and hence an institutionalized arena of discursive action" (1992:110). Within this arena, political and nonpolitical associations are mediators that convey public opinions and concerns to authorities and relay "back to civil society the unwritten rules of the political game" (Veugelers and Lamont 1991:138). They are also active voices in the public debate, at least to the extent that they are given access to it. Competing discourses challenge prevailing understandings, so that "assumptions previously exempt from contestation will have to be publicly argued out" (Fraser 1992:124).

Clearly, the activities of national civil rights organizations, public conflict between pro-choice and pro-life organizations, and even efforts by environmental organizations have put a diversity of issues onto the public stage, challenging the assumptions guiding our social and material relations and in some cases even influencing legislative and policy change. One recent example illustrates the ability of national social movement organizations to provoke such normative contests.

In 1996, the U.S. Congress debated the issues of gay and lesbian marriages and employment discrimination based on sexual orientation. Newspapers ran extensive coverage, prominent television news magazines included segments on gay and lesbian marriages and families, and the nightly news carried coverage of Congressional testimony. In this case, organizations such as the LAMBDA Legal Defense Fund and the National Gay and Lesbian Task Force literally constructed these concerns as a matter for public debate, mobilizing for passage of employment protection at the same time that President Clinton signed the 1996 Defense of Marriage Act (which defines marriage as a heterosexual partnership and allows states to disregard the legality of same-sex marriages performed in other states). Extensive visibility of this sort has the downside of increasing public backlash; but, in bringing issues to public notice, national organizations introduce a new debate and a new moment in the continuous process of "political settlement" (Foley and Edwards 1996).

The visibility of national associations is also implicated in the formation of counterpublic spheres, which operate as spaces for marginalized groups to construct alternative models of participation and community (Fraser 1992). "Subaltern counterpublics" represent "parallel discursive arenas where members of subordinated social groups invent and circulate counter-discourses to formulate oppositional interpretations of their identities, interests, needs" (Fraser 1992:123). Even those members of the constituency who are not directly involved in such discourses have access to them through a variety of media forms—in particular, movement-affiliated newspapers and, increasingly, internet resources such as websites and "chat rooms"—that can ground the kind of symbolic affiliation and collective identity discussed in the previous section.

Conclusion

My purpose here has been to analyze the conceptual treatment of national social movement organizations in current debates over civil society and the decline of social capital in the United States. In contrast to the tendency to dismiss such organizational activity, I argue that national SMOs play a critical role in civil society and the production of social capital by providing an infrastructure for collective action, facilitating the development of mediated collective identities that link otherwise marginalized members of society, and shaping public discourse and debate.

Implicit in the arguments laid out is the view that civil society is not only multidimensional, incorporating local and national social formations and organizations, but that it is also multipurposeful. Certainly face-to-face interactions, local institutions, and embedded social relations promote integration, participation, and some degree of concern for one's neighbors. Even more certainly, to the extent that such interactions cut across and link otherwise homogeneous segments of society—be they organized along racial, class, ethnic, or other status lines—the public good would seemed to be better served. We know, however, that in actuality such bridging social relations are exceptional and difficult to maintain. Patterns of within-group sociability and solidarity still follow racial and class lines, reflecting very real cleavages in the political-economic system. At the same time, identity groups have begun to be constructed across local and even national boundaries, requiring the development of infrastructures that bring together dispersed individuals into some form of collective identity. My argument is that national political organizations serve this purpose and reflect, in part, a newly developing logic of collective identity and social capital formation.

National mobilization is difficult, if not impossible, to sustain without corresponding investment in community infrastructures and institutions. Still, it may be the only option for some groups whose structural location and resource opportunities are limited—by geography, economic constraints, or histories of domination and repression. Ironically, such groups are also the least likely to have the resources necessary to launch national organizations in the first place. By then ignoring their national organization building, their efforts and claims are further marginalized. Because they organize nationally, they are not "really" a community, or they lack social capital, or they are not legitimate members of the civic community—despite evidence to the contrary.

Global Civil Society?

Transnational Social Movement Organizations and Social Capital

JACKIE SMITH

An important function of civil society is to generate social capital that, in turn, contributes to the operation of the broader political order. As noted in the introduction to this volume the neo-Tocquevillean approach to civil society emphasizes its role in promoting effective democratic governance by socializing citizens and enhancing their civic skills. By contrast, the representative or contestatory perspective on civil society that is more typical of Latin American and European analysts sees a strong civil society as protection against an undemocratic or unjust regime. Putnam and other scholars using the civil society concept have excluded social movement organizations from their notion of civil society because they lack the face-to-face contact Putnam claims is crucial to cultivating social trust and social capital. Also, social movements violate the notion that a strong civil society is composed of organizations that bridge social and political cleavages rather than reinforce them. In contrast to this negative interpretation of social movements, many scholars of international relations might be criticized for celebrating what may be viewed as an overly optimistic impression of a growing "global civil society" (Falk 1987; see, e.g., Walker 1995; Wapner 1995). The most striking of the differences in contemporary discourses on national versus transnational civil society is that, while the former attempts to ignore political change organizations, the latter treats the transnational versions of political associations as the main indicators of a growing "global civil society" (Wapner 1996; Willetts 1996).[1] One important difference in the two approaches may lie in the fact that, while political scientists and sociologists exploring national politics typically begin with the assumption of

Revised from an article of the same title in *American Behavioral Scientist* 42, no.1 (1998): 93–107.

a national polity, international relations scholars have had to defend the notion that an international polity exists.

The optimism of some "postrealist" international relations scholars stems from the dominance of state-centric, realist perspectives in international theory that assume states to be the major—if not the only—influential actors in the correspondingly named field of inter*national* relations. Moreover, until quite recently (and especially after the end of the Cold War), states were widely treated as unitary actors motivated by a common geopolitical logic, and thus politics within states was viewed as largely irrelevant to international relations. Thus, in international relations, a fascination with rising levels of transnational, or nonstate, interaction (measured in terms of volume of international mail or the frequency of international air transport) gave way to new attempts to map the growth of various kinds of transnational nongovernmental organizations (Keohane and Nye 1972; Skjelsbaek 1972). These observations typically served as evidence challenging state-centric models of international relations, and they helped back the argument that scholars must account for actors and processes beyond the traditional scope of the discipline. In contrast, analysts of national politics could hardly ignore how advocacy groups, citizens' associations, lobbyists, and others influence national political processes.

A further difference is these scholars' assessments of the relationships between politically engaged elements of civil society and political institutions. Foley and Edwards criticize the exclusion of social movements from the concepts of either conceptualization of civil society, since these are often "the central bearers of democratizing pressures within Western democracies" (Foley and Edwards 1996:47). Indeed, by excluding social movements from the concept of civil society, researchers may overlook a significant causal variable. For instance, Tilly's (1984) work on the emergence of national social movements demonstrates the strong relationship of social movements to the development of national political institutions. And interactions between movement actors and agents of the state have helped to shape contemporary interest-group politics and the institutions and procedures governing the right to free speech (Clemens 1997; McCarthy, McPhail and Crist 1995). Moreover, tax laws and litigation have substantial impacts on the character and scope of citizens' engagement in political processes (McCarthy, Britt, and Wolfson 1991; Pring and Canan 1996). But those advancing either the neo-Tocquevillean or contestatory approaches to the civil society argument generally fail to acknowledge the interactive processes that have shaped how citizens can relate to their political institutions.

The institution-shaping role of political change organizations is perhaps more obvious when one examines international political institutions, which have developed most dramatically over the last century. Transnational social movements and other civil society organizations have been important forces shaping the structures of international political institutions and influencing their operations. For instance, transnational actors seeking to protect non-combatants during wars were crucial to advancing the Geneva Convention, which provides international legal protection for civilians (Chatfield 1997). Also, transnational social movement organizations working for environmental protection, human rights, and disarmament have been essential to effective monitoring and implementation of international treaties (Clapp 1994; Roebuck 1997; Smith 1995). One can not only argue that transnational social movements have influenced the formation and functioning of international institutions but that, in doing so, they have helped to expand participation in (i.e., to democratize) the international polity. Such actions demonstrate that transnational social movements indeed serve to stimulate the creation of "networks, norms and social trust that facilitate coordination and cooperation for mutual benefit" (Putnam 1995:67). Thus, can they be left out of considerations of civil society and social capital formation?

Minkoff (this volume) demonstrates that national social movement organizations help generate important forms of social capital within national societies. Drawing upon her analysis, four claims can be made about how a growing transnational social movement sector affects the development of global civil society. First, transnational social movement organizations (TSMOs) signal the presence of much broader transnational social networks. Case study research on both national and transnational social movement organizations supports this claim, revealing that social movement organizations typically emerge from pre-existing networks or associations that facilitate interactions among individuals with shared interests. Second, as the population of TSMOs develops (both quantitatively and qualitatively), they will provide new and ongoing opportunities for marginalized groups to influence global political change. Third, TSMOs help bring together constituencies—such as unskilled migrant laborers in varied national contexts—that lack natural ties, or that have "thin infrastructures" that frustrate collective action (McCarthy 1987).[2] Fourth, and perhaps most important, is the fact that TSMOs help generate and guide a transnational public discourse and debate around global problems. Because international treaty making has traditionally excluded all of "civil society," these organizations are generating important infrastructure to enable more democratic accountability in international decision making.

TSMOs and Global Social Infrastructures

Extensive evidence shows a dramatic expansion in both the numbers of transnationally organized social movement organizations and the levels of participation by transnational and national social change groups in international political processes (Willetts 1996). This growth parallels the formation of other types of associations, ranging from business interest groups to recreational and professional associations that transcend national borders (Skjelsbaek 1972; Union of International Associations 1996).

Between 1953 and 1993, the population of TSMOs grew from around 100 to more than 600 organizations (Smith 1997a). This trend parallels the growth in intergovernmental organizations facilitating international cooperation around issues of trade and economic coordination and around collective problem-solving efforts, such as peacekeeping and environmental protection. Thus, the growth of TSMOs can be read as a response to the growing tendency of states to turn to inter-state negotiations to solve problems related to increasingly porous national boundaries. But historic evidence shows that transnational SMOs were also partly responsible for generating pressure for multilateral responses to global interdependencies, as they pressed governments to advance the United Nations and the World Health Organization, among other international agencies (Chatfield 1997; Robbins 1971). Parallel to changes in the demand for transnational political activism was a proliferation of technologies that facilitated transnational communication and transportation. These technologies enabled governments, businesses and social movements to organize across national boundaries on a much larger scale than they had in even the early part of the twentieth century (Kriesberg 1997).

Table 1 illustrates the changes in the population of TSMOs over the last part of the twentieth century. Over four decades, the population of transnational SMOs grew almost sixfold. While human rights has been the focus of roughly a quarter of all TSMOs throughout the period, the fastest organizational growth in more recent years has occurred around environmental issues.

The evidence presented in table 1 demonstrates the claim that a dynamic transnational social movement sector exists. A large organizational infrastructure independent of governments facilitates transnational interaction and cooperation for social or political change. But how "global" is this infrastructure? How much transnational interaction is implied by the existence of each organization? These questions are addressed in a preliminary way here in order to assess the extent to which transnational SMOs may be seen as agents that help generate social capital among activist populations that cross national boundaries.

TSMOs tend to be based in the Northern hemisphere, and a disproportionate number are located in cities like London or New York.[3] This organizational distribution in part reflects global inequities, but it also results from strategic organizational choices: telecommunications are more reliable and often cheaper in more industrialized regions, and transport to and

TABLE 1. TSMOs by Issue Area

	1953[a] % *(N = 110)*	*1973*[a] % *(N = 183)*	*1993* % *(N = 631)*
Human rights	30	22	27
Environment	2	5	14
Women's rights	9	9	10
Peace	10	8	9
Multi-issue/world order	7	7	8
Development	3	4	5
Other[b]	39	45	27

Source: Yearbook of International Organizations

   [a] Data for 1953 and 1973 were collected in collaboration with Kathryn Sikkink.

   [b] "Other" category includes groups working for, e.g., Esperanto, ethnic liberation, international law, monarchism, anti-communism, etc. With the exception of Esperanto groups, the "other" category includes groups working on issues that were the focus of no more than 2% of all groups in each year.

from these places far more convenient, thus facilitating transnational organization. Also, many TSMOs seek to monitor government behavior in inter-state negotiations or to otherwise engage international institutions such as the United Nations, and the decision to locate in New York or Geneva may be purely strategic.[4] Moreover, there is clearly a trend showing that TSMOs are increasingly based in developing countries and that they are attracting members and staff from regions once unrepresented in transnational activist circles. For instance, in 1953 just 5 percent of all TSMO secretariats were based in developing countries. By 1993 this figure had risen to 23 percent. This is due in part to an increase in funds from governments and from private (mostly U.S.-based) foundations that have helped support nongovernmental organizations in developing countries and have subsidized their participation in international meetings.

While we see evidence here of a global social infrastructure for activism, its development has been uneven, largely reflecting existing patterns of inequality in the inter-state system. Nevertheless, the growth in the sector—particularly over the last decade—documents dramatic changes in how people organize themselves and suggests that changes in the global economic and political orders have affected many forms of social relations embedded within state structures. Inferring from our understandings of national SMOs that these groups serve as traces of a wider web of associations and networks formed for reasons other than promoting social change, we see a vast, if uneven, global social infrastructure that constitutes an emerging "global civil society." But whether TSMOs are generators of social capital that is relevant in a global polity remains an open question, especially since the concept of social capital implies trust, which some claim results more from face-to-face interaction than from loose affiliations with broadly based and remote organizations. In the following sections I develop further an explanation for the emergence of a transnational social movement sector that draws from theories of national social movements and assesses the role of TSMOs in social capital formation within a global political system.

Structuring Opportunities for Transnational Mobilization

The emergence of transnational SMOs suggests that social change advocates face new threats or opportunities requiring interest articulation structures that transcend local and national polities. Increasingly, influential international bodies that govern international trade, promote universal health and human rights standards, and manage global problems, such as military and environmental security, directly affect the daily lives of individual citizens. Nevertheless, rules of international diplomacy prevent routine participation in inter-state policy decisions by actors other than national governments. TSMOs represent one response to this deficit of infrastructures for articulating and representing the interests of citizens in inter-state decision arenas. Bringing together activists from more than two countries around a particular set of social change goals, these organizations promote transnational collective action in response to global changes. Once formed, TSMO structures provide ongoing resources for global activism, just as national SMOs provide enduring opportunities for marginalized groups to engage in political change efforts (Minkoff, this volume). In some cases, particularly in international negotiations around human rights and the environment, TSMOs have helped to defend and even to expand the access of movement actors to international agencies.

Transnational SMOs help increase the political resources available to advocates of social change. By relating a national or subnational conflict to international laws or norms, they raise the stakes for the government to a new level, where its relations with other states may become part of the cost-benefit equation. Activists within a given country can appeal to international institutions and states outside the targeted government's boundaries in order to bring external pressure upon that government, creating what Keck and Sikkink have called a "boomerang effect" (1998). For instance, human rights activists in Argentina were able to activate their international networks to bring pressure on the Argentine government in the form of U.S. trade sanctions and international criticism at the UN (Pagnucco 1997; Sikkink 1993).

In other cases, TSMO structures help to link an apparently local problem to its global sources. Greenpeace's campaign to end international trade in toxic wastes involved work to cultivate ties with local groups in order to help link these local anti-toxics actions with a global effort to strengthen an international treaty banning international trade in toxic wastes. The Greenpeace campaign involved visits to local groups in Africa, the publication of a "Toxic Trade Update" to inform activists about international legal efforts, and organizing kits to help activists tie their local actions to global political efforts. The presence of a transnational organization—Greenpeace—with the resources to coordinate a global campaign to eliminate the international spread of toxic wastes enabled local groups to relate their own struggles to a broader campaign. Whereas local efforts might only succeed in plugging up the drainage pipes through which wastes flowed, when linked to the global campaign they became part of an effort to eliminate the sources of wastes. Moreover, Greenpeace—with the help of local activist groups—dramatized the local effects of and opposition to toxic dumping, raising the costs of continuing the waste trade (see Smith 1999). The presence of transnational organizations, prepared to organize global campaigns and strategically link local conflicts with global policy processes, enabled these local/global links to be made.

Another way that TSMOs help provide ongoing opportunities for transnational collective action is by providing structured opportunities for activism, in the form of staff and volunteer activities as well as internships. Participation in a movement organization is very likely to shape participants' political views and future activism, as studies like Doug McAdam's *Freedom Summer* have demonstrated. Marullo, Pagnucco, and Smith's analysis of changes in how U.S. peace movement organizations framed the problems they sought to address showed that activism itself can generate new, often more radical, views of the sources of a problem and of its solutions. That study found that the trend among peace movement organizations was a move from more nationally defined strategies for promoting international peace to ones demanding internationalist approaches requiring more substantial policy shifts. Thus, the operation of social movement organizations should be seen as contributing to the ongoing initiation, training, and political socialization of movement participants. Although many transnational SMOs have minimal resources,[5] their collective presence signals many opportunities for individuals to participate in and learn about transnational collective action. Such movement-structured learning opportunities may be particularly important in transnational activism, which demands knowledge of a variety of cultural contexts as well as an understanding of complex international political processes and law.

Forging Links among Constituencies with "Thin Infrastructures"

Transnational social movement organizations serve as mediators between local interests and identities and global institutions. Their work, consequently, may be generating social capital relevant to groups that are marginalized in their own national polities, including political dissidents, the very poor, women, and religious minorities. This directly parallels the role Minkoff has observed in her analysis of national SMOs. The national groups Minkoff observed served as a source of empowerment for activists who are disempowered and isolated in their local communities. A similar claim can be made about transnational organizations, which—by relating various local problems to common global, structural sources—create common interests among otherwise diverse members.

Analysts of social capital have excluded national social movement organizations from their analyses because these groups are typically characterized by what McCarthy calls "thin infrastructures" (1987). Scholars like Putnam have claimed that such organizations lack the face-to-face contact deemed necessary to generate trust on the part of their participants. If this is the case, transnational SMOs can be especially irrelevant to the study of social capital formation, given geographic and resource constraints that limit interpersonal contacts among participants. Despite limited routine, face-to-face communication among members, as proponents of the claims of groups that are marginalized in their own political communities, TSMOs produce a "symbolic affiliation and social integration" that can be crucial to sustaining activist energies in the face of local apathy or even hostility (Minkoff, this volume). Social movement activists around the world increasingly find themselves faced with problems that are beyond the domain of national policy frameworks. International trade agreements reduce governments' ability to enact their own environmental and labor legislation, international environmental and security treaties prohibit certain activities, and World Bank and IMF lending policies strongly influence national fiscal and budgetary decisions, forcing groups seeking to change local practices to focus their energies well beyond their national capitals to centers of international decision making. The transnational identities cultivated in transnational social movements may be essential to sustaining activism around global problems.

The links generated by TSMOs among constituencies that have thin social infrastructures can serve to promote collective identities among culturally diverse individuals who might otherwise feel isolated and powerless. Such groups may include victims of human rights abuses, displaced peasants who are victims of large, state-run (and often World Bank–funded) development projects, local villagers living near toxic waste dumps, and laborers whose governments are engaged in a "race to the bottom" (in terms of social and economic regulation) to compete for international investment. In all of these and other cases, events and policies in the international system directly impact individuals' experiences. But the transnational sources of their problems make local or national action alone unlikely to improve their situations or to prevent new victims.

One illustration of the transnational identities fostered by TSMO action is found in EarthAction, a broad transnational coalition of local, national, and a number of international associations that promotes environmental justice, human rights, and peace. EarthAction's international campaigns typically result in hundreds of letters from around the world to affiliated organizations engaged in struggles with authorities and to government officials—many of whom don't expect international attention on local issues such as logging in Clayoquot Sound in western Canada. As the local group working on this issue, the Friends of Clayoquot Sound, stated in a letter to EarthAction, "the written letters of support that [EarthAction] initiated have really empowered our efforts here in Clayoquot Sound. We don't feel alone anymore. . . . [P]lease tell those who sent letters of support . . . how *very very* much we appreciated them doing that" (emphasis in original). In another case, a local indigenous peoples' coalition in Brazil wrote to request EarthAction's support of their cause: "We desperately need world-wide support to get the Brazilian government to demarcate our indigenous lands. Here in Brazil, the human rights movement alone is not strong enough to face the powerful political, military and economic forces. Change will only happen when the Brazilian Government feels global pressure." Partner organizations contacted in telephone surveys repeatedly expressed their appreciation for the work EarthAction does to remind them they are not alone in their struggles (EarthAction 1994, 1995). Brysk's analysis of transnational environmental cooperation in South America demonstrated a similar dynamic: She showed that South American indigenous leaders found more ready allies in northern-based environmental groups than in their own national, urban-based environmental associations (Brysk 1996:47).

While some transnational campaigns are quite successful in supporting transnational identities, the obstacles to doing so can hardly be overstated. Indeed, one of the earliest transnational movements, the Socialist International, broke down along nationalist lines with the outbreak of World Wars I and II (Chatfield 1997). Clearly, transnational activists in the latter years of the twentieth century have advantages in transportation and communication that those in the early part of the century lacked, but where communication is not a problem, frequently cultural or experiential differences complicate the formation of collective identities. For instance, Gabriel and

Macdonald's study of Mexican and Canadian womens' organizing efforts illustrates the challenges of transnational organizing where victims of the same global phenomenon—namely regional economic integration—frame their problems and solutions differently (1994). In the Canada/Mexico case, transnational identity formation was complicated by differences in experiences and needs of middle-class Canadian activists, immigrant Canadian workers, and poor Mexican women. Efforts to confront differences and to interpret their implications for strategy proved crucial to furthering any collective action by women in these two national contexts (Gabriel and Macdonald 1994).[6]

Strengthening the Global Public Sphere

Formed by agreements among states, international institutions generally exclude nonstate actors (and among these TSMOs) from any formal role in decision-making processes. Where participation is allowed, such as in the global conferences like the UN Conference on Environment and Development (1992), national governments define the parameters of nongovernmental organizations' access to and participation in international meetings. TSMO participation in international politics helps enfranchise individuals and groups that are formally excluded from participation in international institutions. It strengthens the global public sphere by mobilizing this disenfranchised public into discussions of global issues, thereby democratizing the global political process. It provides information channels and opportunities for transnational dialogue and learning that contribute to the realization of commonalities in experiences of global problems and to the emergence of transnational identities.

Within inter-state political contexts, TSMOs raise concerns about economic justice, human rights, and environmental integrity that are often ignored in negotiations among states concerned principally with gaining political, military, or economic advantages. Their participation, in other words, widens the discussion of what constitutes the global public good, and it challenges the prerogative of governments and transnational corporations to define that good for all people. TSMOs also help generate alternative policy proposals to global agendas and to advance these proposals through the policy process. Thus they expand both the global issue agenda and the range of policy proposals governments consider as they seek to address global problems.

In the 1980s a TSMO called Parliamentarians for Global Action worked to renew international consideration of a comprehensive nuclear test ban treaty. Their efforts to initiate a new forum for considering the treaty drew governments' and a global public's attention to an issue that powerful nuclear states (namely the United States and Britain) wished to keep off the global agenda.[7] The Greenpeace campaign mentioned above served to focus international negotiations on a clause in the Basel Convention, governing international trade in hazardous wastes, that created a loophole enabling companies to elude a ban in toxic waste trading. Both campaigns included efforts to expand public debate on the issues they raised, and they worked to go beyond the boundaries of what governments and powerful economic actors would have liked to see. Indeed, the history of diplomacy demonstrates the distaste government leaders have traditionally had (and continue to have in many cases) for public involvement in global policy debates. Greater public awareness of international debates and enhanced participation in global decision-making processes come at the expense of governments' historic monopoly of influence (perceived if not actual) over their foreign affairs.

Beyond raising the concerns of politically marginalized groups to global political agendas, TSMOs help channel information between local and national constituencies and political leaders. By attending and monitoring international negotiations, they provide local activists with access to information that would otherwise be unavailable to them. Their presence signals to governments that their statements and actions in what at one time were highly secretive and closed meetings among diplomats are being scrutinized by their home constituencies. Facing similar pressures from transnationally organized constituents and parliamentarians, governments in international negotiations may be more open to concessions that they would otherwise have resisted. TSMOs' campaigns help generate public attention to otherwise obscure intergovernmental negotiations, thus increasing government accountability in these arenas. TSMO activities help democratize global politics by providing avenues for actors other than governments to influence the public agenda and the decisions taken in global political contexts, by increasing governments' accountability to a global public, and by expanding public debate about the issues considered in international contexts. In other words, they are serving to build up the infrastructures of global civil society and to strengthen them vis-à-vis the inter-state system.

Conclusions

This analysis suggests that, even without face-to-face contact, transnational social movements can generate social capital that is crucial to democratizing the global political process. Moreover, it suggests that transnational political associations are one of the more important civil society actors in the global polity. Their work to target international decision-making processes and to mobilize local and national groups around global policy issues provides the only democratic oversight and participation in international politics. Thus, they are the main forces working to provide democratic accountability within an evolving global governing framework.

As Foley and Edwards have argued, the state/society dichotomy is inappropriate for understanding relationships between the state and politically engaged actors in civil society. State institutions have evolved through *interactions* between government agents, electoral or legislative actors, and elements of civil society—some of which are organizations specifically designed to intervene in politics to protect or advance particular policy goals. Of course, some social agents may choose *not* to play the political game and may even seek to overturn existing power relationships. Many actors—including many social movements—seek either to mitigate the effects of power imbalances within the existing political order, defending marginalized groups from further disenfranchisement, or to actively advance alternative policies. By ignoring the important mechanisms of interaction between the political system and both the neo-Tocquevillean emphasis on socialization and the contestatory emphasis on representation—namely political organizations and institutions governing associational and political life—traditional approaches have overlooked an important conceptual link between civil society and its consequences for governance and democratic participation.

The expansion of transnationally organized citizens' associations in general and of transnational social movement organizations in particular reflects a deepening global civil society. The transnational social movement sector, moreover, appears to be the most promising source of enhanced democratic participation in the emerging global polity. One of the important implications of the transnationalization of social movements (and of transnational social capital formation) is that advocates from widely varying cultural settings may share more with each other than with their compatriots. For instance, environmentalists from Oregon may feel more affinity with indigenous anti-logging activists in Indonesia than with their next-door neighbors. Following the arguments of Edwards and Foley, such individuals share a trust and affinity that stems from "their access to and appropriation of the same cultural reserves from which they construct their separate identities" (1997:670). Transnational social movements are the carriers and disseminators of global cultural reserves.

Transnational social movement organizations provide opportunities for activists to engage in international dialogue on global problems. They do this through newsletters, e-mail and Internet communications, as well as through periodic international meetings and conferences. So while face-to-face contact is limited in transnational organizations, it is still an important part of their operations. Such transnational dialogues are important for sustaining transnational activity because, although their problems stem from similar *causes*, activists in different national contexts often do not feel the same *effects*. Thus we saw that Mexican and North American women have recognized that their economic difficulties grow from NAFTA, but this recognition alone was not sufficient to generate collective action. Transnational dialogues within TSMOs have been an important part of the search for collective solutions here. In short, variation in the experiences of the effects of economic and political globalization can hamper transnational collaboration for social change. But transnational SMOs provide a mechanism for articulating, recognizing, and confronting transnational differences in viewpoints and priorities that are caused by class, race, gender, and national political contexts. The ability to engage in such transnational dialogue—either face-to-face or via newsletter or e-mail—is a necessary component for the formation of social capital and for the strengthening of a global civil society.

Transnational dialogues and perspectives on global problems also influence how movement participants define their own national political strategies. The transnational structure of TSMOs enables them to focus on the international political system so that they can relate international treaties and negotiations to specific national contexts. Thus, organizations like EarthAction have emerged to help movement actors decide how best to focus pressure on their national governments so that they can contribute to more effective *global* policies. Background information and tactical recommendations provided by TSMOs influence how national movement actors think about how their own government's policies relate to the broader global system.

Social movement organizations provide important links between the social organizations and infrastructures typically considered part of "civil society" and the inter-state system. The communications networks embedded in TSMOs—even though they lack direct interpersonal contact—help to generate cultural reserves and mobilizing frames relevant to global political debates. Their work to promote change has both influenced the structures of inter-state relations and democratized the international system. The process has been unequal, and the patterns of social movement mobilization still favor groups with relatively greater resources and access to political and economic institutions. At the same time, transnational social movement mobilization promises more than any other contemporary trend to help break down rather than reproduce existing global inequalities.

Social Capital as Social Movement Outcome

MARIO DIANI

Most contributions to this volume—and indeed most network research (Wellman and Berkowitz 1988)—view social capital as a determinant of social action, both constraining and enabling actors. However, social capital may also be treated as an outcome of action, as the latter persistently generates new types of interdependence and sometimes new solidarities (Cook and Whitmeyer 1992; Emirbayer and Goodwin 1994).[1] In this chapter, I outline an approach to social movement outcomes, focusing on their capacity to create new forms of social capital.

Although scholars have devoted substantial attention to the long- and short-term consequences of social movements (Gamson 1990[1975]; Giugni, McAdam, and Tilly 1999), conclusive evidence is still small (Burstein, Einwohner, and Hollander 1995; Kriesi, Koopmans, Duyvendak, and Giugni 1995, ch. 9; della Porta and Diani 1999, ch. 9; Giugni et al. 1999). The identification of causal paths linking movement actions to certain outcomes has proved to be a major problem.[2] How can we credit social movements with responsibility for macro-level changes (e.g., in gender relations, or in attitudes to the natural environment) that might as plausibly—often, more plausibly—be the outcome of far broader cultural and socioeconomic processes?

Many available analyses suffer from an unsatisfactory conceptualization of "movement outcomes." They focus largely on the determinants of success or failure, or on the factors accounting for different outcomes—however defined—rather than discussing what an outcome is (Giugni 1999). But as long as we keep defining outcomes as broad changes in policies, cultural perspectives, or lifestyles, we shall hardly move toward the sophisticated theories

I am grateful to Hank Johnston, chief editor of *Mobilization*, where a longer version of this piece was originally published (Diani 1997), for his authorization to reprint the article here.

that scholars like Tilly (1999) advocate. The problem of causal attribution will resurface again and again. A more modest approach would be to scale down our ambitions for causality claims and focus on the *structural preconditions* that may facilitate or constrain movements' attempts to influence both politics and culture. We should look at the social networks that movement actors are involved in and their evolution over time. To the extent that network position indicates influence and power (see Knoke 1990, ch. 1), social movement outcomes may be conceived as movements' capacity to achieve more central positions in networks of social and political influence.

To tackle these problems we have to reconstruct the linkages that connect movement actors to each other and to their social milieu. This would enable us to (a) assess the strength of ties among movement actors, and therefore their capacity to mobilize effectively at different times; (b) identify the movement allies in the polity and in other social circles, and their own social centrality, in order to assess the potential for influence that these linkages represent for the movements; (c) evaluate both the integration of movement leaders, representatives, and prominent figures into broader elite networks, and their centrality within movement networks. We must also discriminate between ties that are purely instrumental and do not presuppose any lasting social bond—for example, the occasional alliance between movement organizations and a political patron—from those that entail some degree of solidarity and mutual recognition. The latter are at the core of our concern here.

Social Capital as Movement Outcome

Social networks are universally regarded as a constitutive component of social capital. Accordingly, we can easily reformulate many studies of social movement processes in terms of social capital. First, the rise of collective action and its subsequent developments are affected by the distribution of social capital within potential movement constituencies. Mobilization processes rely heavily upon previous networks of exchange and solidarity (Klandermans, Kriesi, and Tarrow 1988; McAdam 1988; Gould 1995); individual involvement in collective action depends upon identification with other members of the social group, and mutual trust (Pizzorno 1978); and alliance building is easier when movement organizations share some core activists and can thus rely upon interpersonal channels of communication (Diani 1995, ch. 5). Second, we can also point to the importance of social capital as linking movement actors to political and social elites. For example, it may encourage more open attitudes among the elites toward political challengers and therefore improve the "political opportunity structure" for the latter.

Addressing the relationship of social capital to movement outcomes is less straightforward. In our own terms, while bonds based on collective solidarities—that is, social capital—show a strong capacity to persist even over long time spans (Rupp and Taylor 1987; Gould 1995), they rarely go through different political phases unchanged: on the contrary, new social bonds and new identities are also constantly generated (Melucci 1984). This applies to relationships between movement activists and sympathizers, as involvement in collective action creates new solidarities that often persist even when protest activities fade away. It also holds true, though, for links between social movements and their environment. While these linkages may not necessarily result in strong identities, they nonetheless create opportunities for exchange and communication among different social milieus. For example, social movements are often the breeding ground for new political leaders, who may gain recognition by political elites as representatives of previously excluded interests (Gamson 1990). Available—if still unsystematic—empirical evidence shows the influence of movement organizations in the policy process to be positively related to their leaders' integration among political elites (Knoke and Wisely 1990).

In other words, social movements do not merely rely upon existing social capital: they also reproduce it, and sometimes create new forms of it (Sirianni and Friedland 1995). We can regard their performance in this regard as an indicator of their social and political impact. This implies moving our focus away from causality, which can be properly addressed only at the cost of restricting our investigations to specific movement organizations or protest campaigns and concentrating instead on the preconditions of success, that is, on the structural position occupied by movement actors after phases of sustained political and/or cultural challenge. The structural location of movement organizations, activists, and sympathizers in broader societal networks affects their potential impact on policy making and/or on the production of cultural norms and codes. The central problem is no longer whether and how mobilization campaigns determine specific changes at different levels of the political and the social system. It becomes instead whether they facilitate the emergence of new networks, which in turn allow advocacy groups, citizens' organizations, action committees, and even single individuals to be more influential in processes of political and cultural transformation.

Forms of Movement-Generated Social Capital

I will illustrate the argument presented above by distinguishing between the *political* and the *cultural* impact of social movements, and between their *internal* and *external* impact (Rucht 1992). By political impact I refer to the complex of activities meant to affect all stages of the political and policy process. By cultural impact I mean the even broader set of actions meant to shape the processes by which contemporary societies produce and reproduce moral standards, information, knowledge, and life practices.

The "internal vs. external" distinction separates the impact of movement action on the movement's chances to mount further challenges at later stages (internal impact) from the movement's capacity to build bridges to its social environment. On the one hand, movements consist of networks of actors who exchange resources and information and share solidarity and beliefs (Diani 1992). In this perspective, assessing the outcomes of a social movement—even better, of a sustained series of protest activities and/or countercultural initiatives—entails assessing these networks at the conclusion of a wave of collective action. The impact of collective action will be stronger where permanent bonds of solidarity have emerged during the conflict. It will be weaker, in contrast, where collective action has consisted mainly of ad hoc, instrumental coalitions, without generating specific new linkages. In the former case, the newly created social capital is expected to increase the capacity of a movement to mobilize in the future. It will also affect the production and circulation within the movement of ideas, cultural practices, and alternative lifestyles.

On the other hand, movement actors will be more influential when their linkages to their environment—especially to political and cultural elites— are stronger and more extended. In this perspective, the impact of a social movement will be greater when, at the conclusion of a wave of collective action, there is greater integration of movement leaders and activists within elite circles (nationally, locally, or simply within the associational networks of their societies), than there was before the collective action began. Stronger ties of movement intellectuals to the social circles (mass media, corporate cultural operators, intelligentsia) that generate dominant interpretations of reality will also lead to greater movement impact.

Social Capital and Movements' Mobilization Capacity

Let us start our exploration with the most obvious example of social capital creation by social movements, namely, the impact of social movement mobilizations on subsequent collective action. Protest groups' chances of success are greater the stronger their roots in the communities they want to mobilize (Woliver 1993). Similarly, protest waves produce solidarities that last after the most contentious phases are over and provide favorable ground for later insurgency (Melucci 1984; McAdam 1988).

However, not all mobilization campaigns necessarily have the same effects on the production of social capital, as environmental and antinuclear mobilizations in Italy suggest. Between 1976 and 1978 massive antinuclear opposition developed for the first time (Diani 1994). Demonstrations took place, and antinuclear forces organized summer-long camps on proposed new plant sites. However, the antinuclear front was deeply divided. Radical left-wing organizations, opposing nuclear power in the context of their global challenge to capitalist forms of production, established only occasional alliances with moderate opponents. Moreover, the early antinuclear committees founded by concerned scientists and environmentalists failed to overcome the potential for dispute over divergent partisan affiliations and disagreements about strategies.

During that early phase of antinuclear action, little social capital was produced in the movement. Factionalism and ideological incompatibilities largely dominated the early timid attempts to forge a sense of common purpose among antinuclear forces. No permanent coordinating networks emerged from the conflict, nor did solid ties of mutual trust develop among the different actors in the campaign. Failure to develop extensive ties among critics of nuclear power in the late 1970s affected the structure of the environmental movement in the mid-1980s. Even then, systematic cooperation among movement organizations with different approaches developed only among the most central, core organizations. At the grassroots level, barriers between groups with different orientations (in particular, between conservation and political ecology groups) persisted, especially when activists had different political backgrounds. Having or not having been active in political ecology or other new social movement groups in the 1970s still represented for many 1980s activists a criterion for selecting allies (Diani 1995:118–26).

What lessons can we draw from this example? First of all, personal involvement in collective action at a given time was not merely a predictor of later participation; it also produced loyalties and identities that in turn affected the pattern of interorganizational exchanges during new mobilization campaigns. Second, collective action does not just produce ties and solidarity and, therefore, social capital, without further qualifications. Rather, the type of social capital being produced seems to vary according to the salience of political cleavages and identities. In the 1970s, bonds and mutual trust developed among those activists who shared a given perspective on environmental problems (for simplicity, either a conservationist or a political ecology perspective), but not among those holding different views. Therefore, the temporary coalitions that developed locally during the first wave of antinuclear opposition created the preconditions for the later growth of a political ecology sector in Italy. However, these ties were not strong enough to overcome traditional left-right barriers, which largely prevented cooperation among conservation associations, local opponents of nuclear energy, and more radical groups. On the contrary, fallout from these differences persisted well into the 1980s. In conclusion, while the early antinuclear movement in Italy had some effect in slowing down the construction of nuclear plants, its impact in terms of social capital was quite modest. When environmental action restarted in the early 1980s and took momentum after the Chernobyl accident, movement activists could rely upon previous linkages and mutual trust only to a limited extent.

Social Capital and Movement Subcultures

Sometimes the community ties and associational linkages in which both activists and prospective constituents are embedded present a distinctive subcultural profile. Contemporary ethnonationalist movements, especially those that developed in authoritarian regimes, from Franco's Spain to the Soviet Union, have largely relied upon previously existing solidarities in such cultural institutions as the local churches (Johnston 1994). Social movements also create new cultural infrastructures. This may be particularly evident after intense phases of political contention, such as in Italy in the second part of the 1970s (Melucci 1984); but it is a permanent feature of contentious collective action, as shown by the American women's and lesbians' movements (Taylor and Whittier 1992; Taylor and Van Willigen 1996).

The infrastructures that provide movement sympathizers with opportunities for alternative lifestyles, broadly understood, may take several distinct organizational forms. They may be close to the traditional model of the secluded, "world-rejecting" countercultures, or to the model of the religious sect (Leger and Hervieu 1983; Robbins 1988). Other times, symbols and lifestyles adopted by movement activists are quickly integrated into mass culture, thus depriving them of their antagonistic potential (Sassoon 1984)—the transformation of punk counterculture into punk fashion being an obvious example.

Somewhere between radical isolation and total incorporation, however, lie intermediate outcomes closer to the concerns of this chapter. Often, movement activists create cultural and social organizations that are part of broader countercultural networks. Leisuretime venues such as youth and social centers, urban communes, and cultural associations, or alternative businesses such as bookshops, cafes, food shops, and alternative media are usually related through networks that involve their members, customers, patrons, and/or clients, as well as those who make a living from them (Melucci 1984; Taylor and Whittier 1992). The ties that develop in such milieus should not be reduced to pure market relationships, although this component is obviously present. By participating in these activities—for example, by supporting cooperative banks and ethical investment funds—

people may demonstrate their commitment to specific causes or their willingness to differentiate themselves from ordinary consumption behavior. By doing so, they also strengthen specific solidarities and identities.

But why focus on social networks rather than simply note the existence of alternative activities? First, the strength of ties between pairs of alternative agencies, as measured, for instance, by the number of "clients" they share, testifies to the capacity of a specific movement subculture to reproduce itself, albeit in changing forms, and to resist market absorption. This may have important practical implications. For example, the existence of strong subcultural ties may have helped gay communities to better face the spread of AIDS in several Western European countries (Kriesi et al. 1995:225–30).

Second, it is important to ascertain the presence of actors capable of bridging different activities of a countercultural sector. In movement subcultures, centralized forms of leadership are usually neither wanted nor necessary (Melucci 1984; Diani and Donati 1984). Yet the circulation of ideas and identifying symbols is crucial for the reproduction of alternative identities. Strongly connected networks are also essential to spread practical information that can keep a subculture alive. While information often circulates through interpersonal networks, the role of specific agencies is also crucial. Among these, alternative media play a distinctive role.

For example, an independent left-wing radio station based in Milan, Radio Popolare, has been a crucial resource for the social movement sector since the late 1970s (Diani and Donati 1984; Donati and Mormino 1984). Not only does it represent an independent source of information about local and nonlocal events, it also directly promotes activities (concerts, mass parties and feasts, leisuretime activities, public debates) that have largely defined a left-wing, alternative lifestyle in Milan. Its obvious centrality as a communication hub at a time of decreasing alternative grassroots action has rendered this broadcasting station so influential that it may even be regarded as a specific source of collective identity. "Siamo dell'area di Radio Popolare" (We belong to the area of Radio Popolare), a group of listeners replied when asked to define their political and cultural identity. Local groups, cultural associations, and single individuals wishing to promote a specific cause regularly use the radio station to spread their messages to an audience that they know shares their basic values. The linkage that radio stations or other alternative media create among their audience is indeed based on solidarity and mutual recognition (first among these organizations and the individuals in their audience, and then among the individuals themselves through the intermediation of the alternative media). One may thus conclude that broadcasting stations and other movement cultural agencies play a double role: they represent an organizational resource for the movement, and at the same time a source of social capital.

Social Capital in the Political Process

The role of social movements in policy making and political representation
is another crucial area of investigation for those interested in social movement consequences, and one that has attracted much attention. From our
perspective, it is important to ask about the integration of social movement
actors within their broader communities, and about their capacity to mobilize consensus outside movement subcultures. The influence of personal
networks over individual orientations, beliefs, and behaviors has long been
recognized (Lazarsfeld, Berelson, and Gaudet 1948). Here our problem is
how to measure the influence of movement actors in these micronetworks.
Network approaches have usually focused on the form and composition of
ego-networks, that is, on the set of actors directly connected to a given individual, and on the ties among them (Knoke 1990:40–43). It would be
interesting to check whether individuals with backgrounds in or sympa-
thies for a given movement or set of movements play influential roles in
networks of informal discussion. In particular, does the influence of social
movements increase if they strengthen their roots among "opinion makers" in these micronetworks?

Available research points in this direction. Kriesi (1988) has analyzed
the relationship between Dutch citizens' inclination to support the petition
against deployment of cruise missiles in 1983 and their integration in
countercultural networks. This was measured by a questionnaire item asking for the number of members and/or sympathizers of different social
movements every citizen was connected with (1988:50–54). Kriesi demonstrates that the presence of ties between "ordinary" citizens and movement
activists increased the probability that the former would sign the petition
without specific encouragement from antimissile campaigners. In other
words, the resources required to mount effective protest against cruise
missiles were fewer where social movements could count on solid personal
roots in local communities. In our terms, the presence of social capital in
the form of local integration of activists increases both awareness about activists and movement groups and trust in movement members. This in turn
might facilitate their mobilization attempts.

Part of the social capital controlled by social movements also consists of
their leaders' integration in broader social and political elite networks. In
particular, studies conducted by Laumann and Pappi (1976) and Galaskiewicz (1979) have shown that "people and organizations that were more
central [in community networks] were: (1) seen by other community actors
as more influential in community affairs; (2) more likely to become active
in community controversies; (3) more likely to achieve their desired outcomes for these events" (Knoke 1990:130). One may look at the structural

position of individuals from social movement networks among elites in order to estimate a movement's impact on a political system. In this case, looking at the configuration of network ties is a useful corrective to the naive assumption that the cooptation of movement leaders is automatically a sign of movement success. The co-optation of leaders may result in the simultaneous weakening of their ties to the rest of the movement. In order to check this it would be useful to investigate to what extent they (1) become integrated in new elite networks while (2) remaining integrated in old movement networks. If both occur, this intermediate position allows coopted movement leaders to act as "brokers" between otherwise noncommunicating worlds, and thus to create new social capital for movement organizations (Marsden 1982; Gould and Fernandez 1989).

For example, representatives of the postpartum support and breast cancer movements in the United States have managed to develop conspicuous collaborative ties to health professionals, doctors and administrators, and scientific researchers. They have been recognized as legitimate participants in cultural and political debates on these issues but have never loosened their ties to the grassroots of these movements (Taylor and Van Willigen 1996). In this case, new social capital has clearly been created. In contrast, one should not conclude from the simple hiring of former environmental leaders as consultants to top corporations that the environmental movement has increased its social capital and therefore its influence. This may well be a plausible hypothesis, but it should be tested by looking at the persistence of the ties between the "Green" consultants and their former groups. Should relationships of mutual trust persist between the former and the latter, then the claim that the influence of the movement has increased would be substantially strengthened.

Social Capital and Cultural Change

Identifying the impact of social movements on cultural change is even more complex. Here I can offer only a very tentative discussion of how social capital generated by social movements may shape intellectual production, dissemination and diffusion of innovation, and community organizing.

Intellectual Production. I mean by this the activities and the institutional and organizational contexts in which new ideas are elaborated and circulated, artistic standards are set, criteria of taste are defined, technological innovation is developed, and moral and ethical principles are redefined, challenged, or reinforced. This conceptualization represents culture as an elite-driven process. A network approach may help us assess the structural position of individuals and organizations in networks of intellectual production. One example is the position of activist scientists in their respective academic and professional networks. For instance, in the last decades, many scientists voiced their opposition to nuclear power or, earlier, to the Vietnam War. They have also played the role of "mediators" between antinuclear and peace movement organizations, on the one hand, and the political and scientific establishment, on the other (Moore 1999). By doing so, they increased the movements' opportunities. Thus, the centrality of activist scientists in their professional communities is an indicator of the scope of protest movements in areas like peace, energy, and environmental protection and the amount of support and legitimacy they have secured.

Another example comes from the democratic movements in Eastern Europe in the late 1980s (Johnston 1994). While political repression largely prevented explicit political opposition, artists had long played critical roles as dissenting voices in those countries. Artists with strong ties both to global artistic milieus and to underground forces of change in their own countries helped circulate oppositional ideas before the socialist regimes collapsed and also proved to be powerful organizational resources after processes of change began (Johnston and Snow 1998; Glenn 1999). Vaclav Havel and the theater networks in Czechoslovakia and the ethnographic filmmakers in Estonia are cases in point. The capacity of oppositional movements to develop ties of mutual trust within artistic milieus, and therefore to generate social capital, could therefore be regarded as an important indicator of their success in the period preceding democracy.

Dissemination and Diffusion of Innovation. This corresponds to the more or less structured organizational practices by which new ideas are spread and new patterns of behavior and lifestyles are supported. Here again the range of examples is quite broad. We may look at the structural position of the economic actors engendered by social movements: for example, at the place of alternative shops, cafes, and cooperatives within their broader markets. As noted above, participation in such activities may be an opportunity to generate or consolidate social capital among movement sympathizers. At the same time, however, the capacity of movement organizations to reach beyond their current constituencies is also crucial for cultural diffusion. This may further increase the amount of social capital that movements control by creating regular ties among movement agencies, their clients, and other economic operators in their sectors.

Another possible focus is the impact of movement organizations in educational institutions. While it may be difficult for sympathetic teachers to speak up openly on political issues, they may address the moral and ethical dimension of social problems. Therefore it may be important to explore the connections between movements and educators or educational institutions. For example, most core environmental organizations develop cooperative strategies with schools, either through sympathetic teachers or the joint promotion of environmental education initiatives, or both. These activities are often made possible by personal linkages between schools and movement organizations, as well as by broader feelings of mutual trust. Both may be regarded as a reflection of movements' capacity to generate social capital.

Both intellectual production and dissemination are strongly affected by the media. The media system is first of all an arena in which themes are discussed, grievances are turned into public issues, competing definitions of reality clash, and cultural diffusion takes place; but the media are also specific actors with their own agendas and a considerable capacity to shape public perception of the problems (Hannigan 1995, ch. 3; van Zoonen 1996; Gamson 1999). Strong relations to the media system are therefore crucial for movement organizations. When social movements can create specific media agencies, these nonetheless need to be integrated into broader, professional media networks to be perceived as reliable sources of information, and thus extend their reach beyond movement boundaries. New Left radio stations in Italy often represented the broader independent radio sector, developing cooperative linkages to commercial stations on specific issues. This has once again extended the social capital they may rely upon, as well as increasing their potential for influence. More frequently, however, movements' access to the media depends on personal linkages. In the environmental or the women's movements, former activists- or sympathizers-turned-media-professionals are the most obvious channel for challenging groups. Frequently, however—especially in relation to issues with strong technical content, like most environmental ones—movement organizations become a major source for journalists who may not have previous ties to them (Donati 1996; Szerszinski 1995; van Zoonen 1996). While existing social capital facilitates movements' access to the media, news-gathering practices in turn facilitate the growth of new ties among movements, reporters, and editors.

Community Organizing. Movement organizations often move their focus away from political organizing toward a broader range of voluntary and cooperative initiatives aimed at community problem solving (Sirianni and Friedland 1995). Movement organizations or individuals with a history of movement activism have proved capable of establishing cooperation with community groups, public agencies, religious and lay foundations, and even private businesses. Environmental movement organizations increasingly collaborate with innovative industries to promote environment-friendly commodities and sustainable production technologies (Yearley 1992, ch. 3). Women's movement organizations join forces with public agencies, charities, and voluntary associations to promote self-help groups, battered women's shelters, and other not-strictly-political (albeit far from apolitical) activities (Taylor and Van Willigen 1996).

The recent development in Western countries of cooperative rather than confrontational relationships between social movement sectors and national and community elites marks a substantial change from the 1960s and 1970s. While not all forms of community organization are equally close to social movement milieus, nor have they necessarily originated from past social movement activities, substantial cross-fertilization between contentious and noncontentious collective action still seems to have taken place: "Activist social networks . . . have focused on problem solving, and developed new forms of local collaboration and civic education" (Sirianni and Friedland 1995).

Conclusion

Social movement analysts have traditionally treated social networks as predictors of collective action. Here I have reversed the causal order of the relationship and have focused on social movements' capacity to generate new ties and solidarities. In particular, I have suggested that the concept of social capital provides a useful analytical tool for understanding different types of movement influence and assessing social movements' potential to effect political and cultural change. By facilitating communication and strengthening trust and solidarity, social capital increases actors' control over their own lives. There is no reason why this general principle should not apply to social movements. To the contrary: as political challengers and/or advocates of cultural innovation, social movements both rely crucially on previous social capital and have to be able to generate new forms of it if they are to exert a lasting influence over their social environment.

IV

Social Capital Reconsidered

Editors' Introduction

Just what is social capital? Is it a "precise, ingenious, and fruitful" analytical concept with a distinctive though carelessly used analytic payoff, as Andrew Greeley argues below? Or is it simply an amalgam of time-worn notions from the 1950s and 1960s, that, with a bit of plastic surgery and a savvy public relations campaign, got a fresh, new look in the 1990s? Will social capital turn out to be little more than a passing intellectual fad, or does the concept capture something that actually shapes the outcomes of individual and collective actions as significantly as the current debate suggests?

The preceding chapters in this collection have generally treated social capital as a powerful social resource capable of facilitating individual and collective endeavors, though they differ in how they define the central concept. Variations in the availability or "use-value" of social capital, the authors assembled here argue, help explain a wide range of social processes and human relationships. The five essays in this final section take on the questions raised above and attempt to clarify the concept of social capital and differentiate between more and less useful ways in which it has been used in recent research.

Ken Newton argues persuasively for greater precision in attempting to specify the underpinnings of cooperation and civic engagement in contemporary democracies. He distinguishes three facets of the social capital argument: norms (particularly trust), networks, and consequences. Newton stresses the changing nature of trust in different social contexts, differentiating between three forms of trust—thick, thin, and abstract—and elaborating their relevance for the social capital debate. Newton also suggests that the role of voluntary associations in producing the societal benefits attributed to social capital are probably overstated by neo-Tocquevillean analysts. Instead he argues that new social forms of the kind discussed above by Debra Minkoff and Jackie Smith, as well as the pervasive institutions of school and workplace, may be important sources of civic engagement in contemporary societies.

The essays by Andrew Greeley and Jim Youniss, Jeff McLellan, and Miranda Yates respectively examine structural and social-psychological approaches to social capital. Greeley elaborates on the networks, or structural, facet of social capital. Greeley revisits James Coleman's original conceptualization of social capital, arguing for a "social structural" rather than "social-psychological" interpretation of the concept. He also notes that according to Coleman social capital was a value-neutral social resource—equally capable of facilitating the activities of church-based community volunteers and those of street-corner drug crews. The analytic utility of Coleman's conception of social capital is illustrated by examining the striking role of religious congregations in promoting one important form of civic engagement—volunteering. Youniss, McLellan, and Yates take a developmental approach to citizenship formation by first reviewing studies reporting links between youth's participation in organized activities and civic behaviors and civic engagement in later adulthood. They argue that youth participation can be seminal in constructing a civic identity that includes a sense of agency and social responsibility oriented toward sustaining the community's well-being in later adulthood.

Richard Wood uses the concept of social capital to analyze grassroots political action among the urban poor and working classes in the contemporary United States and illustrates the "contestatory function" of civil society in providing a counterweight to elite economic and political power. Rather than addressing the civil society debate directly, Wood does so implicitly by linking social capital to a concept of political culture defined quite differently than in the "civic culture" strand of political science critiqued by Foley and Edwards (1999) and by the editors in the next chapter. Wood examines the intersection of social capital and political culture in the work of organizations challenging antidemocratic public policy; he further highlights both the utility and the limitations of social capital as a construct for analyzing civil society.

In the final essay the editors ask whether and under what definition the concept of social capital provides analytical leverage capable of furthering our understanding of the political process in contemporary democracies. They consider recent empirical research to clarify the notion of social capital, theoretically distinguishing between approaches that center attention on "social trust" as a prime indicator of social capital and those that take a more decidedly social structural view. Following Bourdieu, the editors contend that resources in general, attitudes and norms such as trust and reciprocity, and social infrastructures such as networks and associations cannot be understood as social capital by themselves. Social relations may or may not facilitate individual and collective action—and therefore operate as social capital—depending on the specific contexts in which they are generated. The essay concludes by elaborating a "context-dependent" and "networked" definition of social capital as access plus resources.

Social Capital and Democracy

KENNETH NEWTON

... those who liked one another so well as to joyn into Society,
cannot but be supposed to have some Acquaintance and Friendship together, and some Trust one in another.
JOHN LOCKE, *Second Treatise on Government*

The Nature and Origins of Social Capital

Social capital may be understood and defined in terms of (a) norms and values (b) social networks, or (c) consequences—voluntarily produced collective facilities and resources. These three elements are no doubt closely related in the real world, but to run them together or to include two or three
in the same definition creates conceptual confusion, makes unwarranted
assumptions, and is likely to muddle empirical questions. Therefore, the
first section of this chapter considers the three aspects of social capital and
their possible relationships. The second and third sections raise empirical
questions arising out of the theoretical implications of the first part.

Norms And Values

According to the norms and values approach, social capital consists of subjective values and attitudes of citizens that influence or determine how they
relate to each other. Particularly important are attitudes and values relating
to trust and reciprocity, because these are crucial for social and political

Revised from an article of the same title in *American Behavioral Scientist* 40, no. 5 (1997):
575–86. I would like to thank the Wissenschaftszentrum Berlin fur Sozialforschung where I
spent a sabbatical year in 1996–97 writing the original version of this article.

stability and cooperation. Treated in this way, social capital focuses on values and attitudes involving the cooperation, trust, understanding, and empathy that enables citizens to treat each other as fellow citizens, rather than as strangers or potential enemies. It is a social force that binds society together by transforming individuals from self-seeking and egocentric calculators, with little social conscience or sense of mutual obligation, into members of a community with shared interests, shared assumptions about social relations, and a sense of the common good. Trust and reciprocity are crucial aspects of social capital, and as Simmel wrote, trust is "one of the most important synthetic forces within society" (1950:326).

Reciprocity does not entail the tit-for-tat calculations of rational-choice theory in which participants can be sure that a good turn will be repaid quickly and automatically. Generalized reciprocity is based on the assumption that today's good turns will be repaid at some unspecified time in the future, even by an unknown stranger (Sahlins, 1972). Therefore, it involves uncertainty, risk, or vulnerability (Misztal 1996:18; Kollock 1994:319; Luhmann 1988). To put it the other way around, daily life involves so many small risks that it is impossible without some trust in fellow citizens. Social capital is therefore responsible for converting the Hobbesian state of nature, in which life is nasty, brutish, and short, to something less dangerous and more pleasant. It forms the foundations of a cooperative and stable social and political order that encourages voluntary collective behavior; it generates the good will and understanding necessary for the peaceful resolution of conflict.

In some ways social capital is the modern social science analog of fraternity, which dropped out of political discussion in the late twentieth century. In the era of Reagan and Thatcher it was often assumed that only liberty mattered for democracy, and even then a narrow economic definition of liberty—market freedom. As the 1990s progressed, it was realized that democracy is much more than liberty, requiring a range of values, attitudes, and assumptions of the kind that comprise social capital. For that matter, even the economic transactions of the market are built upon the trust that turns "rational fools" into effective cooperators (Arrow 1972:357; Coleman 1988; Fukuyama 1995b). More generally, fraternity (or social capital) turns a self-defeating concern with individual liberty into a sustainable concern for collective liberty and social justice.

Networks

Some writers focus on social networks of individuals, groups, and organizations as the crucial component of social capital because an ability to mobilize a wide range of personal social contacts is crucial to the effective functioning of social and political life (see, for example, Kolankiewicz 1994:149–51). Although social networks and social trust may be closely related, there are two reasons why they should be kept separate conceptually. Norms and values are subjective and intangible; social networks and organizations are objective and observable. The first is "cultural," the second "social structural" (see Wood, this volume). Second, if we are to understand the nature and origins of social capital, it is important to keep norms and networks theoretically distinct. Simply stated, do close social networks generate the trust necessary for civilized social and political life, or is it the existence of widespread trust that makes the development of social networks possible in the first place? According to Tocqueville and Mill, networks of voluntary activity create trust and cooperation. Mill (1910:164) regarded associations as a means of "mental education," and Tocqueville believed them to be "the great free school" of American democracy. According to Pateman "we learn to participate by participating" (1970:105). Ostrom claims that "[n]etworks of civic engagement foster robust norms of reciprocity" (1990:206). And Putnam writes that "people who join are people who trust. . . . [T]he causation flows mainly from joining to trusting" (1995:666). Nevertheless, it is difficult to see how social networks can be created without trust to start with. The chicken-and-egg problem is difficult enough without confusing possible causes and possible effects in the same definition.

Outputs

"Social capital," wrote Coleman, "is defined by its function. . . . Like other forms of capital, social capital is productive, making possible the achievement of certain ends that in its absence would not be possible" (1988:98). Putnam also partly defines social capital in terms of its ability to "improve the efficiency of society by facilitating co-ordinated actions" (1992:167). Sometimes these products are physical—a village hall produced by voluntary effort—but they may also be common supply of fish from a lake, or grass from a village pasture (Ostrom 1990), or a crop harvested, or the capital accumulated by a rotating credit association (Ardener 1964; Geertz 1962). In modern society, examples include babysitting circles, community watch schemes, car pools, streets parties, and charitable goods and services.

It is not possible to define any social phenomenon in terms of its function or product, because the same phenomenon may have different functions or products, and different phenomena may share the same functions. Moreover, to include products or functions in a definition is also to confuse matters of definition with matters of empirical investigation. Social capital may indeed generate collective goods and services, a possibility that makes the concept especially interesting, but we should not assume that it does, and we must not include goods and benefits as part of the definition. Rather, ask the empirical question: Does social capital help generate collective goods and services, and if so, under what conditions?

Models of Democracy and Social Capital: Communal Society, Mechanical Solidarity, "Thick" Trust and Primary Democracy

"Thick" trust is an essential ingredient of small face-to-face communities (Williams 1988:8) where there is mechanical solidarity, or *gemeinschaft*, generated by intensive, daily contact between people, often of the same tribe, class, or ethnic background. Such communities are generally socially homogeneous, isolated, and exclusive and impose the strict social sanctions necessary to reinforce thick trust (Coleman 1988:105–108). Classic examples are tribal societies; but Western variations may be found in small, homogeneous, and isolated communities in rural peripheries or on remote islands. The West may also have pockets of "thick" trust formed in total institutions such as small sects, churches, ghettos, and minority communities. These tend to generate thick internal trust combined with distrust of wider society.

The thick trust of small, closely integrated groups is likely to be associated with simple forms of primary democracy involving direct political participation. In the modern world this is restricted to a few exceptional cases: New England towns and their meetings; small, alternative communities; isolated and homogeneous communities; and some special organizations. Primary democracy is generally impossible in modern large-scale states.

Voluntary Associations, Organic Solidarity, and "Thin" Trust: The Tocquevillean Model of Civic Virtue

Modern society is based upon the "thin" trust that is associated with the organic solidarity, or *gesellschaft*, of looser secondary relations. Particularly important are the overlapping and interlocking networks of voluntary associations, as so many writers claim, from Tocqueville, Mill, Durkheim, Toennies, Simmel, and Weber to the recent social capital literature. Thin trust is the product of weak ties, which, according to Granovetter's celebrated article (1973), constitute a powerful and enduring basis for social integration in large-scale society (see also, Evans and Boyte 1992).

In the Tocquevillean model, face-to-face interaction in formally organized voluntary organizations is essential for generating democratic norms among citizens (1968:355–59). Such organizations teach citizens the civic virtues of trust, moderation, compromise, and reciprocity and the skills of democratic discussion and organization. These are what might be labeled internal effects, but there are also external effects. Externally, multiple and overlapping groups create cross-cutting ties that bind society together across the faultlines of its own internal divisions and produce pluralist competition among different interests. Edwards and Foley (this volume) refer to the internal effects in terms of socialization for citizenship and to the external effects as representative or contestatory.

Are voluntary organizations really so important for social capital? It might be argued that school, family, work, and community are likely to have stronger internal effects, partly because they usually take up more time than voluntary organizations, and partly because they involve stronger emotional commitment. Quite large minorities of people in Western societies belong to no organizations at all, and only that small stage-army of largely middle- and upper-class activists and joiners devote much time to them.

It seems implausible to ascribe a crucial role to voluntary organizations if they account for only a few hours a week or month for a small minority of people. As Levi argues, "trust is more likely to emerge in response to experiences and institutions outside the small associations than as a result of membership" (1996:48). It is not surprising, therefore, that Coleman stresses the importance of the family and school in the development of social capital (1988:109–16), while Putnam stresses the family alone as the most important form of social capital (1995:73). The family, not associations, may in fact be the most fundamental source of social capital. Putnam also presents data showing that education is by far the strongest correlate of both trust and organizational membership (1994:667; see also, Verba et al. 1995:514; Uslaner n.d.:30). According to Verba et al. "Workplaces provide the most opportunities for the practice of civic skills, churches the fewest" (1995:320). The voluntary sector may not even be a particularly important source of social capital compared with family, work, education, and neighborhood.

Even if we were to accept the Tocquevillean model of civic virtue, there are still problems. To place a high level of trust in ordinary people (horizontal trust) is one thing; to place the same level of trust in politicians (vertical trust) is another. As Putnam puts it: "I might well trust my neighbors without trusting city hall, or vice versa" (1994:665). Similarly, I may trust some types of people, not others. Some organizations may promote generalized trust among a variety of citizens, while others divide their members from the rest of society. This underlines the need to distinguish norms from networks and to ask the empirical question: What kinds of networks and associations bear on what sorts of trust?

A third problem with the Tocquevillean model is its assumption that so-cial capital is a bottom-up phenomenon—that it is generated by grassroots participation. There is probably a close association between membership in voluntary organizations, political attitudes, and political activity (Verba and Nie 1972:184–87; 1996; Van Deth 1966:13–16), but this association is strongly influenced by social and political structures, as other chapters by Edwards and Foley, Berman, Whittington, and Heying in this volume argue. (See also, Tarrow 1996:394–95; Levi 1996:50). "What role orga-nized groups in civil society will play," write Foley and Edwards, "depends crucially on the larger political setting" (1996:47). For example, the move toward market competition, individualism, and elite withdrawal from com-munity politics in the 1980s may have helped to undermine the sense of trust and cooperation between citizens. A task for research is to explore the empirical connections between government policies, economic structures (see Heying, this volume), and social capital.

Modern Democracy:
Imaginary Communities, Abstract Trust, and the Mass Media

If we can distinguish usefully between thick and thin trust, perhaps we can go one step further and talk of abstract trust found in "imaginary," "empa-thetic," or "reflexive" communities. According to Misztal, trust may range along a continuum from the personal to the abstract, and, if so, the abstract form may be of growing importance in modern society (1996:72). This is because its growing size, impersonal nature, complexity, fragmentation, and speed of change make it increasingly difficult to depend upon either personal or impersonal forms of trust. As Luhmann (1988) argues, the modern world is full of complexity, uncertainty, and risk; abstract trust makes this more manageable.

In contemporary society the institutions of the mass media and educa-tion may be of particular and growing importance for the generation of ab-stract trust. Education provides us with a common background knowledge of society and its history, which facilitates the social interaction of other-wise disparate individuals, and schools teach the art of cooperation by means of collective learning tasks, team games, school plays, bands, and joint activities of many kinds. They also develop an understanding of ab-stract ideas such as citizenship, trust, fairness, equality, universalism, the common good, and the golden rule. At any rate, those with higher educa-tion demonstrate high levels of trust and organizational membership (Put-nam 1995b).

There is strong disagreement about the effects of mass media (Norris 1996; Newton 1996; see also, Greeley, this volume), but it is possible that they, too, help to generate abstract trust by acting as a force for cognitive mobilization (see, for example, Inglehart 1990:335–70; Dalton 1988:18–24; Sartori 1989). Others emphasize the capacity of the mass media to induce fear, isolation, political ignorance, low competence, and apathy—the "video-malaise" school of thought, upon which Putnam (1995b) draws when discussing the decline of social capital in the United States. I can do no more here than point out the potential importance of the media in relation to social capital, particularly their possible role in the generating of abstract trust.

There is some evidence for the existence of generalized and abstract trust in modern society. In their research on citizenship in Britain, Conover and Searing write:

> Today, blood and birth, like socialization and residence, are less important. . . . Culture is what counts. . . . [N]early two thirds said they regarded as "British" people from the Falklands and Gibraltar, people who were not born in Britain and perhaps not born of parents born in Britain, people who were definitely not socialized in Britain and, of course, were not residents of Britain either. . . . [N]ational communities are imagined communities. (1995:16, 18)

Similarly, interpersonal trust among citizens in the member states of the European Union is increasing (Niedermayer 1995:237). This may be due to individual processes, such as education, travel, or media consumption, or to the absence of war, or to top-down processes created by the European Community; but the populations of the EU are showing a growing capacity for abstract trust in the citizens of other countries, even though they may rarely meet them.

Voluntary Organizations and Social Capital

Different types of voluntary activity may have very different implications for social capital (see Stolle and Rochon, and Eastis, this volume). At one extreme there are formal organizations with written constitutions, elected officers, appointed staff, and bureaucratic premises; at the other there are amorphous networks of individuals who meet casually and irregularly to play darts, discuss a book, study religion, raise consciousness, organize a street party or a neighborhood watch scheme, run a babysitting circle or a carpool, organize a support group, drink in a bar, or play football in the park. Social science research favors the study of formal organizations because they are easier to identify, but they may be less relevant to modern social capital insofar as they tend to involve members only rarely or marginally in their daily activities. They are also likely to be the vertical and hierarchical organizations of which Putnam (1993a:173) speaks. The more informal networks, with horizontal linkages, may now be more important for the creation of abstract trust in modern society. Their direct external effects may be small, but their internal effects on participants may be large, and in this way their indirect external effects on social integration and social capital may also be of cumulative importance.

In recent decades there has been a growth of two newer kinds of formal organizations. The first, dating back to the 1970s (Gittel 1980), are professionally organized, businesslike associations that tend to be remote from their members but provide them, at arms length, with benefits and services. Although checkbook organizations of this kind may contribute to pluralist democracy (external effects), they may have little impact on social capital (internal effects). The second of the newer type of organization, the new social movements, or national social movement organizations (SMOs) are more controversial, some arguing that they are largely irrelevant to civil society and social capital, others saying that they "produce a kind of symbolic affiliation and social integration" (Minkoff, this volume).

There is, however, evidence that groups with a largely internal effect are growing in numbers and importance in modern society. According to Wuthnow (1994), there has been an expansion of such loose-knit, more-or-less organized, weak-obligation support groups in America in recent times. Barton and Silverman (1994) focus on another example in their study of the growth of common-interest communities. The literature on the new social movements also characterizes them as "network of networks"; they are more loose-knit and less bureaucratic and hierarchical than traditional parties and interest groups (Neidhardt 1985; Neidhardt and Rucht 1993; Tarrow 1994:187–98). Danish research also suggests a growing number of user groups, made up of decentralized and informal networks (Gundelach and Torpe 1996).

Putnam, quoting Wuthnow on "the weakest of obligations" feature of small support and caring groups, suggests that they "need to be accounted for in any serious reckoning of social connectedness," though "they do not typically play the same role as traditional civic associations" (1995:72). They are nonetheless an increasing feature of modern society, and *some* of them in *some circumstances* may well be more important than more formally organized voluntary associations in the formation of social capital. For some people, at some times, in some places they are sporadic and with little internal influence on participants; for other people at other times, they may provide a relatively strong experience with strong internal effects.

For example, a Danish study by Gundelach and Torpe distinguishes between the "classical" formal organizations of the Tocqueville type and what the authors call network associations. The latter are loose, informal, and personal forms of association that have a strong impact on the attitudes and behavior of participants. The authors conclude that "we should study other mechanisms of creating democratic values than the voluntary associations and . . . develop new theories of democratic values which take the character of the present society into account" (1996:31).

Another study of political participation in Britain (Parry et al. 1992:86–87) distinguishes between "[f]ormal groups such as trade union and interest groups which give an impetus to action [by virtue of] the existence of institutionalised channels of communication," and "informal or *ad hoc* groups of neighbors concerned over a local development or parents worried at some proposed change in local schooling." The evidence shows that group resources, formal and informal, are important for political participation, and that informal groups are at least as important as formal ones in generating satisfaction with political action (281), in educating their members both cognitively and effectively (289–90), and facilitating political action (423, 427), particularly in local politics (319). Perhaps their most interesting finding is that slightly more effort is involved in participation in informal groups (275). At best this is only circumstantial evidence, but it does suggest that informal groups may be no less important than formal ones in the formation of social capital (see also, Foley and Edwards 1997).

Conclusions

Putnam defines social capital as "features of social organization, such as trust, norms, and networks, that can improve the efficiency of society by facilitating coordinated actions" (1993a:167; see also, Putnam 1995b: 664–65). This definition includes three conceptually different aspects of social capital—norms, networks, and consequences. The advantage of the definition is that it combines three aspects of social capital in an interesting and provocative way; the disadvantage is that it runs different concepts together that should be separated, the better to study their empirical relationships. If we separate the three aspects of social capital, then a series of questions arises about its nature, causes, and consequences.

- Are norms of trust generated by social networks and organizations? Do voluntary organizations engender the civic virtues of trust and reciprocity, or are those who join trusting in the first place?

- Are schools, families, workplaces, and neighborhoods more important than voluntary organizations for the generation of social capital?

- What sorts of networks, associations, and organizations are best at generating social capital? What, on the contrary are responsible for the "dark side of social capital" and produce conflict, division, and the mischief of faction?

- What sorts of organizations improve the integration and efficiency of society by facilitating coordinated actions and making it possible to produce socially useful goods and services?

In short, to separate the three main dimensions or aspects of social capital is to raise a range of important questions about their relationships—in effect, to ask about the nature, causes, and consequences of social capital. The answers to such questions may require us to adapt the classical Tocquevillean model to fit contemporary conditions.

Coleman Revisited

Religious Structures as a Source of Social Capital

ANDREW GREELEY

The late James Coleman's concept of social capital has been misused in the current debate about the alleged decline of civic and ethical concern in America. Social capital, as Coleman defined it, is a potentiality that inheres in social structures and not a dependent variable. It is a resource available in social structures which facilitates actors who wish to seek certain goals and as such is neither good nor bad. Coleman's concept is a useful and even brilliant analytic tool which has been perverted in the present discussion, thus blinding us to the importance of examining social structural resources for and influences on human behavior. The article uses Coleman's meaning of the term to explore the influence of religious structures on one kind of civic participation in America and finds that such structures affect not only religious projects but secular ones too.

The term "social capital" has been misused and abused in American so-cial science, with little regard for its precise meaning, as part of the ongo-ing campaign of certain "pop" social scientists to announce the decline of society in the United States. The campaign, which has gone on as long as there have been social scientists in the United States, received new impetus from the work of Bellah and his colleagues (1985) reporting on the decline of "civic culture" and more recently in the work of Putnam (e.g., 1995), who seems to have been the first one to hail the decline of "social capital" to considerable academic and popular acclaim.

Revised from an article of the same title in *American Behavioral Scientist* 40, no. 5 (1997): 587–94. I am grateful for help in my work on volunteering to Gary Becker, Albert Bergesen, Ann Beutel, Sean Durkin, Virginia Hodgkinson, Michael Hout, Wolfgang Jagodzinski, Elihu Katz (for teaching me about social structure long ago), Doug McAdam, Margaret Marini, and the late James S. Coleman.

Bellah has often been refuted (Greeley 1992, for example), and Putnam's argument has been devastated by Ladd (1996). Only the most naive, however, would believe that these refutations will have any impact on the consumers of pop social science, particularly as they comment on American society in the mass media.

It might nonetheless be useful to return to the late James Coleman's original use of the words "social capital" and try to restore his meaning to the word so that those who care about precision in social science will be able to tell who is using the word properly and who is using it to mean everything and nothing. I will then endeavor to illustrate Coleman's meaning by analyzing how religious structures contribute to the engendering of social capital for voluntary community service.

Coleman's Model

Coleman (1988) introduced the term as part of the major project that occupied the final years of his life—the building of a bridge between sociology and economics (in particular the economics of the Chicago School), between the concept of the "socialized" notion of humankind and the "rational choice" notion. "My aim," he says, "is to import the economists' principle of rational action for use in the analysis of social systems proper, including but not limited to economic systems, and to do so without discarding social organization in the process. The concept of social capital is a tool in aid in this." Social capital, he tell us,

> is defined by its function not a single entity but variety of different entities, with two elements in common: they all consist of some aspect of social structures and they facilitate certain actions of actors—whether persons or corporate actors—within the structure. Like other forms of capital, social capital is productive, making possible the achievement of certain goals that in its absence would not be possible. Like physical capital and human capital, social capital is not completely fungible but may be specific to certain activities. A given form of social capital that is valuable in facilitating certain actions may be useless or even harmful for others.
>
> Unlike other forms of capital, social capital inheres in the structure of relations between actors. It is not lodged either in the actors themselves or in physical implements of production. (S 98)

Coleman then goes on to illustrate a number of examples of relational structures that generate social capital—the New York wholesale diamond market, South Korean radical youth "study groups" based on town or school or church of origin, support networks for children in Detroit and

Jerusalem, and the Kahn El Khalili market in Cairo. (He might have added organized crime families, whether Mafia or drug gangs.) He concludes, "Just as physical capital and human capital facilitate productive activity, social capital does as well. For example, a group within which there is extensive trustworthiness and extensive trust is able to accomplish much more than a comparable group without that trustworthiness and trust" (S 100).

Next Coleman details a number of aspects of social structures that can generate social capital:

- Obligations, expectations and trustworthiness of structures—such as are found, for example, in the rotating credit associations of Southeast Asia.

- Informational channels—such as networks that provide data about available jobs (my example, based on Wilson 1996).

- Norms and effective sanctions—such as those against crime in certain neighborhoods.

- Closure of social networks, in which all actors interact, one with another.

- Multiplex relationships in which resources of one relationship can be appropriated for use in a second relationship (in conversation, Coleman often referred to the multiplex relationships in which faculty colleagues are also parents of students in the same school—such as the University of Chicago Lab School).

He strongly emphasizes the social capital inherent in parent-child relationships, and also its variability, depending on the nature of the family social structure. He urges survey analysts to consider asking not merely about parental education but about how parents relate to their children in facilitating their educational development. More important, he suggests that the absolute level of parental education is the time and energy parents invest in helping children with their studies.

Finally, he analyzes the dropout rates of Catholic and other religious schools as compared to public and nonreligious private schools (holding constant background variables) to demonstrate that the "multiplex" relationship between religious structure and educational structure generates considerable social capital in holding down dropout rates. (Bryk 1994 demonstrates that much of the extra net effectiveness of Catholic schools can be attributed to their tighter community structures.)

The Coleman model is precise, ingenious, and fruitful. It provides a perspective for looking at human social structures that enables the analyst to look for the work of this powerful social resource in human relationships, effecting either human capital (as in the case of families and schools) or profit (as in the case of the diamond market or the Cairo marketplace). Social capital is a dimension of human social structures whose importance is both obvious and little noticed. It is, in this writer's opinion, *sociological par excellence*. It does not yield to the propensity of much sociological analysis to fall back on social psychological explanations. Yet it does not enter into most sociological model formation.

I argued often with Coleman that there was a tension between his social capital perspective and his notion that "natural relationships" were being replaced by "artificially created" relationships. It seemed to me that (a) in fact the "natural relationships" remain and "artificial relationships" have expanded and (b) in most cases of social capital the structures have taken on the intensity of natural relationship. In our time one has more relationships that take on many of the traits of "natural relationships."

I trust it will be perceived that, as Foley and Edwards (1996, 1999) observe, for James Coleman social capital is neutral (see also Foley, Edwards, and Diani, this volume). Where it is present it facilitates the goals of actors, whether those goals be morally and socially desirable or not. It is therefore not always a "good thing" as much of the current fuzzy-minded discussion about the decline of social capital would seem to suggest.

Moreover, the suggestion that social capital is on the wane is an oxymoron. Social capital is not an appropriate dependent variable to measure the civic health of a society. One can speak of a decline of social capital only if one is able to prove that either the social structures of a society are on balance declining or that existing social structures do not generate as much social capital as they "used to" in the happy days of Alexis de Toqueville. But how does one count and then analyze all the structures of human relationships in a society? And how does one measure the potential at some time in the past? The most one can do is to analyze specific social-capital–enhancing structures in the present and compare them with similar structures in the past—such as the Cairo market or the New York diamond market or the Mafia (in Chicago usually called "The Outfit" or "The Boys on the West Side").

Moreover, if a given network of relationships does not generate in fact (rather than merely in the selective memory of a once "golden age") the social capital it once did, it does not follow that the presumed total amount of social capital in the society is declining. Maybe the Mafia has less social capital then it once did (though that is by no means certain) but maybe that has been compensated for by the increase in social capital in the drug gangs.

The appropriate dependent variables to measure a decline in civic and social responsibility are behaviors in which actors act to enhance the general welfare. But there are many such behaviors and many measures of them. Responsible social science does not rush to conclusions based on only a few such measures. The General Social Survey data show a decline in organizational membership in the United States, but the World Values Study data show an increase—in great part because the WVS lists organizations like community groups and environmental groups about which the General Social Survey had not begun to ask in 1972. If one is responsible, one is very cautious about making sweeping generalizations concerning American society, if only because empirical results are usually far grayer than such generalizations.

An Illustrative Analysis

I have used the volunteer phenomenon in the United States to indicate that social and ethical concern are if anything increasing (Greeley 1997a; 1997b). Americans are significantly more likely to volunteer than any other country in the World Values Study, and American volunteer rates increased dramatically between 1981 and 1990. Moreover, in all the countries studied, religious organization membership and church attendance (except in Ireland) were strong predictors of volunteer service. Indeed, after social structural and general organizational membership variables are held constant, these two religious variables reduce to either insignificance or near-insignificance the differences between the United States and other countries in volunteer rates. Thus 47 percent of Americans and 30 percent of West Germans volunteer; but if American religious attendance and religious membership rates are reduced to the level of West German rates, the proportion volunteering is not significantly different between the two countries. If one estimates a volunteer hour is worth the average salary paid to an American worker, the extra level of religious behavior in the United States (in comparison to West Germany) adds the equivalent of $70 billion a year to the American economy.

This finding by itself does not necessarily prove that religious structures are generating social capital. Probably attending church with others and belonging to organizations with them creates structured relationships that facilitate volunteering. One would like to know, however, whether in fact it is the religious structures themselves that lead to the act of volunteering. Fortunately, data from Independent Sector research (Hodgkinson 1995) enable one to address that question directly: "How did you first learn about the volunteer activities you have been involved in for the past twelve months?" Respondents could answer either "through participation in an organization" or "asked by someone." Among the responses available under "organization" were "church, synagogue or temple," and under "someone" was "someone at my church or synagogue." Thus one has two direct measures of social capital at work.

In the 1992 adult sample (n = 5398) 52 percent of Americans had volunteered and 28 percent of the volunteers, by far the largest proportion, volunteered for religious projects (table 1). Moreover, of the volunteers,

TABLE 1. Social Capital for Volunteering in Religious Structures

Type of volunteer	% of all volunteers	% motivated by religious structures
Health	13	26
Education	16	35
Religious organizations	28	95
Human services	12	29
Environment	6	12
Public/society benefit	7	16
Recreation-adults	7	13
Arts, culture, humanities	6	14
Work related	7	20
Political	5	33
Youth	14	33
Private	2	8
International/foreign	2	5
Informal/alone	23	50
Other	2	4
All	52	34

$N = 5,398$

34 percent said that religious structures (either organizational or inter-personal) were responsible for their volunteering. While it is not unexpected that these religious structures would affect 95 percent of those who volunteer for religious projects, it is impressive that the religious structures also strongly affect many other kinds of volunteering—informal (50 percent), education (35 percent), political (33 percent), youth (33 percent), human services (29 percent), health (26 percent), work-related (20 percent), and public benefit (16 percent). Religion (i.e., religious structures) generates social capital not only for its own projects but for many other kinds of voluntary efforts. It is far and away the strongest resource available to those whom James Coleman would doubtless have called "voluntary actors."

Furthermore, in the 1990 teen sample (table 2), although the patterns of volunteering are somewhat different (religious projects down, arts, environmental, and informal up), virtually the same proportions of teens as adults volunteer (54 percent) and report influence by religious structures (32 percent). Thus volunteering, much of it generated by social capital associated with religious structures, seems to have become an accepted part of American life among both the young and the not-so-young. The social capital generated by religious structures supports not only formally religious volunteering but "secular" volunteering as well.

With these baseline measures, the impact on voluntary service of social capital within religious structures can be monitored through the years. If

TABLE 2. Social Capital for Volunteering in Religious Structures

Type of volunteer	% of all volunteers	% motivated by religious structures
Health	16	25
Education	13	19
Religious organizations	17	32
Human services	2	31
Environment	23	41
Public/society benefit	25	40
Recreation-adults	7	34
Arts, culture, humanities	28	37
Work related	29	52
Political	7	14
Youth	27	43
Private	20	37
International/foreign	8	8
Informal/alone	47	75
Other	16	30
All	54	32

$N = 1,705$

there is a notable decline of the influence of religious structures, accounting for about a third of the volunteers, then one can fairly say that this form of social capital is eroding in this particular structure in relation to this particular activity. However, such a finding, while important, addresses only one form of social capital in relation to one specific kind of activity. Other structures might replace religious social capital in mobilizing volunteers. Religious social capital might continue to affect other actions (such as in schools), perhaps more strongly. Hence society-wide generalizations about the decline of social capital could not be made on the assumed decline of this particular manifestation of it. Thus one perceives the folly of the present broad generalizations about American society on the basis of skimpy data which do not measure social capital at all.

Conclusion

Unlike James Coleman, most American social scientists tend to avoid religion whenever possible, save when they can show it has negative effects. This analysis demonstrates the folly of such bigotry. Religion is (at least potentially) a powerful and enduring source of social capital in this country, and indeed of social capital that has socially and ethically desirable effects. Only the deliberately blind will continue to ignore religions as a source of social capital or deal only with their negative effects.

Note that this analysis in its present form would not have occurred to someone who had not read Coleman's article or who had not learned to view social reality the way Coleman did. Nor would it have occurred if the Independent Sector had not asked questions that made analysis of social capital possible. Yet there is substantial intellectual payoff in understanding American society in the confluence of these two phenomena. The present writer, who can hardly be said to be unaware of the importance of religion in this country, was nonetheless surprised and impressed by the impact of religious structures in "secular" volunteering. The story of religiously linked relationships has a powerful impact not only on the story of religious generosity but on the story of "secular" generosity as well.

This analysis also illustrates how Coleman's discovery of social capital ought to be used: it is an analytic tool suitable for investigation of specific social structures and, as such, is a useful weapon in the armory of the social scientific analyst. It has been a long time since Katz and Lazerfeld (1955), and yet American sociology (in particular) still seems curiously innocent of the sociological (i.e., social structural) imagination and pathetically inclined to fall back on social psychological explanations or ritualistic invocation of the evils of television.

That this brilliant and potentially useful concept could be blurred and perverted as a weapon for those who wish to indulge in the popular game of lamenting all the things that are allegedly wrong with this country is a depressing commentary on just how stupid social scientists can become when they take on the roles of biblical prophets or Puritan divines.

A Developmental Approach to Civil Society

JAMES YOUNISS, JEFFREY A. MCLELLAN,
AND MIRANDA YATES

This paper brings a developmental perspective to the ongoing discussion of the erosion of civil society in the United States. Instead of asking which social structural factors account for the waning of civil society (Putnam 1995, 1996), we focus on the question of how individuals become adults whose civic engagement sustains, reforms, or transforms civil society. We will show the value of framing the problem in terms of the construction of *civic identity*, which entails the establishment of individual and collective senses of personal agency, social responsibility, and political-moral awareness (Yates and Youniss 1996; Youniss and Yates 1997).

We begin with a review of studies that report a linkage between certain kinds of social participation during youth and civic engagement by these same persons later in adulthood. We then show how the concept of *civic identity* may account for the developmental linkage. Finally, we review other studies that illuminate the process by which youth's participatory actions shape political-moral aspects of a critically minded civic identity. Our developmental approach is presented to explain how some, more than other, individuals within any cohort or generation become committed to civil society. Most commentators on contemporary culture overlook the issue of development, preferring to contrast the fragility of present civil society with earlier eras in American history. The contrast is abetted by a detective story plot that searches for causes in social structural change. Probable suspects include new demands of work, family dissolution, isolating effects of television, and the like. An advantage of our developmental approach is that it directly addresses the question of how

Revised from "What We Know About Engendering Civic Identity," in *American Behavioral Scientist* 40, no. 5 (1997): 620–31. This research was sponsored in part by the William T. Grant Foundation.

civil society may be generated in any era and how individuals come to differ in their civic engagement in any era. Thus, instead of positing civil society as a given from which the nation has recently deviated, we focus on processes by which civic commitment develops within individuals who are constructing their personal and social identities.

Youth Participation and Adult Civic Engagement

Without a developmental perspective, Putnam's essays offer a top-down approach to civic engagement. He claims that voting, joining groups, and trusting others have declined across generations during the present century. He attributes the unraveling of the civic fabric to changes in the macro social structure. We take an alternative approach that seeks to understand how individuals develop civic engagement across a range of structural conditions and, thus, are able to participate in the renewal and continual reform of civil society.

The youth era is particularly opportune for shaping the development of identity, with its civic component. The studies we will review demonstrate that participation in organized, norm-bearing groups during youth differentiates civic engagement in adults several years later. In contrast to the search for structural causes of "social capital's strange disappearance," we focus on what is already known about generating civic engagement in individuals and generations of youth.

Table 1 synthesizes data reported by Ladewig and Thomas's (1987) retrospective study of former members of 4-H. In 1985, adults (mean age around 43 years) listed their current membership and leadership in local civic, service, church, and professional groups. They also recalled their membership in youth organizations roughly twenty-five years previously. The sample was purposely comprised of adults who had likely been former 4-H members, but it also included adults who belonged to other youth groups (e.g., Boy Scouts, YMCA) or to no youth groups.

The left two columns present odds ratios for the likelihood of current membership in voluntary groups of former 4-H members compared with adults who belonged to no youth groups. Ratios in the first column demonstrate that former 4-Hers, compared with former non-members, are more likely to be members of each type of group; for example, former 4-Hers are 1.99 times more likely to belong to civic groups and 1.81 times more likely to belong to business groups. The next column reports ratios for currently being an officer in these voluntary groups. Former 4-H members are considerably more likely than former nonmembers to hold leadership positions; for instance, 2.89 times more likely to be officers in civic groups or 1.61 times more likely to be officers in business groups.

TABLE 1. Likelihood of Adult Participation in Voluntary Organizations as a Function of Participation during Youth (Ratios compare youth participants to nonparticipants)

Adult organization type	Youth 4-H		Other youth organizations	
	Member	Officer	Member	Officer
Civic	1.99[a]	2.89	2.13	3.02
Business	1.81	1.61	1.52	1.00
Community	1.97	2.33	1.64	1.83
Agriculture	4.26	7.17	2.63	3.83
Political	3.79	3.20	3.96	2.20
Church	1.84	1.89	1.50	1.55

[a] To be read: Adults who belonged to 4-H during their youth are 1.99 times more likely to be members of civic organizations today than are adults who were not 4-H members during their youth.

The right-hand columns report odds ratios comparing adults who had belonged to youth organizations other than 4-H, with adults who had not belonged to any youth groups. The results are nearly identical to those for 4-H members. Having belonged to Scouts or the YMCA during youth increased the likelihood of membership and office holding in voluntary groups for adults in 1985.

Beane, Turner, Jones, and Lipka (1981) studied adults in 1979 who, as high school seniors in 1945–1949 in northwestern Pennsylvania, participated in a community-based planning project. For four consecutive years, a particular teacher's senior class in civics education assisted the local town government in planning for urban growth. Each class collected and analyzed data under the teacher's supervision and in coordination with town officials. Other seniors in the same school who did not work on this project served as a comparison group. Thirty years later, Beane et al. located the school's alumni, 28 percent returned a questionnaire. According to responses from 26 of the participants and 56 nonparticipants, participants in the planning project, compared with nonparticipants, were 4 times more likely to have been members and 2 times more likely to have been officers in voluntary civic or service organizations over the past 30 years.

Hanks and Eckland (1978) report data from 1,827 adults who had been high school sophomores in 1955 and were part of a national sample of 97 high schools surveyed by the Educational Testing Service. The longitudinal sample was composed of adults who attended 42 of these schools and who were contacted by mail 15 years later. It was found that participation in extracurricular activities in high school predicted adult membership in voluntary associations, independent of socioeconomic status, academic aptitude, and grade-point average. Membership in voluntary associations in 1970 also was significantly associated with voting and with trust in the political system. The critical factor of participation in extracurricular activities during high school included school publications, debate-political clubs, social service groups, drama, music, or science clubs, and student government.

Otto (1976) looked at males who were born in 1940, initially sampled as 17-year-old high school students in Michigan in 1957, and followed up as adults in 1972. Of the original 442 students, 327 were located in 1972 and sent questionnaires about their current political behavior, among other things. As with Hanks and Eckland, adults recalled their extracurricular activities during high school and listed their current membership in voluntary associations (e.g., labor unions, church clubs) and described their current civic behavior (e.g., voting, donating money to political candidates). Otto reported that high school extracurricular activities significantly predicted adults' participation in voluntary associations and political activities, when socioeconomic status and educational achievement were controlled.

Verba, Schlozman, and Brady (1995) reported on a 1990 sample of 15,053 adults who were contacted by telephone in 1989 and on a subsample of 2,517 adults who were interviewed in depth. When asked about voting, working on campaigns, protesting, and the like, 71 percent of the sample said they had recently voted, 6 percent had participated in protests, and 17 percent had taken part in local community activities. Also, 79 percent of the sample reported current involvement in one or more voluntary association (e.g., religious, ethnic, senior citizens, charitable, political, business, cultural). When factors that predicted adult political and associational involvement were explored, regression analyses showed that the two strongest predictors were participation in school government and membership in school clubs or interest groups, excluding athletics.

The Development of Civic Identity

Our thesis is that participation in organized groups during one's youth has a lasting impact for two reasons. Practically, it introduces youth to the basic roles and organizational processes required for adult civic engagement. Personally, it helps youth incorporate civic involvement into their identity during an opportune moment in its formative stages. Such construction of identity in turn persists and mediates civic engagement through adulthood. The formation of civic identity, then, is the hypothesized developmental link across time and the factor that differentiates adults in the degree of their civic engagement.

Verba et al. (1995) propose that organized activities in "American high schools [provide] hands-on training for future [civic] participation." Activities in organized groups "give opportunities to practice democratic governance" (425). Participation in school government, production of a yearbook, and community service projects teach youths that their individual and collective actions make a difference in their high school and wider community. Verba et al. further propose that participation introduces youth to forms of political discourse and role-taking in the broad sense of seeking mutual understanding among people with alternative perspectives.

Organizations typically provide experience in following disciplined protocols that is tantamount to training in civic practices. For example, involvement in teams or dramatic productions teaches youth how to coordinate actions and balance respective roles, to produce collective results that are greater than what any individual alone could achieve. In producing a yearbook, for instance, youth experience the virtues of coordinating a variety of talents that are focused on a shared goal. When editors, reporters, photographers, layout artists, and salespeople play their respective roles, the result is clearly greater than the individual parts. As these coordinated actions enhance one another, they also benefit the larger community.

Theorists usually do not specify the detailed practices needed to sustain civil society. When one asks why adults join groups, which social practices they must use, or what they hope to accomplish thereby, an answer may be found in the developmental picture that emerges from an analysis of youth organizations. The experiences that participation provides allow youth to see that actions are interdependent, that group discipline serves a common purpose, that differences among participants can be negotiated, and that multiple perspectives can be coordinated. In addition to these elemental organizational practices, youth are also exposed to direct effects of cooperative effort, effort that enhances one's own actions and benefits other persons.

Civic Identity

In addition to offering practice with group processes, many youth organizations typically provide direct exposure to explicit ideological orientations or worldviews. For instance, in 4-H and church groups, explicit ideologies inform practices by justifying service projects as contributing to the community's good. The 4-H pledge illustrates the point well: "I pledge my head to clearer thinking, my heart to greater loyalty, my hands to greater service, and my health to better living . . . for my club, my community, my country, and my world."

As Erikson (1968) observed, ideological clarification is important for youth, who are in the midst of constructing their identity. In our pluralistic society, which has also targeted youth as a commercial market, youth need assistance in differentiating alternative interpretations of daily events.

Ideological positions help youth sort through a vast array of options and facilitate the task of finding meaning that has transcendent value. As youth seek meaning that also has historical legitimacy, established groups provide opportunities for exploring options. Membership in groups allows testing of ideological positions, which can then be rejected or incorporated into their developing ideologies. The ideological component of groups, of course, remains important for adults as they decide which groups to join and support or whether to join at all (Zald, 1995).

Flanagan et al. proposed that organized groups that provide youth with experience in community service connect them "to the broader polity and, in that process [, help them] develop an understanding of themselves as civic actors" (1997:3). We have argued similarly from our studies of high school students who proceeded through a year of community service at a soup kitchen for the homeless (Yates and Youniss 1996; Youniss and Yates 1997). As the year progressed, students started to view the people they served, no longer stereotypically as "the homeless," but as individuals with various problems and complicated life histories. Students also started to assess themselves consciously as being in fortunate positions relative to homeless persons, but equally often as being potential actors in the reforms needed to redress poverty and related problems. Students also began to raise questions about the political system that allowed homelessness to expand, and about political choices regarding accessible housing, job training, and welfare reform. Finally, students also addressed moral and ethical aspects of homelessness: Who has responsibility to attend to this problem? And what does justice demand regarding income inequality?

We propose that the raising of these questions at this moment in development illustrates how active participation in social service can contribute to the formation of identity. Service allows youth to see society as something human actors with political and moral goals are always constructing and shaping, rather than as an unchanging, preformed object. Instead of viewing themselves as too young to have power, youth observe that their actions are helpful to individuals who are homeless, and they begin to comprehend how poverty comes about and what are its consequences. Instead of thinking of society as determined by impersonal forces, youth recognize that agency brings responsibility for the way society is and for the well-being of its members.

It seems reasonable to propose that, as youth raise these questions, they are reflecting on their relations to the broader polity and making choices about their roles in it (Flanagan et al. 1997). Participation in the remediation of social problems stimulates the civic aspect of identity just when youth are beginning to articulate the extent of their agency, their social responsibility to others, their part in political processes, and their commitment to moral principles.

When young people's emergent identities are based on civic behavior (Verba et al. 1995), they may take a different direction in their identity development than will youth who, for whatever reasons, lack participatory experience. Erikson argues that organized involvement in society provides youth with a sense of *cultural consolidation* that stems from acting jointly and successfully (1968:31–33). Participation adds social meaning to identity by providing specific information about being a civic actor, along with like-minded others, in the building of society. Individuals thus construct society by their practices and, in the process, become an essential part of it (Giddens 1983). The individual and society are not separate entities but complementary parts of a single relationship.

Examples of the Making of Civic Identities

Thus far we have proposed that youth experiences in organizations may foster adult participation via the learning of organizational practices and seeing oneself as a participant in the making of society. We will now review a second set of studies that provides evidence for three aspects of civic identity that are not so evident in the studies reviewed above. One is the collective component essential to the concept of civic identity. Another is awareness of the political and moral dimensions of society. And the third is that civic identity can be critical as well as supportive of existing society. The studies to be considered involve the same cohort of youth as the studies above, but focus the definition of participation on active attempts to reform society. A select portion of the cohort that came of age in the 1950s and 1960s was engaged in a collective political effort to achieve social justice and civil rights through concerted public action. In contrast to school-based participation in extracurricular activities, these actions were patently political, consciously critical, and grounded in ideological and moral justifications.

Much has been written about the activists of this generation who participated in social movements to secure civil rights and racial equality in the American South, to reform governance on the nation's college campuses beginning with the "free speech" movement at Berkeley, and to sway public opinion for or against the United States' military involvement in Vietnam. We propose now to make use of what these studies tell us about the processes by which lasting political and moral components are incorporated into youth's identities. Inspection of these movements gives a magnified view of the formative processes that take place when political involvement and moral commitment are heightened. DeMartini (1983) reviewed seven studies that examined documented participants, compared them to nonactivists, and followed them from three to eleven years later. It was consistently found that participants who held radical to liberal political views in their youth became less radical but retained their left-of-center outlooks, both absolutely and in comparison with nonactivists, over time. This was true of civil rights activists (two studies), Berkeley Free Speech participants (three studies), and anti-war protesters (two studies). DeMartini concluded that participants had not "blended into a political mainstream and become indistinguishable from age cohort members with comparable educational background who were nonactivists" (199)—the radical turned stockbroker, Jerry Rubin, notwithstanding.

Participants also remained distinct from nonparticipants on measures of political and civic activism. For example, White adults who as students had participated in civil rights demonstrations in Florida were 10 times more likely 11 years later to have participated in political demonstrations and 1.49 times more likely to have participated in conventional political activities such as working on electoral campaigns. Although free speech participants had become less radical in their outlook over time, they belonged to more voluntary associations as adults than did the nonparticipants. Finally, antiwar protesters were more likely than nonparticipants to have given money to a political candidate, attended a political rally, contacted a public official, and attempted to influence other people's voting choices.

Two more recent reports are focused on former participants in the 1950s and 1960s Southern civil rights movement. Both studies had comparison groups of nonparticipants and report findings that support the youth-to-adult identity linkage. McAdam (1988) studied participants in the 1964 Freedom Summer project in which students, mainly from elite colleges in the North, spent the summer in Mississippi registering Black voters and educating unschooled Black children. McAdam described the collective nature of this experience, which included recruitment procedures, group training, the shared tragedy of having three fellow workers killed ten days into the project, and tensions from police harassment and beatings.

Twenty-five years later, McAdam surveyed the participants, along with a comparison group that had been selected to participate but was unable to do so. He also interviewed subsamples from both groups. The majority of participants, compared with nonparticipants, held more liberal views, were more conventionally and unconventionally politically active, belonged to more voluntary groups, and had more often chosen careers in the education and service sector. Participants' adult political views had not remained restricted to civil rights causes, but took various paths from that seminal event to, for example, movements for free speech, action against the war, promotion of feminism, and environmental protection.

McAdam concludes that the Mississippi experience had engendered skills of political action along with a sense of generational potency for social change. As one interviewee said: You realized you belonged "to something larger than" yourself (137). "You felt like you were part of a . . . historic movement. . . . You were . . . making a kind of history and . . . you were . . . utterly selfless and yet found yourself" (138). This is precisely what other observers of participants in the civil rights struggle found. For example, one of the participants studied by Coles and Brenner said: "When I go near a voting registrar in Mississippi I feel I'm dueling with the whole history of my race and the white race. It gets you just like that, in your bones. You're not just a person who is scared. You're doing something for the books; for history, too" (1965:910).

In a parallel study, Fendrich (1993) reported on the lives of Black college student participants in the civil rights movement at Florida A & M University, where over 60 percent of the student body during the 1950s and 1960s participated in sit-ins and other demonstrations. Fendrich estimates that one in six demonstrators suffered arrests, one in twenty was jailed, and one in ten was beaten by police authorities. Activities started with a bus boycott in Tallahassee in May 1956 and continued through the 1960s. Hence, successive cohorts of students maintained the activist tradition almost as a rite of passage in what Fendrich called a *baptism of political protest*.

Fendrich tracked students for ten years (one of the studies cited by De-Martini 1983) and then twenty-five years after college, assessing their political and civic behavior. The title of his book, *Ideal Citizens*, conveys his major findings. Twenty-five years later, 63 percent of the participants had earned graduate degrees, 93 percent voted regularly, 49 percent had joined a political party, 31 percent took active roles in political campaigns, 30 percent had worked in groups devoted to solving local problems, and 11 percent had attended protest meetings. Each of these statistics exceeds that found in the general population, but it was not the case that each differentiated Fendrich's participants from nonparticipants. Fendrich attributes the similarities to the fact that all Black college graduates of this era shared to some degree a generational experience that shaped the trajectory of their life. This generation was offered novel opportunities to further its education, to enter careers previously closed to Blacks, and to achieve financial rewards unavailable to their parents' generation. They were not only baptized in protest but confirmed in opportunity that led to advancement and ideal citizenship.

These studies clarify the outcomes of participation—conscious involvement in collective action against established norms. Participation clearly thrust actors into the political arena in a conscious effort to challenge and overturn the prevailing system. Further, these actions were justified with an articulated moral and ethical position espousing universal rights and principles of social justice. Because practices that defined youth participation were not identical with the actions that subsequently defined adults' civic engagement, one needs to specify their linkage. We propose that participation helped establish civic engagement as a basic element in youth's identities during their formative period. Having sat in at a lunch counter and suffered police harassment, in itself, cannot explain voting or working on a political campaign twenty-five years later. But students who sat in and were arrested may have learned that their individual and collective actions gave them agency and that *their* having taken responsibility encouraged others to take responsibility also. Having acted with a clear sense of the political processes that sustained segregation and of what was necessary to undo it may have engendered lasting trust in these processes. And because these studies deal with positions taken in opposition to the status quo, (ideological conviction and moral justification) they have special relevance. Although adults do not necessarily hold the same ideological positions they held as protesting youth, they have remained committed to viewpoints that propel them to act twenty-five years later, for instance, to protect the environment or seek social justice for the homeless. In sum, the concept of civic identity is useful for explaining continuity in civic orientation expressed through different behaviors over time.

Conclusion

A top-down analysis of civil society, moving from macro social structure down to civic behaviors, leaves us with the sense that great social forces have altered the course of America's civic orientation. The search for causes puts us in a state of rumination and brooding. If macro forces have led us to become a nation of individualists or materialists (Bellah et al. 1985; Etzioni 1992), one is left with few options for how to combat this unsatisfactory situation. Even if causes could be identified, one would know little about the processes by which civil society is formed and could be reconstituted.

We propose that a developmental analysis helps to remedy this impasse. We have cited studies that show how individuals acquire practices that are constitutive of civic identity. Participation in organizations and movements provides experience with normative civic practices and ideologies and also shapes youths' emerging identities in a long-lasting way. Participation in high school government, on the one hand, and in social-political reform, on the other, launches youth on a developmental path toward constructive citizenship.

These findings allow us to set aside the not so fruitful question of how civil society disappeared, in favor of the more generative inquiry into how we can enhance youth's opportunities for active participation in the reform and renewal of contemporary society. Numerous models are available, including mandatory military service, as in Israel or Turkey, as well as voluntary service directed to community problems (Yates and Youniss 1999). By affording youth meaningful participatory experiences, we allow them to discover agency, assess their responsibility, acquire a sense of political processes, and commit to a moral-ethical ideology.

Each generation's task is to make sense of the social conditions given to it and to renew society by making new history. Representatives of the political left (Flacks 1988) and right (National Association of Secretaries of State 1999) bemoan the fact that contemporary youth seem to have shirked their generational obligation. Rather than work at making history, this generation seems content to take the rewards that prior generations have earned, leaving the future in the hands of a few leaders. Clearly, there is a tendency to blame contemporary youth, even to demonize them, for the sorry state of civil society. We believe a more productive remedy is to recognize the older generation's duty to support youth's quest for identity. Youth seek transcendent meaning. This entails locating themselves in history by adopting ideological traditions that older generations have sustained and that still merit respect. Contrary to popular psychology's image of identity as a private existential struggle, youth make identities by joining with others in respectable causes. Adults' duty in this process is to afford participatory experience in which youth can join them so that together they participate in renewing civil society.

Identity is not given but must be constructed. In our pluralistic society, one must make sense of contradictory options and resolve difficult tensions (Calhoun 1994). We recognize that a civic identity may orient individuals toward sustaining society as it is, or it may lead to challenging the status quo in the spirit of reform (Foley and Edwards 1996). Our goal was not to assess which kinds of experiences lead to which of these outcomes. Rather it is to outline a developmental process in which the construction of individuality and of society are complementary so that citizenship is built into the self's very definition.

Political Culture Reconsidered

Insights on Social Capital from an Ethnography

of Faith-based Community Organizing

RICHARD L. WOOD

This chapter uses the concept of social capital to analyze grassroots democratic action, and strives to illustrate both the utility and the limitations of social capital as a construct for analyzing civil society.[1] I focus on explicitly political action among subaltern social groups: the urban poor and working classes in the contemporary United States. This case study and my overall theoretical thrust highlight the "contestatory function" of civil society in providing a counterweight to elite economic and political power. My account shares the European and Latin American emphases on the political dimensions of civil society, especially its role in reshaping the public sphere and holding it accountable to the interests of the majority (see the introductory chapter to this volume by Bob Edwards and Michael Foley).

The research reported here comes from a broader study entailing three years of ethnographic work within one faith-based community-organizing federation in the mid-1990s, supplemented by interviews in six other such federations in recent years. Further analysis from this research can be found in Wood (1995, 1999) and in a forthcoming book. Rather than addressing the civil society debate directly, this chapter does so implicitly by linking social capital to a concept of political culture quite different from that of the "civic culture" strand of political science. Defining political culture as the cultural dynamics internal to political organizations (but constructed partly by drawing on cultural elements from the wider society), I examine the

The main body of this paper appeared as "Social Captial and Political Culture: God Meets Politics in the Inner City," in *American Behavioral Scientist* 40, no. 5 (1997): 595–605.

intersection of social capital and political culture "on the ground," in the work of organizations challenging antidemocratic public policy.

An initial narrative section describing a typical public action carried out under the aegis of faith-based community organizing provides a taste of the kinds of political action analyzed here. Later sections draw on the concept of social capital to explain the effectiveness of this kind of organizing, then suggest aspects of political culture relevant to "making democracy work" but not addressed adequately by the social capital framework. Finally, in the conclusion I outline what this kind of grounded ethnographic analysis suggests for the project of reconstructing the social capital conceptual framework.

Narrative: Faith-Based Community Organizing in Action

Rain was falling on a dark evening in March 1994 in Oakland, California. East 14th Street is the main artery through a densely populated but run-down section of the city, hard hit by the loss of manufacturing jobs associated with American economic restructuring over the last fifteen years. Once a belt of solid blue-collar neighborhoods, East Oakland by the mid-1990s was an area of concentrated poverty and shuttered factories. Hard by East 14th Street looms the enormous hulk of what was once a major Montgomery Ward retail store, abandoned now for over ten years.

Despite the rain and the darkness, people congregated steadily at the St. Elizabeth School cafeteria. By 7:30 P.M., the cafeteria was overflowing, some 350 people crowding into the space. Some 90 percent were Latino, with some "Anglos" (actually mostly descendants of Portuguese, Irish, and Italian immigrants) and African Americans scattered through the crowd.[2] Behind the front speakers' table hung a large "Oakland Community Organizations" banner. OCO is the local incarnation of the Pacific Institute for Community Organization (PICO), a national network of urban community organizing federations based in religious congregations.

In the front, two tables stood on either side of a podium. At one sat the local PICO members who led this action: Roberto Montalvo, Haydee Salgado, Manuel Arias, a translator, and the pastor, Fr. Ignatius de Groot. At the other table sat the "target" of the action: City Council member Ignacio De la Fuente. At the back of the cafeteria were reporters for a local television station and the local newspaper.

The meeting began with a welcome and "credential" of OCO by Fr. de Groot, in English and Spanish:

> OCO is a federation of 18 churches representing 25,000 families throughout
> Oakland. . . . we work through a process of one-to-one contacts to identify

the community's concerns and priorities, and to take action for changing things. In the past, we have successfully moved Oakland to improve street lighting in neighborhoods throughout the city and to establish the Aviation Academy in the schools. Our goal is to represent the community.

During the rest of the meeting, participants spoke in whichever language they felt most comfortable, and summary translations were provided into the other language. Ms. Salgado, a laywoman, led an "opening reflection":

> How beautiful it is to see this group meeting here, united and working together to improve our community. . . . In preparing this reflection, I thought about many things: especially how we must have faith, a faith that leads us to action. [She reads and reflects briefly on Jesus' Parable of the Talents in Matthew 25, connecting the passage with the life and work of George Washington Carver.]
> God has given us a place, and asks us what we are going to do with it. . . . Part of the place God has given us is this street and that huge [Montgomery Ward] building that has been unused for ten years. We want to make this place something to serve everyone, something for the community.

Next, three Latino leaders gave the "Background Research Report," as others projected slides showing the building and its surrounding area:

> This building has sat empty for 10 years. It is a symbol of blight and neglect that plague our neighborhood. . . . But let's not concentrate on the negative: let's use our imaginations. What could be here? Food stores, a job training center, a police substation. . . . We could have these things, but Montgomery Ward refuses to sell the property and is not willing to invest in it. . . . [They go on to describe various retailers' interest in building on the site, and the city's ability to use eminent domain laws to take over property abandoned this long.] We have done our homework. We know that, given all these interested parties and the city's leverage over Montgomery Ward, we have faith that we can turn this dream into a reality: that's why we're here. . . . "Montgomery Ward, let's do it now!" [Applause]

Fr. de Groot, moderating the meeting, introduced the next portion of the action, saying: "Now comes the most important part of our meeting: questions about what can be done, what our guests are willing to do."

Residents from the local neighborhood, trained as leaders through their participation in PICO, presented Mr. De la Fuente with a series of questions, focused on gaining his express commitment to three goals: to push forward in negotiations with Montgomery Ward to either redevelop the site or sell it to someone who will; to work actively with OCO in doing so; to give the assembled people a time line showing what concrete steps would be taken and when. In addition, they asked the councilmembers to commit to taking over the property using the city's power of eminent domain, should the corporation fail to redevelop or sell the property. The latter is crucial, for it represents the threat of exerting State power over against the interests of corporate capital.

Under close questioning, Mr. De la Fuente committed to all three goals and to use of eminent domain powers, noting that he and the city were already engaged in negotiations with Montgomery Ward. Throughout, the meeting remained relatively amicable, with only minor conflict over how long Mr. De La Fuente would be allowed to hold the floor; however, this amicability concealed significant conflict, as will be discussed below.

Once the leaders had gained these commitments from their representatives, Fr. de Groot summarized the meeting:

> I think we're moving!! [Applause] I have been here 6 years, and the only change I have seen has been more graffiti on that building. Now I feel a sense of going forward, of movement. And we will see to it that this continues!

He then asked Mr. De la Fuente to report back to OCO leaders, "who will report back to all of you." The action closed with a prayer led by Sister Mary Virginia:

> Lord, I feel energy and excitement here I have not felt before.... You are not a God of emptiness, not a God of waste, not a God of irresponsibility.... You want us to have life, to have life to the full. Strengthen our energy, strengthen us, to bring life to what is dead, to fill what is empty, for our children, and for the children of the future.

The meeting ended with the group applauding and PICO leaders gathering for an evaluation meeting. The action would receive extensive coverage in the media, including a highly sympathetic report on local television news and a prominent story in the local newspaper.

By early 1996, the Montgomery Ward building would begin coming down—albeit with interminable delays, occasioned by lawsuits in the name of historic preservation.

Projecting Power into the Public Realm

The following account briefly summarizes a fuller argument made elsewhere (Wood 1995). Putnam has been accused (wrongly, I believe) of theorizing that strong reserves of social capital substitute for political institutions or for relatively egalitarian economic development in making democracy work. My key thesis is not this, but rather—as Putnam does argue—that, in the complex causal processes of social history, certain kinds of political culture help to shape and sustain such political institutions and economic relations.

A note on the term "political culture" is relevant here, especially since Putnam has apparently denied that his position has to do with culture at all (Tarrow 1996). Laitin's account of "the two faces of culture" (1986) provides a theoretically sophisticated way of understanding the confusion of terms: One face of culture, made up of the interpersonal ties and relational networks in which people are embedded, is closely related to social structure. The other face includes the symbols, language, values, and assumptions people use to interpret their world, more closely reflecting common usage of the term "culture." "Social capital" as conceptualized by Putnam provides a useful way of discussing the first face of culture as it relates to political life, and thus should rightly be seen as a concept of political culture. As I will later argue, understanding the second face of political culture demands a conceptual framework broader than that of "social capital."

In the last 15 years, the kind of community organizing effort described above has probably become the most extensive and successful effort by low-income urban residents (both citizens and undocumented residents) to shape the social, political, and economic conditions of their existence (Hart 2000). Four major networks sponsor faith-based community organizing "federations" in some 120 metropolitan areas around the country. The networks are the Industrial Areas Foundation (IAF), the Pacific Institute for Community Organization (PICO), Gamaliel, and DART. Each local "federation" is sponsored by 10 to 40 local religious congregations, but is separately incorporated and staffed. Roman Catholic, historic black Protestant, and mainline white Protestant congregations make up the bulk of these federations, but evangelical Christian, Jewish, Unitarian, and other congregations are also involved.

The model of organizing varies somewhat across the four networks, but they all share fundamental similarities that combine tactics popularized by the legendary organizer Saul Alinsky (1946, 1971) and elements drawn from more recent organizing work. The community organizing staff of the federation work through local congregations, at the invitation of the pastor or governing board. Through "one-to-one" meetings or "house meetings," the organizer strives to identify relevant issues and enlist the participation of natural leaders within the congregation. These typically include both persons in formal leadership roles and, at least as important, those without formal roles but whose opinions and character are respected widely by others. Eventually, the organization selects a specific issue and solution strategy to pursue, through a combination of (1) this grassroots consultation; (2) "research" meetings with city staff, government bureaucrats, academic experts, consultants, etc.; and (3) the organizing staff's own outside research, often through the larger networks.

Once an issue has been chosen and a solution strategy identified, the organization must select a "target": a person with the decision-making authority to implement the solution strategy. For simpler issues, this is often a single government official. For more complex issues, a majority of members of a city council, school board, or key leaders in the state legislature may be targeted. The organization then strives to build momentum toward an "action" or "accountability session," synonyms for the kind of public event described above. At these events (which may be sponsored by a single congregation or a citywide federation), the target is asked to commit to the proposed solution, and often to working with the organization in implementing it.

Throughout this process, the better organizers focus on both mobilizing a sufficient number of participants to win the issue and positioning the organization to accumulate power for the long term. The former involves not only their own work, but asking church members to do one-to-ones and house meetings and asking church pastors to make announcements and encourage participation as well. Organizational accumulation of power involves selecting gradually higher-level issues to engage, escalating conflict when targets reject the organization as a participant in public affairs, and strategically entering into (nonpermanent) collaborative relationships with political leaders in order to influence major issues.

Through this process, federations around the country have moved from being able to influence only the neighborhood-level issues that are the fodder of traditional community organizing (e.g., stop signs, more police, better parks) to far more significant initiatives. This has been possible because, at a period of American history when turning out a hundred attendees at an event makes an organization a player in the political arena, these federations regularly turn out a thousand members (and at times two thousand or more) for citywide actions. With such numbers, they project sufficient power into the public arena not only to affect specific decisions, but to shape future policy formulation.

In New Orleans, this kind of organizing has been a key political base for significant police reform efforts. In Texas, it has helped restructure local-level power relationships between poor, working, and middle-class Hispanic neighborhoods and historically dominant white political institutions (Warren 1995). In California, it has led to increased funding for public education, a higher minimum wage, and money for school-to-work transition programs (Wood 1995). In Milwaukee, it has forced financial institutions to end red-lining of minority residents, through pressure brought to bear under the Community Reinvestment Act (Appleman 1996). In Baltimore and New York, it helped bring about large-scale reworking of public housing programs. Significantly, as shown in the Montgomery Ward action above, some federations have accumulated sufficient power to exert pressure on private capital through the leverage of the State; this represents a qualitatively different level of power than exerting pressure on elected leaders, since corporations are structurally insulated from democratic pressure.

Analysis: Social Capital and Political Power

The research summarized here did not attempt the kind of quantification of social capital carried out by Putnam and his collaborators—rather elegantly in Italy (1993) and less convincingly in the United States (1996), and more recently by Pamela Paxton (1999) and others. Rather, I use the social capital conceptual framework as one theoretical lens through which to understand the differential success of various faith-based organizing efforts.

How, then, can we understand the relative success, vis-à-vis other mobilizing efforts, of faith-based efforts to organize low-income Americans for political engagement? Resource mobilization perspectives provide one possible explanation: churches channel economic and other material resources to movements, thus helping them succeed. In work reported elsewhere (Wood 1995), the current research controls for this by comparing two efforts at community organizing with comparable access to material resources, organizing in identical neighborhoods and with similar potential bases of participants, but with different cultural strategies: one appealing to religious identity, the other appealing to racial identity. Thus, resource mobilization cannot explain their differential success.

I argue that thinking of social capital as a resource does explain the relative success of faith-based organizing, as follows: Think of trust, social networks, and norms of generalized reciprocity (Sahlins 1972) as pools of social capital generated and flowing within societal institutions, including religious communities—more precisely, in specific kinds of religious communities. Community organizers essentially work through church-built social networks to draw on these reserves of trust and reciprocity in order to build what they term a "power organization"—and then project that power into the public arena to reshape the life conditions and structural pressures in urban America.

Why would faith-based organizing be any more successful at this than other efforts? Because in many urban areas those settings that previously generated trust and sustained broad social networks have deteriorated badly: unions, blue-collar workplaces, cultural associations, families, etc.

(W. J. Wilson 1996). Religious congregations are among the few institutions still active in many poor neighborhoods. The sophisticated survey work of Verba, Schlozman, and Brady (1995) suggests that religious institutions may be exceptional in their tendency to foster democratic skills in egalitarian ways across divides of class, race, and gender; it may well be true that they do likewise with social capital. At least, organizers believe so: Denise Collazo, now the director of PICO's federation in San Francisco, notes:

> In most neighborhoods people don't know each other anymore. It's not like before when you knew everyone and knew everyone's business and their kids and everything—neighborhoods have changed in the past thirty years. But in the church most people have known each other. Their kids have been raised with each other and so I think just the level of relationship that you have to start with is bigger and broader with the churches.

Likewise, Peter Phillips, a PICO organizer in Florida notes the importance of the interpersonal trust provided by churches:

> It gives you an incredibly strong forum when a local congregation decides to organize, because you might start with 15 or 20 people who are already in relationship and that have trust and commitment. They go out and bring people in who don't go to church here but what is so nice is that you've got these fifteen to twenty people that already trust one another and are in relationship. The problems that neighborhood organizing has where people start having turf battles with one another are not present. Here the new people kind of integrate into an already committed and developed group of leaders that are working together in love and respect. The congregation provides that.

But not all religious congregations do so equally. Rather, religious congregations differ in the levels of trust they generate among members, the extent of the social networks they sustain, and the character of those networks. By measuring these components of social capital, one could thus measure whether differing stores of social capital influence the congregations' success in projecting public power through community organizing; though not pursued here, such an approach would mirror Putnam's work on Italy. (See Warren 1995 for an insightful application of the concept of social capital to a different faith-based organizing network, the IAF.)

Note, too, that community organizing federations are not necessarily parasitic upon the social capital reserves of religious congregations. The best federations also help the congregations increase their own stores of social capital. In particular, they extend social networks more fully toward greater numbers of church members, and they generate cross-connections between church networks that previously were isolated from one another. For example, the organizing effort described above helped connect disparate groups at St. Elizabeth (readers, charismatic prayer groups, choirs, traditional Catholic fraternal groups, etc.) into a more cohesive parish community. Where this does not occur, community organizing must be considered parasitic on religious congregations; where it does, community organizing federations and individual congregations can become truly symbiotic.

Beyond Politics?

The relatively collaborative relationship between political leaders and the PICO leaders depicted in the political action at St. Elizabeth obscures a crucial underlying reality of community organizing: Political conflict is a constitutive element of the organizing process and underlies much of the success such efforts have enjoyed—including their collaborative relationships with political partners. In many ways, conflict is the lifeblood of these organizations, providing the drama that sustains members' interest and serving as both the whetstone on which their political skills are sharpened and the antidote to efforts by economic or political elites to manipulate the organization.

The minor struggle between City Council member De la Fuente and the PICO leaders over who would control the meeting offers a case in point: it shows PICO's refusal simply to be used as a political tool. More significantly still, though Mr. De la Fuente had worked with local PICO leaders on various projects, only a week before the action described above, he had informed them he would not attend. This led to a sharp conflict and angry phone calls accusing him of disrespecting and manipulating them, and a threat to embarrass him publicly by holding the action with his name on an empty chair in front. Ultimately, the councilmember canceled another meeting in order to attend. Thus, the benign public face of mutually beneficial political collaboration often belies—and from the point of view of community organizations relies upon—a deeper reality of conflict and strategic positioning. Analysts, funders, and community organizers who fail to appreciate this may see "replenishing social capital" as a cure-all for what ails American democracy. Current thinking holds that regenerating social capital indeed holds democratic promise but that this promise often remains on the horizon until connected to explicitly democratic political organizing—organizing that often includes more, rather than less, conflict.

Rather than offering a way beyond politics, community organizing as a way of projecting social capital–based power into the public arena offers precisely a way into more democratic politics. Social capital as conceptualized by Putnam indeed provides a conceptual framework for helping to understand what makes democracy work—but properly understood, it leads precisely to the hard work of politics, rather than to an illusory, conflict-free civil society.

Beyond Social Capital: A Second Face of Political Culture

Finally, Laitin's "second face of culture" suggests a whole second arena of political culture that a conceptual framework centered on social capital fails to address.[3] If the first face of political culture concerns the way social capital helps structure people's daily lives, this second face of political culture draws attention to the symbolic, linguistic, and interpretive elements through which people make sense of politics. That is, in addition to interpersonal ties and the benefits that go with them (networks, trust, reciprocity—the first face), we must pay attention to how shared cultural elements (symbols, meanings, assumptions—the second face) help either to enable or constrain people's efforts to engage together in social action. The organizational culture literature (Zucker 1988; Wood 1994, 1999) suggests one such route: the symbolic elements shared among members of religious communities help stabilize and institutionalize communities and the organizing efforts they sponsor. As PICO organizer Collazo continues:

> I think one most important thing is that [faith-based community organizing] is value-based and [people have] the Bible and the specific stories we all know. We have all heard or have all been brought up hearing and using these examples or symbols as the reason why we do this.

Peter Phillips also recognizes this:

> They [the churches] provide more of the long-term vision and guidance and stability to the organizations. The congregations are much more stable than the organizations because they have been there for hundreds of years.

Beyond simply stabilizing organizations, elements of the second face of culture enable political engagement in other ways. How group members interpret the conflict inherent in political organizing matters greatly for their effectiveness. Also important is whether they have interpretive elements through which to make sense of being in conflict with a given political leader one month, in partnership with him the next. Finally, the inclination to engage in this-worldly social action in the first place (as opposed, say, to prayer alone) is also partly the product of this second face of a group's culture. Elsewhere, I analyze how this second face of culture shapes political dynamics in community organizing (Wood 1999). Here, I simply note that all these factors are at work in the opening narrative of this chapter: Haydee Salgado's calling people to this-worldly responsibility, her interpretation of faith as "a faith that leads us to action," and her invocation of God's strength to assist the people's efforts all represent this second face of culture. The priest's implicit endorsement of conflict with political leaders, as long as this conflict remains within ethical bounds and serves community interests, provides an interpretation that others can imitate. In a forthcoming book, I explore how the religious symbols, ethical worldviews, and ritual experience of different congregations shape their members' political engagement.

Conclusion

This ethnographic look at the micro context of democratic political action suggests several insights relevant to the themes of social capital and civil society. See the concluding essay of this volume for the editors' synthesis of key insights; here, I note the ways in which this chapter dovetails with their conclusions and where it may suggest continuing conceptual reconstruction and further empirical research.

Clearly, the thrust of this analysis shares the editors' emphasis on the political dimensions of civil society, seeing at least as much democratic importance in political conflict as in consensus. Likewise, my analysis does not rely on the assumption that generalized social trust represents a key independent variable leading to healthy democracy. Indeed, I share their stance that measuring trust at this aggregate level obscures far more than it reveals about democracy. Finally, as the editors note in the conclusion that follows, "context counts," and the role of social capital in fostering democracy is context dependent and must be linked to more social and structural factors. Their claim that social capital must be conceptualized as access *and* resources pushes the debate in the right direction. In understanding social context, my intellectual taste runs in favor of ethnography as a way of grounding social scientific analysis; but rigorous measurement of the right analytic variables is also crucial.

But in keeping with our shared belief that conflict—political and intellectual—fosters progress, I dissent from whatever emerging consensus may be embedded in Foley, Edwards, and Diani's fine concluding synthesis. If I understand them correctly, they think the quality of the "network ties" component of social capital is irrelevant for understanding democratic outcomes—that is, that network ties facilitate access, regardless of the quality of those ties. This allows them, rightly, to reject the generalized social trust argument. But what of *particularized* social trust? As the editors note, *localized* relationships that embody high levels of mutual trust may powerfully facilitate social action, say among subaltern groups pushing for expanded democracy. Likewise, if the key challenges for expanding democracy include reconstituting a public realm and creating democratic subaltern spaces, "horizontal" ties may offer important advantages over vertical ties. This suggests continuing analytic attention to the quality of network ties. It also reopens the matter of whether the "socialization" function of civil society may in fact be important. Edwards and Foley provide an opening for this socialization function in their concluding allusion to the importance of strategic choices. Surely, good strategic choices entail leadership, which is dependent on socialization—albeit socialization for political agency, not for submission to political elites.

Social Capital Reconsidered

MICHAEL W. FOLEY, BOB EDWARDS, AND MARIO DIANI

Since Robert Putnam's 1995 "Bowling Alone" article popularized the concept of social capital, many scholars have adopted it, both in empirical research and in argumentative pieces directed toward readers of journals of opinion. Political scientists and sociologists have dominated empirical research, but economists and other social scientists have also taken up the notion in studies ranging from renewed tests of the thesis of a "decline in social capital" in the United States to analyses of the impact of social capital on economic performance, public health, or delinquency among teenagers. Others have explained variations in the kinds and value of social capital as resulting from cross-national differences in the predominance of politicized versus "civic" groups operating in a society[1] or from historical changes in the structure of local economies.

As we noted in the introduction, research in this field has been driven by different theoretical approaches. Putnam's work has led many political scientists and economists to focus on the relationships among associations and trust as well as other attitudes and norms, on the one hand, and the ways any or all of these affect social, economic, and political outcomes, on the other. At the same time, other social scientists, mostly sociologists, have adopted versions of the social capital concept that are more in keeping with the social structural versions enunciated by Coleman (1990) and Bourdieu (1986), in that they emphasize individual and organizational social ties in predicting individual advancement or collective action.

In this concluding chapter, we review empirical work in the hope of clarifying the notion of social capital theoretically. We distinguish those approaches which center attention on "social trust" as a prime indicator of social capital and those which take a more decidedly social structural view. Following Bourdieu, we contend that resources in general, attitudes and norms such as trust and reciprocity, and social infrastructures such as networks and associations cannot be understood as social capital by them-selves. Social relations may or may not facilitate individual and collective action—and therefore operate as social capital—depending on the specific contexts in which they are generated. Moreover, given the context-dependent nature of social capital, access to social resources is neither bro-kered equitably nor distributed evenly, as Bourdieu explicitly recognizes. For social relations to turn into social capital we need the perception that a specific resource exists and some form of social relationship that brokers individual or group access to those particular social resources. The latter can be socially organized at the level of dyads, informal networks (Burt 1997; Heying, this volume), voluntary associations (Eastis, this volume), religious institutions (Wood, this volume), communities (Bebbington 1997; Schulman and Anderson, this volume), cities (Portney and Berry, this volume), or national (Minkoff, this volume) and transnational (Smith, this volume) social movements. The specific social context of social capital not only influences its "use value"; it also affects access to specific social re-sources.

We consider, first, work that takes social capital as an independent vari-able, conceived in essentially social-psychological terms. Then, we turn to research informed by more social structural conceptions of social capital. Finally, we consider research that treats social capital as a dependent vari-able. In the concluding sections, we lay out what we consider to be key components of a concept of social capital capable of delivering on the promise of the term.

Social Trust and Social Capital

Scholars who privilege survey analysis in their approach to social capital (mainly political scientists) tend to conceive of the latter as something that inheres in individuals (norms and attitudes such as trust). In this approach, social capital is an individual attribute and a fully portable resource, the value of which does not fluctuate as the individual moves in and out of nu-merous social contexts. When social capital is measured at the national level by aggregating survey responses into a "grand mean," it is impossible to distinguish the impact of localized social contexts on its generation. Once we take seriously the context-specific character of social capital in Coleman's or Bourdieu's sense, political scientists' efforts to resurrect the civic culture argument under the rubric of social capital appear to get the relationships exactly the wrong way around. The norms and values of the political culture theorists have always been treated as exogenous var-iables, whereas Coleman explicitly casts social capital as endogenous to particular social structural contexts (Jackman and Miller 1998). Moreover, the sorts of effects posited for "generalized social trust," or even the "civic norms" of some of this research, are likely to be highly mediated by much more "local" social structures (Tarrow 1996). Even when "generalized social trust" is taken as survey respondents' assessments of the trustworthiness of their social environment, aggregate scores at the national level can tell us little to nothing about what social groups enjoy trustworthy environments and under what circumstances. Moreover, if analysts wished to examine respondents' assessments of their everyday social environment, rather than the trustingness of the respondents themselves, extant survey data offer more direct indicators.[2]

An example drawn from Coleman's exposition might help make clear what we mean. The presence of norms ensuring that "unattended children will be looked after by adults in the vicinity" constituted social capital for a Jewish acquaintance of his who noted the difference between her old home in the United States and Jerusalem (Coleman 1990:303). Such norms are no doubt borne by individuals. But even their wide distribution may be irrelevant to the peace of mind of parents unless they are active for *their* children (e.g., Arab children as well as Jewish children, Yemenite and Ethiopian Jews as well as those of obviously European origins) in *their* neighborhood (East Jerusalem as well as West; Arab neighborhoods as well as settler communities). The wider the distribution of such norms, no doubt, the more reason I may have to trust my children to themselves (so to speak); but my knowledge that one individual possessed of such a norm is at my small neighborhood park today may be enough to allow me to permit my child to wander over there and hence may constitute social capital for me.

Even more than the distribution of certain norms, the context that makes it possible (or not) for me to rely upon other people's adherence to them determines their significance as social capital. A given neighborhood may have many individuals predisposed to such norms without the neighbors having a sense that theirs is a safe place for children. People's perception that it is so depends upon such factors as the extent to which people are out on the streets, the external reputation of the area, or a dramatic incident "demonstrating" the trustworthiness of neighbors. Conversely, high levels of "generalized social trust"—absent information about who has access to such trust under what conditions—can tell us little about a polity or a community. Context counts, and it counts crucially.

The theoretical difficulties are compounded when analysts attempt to link attitudinal data with macro economic and political outcomes by the opaque character of the aggregate data employed. Cross-national research relying on mean scores at the national level on variables such as social trust, civic norms, or trust in government ignore the significance of varying distributions that may lie behind identical statistical profiles. In this respect, work like that of Ronald Inglehart on "political culture" and Putnam on the "civic culture" in Italy is vulnerable to the same criticism that has been applied in the development literature against the use of per capita GNP as a measure of "development." In both cases, the underlying distributions may reflect wildly varying national or regional patterns.

The elementary statistical point bears reiterating: the same mean may reflect a normal distribution or a bimodal one; the same mean and standard deviation can capture bimodal or relatively flat distributions. Surely it matters whether support for democratic values is (1) normally distributed in a population; (2) represented by a core of activists, organized labor, and peasant groups, but counterbalanced by an antidemocratic upper-middle class and military; or (3) evenly distributed along a continuum ranging from radical democrats to radically antidemocratic elements. Given the fact that most research on these topics ignores such possible differences, it is little wonder that Newton found little correlation among the key variables of Putnam's thesis.[3]

At some lower level the aggregation of individual characteristics could indicate empirically accessible variations in a social context capable of capturing the sorts of expectations and access to social resources Coleman and Bourdieu have in mind, as well as their impact on people's behavior. To return to the earlier illustration, if we are going to talk about social capital at the level of the neighborhood, the norm that neighbors should look after unattended children probably has to be adhered to by some critical mass of residents. More important, that fact would need to be widely known and accepted as a characteristic of the neighborhood before it could generate the expectations that convert those norms to social capital. Aggregate scores on such norms and perceptions at the level of the social network or neighborhood might well describe significant differences among neighborhoods, but they still would not certify real differences in social capital without a closer look at how such differences play out in concrete cases. Aggregating at this level might be empirically difficult or expensive but clearly makes better sense theoretically than doing so at higher levels of analysis.[4]

Similarly, interpersonal trust is certainly important at the level of the firm, organization, or neighborhood. But the sort of aggregate national measures employed in cross-national studies of political culture since Almond and Verba's *The Civic Culture* mask very real differences within societies between the affluent and the poor, white and black, dominant ethnic groups and the marginalized, and political winners and losers, as Newton's survey of the literature shows. Tom Smith's analysis of the data on "misanthropy," operationalized as negative scores on the "social trust" items of the U.S. General Social Survey, raises similar doubts. Smith notes that responses have been shown to be sensitive to both wording and context in the overall questionnaire, and both of these shift over the years in which the

GSS has been administered. A more careful look at the data shows no clear overall trend but reveals that misanthropy ("negative social trust") "is shaped by socioeconomic and minority status, noneconomic life events, religion, and age-cohort." It is higher among "the less educated, those with lower incomes, and those with recent financial reversals," "among subgroups toward the social periphery," among victims of crime and those in poor health, among non-church goers and fundamentalists, and among younger adults" (1997:172–80, 191). Clearly, "social trust" itself depends upon a larger social context than that captured by the usual measures of associational membership. By the same token, its "use value" to individuals will vary systematically in ways scarcely considered by macroanalysis of the sort preferred by most of the political scientists in this literature.

We might sum up these observations with the following axiom: The more the "use value" of social capital is shaped by systematic variations between and within groups, the more distorted will be the connection between the "grand mean" of self-reported attitudes and beliefs among survey respondents and the varying social locations and contexts within which social resources are capitalized and made accessible to people.

Both theoretical and methodological considerations, then, point to the difficulty of sustaining the sorts of claims that have been made about the relationships between social capital, conceived in fundamentally normative terms, and macroeconomic, political, or social outcomes. Work outside the social capital framework on the determinants of political participation in American politics points to a complex interplay of factors influencing the kind and degree of political participation people undertake—including the skills learned through participation in churches, higher levels of education, and networks of mobilization and recruitment (Verba, Schlozman, and Brady 1995; Rosenstone and Hansen 1993). Comparative research on the bases for economic growth in industrial nations suggests that, while cooperation is important, it is won more through conflict, the threat of sanction, and institutions than as a result of exogenously generated trust or norms (Kenworthy 1995, and this volume).

Associations, Social Capital and Social Structure

The political culture approach to social capital assumes that associations facilitate economic growth or democratic performance through their impact on individual norms and attitudes, which in turn have an impact on society through individual behavior (Stolle and Rochon, this volume; Eastis, this volume). Coleman's conception, however, is both more expansive and less indirect. Social capital includes social organization of all sorts, including "appropriable social organization" and "intentional organization"

(1990:311–13). Associations are created for specific purposes but can also be turned to other uses; like informal social networks, they may be appropriated or intentionally created as "investments in social capital." In either case, they are social capital for those who are able to use them, that is, for those who have access to them.

To return to our example: the social capital available in my neighborhood stems not only from the subjective attributes carried around by the individuals who live there, but more profoundly from emergent and existing social infrastructures that facilitate individual and collective actions of many kinds. For example, the PTA, neighborhood churches, the volunteer fire department, local realtors, the area newspaper, and the community policing program might all be employed to reinforce the notion that this is the kind of neighborhood where neighbors look out for one another's children and where unattended children are safe on the street. Or these and other organizations may contribute willy-nilly to the contrary perception. As instances of "appropriable social organization," they may be mobilized directly in the service of social goals (good or bad), whether or not they are particularly good at generating attitudes of trust, norms of reciprocity, or civic engagement in their own endeavors. When a neighborhood child is struck by a drunken driver, his mother might mobilize her network of neighborhood parents gathered in the park for a spontaneous potluck dinner to form a chapter of Mothers Against Drunk Driving. Her brother might enlist the members of the volunteer fire department, up to now better known for misusing public funds for their clubhouse. Other parents join with the police department to lobby the mayor's office to seek a block grant to beef up the town's community policing program. And the mayor, building on the town's growing reputation as an urban "multicultural Mayberry" boosts his own clout with county officials by hosting a waffle breakfast at the local coffee shop for the Democratic candidates for governor and assembly, drawing on the business association, realtors, and the new Crime Watch group for funding and ticket sales.

As these hypothetical examples suggest, the reliance of most political science research on aggregate measures of attitudes and opinions and of a narrow range of behaviors may miss the real meaning and scope of social organization for individual and group efforts. Social organization, both formal and informal, provides multiple resources to individuals and communities. But sheer "associational density" is not enough, just as the mere existence of other-regarding norms among scattered individuals is not enough to make such norms "social capital." Again, aggregate statistics at the national level hardly capture the sort of dynamic sketched above, which depends upon a social context in which social networks, existing organizations, and enterprising individuals conspire to create a cumulative effect that may be absent in other settings, whatever the average level of membership in associations either locally or across the nation. The difficulty of achieving lasting peace in Belfast and Beirut should warn us against assuming that "associational density" has the same meaning in all social and political contexts.[5]

Social structures must be "appropriable" by individuals and groups to really be social capital; their use value as social capital will be multiplied to the extent that they enable multiple linkages across communities and beyond them (Bebbington 1997; Flora, Sharp, Flora, and Newlon 1997). Moreover, as the mention of Northern Ireland and Lebanon suggests, not all examples are so happy as the ones we have sketched here. Social networks and institutions may limit members' connections with the wider community; they may include some and exclude others; they may serve selfish and/or antisocial as well as "civic" ends (Portes and Landolt 1996); and they may battle one another furiously over the nature of the "public good."

Social scientists who have treated social capital as an independent variable have been attentive—to a much greater degree than have proponents of the "political culture" perspective—to the role of informal social networks and formal social organization in providing both individuals and their communities with vehicles for the advancement of their goals. Because the former have tended to conceptualize social capital more as a structural variable than an attitudinal one, even their use of survey data to measure the concept has differed markedly from that of most political scientists. In developing an analytical model of volunteering, for example, Wilson and Musick (1997) employ parsimonious measures of social capital—the number of children living in the household (on the assumption that children help connect adults to other adults) and self-reported informal social interactions—clearly tied theoretically to the extent to which respondents are embedded in social networks. Wilson and Musick find that individuals who report more children in the household and more frequent informal social interactions are also more likely to volunteer.

Social structural variables can also be employed in studies of "meso-level" effects of social capital. In an effort to explain varying development trajectories among six communities in the Ecuadorian and Bolivian Andes, Bebbington (1997) focuses on the presence (or absence) in each community of base and federated organizations and of specific individuals who linked communities to extra-local institutions and resources. The "organizations first helped create the *pre-conditions* for intensification, and then helped catalyze *processes* of intensification" (1997:194). The key individuals played crucial roles in renegotiating existing relationships among state, civic, and market spheres, that is, in establishing *linkages* between local organizations and extra-local agencies. Flora, Sharp, Flora, and Newlon (1997) surveyed elected or appointed officials in a random sample of 1,099 nonmetropolitan communities to test the relationship between local variations in "entrepreneurial social infrastructure"—the community's capacity to accept controversy ("legitimacy of alternatives"); its ability to mobilize resources from diverse sources; and variations in the structure of community networks—and their having undertaken an economic development project. The authors find that an unbiased local newspaper (legitimacy of alternatives), contributions to community projects from several types of financial institutions (resource mobilization), and more extensive network linkages to other communities were significant predictors of economic development activity.

These studies illustrate fruitful and relatively parsimonious models for gathering reliable data on social capital at the same level of social organization as the political or economic outcome of interest. In so doing they avoid entirely the methodological difficulties inherent in aggregating individual attitudes or actions into a single measure of political culture with effects posited at the level of the polity or region.

Explaining Social Capital

A final group of analysts have taken up the task of explaining social capital as a dependent, rather than independent, variable. By seeking to explain patterns in the production, presence, and use of social capital, they must wrestle directly or indirectly with the ways specific social contexts shape the "use value" of social capital and broker access to it. Thus, Heying (this volume) and Schulman and Anderson (this volume) demonstrate the impact of economic restructuring during the twentieth century on production of and access to social capital. Similarly, Portney and Berry (this volume) and Booth and Richard (this volume) make clear that local and national political contexts exert substantial influence on the kind and degree of mobilization of social capital.

Others, notably Stolle and Rochon (this volume), Eastis (this volume). and Booth and Richard (this volume), have shown that different sorts of groups are associated with different sorts of attitudes. Even when analysts focus on the "neo-Tocquevillean," that is, normative, interpretation of social capital, context proves to be important once we ask under what circumstances what sorts of social capital are produced, as in Stolle and Rochon's analysis of differences between type of group and levels of generalized trust, community reciprocity and tolerance among members.

Is It Time to Divest Ourselves of Stock in the Social Capital Concept?

Our answer is a qualified "No." If, on the one hand, social capital is conceived as little more than a stand-in for the old political culture variables, we can see very little use in applying a new label to the traditional stock of terms. We judge that a primary focus on "generalized social trust" (as measured, e.g., by one or more of the three GSS items commonly used for these purposes) is a dead-end. While there is no doubt that trust of some sort is crucial to many social relations, there is little evidence that, when greater or lesser proportions of a population consider themselves to be trustful of "people in general," this has any bearing on the health of democracy or the prospects for economic achievement in a given country. On the contrary, such expressions appear to reflect the peculiar social, economic, and political positions of the respondents: social trust is the result of a social, economic, or political system that works well for some, if not others; it is not the cause of their felicity. Trust, moreover, is not some universal lubricant that oils the wheels of cooperation wherever it is applied. Rather, cooperation is achieved through a variety of mechanisms, not the least important of which is effective government regulation (Kenworthy 1995). Where cooperation succeeds, trust may be presumed to follow.

On the other hand, we find much that is promising in the context-dependent and social structural/relational approaches of Bourdieu and Coleman. Research cited here has shown how interpersonal relations and institutional context may affect outcomes as diverse as individual exploitation of their own human capital, juvenile delinquency, and the success of communities in attracting resources for economic development. At the same time, other work has shown to what extent economic and political context may shape the level and kind of social capital a community may enjoy. Totalitarian and authoritarian regimes may force people to adopt more inward-looking strategies; corporate disengagement or government-mandated professionalization of nonprofit social service provision may undermine community spirit and voluntarism (Garth-Nowland 1998); different sorts of organizations may produce different mixes of self-regarding and civic behavior.

We need to think more seriously about the ways in which the elements of social structure facilitate or constrain individual political participation or collective action and look for sources of data that can capture such phenomena. Verba, Schlozman, and Brady (1995) and Rosenstone and Hansen (1993) have pointed the way in devising new datasets and creatively exploiting older ones to get at such variables. Diani (1995), Minkoff (1995), and J. Smith (1997) have each built extensive datasets focusing on regional, national, and transnational organizations, respectively, each of which has provided considerable leverage for thinking about how the connections and structures embodied in them work. Rose (1998) has designed a survey instrument expressly designed to tap social capital variables and the varying strategies of individuals in employing available social capital for economic survival and advancement.

Finally, the notion of social capital has already proven useful for political scientists and others concerned with understanding local processes of resource mobilization, economic development, and political recruitment and mobilization (Maloney, Smith, and Stoker, this volume). At the same time, social capital research in political science and political sociology need not confine itself to local politics, as the work of Minkoff and Smith cited above demonstrates. What these efforts have in common is attention to the social structures in which social resources are embedded, and to the kind and degree of access to such resources they provide individuals and groups. Understood in this way, the concept of social capital provides useful leverage for uncovering the ways in which individuals, groups, and societies generate, broker, and put to use the noneconomic resources that are crucial to our maneuvering the diverse social settings of which the economists' "marketplace" is only a subset.

"Networking" Social Capital

We close with a look at the recent trend toward a more "networked" conceptualization of social capital and our own attempt to construct a useful model of social capital. Although network analysis holds much promise in research on social capital, one should beware of uncritical, "over-networked" conceptions of it. One example of such conceptions is the widely held assumption that the amount of individual social capital corresponds to the number of network ties the same individual participates in. The expectation is that having more ties, or more diverse ties, increases an individual's likelihood of accessing resources of various kinds. While this may be true under certain conditions, there are also substantial differences among networks in the sorts of resources and the character of the ties they offer.

For example, ties of different intensity may generate access to quite diverse types of resources. While it has been influentially argued that weak ties (i.e., ties with a low emotional involvement) provide better job opportunities than strong ties (Granovetter 1973), weak ties are not always the most effective at generating opportunities. For example, involvement in collective action—in particular, in high-stakes forms of collective action—often depends on strong ties. Della Porta (1988) showed how recruitment to Italian left-wing terrorist groups was facilitated by strong and densely knit personal linkages between current and prospective militants. Differences between strong and weak ties may operate even within the same social milieu. In his analysis of the failure of unionization attempts in a small firm, Krackhardt (1992) found network centrality in friendship (i.e., strong) ties among colleagues to be far more effective at steering employees' opinions than centrality in more neutral (i.e., weak) ties such as advising. In this case, that some individuals were regarded as crucial sources of technical information by their colleagues provided these individuals with a certain degree of access to professional resources, yet that kind of social capital was not automatically converted into resources of political influence when proposals for unionization were put forward.

Under closer scrutiny, apparently similar outcomes may indeed turn out to differ in important ways, reflecting different types of operative social ties. For example, Diani and Lodi (1988) found that the kinds of ties that help in recruiting people to environmental groups changed according to the degree of radicalism of the organizations concerned. Recruitment to radical environmental organizations was frequently facilitated by activists' previous shared experiences of collective action. Adhesion to more traditional conservation groups depended more frequently on private ties, such as personal acquaintances developed in neighborhoods, schools, workplaces, etc., but not in organizations promoting collective action. These researchers suggested that adhesion to more demanding and controversial forms of collective action requires more specific forms of social capital (although they did not use the term), where people are not merely offered opportunities for collective action but are socialized to a critical political perspective; in contrast, adhesion to largely uncontroversial groups—conservation, for instance—could simply depend on the practical opportunities provided by more generic social linkages.

Finally, while more, or more diverse, network ties increase an individual's likelihood of accessing crucial resources in a given sociohistorical context, resources are accessed one tie at a time. As Briggs concludes, "adding just one steadily employed adult to an adolescent's circle of significant ties has dramatic effects on perceived access" (1998:177). Or, as we discussed above, knowing that just one reliable parent is in the neighborhood park enables a child's caregiver to benefit from that social tie. In other words, more ties are better, but one tie might be sufficient to gain access to a crucial resource.

"Context dependency," therefore, means first of all that the mere number and intensity of ties is not necessarily an adequate measure of social capital. It also means, however, that individual (or ego) networks may—and should—be considered as embedded in broader patterns of social relations. In this perspective, the network is the immanent structure (Bourdieu 1986) that influences the "use value" of an individual's network position or ties. The amount of access an individual gains from a network depends on two things. First, it depends on the structure of the network itself and the individual's precise position within it. As the contours of the network change over time, the amount of access to resources that individuals command by virtue of their network attributes also changes. Second, the social location of the entire network within the broader socioeconomic context shapes the ways that specific networks can and cannot link their members to resources. An individual may have extensive access to resources in a specific network, but the network as a whole may be embedded in a declining sector or an oppressed constituency (Edwards and Foley 1997, 1998; Tilly 1998). Recent discussions of social capital from a social structural perspective underline this point in referring to the "linkages" or "social bridges" that local networks need in order to gain access to a greater array of resources (Burt 1992, 1997; Woolcock 1998; Lang and Hornburg 1998; Warren, Brenner, and Saegert 1999).

Network analysis offers inroads into both versions of the "context dependency" of social capital. It offers first of all a set of indicators and concepts to measure the location of specific individual actors within a network, focusing either on the amount of ties they are involved in or on their capacity to act as intermediaries between other actors (Freeman 1979; Scott 1992; Wasserman and Faust 1994; Borgatti, Jones, and Everett 1998). It also allows analysts, however, to examine the structure of global networks to assess to which extent centrality in a specific network may be regarded as an indicator of influence on a broader scale (Scott 1992; Wasserman and Faust 1994). However, network analysis tools are no substitute for a proper understanding of the specific relationships being analyzed. Without some knowledge of the content of ties, and of the specific resources available through networks, we have no way of judging how much social capital an individual or group actually has at its disposal. Whether conceived as the number or diversity of ties, as network position, or as structural attributes of entire networks, networked access is but one component of social capital, albeit a crucial one (Bourdieu 1986; Portes 1998). *Social capital is best conceived as access (networks) plus resources.*

A Model of Social Capital

In closing, we draw together these points in order to clarify a model of social capital. Figure 1 helps illustrate the relationship of social context to social capital and of social capital both to means of access and to the agency of specific actors. The top arrow in the figure denotes the uneven distribution of social resources across specific social contexts in a given society. It signals the fact that the "use value" of resources available in a given context varies according to the location of that context within the larger socioeconomic setting. The second arrow problematizes the question of access to the specific resources present in a given context. That is, in order for such resources, the "raw materials" of social capital, to be converted into social capital, individual or collective actors must perceive

FIGURE I

Broader sociohistorical context

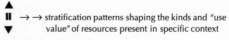

▲
II → → stratification patterns shaping the kinds and "use
▼   value" of resources present in specific context

Resources present within a specific social context

▲
Knowledge that resources are present ← ← **II** → → Access to resources present in the social field
▼

Social capital

Resources accessible (mobilizable) to individual or collective actors in
particular sociohistorical contexts; resources available for use

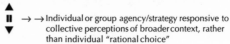

▲
II → → Individual or group agency/strategy responsive to
▼   collective perceptions of broader context, rather
            than individual "rational choice"

Resources utilized (mobilized) for particular
purposes in specific situations

that some specific resource is present within their social field and must have some form of social relationship that provides access to those resources. Social networks provide direct access to both resources and information. They also constitute the most proximate spheres of interaction in which individuals come to perceive resources to be both available and valuable.

Individual or collective actors can be said to have social capital when resources are present and accessible, in other words when they are actually available for use. Thus, social capital = resources + access. Consequently, measures of network attributes should not be treated as direct measures of social capital, any more than the mere presence of some sort of resources should be. Measures of access can be taken as indirect indicators of social capital in the sense that one cannot have social capital available without access, so more means of access increases one's *likelihood* of having greater social capital available for use. Nevertheless, measures of access are better indicators of one's potential social capital than would be some indication of the resources generally present in a given context.

Finally, the bottom arrow of figure 1 indicates the role of individual or collective agency in making use of social capital. Simply because individuals or collective actors have social capital available for use does not mean that they use it immediately until it is exhausted, or that they use it well. The basic distinction between mobilizable resources (social capital) and resources actually used needs to be maintained. Actors may use social capital, for good or ill. While a rich endowment of social capital certainly disposes an individual, group, or community to success (however defined), specific strategic choices in the use of social capital determine actual outcomes.

The formulation captured here has several strengths. First, it explicitly accounts for the context dependency of social capital—not all actors in a group, community, or polity have equal access to the same resources. One reason that social capital is context dependent is because neither of its necessary components (resources and access) is distributed evenly. Thus, a second strength of the view of social capital depicted in figure 1 is that it allows for the stratification of resources and access to be differentiated and investigated individually. A network analytic conception of social capital rightly calls attention to the fact that resources are not equally available to all individuals or collective actors operating within specific geographic or organizational boundaries. But, more broadly, the use value of social capital depends upon how specific networks are embedded within the broader system of stratification, that is, how and why different networks provide access to richer or poorer stores of resources. Both network position and the quantity and quality of the resources available must be examined in any judgment of the value of the social capital available to an individual or group. Finally, this formulation does not implicitly presume that every individual or collective actor utilizes all available social capital all the time. Rather, one can be said to have social capital if one has access to specific resources, yet one can have social capital and not use it at a particular time for a variety of reasons, or not use it well. This allows a clear distinction to be made between the possession of social capital and the use of social capital; in short, agency is problematized as a variable influenced by a range of factors, rather than implicitly presumed to be constant.

Conclusion

The rich empirical work surrounding the notion of social capital over the last five years has demonstrated that the character of "civil society" indeed can have profound impacts not only on individual opportunities, but on possibilities for collective action for groups of all sorts. At the same time, it has made clear the dangers of overgeneralized and undertheorized conceptions of both "civil society" and "social capital." The sorts of mechanisms examined here may serve the interests of mafias and militias as well as those of churches and civil rights organizers. As several of the studies collected here show, moreover, organizations differ tremendously in their effects on individual attitudes, participation, and engagement. However conceived, "social capital" plays out differently in different settings, depending on both informal and formal elements of social organization. Its meaning for the polity is rarely direct or unambiguous and is highly mediated by the character of the polity itself.

Such results should warn us against analyses that lay too much weight on "civil society" conceived as voluntary associations. As Kenneth Newton has argued elsewhere (1997), schools, the home, and the workplace might all be expected to contribute more to building the sorts of skills and attitudes and commitments often ascribed to participation in the associational life of the community. Our review of recent research on "social capital" also suggests that a conception focused on norms and attitudes like "trust" and "reciprocity" yields little new insight and may even undermine understanding where measurement at the national level renders invisible the actual mechanisms by which social relations facilitate or block individual and collective access to resources. In this light, we have argued, a conception of social capital that takes the notion of "capital" seriously and pays attention to the ways in which social ties themselves provide access to resources better fulfills the promise of the concept to provide insight into the critical role of such ties in social differentiation.

The civil society debate has served to focus attention on neglected aspects of social relations. Future research, however, will have to move beyond the broad and contested generalities of civil society to consider the concrete, context-dependent processes by which organizations and informal social ties alike reproduce inequality or transcend it, promote inclusive and cooperative relations, or build boundaries and reinforce hostility. The concept of social capital, properly specified, gives us purchase on some, but not all, of these processes.[6] The studies collected here demonstrate some of the richness of the results.

Notes

Edwards and Foley: Civil Society and Social Capital (pp. 1–8)

1. While Coleman's formulation (1986) is the most well known, in the United States the term can be traced back to L. J. Hanifan's 1920 book entitled *The Community Center* (Boston: Silver, Burdette and Co.), 78–79, and later to Jane Jacobs's *Life and Death of Great American Cities* (1961). In European social thought, Pierre Bourdieu first used "social capital" in 1972, eventually developing the triad: physical capital, cultural capital, and social capital. See Bourdieu (1972) and Bourdieu and Wacquant (1992).

2. For a recent attempt to situate the U.S. debate in its normative context, see Benjamin Barber's "Three Kinds of Civil Society" (1998).

3. Nevertheless, a long tradition of European *and* American thought had concerned itself with the problematic place of groups in modern polities, without, however, invoking the term "civil society." The corporatist tradition represents one distinctive, if disorderly, line of thinking on these issues. See Schmitter (1974). See Pizzorno (1981) and Dahl (1982) for overviews of the issues in the "pluralist" tradition. In the United States, starting with Arthur Bentley's *The Process of Government* (1908), the focus was on the role of so-called "interest groups" in a democratic polity whether adjudged an integral part of the system of representation (Truman 1971) or a source of systematic distortion (Buchanan, Tollison, and Tullock 1980; Olson 1982).

4. The major exception lay in the beginnings of the "communitarian" movement, with Peter Berger and Richard Neuhaus's call for a re-examination of the role of what they called "mediating structures" in contemporary societies. See Berger and Neuhaus (1977).

5. Lester Salamon has convincingly demonstrated the positive effects of the United States' distinctive "public-private partnership" for the growth of the nonprofit sector in this country (1995). He tends to side with those, accordingly, who stress the continuing importance of government in stimulating and supporting private initiative, though much of his recent scholarly effort has been to distinguish sharply the "independent sector" from both market and state (Salamon and Anheier 1992a, 1992b).

6. In recent presentations and forthcoming work, Putnam (2000) has adopted an understanding of social capital that focuses on "networks" and has argued that "social trust" must be understood endogenously, that is, as a reflection of the experiences and social setting in which individuals find themselves and not as an independent variable.

Whittington: Revisiting Tocqueville's America (p. 27)

1. In 1832, a convention called by the legislature of the state of South Carolina declared the federal protective tariff unconstitutional and null and void within the confines of the state and directed the state government to take steps to prevent enforcement of the tariff. The crisis was resolved through a congressional compromise that abandoned the protective tariff. See also, Whittington 1999.

Berman: Civil Society and Political Institutionalization (pp. 32–42)

1. See also, Keith Whittington, "Revisiting Tocqueville's America," in this volume.
2. See also, Sigmund Neumann (1942), Karl Mannheim (1980), and David Reisman (1961).
3. Contemporary neo-Tocquevilleans also share with many of their mass society counterparts the conviction that the mass media (especially television) is the most important culprit in societal and cultural degeneration. See Putnam (1995b). For a review of the literature on the connections between mass culture and society, see Brantlinger (1983).
4. See also, Pinard (1968), von Eschen, Kirk, and Pinard (1971), Jenkins (1983), and Oberschall (1973).
5. Perhaps the most prominent advocate of this view is Mancur Olson (1982).
6. Not surprisingly, an examination of Americans' confidence in their political institutions reveals a fairly steady decline since the 1960s. See Heying, this volume, and Lipset (1995).
7. During the early nineteenth century, for example, associational life in America was spurred on by the rise of mass suffrage and the emergence of mass parties. In Europe this dynamic is even more pronounced with political parties spawning everything from their own soccer clubs to debating societies. See Tarrow (1996) and Skocpol (1996b).

Booth and Richard: Civil Society and Political Context in Central America (pp. 45–55)

1. Putnam's delineation of variable relationships is inconsistent. For example, he suggests that group membership, newspaper readership, and voter turnout constitute elements of social capital in Italy (1995a:66). Yet, in his general argument, group membership is the *source*, not a component, of such social capital.
2. A. L. Seligson (1996), for instance, has shown that membership in communal orgnizations in Central America correlates positively with demands on government and community self-help participation. In contrast, the social capital of interpersonal trust has little impact on participation.
3. For a related argument see also this volume's chapter by Youniss, McLellan, and Yates.
4. We gratefully acknowledge the support given for the collection of these data

by the North-South Center of the University of Miami, the Howard Heinz Endowment-Center for Latin American Studies of the University of Pittsburgh Research Grants on Current Latin American Issues, University of North Texas Faculty Development Grants and Faculty Research programs, the Andrew Mellon Foundation, the Tinker Foundation, the Heinz Foundation, and the University of Pittsburgh. The project was designed and much of the data were collected by a team including Mitchell A. Seligson of the University of Pittsburgh and John Booth. Team members who also directed fieldwork were Ricardo Córdova, Andrew Stein, Annabelle Conroy, Orlando Pérez, and Cynthia Chalker. Guatemala fieldwork was conducted by the Asociación de Investigación y Estudios Sociales (ASIES) of Guatemala. Invaluable assistance and collaboration were provided by the following institutions in Central America: *Costa Rica:* Consejo Superior Universitaria Centroamericana (CSUCA), Maestría en Sociología, and the Universidad de Costa Rica, Departments of Statistics and Political Science; *Nicaragua:* Instituto de Estudios Internacionales (IEI), Universidad Centroamericana; *Honduras:* Centro de Estudio y Promoción del Desarrollo (CEPROD), and Centro de Documentación de Honduras; *Panama:* Centro de Estudios Latinoamericanos "Justo Arosemena" (CELA); *El Salvador:* Centro de Investigación y Acción Social (CINAS) and the Instituto de Estudios Latinoamericanos (IDELA).

5. In mid-1991 surveys were conducted among the urban voting-age populations of El Salvador, Honduras, Nicaragua, and Panama. In 1992 a similar survey was conducted in Guatemala, followed in 1995 by another in Costa Rica. In each a stratified (by socioeconomic level) cluster sample of dwelling units was drawn from the national capital and other major urban centers. Interviewees were chosen using randomizing procedures and following sex and age quotas.

We collected a total of 4,089 face-to-face interviews region-wide, but national sample Ns varied from 500 to 900. To prevent larger country Ns from distorting findings in this analysis, the country samples have been weighted equally to approximately 700 each (total N = 4198). We believe that our samples reflect the opinions of the urban populations of Central America (capital cities and other major cities and towns). We generalize only to citizens of urban areas—roughly half the region's populace.

6. Similar participation modes were found by Verba and Nie (1972), Verba, Nie, and Kim (1978), and Booth and Seligson (1979).

7. See M. A. Seligson and Booth (1993) for a discussion of these schools and the development of the measures used here.

8. The repression measure has been validated by comparison with individual respondent perceptions of violence, and by comparison to other indices of regime repression for these countries (Booth and Richard 1996:1209-10, n. 9).

9. This suggests a possible phenomenon in repressive societies similar to what Brehm and Rahn call a "vicious cycle" of reciprocal disengagement and alienation in the United States (1997:1008).

10. This somewhat counterintuitive finding may merely be an artifact of conditions specific to Central America. Table 1, for instance, reveals that Honduras and Nicaragua, the region's poorest nations, have above average levels of group activism and democratic norms.

11. While gender role expectations may be moving toward an ethos of greater

equality for Central American women, lag times exist before these become embedded in behavior. Parallels can be found in the decades it took after woman's suffrage before women's voter turnout rates caught up to men's.

12. In other research on Central America as well as here we have found support for this connection (Richard and Booth 1995; Booth and Richard 1996).

Rose: When Government Fails (pp. 59–62)

1. Inglehart's definition avoids Putnam's mistake of conflating different elements by defining social capital as "features of social life–networks, norms, and trust–that facilitate cooperation and coordination for mutual benefit" (1997:31). The conflation of networks, norms and trust makes it impossible to use the term social capital to construct a cause-and-effect model.

2. A battery of questions about trust in macro institutions of society showed a majority of Russians distrusting or skeptical about every major institution of their society, and especially about representative institutions of governance.

3. The logic is parallel to Greif's emphasis on the importance of understanding beliefs that represent "individual's expectations with respect to actions that others will take in various contingencies" (1994:915).

Portney and Berry: Mobilizing Minority Communities (p. 75)

1. Low SES is defined as people who had low incomes (between $0 and $15,000) or low levels of schooling (less than a high school education). Middle SES is defined as having either middle income (between $15,000 and $30,000) or middle education (at least a high school diploma and some college or schooling beyond high school). High SES is defined as high income (over $30,000) and high education (a college degree or beyond).

Maloney, Smith, and Stoker: Social Capital and the City (pp. 84–93)

1. The definition of voluntary association used in this paper also encompasses local and neighborhood community-based associations, which other definitions sometimes overlook.

2. Questionnaires were sent out to voluntary and community associations using the Birmingham Voluntary Sector Council mailing list supplemented by additional environmental, professional, and trade union lists. The response rate was 30 percent (n = 387). The dataset covers the variety of different types, functions, and geographical focus (neighborhood to international) of associations in Birmingham.

3. The figure of £17 million does not include all the service level agreements, which would make the financial support currently provided to the voluntary sector substantially higher.

4. For a more detailed discussion of the different factors that influence the nature of the POS, see Maloney et al. (2000).

5. This case study is based on the analysis of documentary evidence and interviews with council officers and community activists in 1998 and 1999. For a more detailed discussion of the changing nature of the race POS in Birmingham, see Maloney et al. (2000).

Stolle and Rochon: Are All Associations Alike? (pp. 143–154)

1. Dietlind Stolle acknowledges the support of the Department of Politics at Princeton University; the Comparative Gender Research School and the Department of Politics and Statistics at Stockholm University; and the Swedish Social Science Data Service at Göteborg University, especially Torbjörn Berglund. We are both indebted to Jason Abbott for research assistance. Special thanks to Nancy Bermeo, Jonathan Krieckhaus, Bob Edwards, Michael Foley, Paul Whiteley, and the Wilson Society of Fellows at Princeton University for their thoughtful comments on earlier versions of this chapter.

2. For further detail on our construction of measures of social capital, see Stolle and Rochon (1998), especially the appendix.

3. (Stolle & Rochon) The data sources consist of the United States General Social Survey merged samples (1983, 1984, 1986); *Svenska Medborgarundersökningen* (Swedish Citizen's Survey) (1987); German *Allbus* survey (1991); and the World Values Survey merged samples of the United States, Germany, and Sweden (1983, 1990).

4. In the United States, race was also controlled. In the Swedish Citizenship Survey, size of community was not measured and so could not be controlled.

5. Our challenge was to construct a typology of associational sectors in the three countries that would make comparisons possible without doing violence to the differences between association types. Table 2 is based on the following scheme:

Political associations: political clubs; political parties; international affairs clubs; peace, environmental, and temperance organizations; Third World and human rights groups.

Economic associations: unions; employers' associations; professional associations; agriculture associations; consumer groups; cooperatives; shareholders' organizations.

Group rights: pensioners; *Vertriebene;* veterans; immigrants; handicapped; animal rights; women's groups.

Cultural associations: associations for preservation of traditional regional, national, or ethnic culture; church groups; literary, music, and arts societies.

Community groups: local action groups; residents' associations; service and welfare organizations; health care groups; parents' associations; voluntary defense associations.

Private Interests: Sport; outdoor; youth; hobby; auto.

Social or leisure groups: fraternities and sororities; social groups; *Heimat* organizations; fraternal organizations.

For further detail on this categorization see Stolle and Rochon (1998:n. 6).

6. The categories of political action, generalized trust/community credit slips, political trust and efficacy, and optimism/tolerance/disapproval of free ridership are aggregations of the variables and scales listed in table 1. We refer to these four clusters of indicators as the "dimensions" of social capital. The statistical procedure in table 2, as in table 1, is analysis of covariance.

7. We deleted the dimension on which the association was least representative in order not to penalize associations of youth, older people, women, and so forth—associations whose defining trait happens to coincide with one of the dimensions of representativeness that we measure.

8. We exclude the World Values Survey from this analysis because its trust indicator is a single dichotomous question and there are no indicators of community credit slips.

9. See Stolle and Rochon (1999) for an examination of national differences in patterns of relationship between associational membership and social capital.

Eastis: Organizational Diversity and the Production of Social Capital (pp. 158–168)

1. Edwards and Foley (1997), Minkoff (this volume), Newton (this volume), and others take issue with this focus, pointing out that action in many other settings— the family, schools, national organizations—is also conducive to and driven by social capital.

2. Other schools of organizational theory would emphasize other influences on internal organizational structure. For example, neo-institutional theorists argue that organizations often adopt "symbolic" structures—mission statements, certain types of research programs—because they are imitating other organizations that have gained a certain level of legitimacy in the task environment. While a more complete framework for the analysis of diversity among voluntary associations would incorporate concepts from other theories in organizational sociology, contingency theory's concepts, at the level of the individual organization, are an adequate basis for the present purposes.

3. Press release announcing Collegium Musicum concert, 24 April 1996.

4. Concert program of the Community Chorus, 16 December 1995.

5. Concert program of the Collegium Musicum, 6 December 1995.

6. Concert program of the Community Chorus, 16 December 1995.

7. Many differences in rehearsal experience are related to size. As musical ensembles get larger, and face-to-face nonverbal communication becomes impossible, the conductor's role in technical matters like keeping time becomes more important. However, size is not the sole determinant for the processes I am discussing here.

8. Separating these aspects of social capital also allows inquiry more in the spirit of Coleman's original conceptualization. While he defined social capital by its function, as the entity that facilitates action within a social structure, he was neither specific about what "facilitation" meant nor did he imply that it was always a positive thing.

9. There are clearly a number of settings in which smaller groups of participants might develop such norms, especially work on one of the committees. I never ob-

served any of these settings and do not consider them here, as they are by definition not open to all participants.

Warren: Power and Conflict in Social Capital (pp. 169–181)

1. This chapter reports some of the findings of a larger research project on the IAF, consisting of in-depth interviews, participant observation, and analysis of documents and newspaper articles conducted between 1993 and 1998 and supported by grants from the American Academy of Arts and Sciences Project on Social Capital, the Louisville Institute of the Lilly Endowment, and the Ford Foundation. The results of the larger research project, including a fuller discussion of the Project QUEST campaign, can be found in Warren (2001). I would like to thank Ernesto Cortes, Jr., and the Southwest IAF network for their assistance in conducting the research and analysis presented here.

2. The East Brooklyn IAF affiliate initiated the Nehemiah Homes affordable housing project, which became the model for federal legislation of that name (Ross 1995). BUILD in Baltimore developed a model "commonwealth" pact to supply college and work opportunities to high school graduates and worked to get the city council to pass the nation's first "living wage" ordinance (Orr 1992). In California the IAF worked to pass a substantial increase in the minimum wage.

3. The IAF may have had a substantial impact on citizen participation in San Antonio while the city's level of activity still remains behind other American cities. The study also covered all of San Antonio, so it may dilute the effects of IAF organizing.

4. From comments made by Ernesto Cortes, Jr., at a seminar held by the Southwest IAF, March 7, 1997, Austin, TX. In the fall of 1999, the East Coast network of IAF organizations launched an effort to get the U.S. Congress to pass legislation requiring all employers to offer a "living wage and benefits standard of at least $25,000."

Minkoff: Producing Social Capital (pp. 183–191)

1. Advocacy organizations pursue conventional grassroots and direct lobbying methods (e.g., contacting policy makers, policy monitoring, grassroots letter-writing campaigns) to influence authorities on behalf of collective interests (Jenkins 1987). Social movement organizations (SMOs) represent unrepresented constituencies with a combination of conventional and confrontational methods, including demonstrations, protests, boycotts, and the like. The national social movement sector (Garner and Zald 1987) includes all SMOs and advocacy organizations with a national movement base that are committed to social movement objectives.

2. Bryant (1993), Cohen and Arato (1994), Foley and Edwards (1996), and Kumar (1993) provide useful discussions about whether and where to draw the boundaries of civil society and the intellectual roots of various perspectives.

3. Coleman (1988) formally defines social capital as a property that inheres in the relations between individuals and social groups that facilitates individual action

(Coleman 1988). Note that this is a nonnormative definition that contrasts with Putnam's interpretation of the concept.

4. Interestingly, Foley and Edwards (1996), who criticize Putnam on a number of grounds, seem to agree with him on this one: they suggest that if national SMOs were dominant movement actors, rather than a minority in comparison with local grassroots organizations, then Putnam would be correct in omitting the extent of new organizational activity in recent decades and asserting a decline in civic participation as a result.

5. An earlier version of Cornell's paper used the term "communities of affinity," which conveys somewhat better the idea that group members feel some connection or affinity with other individuals and not simply to abstract identity symbols. Ken Newton (1997) develops a related concept of "imaginary" or "empathetic" communities built on abstract trust that creates "social solidarity for a community which stretches far beyond the immediate community of known individuals or sporadic contacts." He goes on to note that in modern societies this form of trust is likely to gain prominence, an argument that dovetails with the one made here.

6. Friedman and McAdam (1992) point out the double-sided nature of this process, that "increasingly the diffusion of collective identities and cultural symbols associated with the movement has blurred the boundary between the SMOS and the public" (p. 162). It then becomes something for everyone and operates less effectively as a selective incentive to mobilize tangible participation.

Smith: Global Civil Society? (pp. 194–204)

1. While nonpolitical transnational associations have expanded in numbers, it is those associations seeking to influence global social and political change that have drawn the bulk of analysts' attention.

2. McCarthy uses the term "thin infrastructures" to refer to "infrastructural deficits" that make it difficult to draw large populations who share common social change goals into the political process. These thin infrastructures are characterized by weak communication networks, a lack of face-to-face interaction, and a reliance on modern communications technologies such as mass mailings. In contrast, more readily activated social infrastructures consist of more traditional organizational bases such as churches (McCarthy 1987).

3. This seems to be changing somewhat. In more recent years, a larger percentage of TSMO headquarters have been based in the global South.

4. The question of how connected organizations based in global metropolitan centers are with their local and even national constituencies and whether these organizations are more or less integrated with their constituencies than are transnational organizations based outside global centers bears further investigation. Case study evidence suggests, however, that a tension exists that is similar to that found between U.S. groups based inside and outside the "beltway" (around Washington, D.C.) (Atwood 1997).

5. More than half of human rights TSMOs reported having three or fewer staff people (Smith, Pagnucco, and Lopez 1997).

6. Liebowitz found a similar problem in organizing efforts among U.S. and

Mexican womens' groups (Liebowitz 1997). In another case, dialogue and networking among environmental and development activists have led to a shift in mobilizing frames targeting World Bank policies from one emphasizing environmental conservation toward one that seeks the protection of human rights and the democratization of development processes (Nelson 1996:609).

7. For a detailed discussion of this campaign see Schrag (1992).

Diani: Social Capital as Social Movement Outcome (p. 207)

1. This is by no means a novel argument. Simmel (1955) offered what has become a classic formulation of the point when he stressed the integrative function of conflict not only *within*, but *among* collectivities.

2. See Diani (1997, pp.129–133) for a more detailed discussion of different approaches to movement outcomes.

Wood: Political Culture Reconsidered (pp. 254–263)

1. The author wishes to thank Robert Bellah, Ann Swidler, Robert Cole, Elisabeth Wood, Jerome Baggett, Dana Bell, John Coleman, SJ, Barry Stenger, and the editors of this volume for valuable feedback. Thanks also to the leaders and staff of the Pacific Institute for Community Organization for research access to their inspiring work, and to the Lilly Endowment for research support through the Center for Ethics and Social Policy in Berkeley, California. Please direct correspondence to Richard L. Wood, Department of Sociology, University of New Mexico, 1915 Roma NE, Albuquerque, NM 87131–1166, <rlwood@unm.edu>.

2. This is typical for such "actions" sponsored by single congregations: like American religious congregations, they will often be primarily of a single ethnic or racial group. However, "citywide actions" sponsored by a federation of ten to fifty congregations from a city are usually far more varied in their composition. In Oakland, such actions were typically about a third African American, a third Latino, and a third white, with smaller numbers of other ethnic groups.

3. Note that, for sake of clarity, this discussion switches Laitin's "first face" and "second face" of culture.

Foley, Edwards, and Diani: Social Capital Reconsidered (pp. 266–280)

1. This distinction bespeaks the easy slide into normative concepts occasioned by the adoption, by Putnam and others, of the "civic culture" argument of 1950s political science. Rarely theorized explicitly, its meaningfulness is even more rarely tested. However, Knack and Keefer (1997) attempt to test the conflicting claims that associational participation promotes trust and cooperative habits (Putnam 1995) or harmful rent-seeking behavior (Olson 1983). They find no empirical support for either position, as membership in the Olsonian (i.e., traditional interest) groups appears to have no effect on investment or growth, while membership in Putnamesque groups

(including religious and church organizations; education, arts, music, or cultural groups; and youth organizations) appears "perversely" to harm investment (1997:1273–74).

2. One standard question in the U.S. General Social Survey, for example, asks, "Is there any area right around here—that is, within a mile—where you would be afraid to walk alone?"

3. Jackman and Miller (1996a, 1996b) point to other problems with Putnam's and Inglehart's analyses. They note that Putnam's single-factor solution in constructing his indicator of institutional performance in *Making Democracy Work* does not adequately represent the information in the underlying measures and that re-analysis using the original variables does not support his conclusions. Turning to Inglehart's *Culture Shift in Advanced Industrial Society* (1990), Jackman and Miller find only weak correlations among the key cluster of cultural variables and they note that each of these variables responds differently to changes in economic conditions. In general, they find that "the six 'components' of political culture do not form a coherent general structure" (1996a:648). In a rejoinder to criticisms, they point out that the one variable that remains significant in Granato, Inglehart, and Leblang's reanalysis (1996), McClellands' "need for achievement," is measured in 1990 to predict economic growth from 1960 to 1989 (1996b:700).

4. Achieving such fine-grained precision is not easy. It cannot be done, as some have thought, by simply disaggregating data representative of a larger unit (nation) to "measure" variables at the subunit (state) level (Kawachi, Kennedy, and Lochner 1997). Disaggregating the 1996 National Election Survey into state-level indicators of political activity illustrates the flaws in such an approach. The nationally representative sample (N = 1,714) has a margin of error of ±2.4 percent, yet nine states have zero respondents in the nationally representative sample, six more have between one and four, which means that as state-level samples they would have a margin of error of between ±50 and ±100 percent. Only three state level subsamples—California, Texas, and Virginia—would have margins of error of less than ±10 percent. To make meaningful and reliable cross-state comparisons one would have to use separate random samples from each of the 50 states. For each of these to have a margin of error of even ±10 percent, each state sample would need 100 cases for a total of 5,000 across all 50 states. To gather such data on neighborhoods or even communities would require Herculean data collection efforts and vast resources—a task for the Census Bureau. While using the standard procedure just described at higher levels of analysis—cities, states, nations—would yield reasonably reliable measures, at that level of analysis such aggregate scores, regardless of their reliability, would lack validity, because they would collapse over too many relevant social cleavages and could mask systematic and even extreme differences between geographic or social groupings.

5. Peter Uvin (1998) notes that Rwanda probably enjoyed the highest density of "civil society" in Africa, yet many of these associations contributed indirectly and sometimes directly to the genocide that overwhelmed the nation in 1994. Little of the social capital represented by this "rich associational life" served to prevent or stem the horror, because most of it reflected the racism and structural violence that had characterized Rwandan society since independence. That associational life per se need not automatically generate positive outcomes is recognized by Putnam too

(e.g., 1995b). However, the point is often overlooked in analyses measuring social capital through survey questions, where only broad references to associational participation are made, without further qualification.

6, Charles Tilly (1998), for example, calls attention to other important dimensions of the structuring of individual and group access to opportunity in his elaboration of a framework for understanding the role of categorical schemes in creating and reinforcing "durable inequality" in the interests of "exploitation" and "opportunity hoarding."

Bibliography

Abbott, C. 1981. *The New Urban America: Growth and Politics in Sunbelt Cities.* Chapel Hill: University of North Carolina Press.

Adam, Barry. D. 1987. *The Rise of a Gay and Lesbian Movement.* Boston, Mass.: Twayne Publishers.

Adams, C. T. 1991. Philadelphia: The slide toward municipal bankruptcy. In *Big City Politics in Transition,* ed. H. V. Savitch and John Clayton Thomas. Urban Affairs Annual Review, 38. Beverly Hills, Calif.: Sage Publications.

Alinsky, Saul D. 1946. *Reveille for Radicals.* New York: Vintage Books.

———. 1965. The war on poverty—Political Pornography. *Journal of Social Issues* 21 (January): 41–43.

———. 1971. *Rules for Radicals: A Pragmatic Primer for Realistic Radicals.* New York: Vintage Books.

Anderson, Cynthia D., and Michael D. Schulman. 1999. Women, restructuring, and textiles: The increasing complexity of subordination and struggle in a southern community. Pp. 91–108 in *Neither Separate nor Equal: Women, Race, and Class in the South,* ed. Barbara Ellen Smith. Philadelphia, Pa.: Temple University Press.

Aoki, M. 1988. *Information, Incentives, and Bargaining in the Japanese Economy.* Cambridge, U.K.: Cambridge University Press.

Applebaum, E., and R. Batt. 1994. *The New American Workplace.* Ithaca, N.Y.: ILR Press.

Appleman, J. 1996. *Evaluation Study of Institution-Based Organizing.* Unpublished manuscript, Jericho, N.Y.

Ardener, Shirley. 1964. The comparative study of rotating credit associations, *Journal of the Royal Anthropological Institute of Great Britain and Northern Ireland* 94: 201–39.

Arendt, Hannah. 1973. *The Origins of Totalitarianism.* New York: Harcourt Brace Jovanovich.

Aron, Raymond. 1968. *Main Currents in Sociological Thought: Volume 1, Montesquieu, Comte, Marx, Tocqueville, and the Sociologists and the Revolution of 1848.* Garden City, N.Y.: Doubleday.

Arrow, Kenneth J. 1972. Gifts and exchanges. *Philosophy and Public Affairs* 1 (summer).

Atwood, D. 1997. Mobilizing around the United Nations special session on disarmament. In *Transnational Social Movements and Global Politics: Solidarity Beyond the State,* ed. J. Smith, C. Chatfield, and R. Pagnucco. Syracuse, N.Y.: Syracuse University Press.

Banfield, Edward C. 1958. *The Moral Basis of a Backward Society.* Glencoe, Ill.: Free Press.

Barber, Benjamin R. 1984. *Strong Democracy*. Berkeley: University of California Press.

———. 1995. *Jihad vs. McWorld: How the Planet Is both Falling Apart and Coming Together—and What This Means for Democracy*. New York: New York Times Books.

———. 1998. *A Place for Us*. New York: Hill and Wang.

Barton, Stephen E., and Carol J. Silverman, eds. 1994. *Common Interest Communities: Private Governments and the Public Interest*. Berkeley, Calif.: Institute of Governmental Studies.

Beane, J., J. Turner, D. Jones, and R. Lipka. 1981. Long-term effects of community service programs. *Curriculum Inquiry* 11: 143–55.

Bebbington, Anthony. 1997. Social capital and rural intensification: Local organizations and islands of sustainability in the rural Andes. *The Geographical Journal* 163, no. 2 (July 1997): 189–97.

Bellah, R. N., R. Madsen, W. M. Sullivan, A. Swidler, and S. M. Tipton. 1985. *Habits of the Heart: Individualism and Commitment in American Life*. New York: Harper & Row.

Benson, Lee. 1964. *The Concept of Jacksonian Democracy: New York as a Test Case*. New York: Atheneum.

Bentley, Arthur F. 1908. *The Process of Government: A Study of Social Pressures*. Chicago: University of Chicago Press.

Berger, Peter L., and Richard John Neuhaus. 1977. *To Empower People: The Role of Mediating Structures in Public Policy*. Washington: American Enterprise Institute for Public Policy Research.

Berliner, Joseph. 1957. *Factory and Manager in the USSR*. Cambridge, Mass: Harvard University Press.

Berman, Sheri. 1997. Civil Society and the Collapse of the Weimar Republic. *World Politics* 49: 401–29.

Berry, Jeffrey M. 1989. *The interest group society*. 2nd ed. New York: Harper Collins.

Berry, Jeffrey M., Kent E. Portney, and Ken Thomson. 1993. *The Rebirth of Urban Democracy*. Washington, D.C.: Brookings Institution.

Birmingham City Council. 1994. *Report of the Assistant Chief Executive (Race Relations): Standing Consultative Forum and Black and Minority Ethnic Umbrella Groups (Joint Race Relations Sub-Committee, 28 January 1994)*. Birmingham: Birmingham City Council.

———. 1999. *Report of the Head of Equalities: Review and Development of the Standing Consultative Forum (Equalities Committee, 26 January 1999)*. Birmingham: Birmingham City Council.

Blair, H. 1994. Civil society and democratic development. Washington, D.C.: U.S. Agency for International Development—Center for Development Information and Evaluation.

Blaney, D. L., and M. K. Pasha. 1993. Civil society and democracy in the third world: Ambiguities and historical possibilities. *Studies in Comparative International Development* 28: 3–24.

Booth, John A., and Patricia Bayer Richard. 1996. Repression, participation, and democratic norms in urban Central America. *American Journal of Political Science* 40: 1205–32.

———. 1998. Civil society, political capital, and democracy in Central America. *Journal of Politics* 60, no. 3: 780.

Booth, John A., and Mitchell A. Seligson. 1979. Peasants as activists: A reevaluation of political participation in the countryside. *Comparative Political Studies* 12: 29–59.

———. 1993. Paths to democracy and the political culture of Costa Rica, Mexico, and Nicaragua. In *Political Culture and Democracy in Developing Countries*, ed. E. Diamond. Boulder: Lynne Rienner.

Booth, John. A, and T. W. Walker. 1993. *Understanding Central America.* Boulder: Westview.

Borgatti, Stephen P., Candace Jones, and Martin G. Everett. 1998. Network measures of social capital. *Connections* 21: 27–36.

Bourdieu, Pierre. 1986. The forms of capital. Pp. 241–58 in *Handbook of Theory and Research for the Sociology of Education*, ed. John Richardson. New York: Greenwood Press.

Bourdieu, Pierre, and Loic Waquant. 1992. *Introduction to Reflexive Sociology.* Chicago: University of Chicago Press.

Boyte, Harry C. 1980. *Backyard Revolution: Understanding the New Citizen Movement.* Philadelphia: Temple University Press.

———. 1989. *Commonwealth: A Return to Citizen Politics.* Glencoe, Ill.: Free Press.

Brantlinger, Patrick. 1983. *Bread and Circuses: Theories of Mass Culture and Social Decay.* Ithaca, N.Y.: Cornell University Press.

Brehm, J., and W. Rahn. 1997. Individual-level evidence for the causes and consequences of social capital. *American Journal of Political Science* 41: 999–1023.

Brienes, Wini. 1982. *Organization and Community in the New Left, 1962–1968: The Great Refusal.* New York: Praeger.

Briggs, Xavier de Souza. 1998. Brown kids in white suburbs: Housing mobility and the many faces of social capital. *Housing Policy Debate* 9, no. 1: 177–221.

Brown, L. David, and Darcy Ashman. 1996. Participation, social capital, and intersectoral problem solving: African and Asian cases. *World Development* 24, no. 9: 1467–79.

Bryant, C. 1993. Social self-organisation, civility and sociology: A comment on Kumar's "Civil Society." *British Journal of Sociology* 44: 397–401.

Bryk, Anthony, et al. 1994. *Catholic Schools and the Common Good.* Cambridge, Mass.: Harvard University Press.

Brysk, Allison. 1996. Turning weakness into strength: The internationalization of Indian rights. *Latin American Perspectives* 89, no 23: 38–57.

Buchanan, James M., Robert D. Tollison and Gordon Tullock. 1980. *Towards a Theory of the Rent-Seeking Society.* College Station: Texas A&M University Press.

Bulmer-Thomas, V. 1987. *The Political Economy of Central America since 1920.* Cambridge, U.K.: Cambridge University Press.

Burstein, Paul, Rachel L. Einwohner, and Jocelyn A. Hollander. 1995. The success of political movements: A bargaining perspective. Pp. 275–95 in *The Politics of Social Protest*, ed. J. Craig Jenkins and Bert Klandermans. Minneapolis, Minn. and London: University of Minnesota Press/UCL Press.

Burt, Ronald S. 1992. *Structural Holes.* Cambridge, Mass.: Harvard University Press.

———. 1997. The contingent value of social capital. *Administrative Science Quarterly* 42: 339–65.

Byrne, J. A. 1993a. The horizontal corporation. *Business Week*, 20 December: 76–81.

———. 1993b. The virtual corporation. *Business Week*, 8 February: 98–102.

Calhoun, Craig. 1992. Introduction. In *Habermas and the Public Sphere*, ed. C. Calhoun. Cambridge, Mass.: MIT Press.

———. 1994 Nationalism and civil society. Pp. 304–35 in *Social Theory and the Politics of Identity*, ed. C. Calhoun. Cambridge, Mass.: Blackwell.

Carroll, T. F. 1992. *Intermediary NGOs: The Supporting Link in Grassroots Development*. West Hartford, Conn.: Kumarian.

Charlotte Observer. 1997. Pillowtex to buy Fieldcrest. 12 September.

———. 1985 Cannon union vote likely to echo throughout textiles. 29 September.

Chatfield, Charles. 1997. Intergovernmental and nongovernmental associations to 1945. In *Transnational Social Movements and Global Politics: Solidarity Beyond the State*, ed. Jackie Smith, Charles Chatfield, and Ronald Pagnucco. Syracuse, N.Y.: Syracuse University Press.

Clapp, J. 1994. The toxic waste trade with less-industrialised countries: Economic linkages and political alliances. *Third World Quarterly* 15, no. 3: 505–18.

Clark, J. 1991. *Democratizing Development: The Role of Voluntary Organizations*. West Hartford, Conn.: Kumarian.

Clemens, Elisabeth S. 1997. *The People's Lobby: Organizational Innovation and the Rise of Interest Group Politics in the United States, 1890–1925*. Chicago: University of Chicago Press.

Clemetson, R. A., and R. Coates. 1992. *Restoring Broken Places and Rebuilding Communities: A Casebook on African-American Church Involvement in Community Economic Development*. Washington, D.C.: National Congress for Community Economic Development.

Cohen, C. 1999. *The Boundaries of Blackness: AIDS and the Breakdown of Black Politics*. Chicago: University of Chicago Press.

Cohen, J., and J. Rogers. 1992. Secondary associations and democratic governance. *Politics and Society* 20: 393–472.

Cohen, Jean, and Andrew Arato. 1994. *Civil Society and Political Theory*. Cambridge, Mass.: MIT Press.

Coleman, James S. 1988. Social capital in the creation of human capital. *American Journal of Sociology* (supplement) 94: S95–S120.

———. 1990. *Foundations of Social Theory*. Cambridge, Mass: Harvard University Press.

———. 1993. The rational reconstruction of society. *American Sociological Review* 58: 1–15.

———. 1994. A rational choice perspective on economic sociology. Pp. 166–80 in *The Handbook of Economic Sociology*, ed. Neil J. Smelser and Richard Swedberg. Princeton, N.J.: Princeton University Press.

Coles, R., and J. Brenner. 1965. American youth in a social struggle. *American Journal of Orthopsychiatry* 35: 909–26.

Collins, C. L. 1994. Fieldcrest Cannon." Pp. 213–17 in *International Directory of Company Histories*, vol. 9, ed. Paula Kepos. Detroit, Mich.: St. James Press.

Committee for Economic Development, Research and Policy Committee. 1995. *Rebuilding Inner-City Communities: A New Approach to the Nation's Urban Crisis*. New York: Committee for Economic Development.

Conover, Pamela Johnston, and Donald D. Searing. 1995. Citizens and members: Foundations for participation. Paper prepared for the annual meeting of the American Political Science Association, Chicago, Illinois, September 1995.

Conrad, D. 1991. School-community participation for social skills. Pp. 540–48 in *Handbook of Research on Social Studies Teaching and Learning*, ed. J. P. Shaver. New York: Macmillan.

Conway, M. M. 1991. *Political Participation in the United States*. Washington, D.C.: Congressional Quarterly.

Cook, Karen S., and J. M. Whitmeyer. 1992. Two approaches to social structure: Exchange theory and network analysis. *Annual Review of Sociology* 18: 109–27.

Cornell, S. J. 1996. The variable ties that bind: Content and circumstance in ethnic processes. *Ethnic and Racial Studies* 19: 265–89.

Couch, Carl J. 1968. Collective behavior: An examination of some stereotypes. *Social Problems* 15: 318.

Crenson, Matthew A. 1983. *Neighborhood Politics*. Cambridge, Mass.: Harvard University Press.

Crouch, C. 1985. Conditions for trade union wage restraint. In *The Politics of Inflation and Economic Stagnation*, ed. L. N. Lindberg and C. S. Maier. Washington, D.C.: Brookings Institution.

D'Emilio, J. 1983. *Sexual Politics, Sexual Communities*. Chicago: University of Chicago Press.

Dahl, Robert A. 1982. *Dilemmas of Pluralist Democracy: Autonomy vs. Control*. New Haven: Yale University Press.

Dalton, Russell J. 1988. *Citizen Politics in Western Democracies*. Chatham, N.J.: Chatham House.

Dalton, R. J., and M. Kuechler, eds. 1990. *Challenging the Political Order: New Social Movements in Western Democracies*. New York: Oxford University Press.

Dasgupta, Partha. 1988. Trust as a commodity. Pp. 49–72 in *Trust: Making and Breaking Cooperative Relations*, ed. Diego Gambett. Oxford: Blackwell.

della Porta, Donatella. 1988. Recruitment processes in clandestine political organizations: Italian left-wing terrorism. Pp.155–72 in *From Structure to Action*, ed. B. Klandermans, H. Kriesi, and S. Tarrow. Greenwich, Conn.: JAI Press.

della Porta, Donatella, and Mario Diani. 1999. *Social Movements*. Oxford: Blackwell.

DeMartini, J. 1983. Social movements participation. *Youth and Society* 15: 195–223.

Diamond, L. 1992. Introduction: Civil society and the struggle for democracy. In *The Democratic Revolution: Struggles for Freedom and Democracy in the Developing World*, ed. L. Diamond. New York: Freedom House.

Diani, Mario. 1992. The concept of social movement. *Sociological Review* 40: 1–25.

———. 1994. The conflict over nuclear energy in Italy. Pp. 201–31 in *States and Anti-Nuclear Movements*, ed. Helena Flam. Edinburgh: Edinburgh University Press.

———. 1995. *Green Networks: A Structural Analysis of the Italian Environmental Movement*. Edinburgh: Edinburgh University Press.

———. 1997. Social movements and social capital: A network perspective on movement outcomes. *Mobilization* 2: 129–47.

Diani, Mario, and Paolo R. Donati. 1984. L'oscuro oggetto del desiderio: Leadership e potere nelle aree del movimento. Pp. 315–44 in *Altri Codici*, ed. Alberto Melucci. Bologna: Il Mulino.

Diani, Mario, and Giovanni Lodi. 1988. Three in one: Currents in the Milan ecology movement. Pp. 103–24 in *From Structure to Action*, ed. by B. Klandermans, H. Kriesi, and S. Tarrow. Greenwich, Conn.: JAI Press.

Donati, Paolo R. 1996. Building a unified movement: Resource mobilization, media work, and organizational transformation in the Italian environmentalist movement. Pp. 125–57 in *Research in Social Movements, Conflict and Change*, vol. 19, ed. L. Kriesberg. Greenwich, Conn.: JAI Press.

Donati, Paolo, and Maria Mormino. 1984. Il potere della definizione: Le forme organizzative dell'antagonismo metropolitano. Pp. 349–84 in *Altri Codici*, ed. A. Melucci. Bologna: Il Mulino.

Dore, Ronald. 1986. *Flexible Rigidities*. Stanford, Calif.: Stanford University Press.

———. 1987. *Taking Japan Seriously*. Stanford, Calif.: Stanford University Press.

Durham Herald-Sun. 1998. Businessman has big plans for Fieldcrest Cannon. 9 February.

EarthAction. 1994. Report on 1994 Partner Survey. Amherst, Mass.: EarthAction.

———. 1995. Partner Survey. Amherst, Mass.: EarthAction.

Eckstein, Harry. 1961. *A Theory of Stable Democracy*. Research Monograph 10. Princeton, N.J.: Princeton University Center for International Studies.

Edwards, Bob. 1995. Organizational style in middle-class and poor people's social movement organizations: An empirical assessment of new social movements theory. Diss. The Catholic University of America, Washington, D.C.

Edwards, Bob, and Michael W. Foley. 1997. Social capital and the political economy of our discontent. *American Behavioral Scientist* 40: 669–78.

———. 1998. Civil society and social capital beyond Putnam. *American Behavioral Scientist* 42, no. 1: 124–39.

Eisinger, Peter K. 1973. The conditions of protest behavior in American cities. *Political Studies* 6: 11–28.

Emirbayer, Mustafa, and Jeff Goodwin. 1994. Network analysis, culture, and the problem of agency, *American Journal of Sociology* 99: 1411–54.

Epstein, Barbara. 1991. *Political Protest and Cultural Revolution*. Berkeley: University of California Press.

Erikson, E. H. 1968. *Identity, Youth and Crisis*. New York: Norton.

Esman, M. J., and N. Uphoff. 1984. *Local Organizations: Intermediaries in Rural Development*. Ithaca, N.Y.: Cornell University Press.

Etzioni, A.1995. *Rights and the Common Good: The Communitarian Perspective*. New York: St. Martin's Press.

Evans, Sara M., and Harry Boyte. 1992. *Free Spaces*. Chicago: University of Chicago Press.

Falk, R. 1987. The global promise of social movements. Pp. 363–85 in *Towards a Just World Peace: Perspectives From Social Movements*, ed. S. H. Mendlovitz and R. B. J. Walker. Boston: Butterworths.

Fals Borda, O. 1992. Social movements and political power in Latin America. Pp. 303–16 in *The Making of Social Movements in Latin America*, ed. A. Escobar and S. E. Alvarez. Boulder: Westview Press.

Fantasia, R. 1988. *Cultures of Solidarity*. Berkeley: University of California Press.

Fendrich, J. 1993. *Ideal Citizens*. Albany: State University of New York Press.

Ferguson, Adam. 1995. *An Essay on the History of Civil Society*. Cambridge, U.K.: Cambridge University Press.

Finkelman, Paul. 1987. Slavery and the constitutional convention: Making a covenant with death. Pp. 188–225 in *Beyond Confederation: Origins of the Constitution and American National Identity*, ed. Richard Beeman, Stephen Botein, and Edward C. Carter II. Chapel Hill: University of North Carolina Press.

Flacks, R. 1988. *Making History: The American Left and the American Mind*. New York: Columbia University Press.

Flanagan, C., B. Jonsson, L. Botcheva, B. Csapo, J. Bowes, and P. Macek. 1997. Adolescents and the "social contract": Developmental roots of citizenship in seven countries. In *International perspectives on community service and civic engagement*, ed. M. Yates and J. Youniss. Manuscript.

Flora, Cornelia B., and Jan L. Flora. 1993. Entrepreneurial social infrastructure: A necessary ingredient. *The Annals of the American Academy of Political and Social Sciences* 529: 48–58.

Flora, Jan L. 1998. Social capital and communities of place, *Rural Sociology* 63, no. 4: 481–506.

Flora, Jan L., Jeff Sharp, Cornelia Flora, and Bonnie Newlon. 1997. Entrepreneurial social infrastructure and locally initiated economic development in the nonmetropolitan United States, *Sociological Quarterly* 38, no. 4: 623–45.

Foley, Michael W. 1996. Laying the groundwork: The struggle for civil society in El Salvador. *Journal of Interamerican Politics and World Affairs* 38: 67–104.

Foley, Michael W., and Bob Edwards. 1996. The paradox of civil society. *Journal of Democracy* 7, no. 3: 38–52.

———. 1997. Escape from politics? Social theory and the social capital debate. *American Behavioral Scientist* 40, no. 5: 549–60.

———. 1998. Beyond Tocqueville: Civil society and social capital in comparative perspective. *American Behavioral Scientist* 42, no. 1: 5–20.

———. 1999. Is it time to disinvest in social capital? *Journal of Public Policy* 19: 669–78.

Formisano, Ronald P. 1983. *The Transformation of Political Culture: Massachusetts Parties, 1790s–1840s*. New York: Oxford University Press.

Fowler, Robert Booth. 1991. *The Dance with Community*. Lawrence: University Press of Kansas.

Francis, M. 1996. Dual citizenship. *The Oregonian*, 25 July, B1.

Fraser, N. 1992. Rethinking the public sphere: A contribution to the critique of actually existing democracy. In *Habermas and the public sphere*, ed. C. Calhoun. Cambridge, Mass.: MIT Press.

Freeman, J. 1973. The emergence of the women's liberation movement. *American Journal of Sociology* 78: 792–811.

Freeman, L. C. 1979. Centrality in social networks. I. Conceptual clarifications. *Social Networks* 1: 215–39.

Friedman, D., and D. McAdam. 1992. Collective identity and activism. In *Frontiers in social movement theory*, ed. A. D. Morris and C. M. Mueller. New Haven, Conn.: Yale University Press.

Fritzsche, Peter. 1990. *Rehearsals for Fascism*. New York: Oxford University Press.

Fromm, Erich. 1941. *Escape from Freedom*. New York: Avon Books.

Fukuyama, Francis, 1995a. *Trust: The Social Virtues and the Creation of Prosperity*. New York: Free Press.

———. 1995b. Social capital and the global economy. *Foreign Affairs* (September/October): 89–103.

Gabriel, C., and L. Macdonald. 1994. NAFTA, Women and Organising in Canada and Mexico: Forging a "Feminist internationality." *Millennium: Journal of International Studies* 23, no. 3: 535–62.

Galaskiewicz, Joseph. 1979. *Exchange Networks and Community Politics*. Beverly Hills, Calif.: Sage.

Gamson, Joshua. 1995. Must identity movements self-destruct? A queer dilemma. *Social Problems* 42: 101–18.

Gamson, William. 1990. *The Strategy Of Social Protest*. 2nd ed. Belmont, Calif.: Wadsworth.

———. 1991. Commitment and agency in social movements. *Sociological Forum* 6: 27–50.

Garner, R, and M. N. Zald. 1987. The political economy of social movement sectors. In *Social movements in an organizational society*, ed. M. N. Zald and J. D. McCarthy. New Brunswick, N.J.: Transaction Publishers.

Garreton, M. A. 1989. Popular mobilization and the military regime in Chile: The complexities of the invisible transition. Pp. 259–77 in *Power and Popular Protest: Latin American Social Movements*, ed. S. Eckstein. Berkeley and Los Angeles: University of California Press.

Geertz, Clifford. 1962. The rotating credit association: A "middle rung" in development. *Economic Development and Cultural Change* 10: 241–63.

Giddens, A. 1983. *New Rules of Sociological Methods*. Stanford, Calif.: Stanford University Press.

Gitelman, Zvi. 1984. Working the Soviet system: Citizens and urban bureaucracies. Pp. 221–43 in *The Contemporary Soviet City*, ed. Henry W. Morton. Armonk, N.Y.: M. E. Sharpe.

Gitlin, T. 1987. *The Sixties: Days of Hope, Days of Rage*. New York: Bantam Books.

Gittell, Marilyn. 1980. *Limits to Citizen Participation: The Decline of Community Organizations*. Beverly Hills, Calif.: Sage.

Giugni, Marco. 1999. How social movements matter. Pp. xiii–xxxii in *How Movements Matter*, ed. M. Giugni, D. McAdam, and C. Tilly. Minneapolis and London: University of Minnesota Press/UCL Press.

Giugni, Marco, D. McAdam, and C. Tilly, eds. 1999. *How Movements Matter*. Minneapolis and London: University of Minnesota Press/UCL Press.

Glenn, John. 1999. Competing challengers and contested outcomes to state breakdown: The velvet revolution in Czechoslovakia. *Social Forces* 78: 187–211.

Gould, Roger. 1995. *Insurgent Identities: Class, Community, and Protest in Paris from 1848 to the Commune*. Chicago: University of Chicago Press.

Gould, Roger, and Roberto Fernandez. 1989. Structures of mediation: A formal approach to brokerage in transaction networks. *Sociological Methodology* 19: 89–126.

Graber, Mark. 2001. *Dred Scott and the Problem of Constitutional Evil*. Princeton, N.J.: Princeton University Press.

Gramsci, Antonio. 1971. *Selections from the Prison Notebooks of Antonio Gramsci*. Ed. and trans. Quintin Hoare and Geoffrey Nowell Smith. New York: International Publishers.

Granato, Jim, Ronald Inglehart, and David Leblang. 1996. The effect of cultural values on economic development: Theory, hypotheses, and some empirical tests. *American Journal of Political Science* 40, no. 3 (August): 607–31.

Granovetter, Mark. 1973. The strength of weak ties. *American Journal of Sociology* 78: 1360–80.

Greeley, Andrew. 1992. Habits of the head. *Society and Social Research* 29, no. 4: 74–81.

———. 1997a. *The Strange Reappearance of Civic America: Religion and Volunteering*. [On-line]. Available: <http://www.agreeley.com/articles/civic.html>.

———. 1997b. The other civic America, religion, and social capital. *The American Prospect* 32 (May-June): 68–73.

Greensboro News and Record. 1997. Pillowtex buys out Fieldcrest, joins nation's top linen makers. 20 December.

Greif, Avner. 1989. Reputation and coalition in medieval trade: Evidence on the Maghribi traders. *Journal of Economic History* 49: 857–82.

———. Cultural beliefs and the organization of society. *Journal of Political Economy* 102: 912–50.

Gronbjerg, K., L. Harmon, A. Olkkonen, and A. Raza. 1996. The United Way system at the crossroads: Community planning and allocation. *Nonprofit and Voluntary Sector Quarterly* 25: 428–52.

Grossman, Gregory. 1977. The second economy of the USSR. *Problems of Communism* 26, no. 5: 25–40.

Gundelach, Peter, and Lars Torpe. 1996. Voluntary associations: New types of involvement and democracy. Paper presented to the European Consortium for Political Research Joint Sessions of Workshops, Oslo.

Gurwitt, R. 1991. The rule of the absentocracy: The eclipse of hometown leadership and how some places are coping with it. *Governing* (September): 52–58.

Gusfield, Joseph R. 1962. Mass society and extremist politics. *American Sociological Review* 27, no. 1:19–30.

Habermas, J. 1974. The public sphere. *New German Critique* 3: 49–55.

Hagtvet, Bernt. 1980. The theory of mass society and the collapse of the Weimar Republic: A re-examination. In *Who Were the Fascists: Social Roots of European Racism*, ed. Stein Ugelvik Larsen. Oslo: Universitetsförlaget.

Halebsky, Sandor. 1976. *Mass Society and Political Conflict: Toward a Reconstruction of Theory*. Cambridge, U.K.: Cambridge University Press.

Hall, Jacquelyn Dowd, James Leloudis, Robert Korstad, Mary Murphy, Lu Ann Jones, and Christopher B. Daly. 1987. *Like a Family: The Making of a Southern Cotton Mill World*. Chapel Hill: University of North Carolina Press.

Hall, Peter. 1998. Social capital in Britain. *British Journal of Political Science* 29 (1999): 417–61.

Hanifan. L. J. 1920. *The Community Center*. Boston: Silver, Burdette.

Hanks, M., and B. K. Eckland. 1978. Adult voluntary associations and adolescent socialization. *The Sociological Quarterly* 19: 481–90.

Hannigan, John. 1995. *Environmental Sociology*. London and New York: Routledge.

Hansen, John Mark. 1991. *Gaining Access: Congress and the Farm Lobby, 1919–1981*. Chicago: University of Chicago Press.

Hedlund, Stefan, and Niclas Sundström. 1996. Does Palermo represent the future for Moscow? *Journal of Public Policy* 16, no. 2: 113–55.

Hegel, Georg Wilhelm Friedrich. 1945. *Hegel's Philosophy of Right*. Trans. with notes by T. M. Know. Oxford: Clarendon Press.

Held, D. 1989. *Political Theory and the Modern State*. Stanford, Calif.: Stanford University Press.

Helliwell, J., and R. D. Putnam. 1995. Economic growth and social capital in Italy. *Eastern Economic Journal* 21: 295–307.

Heying, C. H. 1995. Civic elites, civic institutions, and the urban growth dynamic. Doctoral diss., University of North Carolina at Chapel Hill. *Dissertation Abstracts International* 56, 10A.

Hicks, A., and L. Kenworthy. 1998. Cooperation and political economic performance in affluent democratic capitalism. *American Journal of Sociology* 103: 1631–72.

Hirschman, A. O. 1984. *Getting Ahead Collectively: Grassroots Experiences in Latin America*. Elmsford, N.Y.: Pergamon.

Hodgkinson, V., and M. Weitzman. 1989. *Dimensions of the Independent Sector: A Statistical Profile*. 3rd ed. Washington, D.C.: The Independent Sector.

Holt, D. 1991. City leaders back jobs program. San Antonio *Light*, 4 September.

Huntington, Samuel P. 1968. *Political Order in Changing Societies*. New Haven, Conn.: Yale University Press.

Huston, James L. 1993. The American revolutionaries, the political economy of aristocracy, and the American concept of the distribution of wealth, 1765–1900. *American Historical Review* 98: 1079–1105.

Imig, D. R. 1996. *Power and Poverty: The Political Representation of Poor Americans*. Lincoln: University of Nebraska Press.

Inglehart, Ronald. 1988. The rennaissance of political culture. *American Political Science Review* 82: 1203–30.

———. 1990. *Culture Shift in Advanced Industrial Society*. Princeton, N.J.: Princeton University Press.

———. 1997. *Modernization and Postmodernization: Cultural, Economic and Political Change in 41 Societies*. Princeton, N.J.: Princeton University Press.

Jackman, Mary. 1994. *The Velvet Glove: Paternalism and Conflict in Gender, Class, and Race Relations*. Berkeley: University of California Press.

Jackman, Robert W., and Ross A. Miller. 1996a. A renaissance of political culture? *American Journal of Political Science* 40, no. 3 (August): 632–59.

———. 1996b. The poverty of political culture." *American Journal of Political Science* 40, no. 3 (August): 697–716.

———. 1998. Social capital and politics. *Annual Review of Political Science* 1: 47–73.

Jenkins, J. Craig. 1983 Resource moblization theory and the study of social movements. *Annual Review of Sociology* 9: 527–53.

———. 1987. Nonprofit organizations and policy advocacy. In *The Non-Profit Sector*, ed. W. Powell. New Haven, Conn.: Yale University Press.

Johnson, Paul E. 1978. *A Shopkeeper's Millennium: Society and Revivals in Rochester, New York, 1815–1837*. New York: Hill and Wang.

Johnston, Hank. 1994. New social movements and old regional nationalisms. Pp. 267–86 in *New Social Movements. From Ideology to Identity*, ed. E. Laraña, H. Johnston, and J. Gusfield. Philadelphia: Temple University Press.

Johnston, Hank, and David A. Snow. 1998. Subcultures and the emergence of the Estonian nationalist opposition. *Sociological Perspectives* 41: 473–97.

Judis, J. B. 1992. The pressure elite: Inside the narrow world of advocacy group politics. *American Prospect* 9: 15–30.

Kasarda, J., and M. Janowitz. 1974. Community attachment in mass society. *American Sociological Review* 39: 328–39.

Kawachi, Ichiro, Bruce P. Kennedy, and Kimberly Lochner. 1997. Long live community: Social capital as public health. *The American Prospect* (November-December): 56–59.

Keane, J., ed. 1988a. *Civil Society and the State*. London: Verso.

——. 1988b. *Democracy and Civil Society: On the Predicaments of European Socialism, the Prospects for Democracy, and the Problem of Controlling Social and Political Power*. London: Verso.

——. 1988c. Despotism and democracy. Pp. 35–72 in *Civil Society and the State*, ed. J. Keane. London: Verso.

Kearns, Paul R. 1995. *Weavers of Dreams*. Barium Springs, N.C.: Mullen Press.

Keck, Margaret, and Kathryn Sikkink. 1998. *Activists Beyond Borders: Advocacy Networks in International Politics*. Ithaca, N.Y.: Cornell University Press.

Kenney, M., and R. Florida. 1988. Beyond mass production: Production and the labor process in Japan. *Politics and Society* 16: 121–58.

Kenworthy, Lane. 1995. *In Search of National Economic Success: Balancing Competition and Cooperation*. Thousand Oaks, Calif.: Sage.

——. 1996. Unions, wages, and the common interest. *Comparative Political Studies* 28: 491–524.

——. 1998. Economic cooperation in 18 industrialized democracies: Scoring for 1960–89, with tentative scores for 1990–94. Unpublished.

Kenworthy, Lane, and A. Hicks. 2000. Neocorporatism, income distribution, and macroeconomic performance. Unpublished. Department of Sociology, Emory University.

Keohane, R., and J. Nye. 1972. Transnational relations and world politics: An introduction. Pp. ix–xxvii in *Transnational Relations and World Politics*, ed. R. Keohane & J. Nye. Cambridge, Mass.: Harvard University Press.

Kettering Foundation. 1991. *Citizens and Politics: A View from Main Street America*. Dayton, Ohio: Charles F. Kettering Foundation.

Klandermans, Bert, Hanspeter Kriesi, and Sidney Tarrow, eds. 1988. *From Structure to Action*. Greenwich, Conn.: JAI Press.

Klatch, R. 1987. *Women of the New Right*. Philadelphia: Temple University Press.

Knack, S., and P. Keefer. 1997. Does social capital have an economic payoff? A cross-country investigation. *Quarterly Journal of Economics* 112: 1251–88.

Knoke, David. 1990. *Political Networks. The Structural Perspective*. Cambridge, U.K.: Cambridge University Press.

Knoke, David, and Nancy Wisely. 1990. Social movements. Pp. 57–84 in *Political Networks*, ed. David Knoke. Cambridge and New York: Cambridge University Press.

Kolankiewicz, George. 1994. Elites in search of a political formula. *Daedalus* (summer): 143–57.

Kollock, Peter. 1994. The emergence of exchange structures: An experimental study of uncertainty, commitment, and trust. *American Journal of Sociology* 100: 313–45.

Kornhauser, William. 1960. *The Politics of Mass Society*. London: Routledge and Kegan Paul.

Krackhardt, David. 1992. The strength of strong ties: The importance of philos in organizations. Pp. 216–39 in *Networks and Organizations*, ed. N. Nohria and R. G. Eccles. Cambridge, Mass.: Harvard Business School Press.

Kriesberg, L. 1997. Social movements and global transformation. In *Transnational Social Movements and Global Politics: Solidarity Beyond the State*, ed. J. Smith, C. Chatfield, and R. Pagnucco. Syracuse, N.Y.: Syracuse University Press.

Kriesi, Hanspeter. 1988. Local mobilization for the people's petition of the Dutch peace movement. Pp. 41–82 in *International Social Movement Research, Vol.I, From Structure To Action*, ed. Bert Klandermans, Hanspeter Kriesi, and Sidney Tarrow. Greenwich, Conn.: JAI Press.

———. 1995. The political opportunity structure of new social movements: Its impact on their mobilization. Pp. 167–98 in *The Politics of Social Protest*, ed. J. Craig Jenkins and Bert Klandermans. London: UCL Press.

Kriesi, Hanspeter, Ruud Koopmans, Jan Willem Duyvendak, and Marco Giugni. 1995. *New Social Movements in Western Europe*. Minneapolis and London: University of Minnesota Press/UCL Press.

Kumar, K. 1993. Civil society: An inquiry into the usefulness of an historical term. *British Journal of Sociology* 44: 376–95.

Ladewig, H., and J. K. Thomas. 1987. *Assessing the Impact of 4-H on Former Members*. College Station: Texas Tech University.

Laitin, D. 1986. *Hegemony and Culture: Politics and Religious Change among the Yoruba*. Chicago: University of Chicago Press.

Lane, J. E., and S. Ersson. 1990. Macro and micro understanding in political science: What explains electoral participation? *European Journal of Political Research* 18: 457–65.

Lang, Robert E., and Steven P. Hornburg. What is social capital and why is it important to public policy? *Housing Policy Debate* 9, no. 1: 1–16.

Lange, Peter, Michael Wallerstein, and Miriam Golden. 1995. The end of corporatism? Wage setting in the Nordic and Germanic countries. Pp. 76–100 in *The Workers of Nations*, ed. Sanford Jacoby. New York: Oxford University Press.

Laumann, Edward O., and Franz U. Pappi. 1976. *Networks of Collective Action. A Perspective on Community Influence Systems*. New York: Academic Press.

Lazarsfeld, Paul, Bernard Berelson, and Hazel Gaudet. 1948. *The People's Choice: How The Voter Makes Up His Mind In Presidential Campaigns*. New York: Columbia University Press.

Ledeneva, Alena V. 1998. *Russia's Economy of Favours*. Cambridge, U.K.: Cambridge University Press.

Leeson, F. Nevada utility buys PGE for $3.1 billion. *The Oregonian*, 9 November 1999, AO5.

Lerner, Ralph. 1968. The Supreme Court as Republican schoolmaster. Pp. 127–80 in *The Supreme Court Review, 1967*, ed. Philip B. Kurland. Chicago: University of Chicago Press.

Leroux, C., and R. Grossman. Nation of strangers. *Chicago Tribune*, 11 October 1996.

Levi, Margaret. 1996. Social and unsocial capital: A review essay of Robert Putnam's *Making Democracy Work, Politics and Society* 24: 45–55.

Levitan, S., and G. Mangum. 1994. *Federal Human Resource Policy: From Kennedy to*

Clinton. Washington, D.C.: Center for Social Policy Studies, The George Washington University.

Liebowitz, D. J. 1997. Engendering globalization from the Mexican political front. Paper presented at International Studies Association Annual Meeting, Toronto, Canada.

Linz, Juan J. 1975. Totalitarian and authoritarian regimes. Pp. 175–411 in *Handbook of Political Science*, vol. 3, ed. Fred I. Greenstein and Nelson W. Polsby. Reading, Mass.: Addison-Wesley.

Lipset, Seymour Martin. 1995. Malaise and resiliency in America. *Journal of Democracy* 6, no. 3:4–18.

Lofland, J. 1993. *Polite Protesters: The American Peace Movement of the 1980s*. Syracuse, N.Y.: Syracuse University Press.

Lowndes, Vivien, Gerry Stoker, Lawrence Pratchett, David Wilson, Steve Leach, and Melvin Wingfield. 1998. *Enhancing Public Participation in Local Government*. London: Department of the Environment, Transport and Regions.

Luhmann, Niklas. 1988. Familiarity, confidence, trust: Problems and alternatives. Pp. 94–107 in *Trust: Making and Breaking Cooperative Relations*, ed. Diego Gambetta. Oxford: Blackwell.

Luker, K. 1984. *Abortion and the Politics of Motherhood*. Berkeley: University of California Press.

Maloney, William, Graham Smith, and Gerry Stoker. 2000. Social capital and urban governance: Adding a more contextualised "top down" perspective. *Political Studies* 48: forthcoming.

Mannheim, Karl. 1980. *Man and Society in an Age of Reconstruction*. New York: Routledge and Kegan Paul.

Marsden, Peter. 1982. Brokerage behavior in restricted exchange networks. Pp. 201–18 in *Social Structure and Network Analysis*, ed. P. Marsden and L. Nan. Beverly Hills, Calif.: Sage.

Mazaika, Rosemary. 1999. The Grande Ronde watershed program: A case study. *Administrative Theory and Praxis* 21, no. 1: 76–87.

McAdam, Doug. 1983. *Political Process and the Development of Black Insurgency*. Chicago, Ill.: University of Chicago Press.

———. 1988. *Freedom Summer*. New York and Oxford: Oxford University Press.

———. 1995. "Initiator" and "spin-off" movements: Diffusion processes in protest cycles. In *Repertoires and Cycles of Collective Action*, ed. M. Traugott. Durham, N.C.: Duke University Press.

McAdam, Doug, John D. McCarthy, and Mayer N. Zald, eds. 1996. *Comparative Perspectives on Social Movements*. Cambridge, U.K.: Cambridge University Press.

McCarthy, J. D. 1987. Pro-life and pro-choice mobilization: Infrastructure deficits and new technologies. In *Social Movements in an Organizational Society*, ed. M. N. Zald & J. D. McCarthy New Brunswick, N.J.: Transaction Publishers.

McCarthy, J. D., C. McPhail, and J. T. Crist. 1995. Institutional channeling of protest. Conference paper presented in Mount Pelerin, Switzerland.

McCarthy, J. D., and M. N. Zald. 1977. Resource mobilization and social movements. *American Journal of Sociology* 82: 1212–41.

McLaurin, Melton Alonzo. 1971. *Paternalism and Protest: Southern Mill Workers and Organized Labor, 1875–1905*. Westport, Conn.: Greenwood.

McPherson, R., and B. Deaton. 1992. The job training demonstration project. Phase 1: The conceptual design. Unpublished manuscript.

Melucci, Alberto. 1989. *Nomads of the Present*. Philadelphia: Temple University Press.

———, ed. 1984. *Altri Codici. Aree di Movimento nella Metropoli*. Bologna: Il Mulino.

Migdal, Joel S. 1988. *Strong Societies and Weak State: State-Society Relations and State Capabilities in the Third World*. Princeton, N.J.: Princeton University Press.

Mill, John Stuart. 1910. *Utilitarianism, Liberty and Representative Government*. London: J. M. Dent.

Mills, C. Wright. 1959. *The Power Elite*. New York: Oxford University Press.

Minkoff, Debra C. 1995. *Organizing for Equality: The Evolution of Women's and Racial Ethnic Organizations in America, 1955–1985*. New Brunswick, N.J.: Rutgers University Press.

———. 1997. The sequencing of social movements. *American Sociological Review* 62: 779–99.

Mishler, William, and Richard Rose. 2001. What are the origins of political trust? Testing institutional and cultural theories in post-communist societies. *Comparative Political Studies*, in press.

Misztal, Barbara A. 1996. *Trust in Modern Societies*. Cambridge, U.K.: Polity Press.

Moore, James, and Lewis Wingate. 1940. *Cabarrus Reborn: A Historical Sketch of the Founding and Development of Cannon Mills and Kannapolis*. Kannapolis, N.C.: Kannapolis Publishing Co.

Moore, Kelly. 1999. Political protest and institutional change: The anti-Vietnam War movement and American science. In *How Movements Matter*, ed. M. Giugni, D. McAdam, and C. Tilly. Minneapolis and London: University of Minnesota Press/UCL Press.

Morris, A. 1984. *The Origins of the Civil Rights Movement: Black Communities Organizing for Change*. New York: Free Press.

Muller, E. N., et al. 1987. Education, participation, and support for democratic norms. *Comparative Politics* 20: 19–33.

Muller, E., and M. Seligson. 1994. Civic culture and democracy: The question of causal relationship. *American Political Science Review* 88, no. 3: 635–52.

Nagel, J. H. 1987. *Participation*. Englewood Cliffs, N.J.: Prentice-Hall.

National Association of Secretaries of State. 1999. American youth attitudes on politics, citizenship, government and voting. Lexington, Ky.: National Association of Secretaries of State.

Neidhardt, Friedhelm, and Dieter Rucht. 1993. Auf dem Weg in die "Bewegungsgesellschaft"? *Soziale Welt* 44: 305–26.

Nelson, P. 1996. Internationalising economic and environmental policy: Transnational NGO networks and the World Bank's expanding influence. *Millennium: Journal of International Studies* 25, no. 3: 605–33.

Neumann, Sigmund. 1942. *Permanent Revolution*. New York: Harper.

New York Times. 1999. Union victory at plant in south is labor milestone. 25 June.

Newby, Howard. 1975. The Deferential Dialectic. *Comparative Studies in Society and History* 17: 139–64.

Newton, Kenneth. 1976. *Second City Politics*. Oxford: Clarenden Press.

———. 1996. The mass media and modern government. Wissenschaftszentrum Berlin fur Sozialforschung, Discussion Paper FS III 96–301.

———. 1997. Social capital and democracy. *American Behavioral Scientist* 40: 575–86.

———. 1999. Social and political trust. In *Critical Citizens: Global Support for Democratic Government*, ed. Pippa Norris. Oxford: Oxford University Press.

Niedermayer, Oskar. 1995. Trust and sense of community. Pp. 227–45 in *Public Opinion and Internationalized Governance*, ed. Oskar Niedermayer and Richard Sinnott. Oxford: Oxford University Press.

Norris, Pippa. 1996. Does television erode social capital? A reply to Putnam. PS (September): 1–7.

North Carolina Department of Commerce, State Data Center, MIS Section, EDIS Unit. 1997. *Cabarrus County Profile*. Website: <http://cmedis.commerce.state.nc.us/cmedis/outlook/cabacp.pdf>.

Norton, Anne. 1986. *Alternative Americas: A Reading of Antebellum Political Culture*. Chicago: University of Chicago Press.

Nowland-Forman, G. 1998. Purchase-of-service contracting, voluntary organizations, and civil society: Dissecting the goose that lays the golden egg. *American Behavioral Scientist* 42: 108–23.

Oberschall, Anthony. 1973. *Social Conflict and Social Movements*. Englewood Cliffs, N.J.: Prentice Hall.

OECD (Organization for Economic Cooperation and Development). N.d. Website: <http://www.oecd.org.>

———. 1999. *Historical Statistics, 1960–1997*. Paris: OECD.

Offe, C. 1985. New social movements: Challenging the boundaries of institutional politics. *Social Research* 52: 817–68.

Oliver, P., and G. Marwell. 1992. Mobilizing technologies for collective action. In *Frontiers in Social Movement Theory*, ed. A. D. Morris and C. M. Mueller. New Haven, Conn.: Yale University Press.

Olson, Mancur. 1982. *The Rise and Decline of Nations: Economic Growth, Stagflation, and Social Rigidities*. New Haven, Conn.: Yale University Press.

Orr, M. 1992. Urban regimes and human capital policies: A study of Baltimore. *Journal of Urban Affairs* 14, no. 2: 173–87.

Ortega Y Gassett, Jose. 1932. *The Revolt of the Masses*. New York: W.W. Norton.

Osterman, P., and B. Lautsch. 1996. *Project QUEST: A Report to the Ford Foundation*. Cambridge, Mass.: MIT Sloan School of Management.

Ostrom, Elinor. 1990. *Governing the Commons: The Evolution of Institutions for Collective Action*. New York: Cambridge University Press.

Otto, L. B. 1976. Social integration and the status attainment process. *American Journal of Sociology* 81: 1360–83.

Pagnucco, R. 1997. Transnational strategies of the Service for Peace and Justice in Latin America. In *Transnational Social Movements and Global Politics: Solidarity Beyond the State*, ed. J. Smith, C. Chatfield, and R. Pagnucco. Syracuse, N.Y.: Syracuse University Press. Paper presented at the April 1996 meeting of the Midwest Political Science Association, Chicago, Illinois.

Parkin, Frank. 1968. *Middle Class Radicalism*. Manchester, U.K.: Manchester University Press.

Parry, Geraint, George Moyser, and Neil Day. 1992. *Political Participation and Democracy in Britain*. Cambridge, U.K.: Cambridge Univesity Press.

Pateman, Carol. 1970. *Participation and Democratic Theory*. Cambridge, U.K.: Cambridge University Press.

Paxton, Pamela. 1999. Is social capital declining in the United States? A multiple indicator assessment. *American Journal of Sociology* 105, no. 1: 88–127.

Pelczynski, Z. A. 1988. Solidarity and "the rebirth of civil society." Pp. 361–80 in *Civil Society and the State*, ed. J. Keane. London: Verso.

Perrow, C. 1967. A framework for comparative organizational analysis. *American Sociological Review* 32: 194–208.

Pinard, Maurice. 1968. Mass society and political movements: A new formulation. *American Journal of Sociology* 73, no. 6: 682–90.

———. 1971. *The Rise of a Third Party: A Study of Crisis Politics*. Englewood Cliffs, N.J.: Prentice Hall.

Piven, Frances Fox, and Richard A. Cloward. 1979. *Poor People's Movements*. New York: Vintage.

Pizzorno, Alessandro. 1978. Political exchange and collective identity in industrial conflict. Pp. 277–98 in *The Resurgence of Class Conflict in Western Europe*, ed. C. Crouch and A. Pizzorno. New York: Holmes and Meier.

———. 1981. Interests and parties in pluralism. In *Organizing Interests in Western Europe: Pluralism, Corporatism, and the Transformation of Politics*, ed. Suzanne Berger. London: Cambridge University Press.

Porter, M. 1992. *Capital Choices: Changing the Way America Invests in Industry*. Washington, D.C.: Council on Competitiveness.

Portes, Alejandro. 1995. Economic sociology and the sociology of immigration: A conceptual overview. Pp. 1–41 in *The Economic Sociology of Immigration*, ed. Alejandro Portes. New York: Russell Sage.

———. 1998. Social capital: Its origins and applications in modern sociology. *Annual Review of Sociology* 24: 1–24.

Portes, Alejandro, and Patricia Landolt. 1996. The downside of social capital. *The American Prospect* (May-June): 18–21, 94.

Potter, David. 1976. *The Impending Crisis, 1848–1861*. New York: Harper and Row.

Powell, W. W. 1990. Neither market nor hierarchy: Network forms of organization. *Research in Organizational Behavior* 12: 295–336.

Powell, W., and P. DiMaggio. 1991. *The New Institutionalism in Organizational Analysis*. Chicago: University of Chicago Press.

Putnam, Robert D. (with R. Leonardi and R. Nanetti). 1993a. *Making Democracy Work: Civic Traditions in Modern Italy*. Princeton, N.J.: Princeton University Press.

Putnam, Robert D. 1993b. The prosperous community: Social capital and public life. *The American Prospect* 13: 35–42.

———. 1995a. Bowling alone: America's declining social capital. *Journal of Democracy* 6: 65–78.

———. 1995b. Tuning in, tuning out: The strange disappearance of social capital in America. 1995 Ithiel de Sola Lecture. *PS: Political Science and Politics* 29: 664–83.

———. 1996. The strange disappearance of civic America. *The American Prospect* 24: 34–48.

———. 1997. Democracy in America at century's end. Pp. 27–70 in *Democracy's Victory and Crisis*, ed. Axel Hadenius. New York: Cambridge University Press.

———. 2000. *Bowling Alone: The Collapse and Revival of American Community*. New York: Simon and Schuster.

Rahn, Wendy M., John Brehm, and Neil Carlson. 1997. National elections as institutions for generating social capital. Paper prepared for presentation at the 1997 annual meeting of the American Political Science Association, Washington, D.C., August 30–Sept. 1.

Raleigh News and Observer. 1985. Kannapolis: Still feeling change at Cannon. 1 September.

———. 1995. Fieldcrest ordered to make changes. 6 September.

———. 1997. Cannon employees reject union. 14 August.

Rankin, Edward L. 1987. *Cannon Mills Company 1887–1987: A Century of Progress.* Kannapolis, N.C.: Fieldcrest Cannon, Inc.

Reisman, David. 1961. *The Lonely Crowd.* New Haven: Yale University Press.

Richard, Patricia B., and John A. Booth, 1995. Sex and repression effects on political participation and support for democratic norms in urban Central America. Paper presented at the Midwest Political Science Association meeting, Chicago, April 6–8.

Rimer, S. 1996. The downsizing of America: The community trying to regroup. *New York Times News Service.* Reprinted in *The Oregonian*, 20 March, A12.

Robbins, D. B. 1971. *Experiment in Democracy: The Story of U.S. Citizen Organizations in Forging the Charter of the United Nations.* New York: The Parkside Press.

Robbins, Thomas. 1988. *Cults, Converts and Charisma: The Sociology of New Religious Movements.* London and Newbury Park, Calif.: Sage.

Rodgers, Daniel T. 1988. Of prophets and prophecy. Pp. 192–206 in *Reconsidering Tocqueville's Democracy in America*, ed. Stuart S. Eisenstadt. New Brunswick, N.J.: Rutgers University Press.

Roebuck, J. 1997. NGOs and the UN disarmament register. Doctoral Dissertation, Ohio State University.

Rogin, Michael. 1987. *Ronald Reagan, the Movie, and Other Episodes in Political Demonology.* Berkeley: University of California Press.

Room, Graham, ed. 1995. *Beyond the Threshold: The Measurement and Analysis of Social Exclusion.* Bristol, U.K.: Policy Press.

Rose, Richard. 1993. Contradictions between micro and macro-economic goals in post-communist societies. *Europe-Asia Studies* 45, no. 31 419–44.

———. 1998. *Getting Things Done with Social Capital: New Russia Barometer VII.* Studies in Public Policy No. 303. Glasgow: U. of Strathclyde.

———. 1999. Living in an antimodern society. *East European Constitutional Review*, 8, no. 1–2: 68–75.

———. 2000. How much does social capital add to individual health? A Survey Study of Russians. *Social Science and Medicine*, in press.

Rose, Richard, William Mishler, and Christian Haerpfer. 1998. *Democracy and Its Alternatives: Understanding Post-Communist Societies.* Cambridge: Polity Press; Baltimore: Johns Hopkins University Press.

Rose, Richard, and Doh Chull Shin. 2000. Democratization backwards: The problem of third-wave democracies. *British Journal of Political Science*, in press.

Rose, Richard, and Evgeny Tikhomirov. 1993. Who grows food in Russia and Eastern Europe? *Post-Soviet Geography* 34, no. 2: 111–26.

Rosenstone, S. J., and J. M. Hansen. 1993. *Mobilization, Participation, and Democracy in America*. New York: Macmillan.

Ross, T. 1995. The impact of industrial areas foundation community organizing on East Brooklyn: A study of East Brooklyn Congregations, 1978–1995. Doctoral dissertation, University of Maryland, College Park, Maryland.

Rousseau, Jean-Jacques. 1968. *The Social Contract*. New York: Penguin.

Rucht, Dieter. 1992. Studying the effects of social movements: Conceptualizations and problems. Paper for the European Consortium for Political Research Joint Sessions, Limerick, Ireland.

Rueschemeyer, D., E. H. Stephens, and J. D. Stephens. 1992. *Capitalist Development and Democracy*. Chicago: University of Chicago Press.

Rupp, Leila, and Verta Taylor. 1987. *Survival in the Doldrums: The American Women's Rights Movement, 1945 to the 1960s*. Columbus: Ohio State University Press.

Sahlins, Marshall. 1972. *Stone Age Economics*. Chicago: Aldine-Atherton.

Salamon, Lester M. 1995. *Partners in Public Service: Government-Nonprofit Relations in the Modern Welfare State*. Baltimore: Johns Hopkins University Press.

Salamon, Lester M., and K. Helmut Anheier. 1992a. In search of the nonprofit sector. I: The question of definitions. *Voluntas* 3, no. 2: 125–61.

———. 1992b. In search of the nonprofit sector. II: The problem of classification. *Voluntas* 3, no. 3: 263–309.

Sampson, R. J. 1988. Local friendship ties and community attachment in mass society: A multilevel systemic model. *American Sociological Review*, 53: 766–79.

Sandel, Michael J. 1984. The procedural republic and the unencumbered self. *Political Theory* 12 (February): 81–96.

———. 1996. *Democracy's Discontent: America in Search of a Public Philosophy*. Cambridge, Mass.: Harvard University Press.

Sartori, Giovanni. 1989. Video power. *Government and Opposition* 24, no. 1: 39–53.

Sassoon, Joseph. 1984. Ideology, symbolic action and rituality in social movements: The effects of organizational forms. *Social Science Information* 23:861–73.

Schlozman, K. L., and J. Tierney. 1986. *Organized Interests and American Democracy*. New York: Harper and Row.

Schmitter, Philippe C. 1974. Still the century of corporatism? *Review of Politics* 36 (January): 85–131.

———. 1995. Corporatism. Pp. 308–10 in *The Encyclopedia of Democracy*, vol. 1, ed. S. M. Lipset. Washington D.C.: Congressional Quarterly.

Schrag, P. G. 1992. *Global Action Nuclear Test Ban Diplomacy at the End of the Cold War*. Boulder: Colo.: Westview.

Schulman, M. D. and C. Anderson. 1999. The dark side of the force: A case study of restructuring and social capital. *Rural Sociology* 64, no. 3:351–72.

Scott, J. 1992. *Social Network Analysis*. A Handbook. Newbury Park, Calif.: Sage.

Sekul, Joseph D. 1983. Communities organized for public service: Citizen power and policy. In *The Politics of San Antonio*, ed. David R. Johnson, John A. Booth, and Richard J. Harris. Lincoln: University of Nebraska Press.

Seligman, Adam B. 1992. *The Idea of Civil Society*. New York: Free Press.

Seligson, A. L. 1996. Civic association and democratic participation in Central

America: A test of the Putnam thesis. Paper presented at the Midwest Political Science Association, Chicago.

Seligson, M. A., and J. A. Booth. 1993. Political culture and regime type. *Journal of Politics* 55: 777–92.

———, eds. 1995. *Elections and Democracy in Central America, Revisited*. Chapel Hill: University of North Carolina.

Seligson, M. A., and B. M. Gomez. 1989. Ordinary elections in extraordinary times. In *Elections and Democracy in Central America*, ed. J. A. Booth and M. A. Seligson. Chapel Hill: University of North Carolina.

Shi, Tianjian. 1997. *Political Participation in Beijing*. Cambridge, Mass.: Harvard University Press.

Shirley, D. 1997. *Community Organizing for Urban School Reform*. Austin: University of Texas Press.

Shlapentokh, Vladimir. 1989. *Public and Private Life of the Soviet People*. New York: Oxford University Press.

Siedentop, Larry. 1979. Two liberal traditions. Pp. 153–74 in *The Idea of Liberty: Essays in Honour of Isaiah Berlin*, ed. Alan Ryan. New York: Oxford University Press.

Sikkink, K. 1993. Human rights, principled issue-networks, and sovereignty in Latin America. *International Organization* 47: 411–41.

Simmel, Georg. 1950. *The Sociology of Georg Simmel*. New York: Free Press.

———. 1955 [1908]. Conflict. Pp. 11–123 in *Conflict and the Web of Group Affiliations*, trans. by K. Wolff. New York: Free Press.

Simon, Herbert A. 1997. *Models of Bounded Rationality*. Cambridge, Mass.: MIT Press.

Simpson, Richard L. 1991. Labor force integration and southern U.S. textile unionism. Pp. 83–403 in *Research in the Sociology of Work*, vol. 1, ed. by Richard L. Simpson and Ida H. Simpson. Greenwich, Conn.: JAI Press.

Sirianni, Carmen, and Lewis Friedland. 1995. Social capital and civic innovation: Learning and capacity building from the 1960s to the 1990s. Paper presented at the American Sociological Association Annual Meeting, Washington, D.C.

Skjelsbaek, K. 1972. The growth of international nongovernmental organizations in the twentieth century. Pp. 70–92 in *Transnational Relations and World Politics*, ed. R. Keohane and J. Nye. Cambridge, Mass.: Harvard University Press.

Skocpol, Theda. 1996a. The Tocqueville problem: Civic engagement in American democracy." Presidential address for the annual meeting of the Social Science History Association, New Orleans, 12 October.

———. 1996b. Unraveling from above, *The American Prospect* 25: 20–25.

Skocpol, Theda, and Kenneth Finegold. 1982. State capacity and economic intervention in the early New Deal. *Political Science Quarterly* 97: 255–78.

Smith, H. 1995. *Rethinking America*. New York: Random House.

Smith, Jackie. 1995. Transnational political processes and the human rights movement. Pp. 185–220 in *Research in Social Movements, Conflict and Change*, vol. 18, ed. L. Kriesberg, M. Dobkowski, and I. Walliman. Greenwood, Conn.: JAI Press.

———. 1997a. Characteristics of the modern transnational social movement sector. In *Transnational Social Movements and World Politics: Solidarity Beyond the State*, ed. J. Smith, C. Chatfield, and R. Pagnucco. Syracuse, N.Y.: Syracuse University Press.

———. 1997b. Global politics and transnational social movement strategies: The transnational campaign against trade in toxic wastes. In *Cross-National Influences and Social Movement Research*, ed. H. Kriesi, D. D. Porta, and D. Rucht.

———. 1999. Global politics and translational social movement strategies: The transnational campaign against trade in toxic wastes. Pp. 170–88 in *Social Movements in a Globalizing World*, ed. H. Kriesi, D. D. Porta, and D. Rucht. London: MacMillan.

Smith, Jackie, George Lopez, and Ronald Pagnucco. 1997. *Report on a Survey of Transnational Human Rights NGOs* (occasional paper). South Bend: The Joan B. Kroc Institute for International Peace Studies.

Smith, Tom W. 1997. Factors relating to misanthropy in contemporary American society. *Social Science Research* 26: 170–96.

Smith-Rosenberg, Carroll. 1986. *Disorderly Conduct: Visions of Gender in Victorian America*. New York: Oxford University Press.

Solomos, John, and Les Back. 1995. *Race, Politics and Social Change*. London: Routledge.

Soskice, D. 1990. Wage determination: The changing role of institutions in advanced industrialized societies. *Oxford Review of Economic Policy* 6, no. 4, 36–61.

———. 1991. The institutional infrastructure for international competitiveness: A comparative analysis of the UK and Germany." In *Economics for the New Europe*, ed. A. B. Atkinson and R. Brunetta. New York: New York University Press.

Stampp, Kenneth M. 1990. *America in 1857: A Nation on the Brink*. New York: Oxford University Press.

Standard and Poor's Register of Corporations, Directors and Executives, United States and Canada. 1931, 1961, 1991. New York: Standard and Poor's.

Stoecker, R. 1997. The CDC model of urban redevelopment: A critique and an alternative. *Journal of Urban Affairs* 19, no. 1: 1–22.

Stoker, Gerry. 1997. Local government reform in Britain after Thatcher. Pp. 225–34 in *Public Sector Reform*, ed. Jan-Erik Lane, London: Sage.

———. 1988. *The Politics of Local Government*. Basingstoke: Macmillan.

Stoker, Gerry, and David Wilson. 1991. The lost world of British local pressure groups. *Public Policy and Administration* 6: 20–34.

Stoker, Gerry, and Stephen Young. 1993. *Cities in the 1990s*. Harlow: Longman.

Stolle, D. 2000. Communities of trust: Social capital and public action in comparative perspective. Doctoral dissertation, Department of Politics, Princeton University.

Stolle, D., and T. R. Rochon. 1998. Are all associations alike? Member diversity, associational type, and the creation of social capital. *American Behavioral Scientist* 42: 47–65.

———. 1999. The myth of American exceptionalism: A three nation comparison of associational membership and social capital. In *Social capital and European democracy*, ed. J. van Deth, M. Maraffi, K. Newton, and P. Whitely. London: Routledge.

Stone, C. N. 1989. *Regime politics: Governing Atlanta, 1946–1988*. Lawrence: University Press of Kansas.

Streeck, W. 1992. *Social Institutions and Economic Performance*. Newbury Park, Calif.: Sage.

Swank, D. 1996. Culture, institutions, and economic growth: Theory, recent evidence, and the role of communitarian polities. *American Journal of Political Science* 40: 660–79.

Swenson, P. 1991. Bringing capital back in, or social democracy reconsidered: employer power, cross-class alliances, and centralization of industrial relations in Denmark and Sweden. *World Politics* 43: 513–44.

Szerszinski, Bron. 1995. Entering the stage: Strategies of environmental communication in the UK. In Framing and Communicating Environmental Issues, Research Report, Commission of the European Communities, DGXII, ed. Klaus Eder, Florence and Lancaster: European University Institute/CSEC, University of Lancaster.

Tarrow, Sidney, 1994. *Power in Movements, Social Movements, Collective Action and Politics.* Cambridge, U.K.: Cambridge University Press.

———. 1996. Making social science work across space and time: A critical reflection on Robert Putnam's *Making Democracy Work. American Political Science Review* 90: 389–97.

Taylor, Charles. 1990. Modes of Civil Society. *Public Culture* 3: 95–118.

Taylor, Marilyn. 1997. The impact of local government changes on the voluntary and community sectors. Pp. 74–117 in *New Perspectives on Local Government*, ed. Robin Hambleton. London: Joseph Rowntree Foundation.

Taylor, Verta. 1989. Social movement continuity: The women's movement in abeyance. *American Sociological Review* 54: 761–75.

Taylor, Verta, and Marieke Van Willigen. 1996. Women's self Help and the reconstruction of gender: The postpartum support and breast cancer movements. *Mobilization* 1: 123–42.

Taylor, Verta, and Nancy Whittier. 1992. Collective identity in social movement communities: Lesbian feminist mobilization. Pp. 104–32 in *Frontiers in Social Movement Theory*, ed. A. Morris and C. McClurg Mueller. New Haven: Yale University Press.

Teachman, Jay D., Kathleen Paasch, and Karen Carver. 1996. Social capital and dropping out of school early, *Journal of Marriage and the Family* 58 (August): 773–83.

———. 1997. Social capital and the generation of human capital. *Social Forces* 75, no. 4: 1343–59.

Tillman, A. D. 1998 *Corporate contributions in 1996: A research report.* New York: The Conference Board.

Tilly, Charles 1984. Social Movements and National Politics. In *Statemaking and Social Movements: Essays in History and Theory*, ed. C. Bright and S. Harding. Ann Arbor: University of Michigan Press.

———. 1998. *Durable Inequality*. Berkeley and Los Angeles: University of California Press.

———. 1999. From interactions to outcomes in social movements. Pp. 253–70 in *How Movements Matter*, ed. M. Giugni, D. McAdam, and C. Tilly. Minneapolis, Minn., and London: University of Minnesota Press/UCL Press.

Time. 1996. Bowling together: Civic engagement in America isn't disappearing but reinventing itself. 22 July.

Tocqueville, Alexis de. 1968. *Democracy in America.* London: Fontana.

———. 1969a. *Democracy in America.* Ed. J. P. Mayer. Garden City, N.Y.: Doubleday.

———. 1969b. *Democracy in America.* New York: Harper and Row.

Tolbert, Charles M., J. J. Beggs, and G. D. Boudreaux. 1995. *PUMS-L Data and As-*

sociated Files: CD-Rom Edition. Machine-readable data files prepared by the Louisiana Population Data Center, Louisiana State University and LSU Agricultural Center. Baton Rouge: The Center.

Truman, David B. 1971. *The Governmental Process: Political Interest and Public Opinion.* 2nd ed. New York: Knopf.

Tyrrell, Ian R. 1979. *Sobering Up: From Temperance to Prohibition in Antebellum America, 1800–1860.* Westport, Conn.: Greenwood Press.

Union of International Associations. 1996. *Yearbook of International Organizations.* Brussels: Union of International Associations.

United Nations Development Programme (UNDP). 1993. *Human Development Report.* New York: Oxford University Press.

Uslaner, Eric M. N.d. Faith, hope, and charity: Social capital, trust, and collective action. Mimeo.

———. 1999. Morality plays: Social capital and moral behaviour in Anglo-American democracies. In *Social Capital and European Democracy,* ed. J. van Deth, M. Maraffi, K. Newton, and P. Whitely. London: Routledge.

Uvin, Peter. 1998. *Aiding Violence: The Development Enterprise in Rwanda.* West Hartford, Conn.: Kumarian Press.

van Deth, Jan W. 1996 Social and political involvement: An overview and reassessment of empirical findings. Paper presented at the Joint Sessions of Workshops of the European Consortium for Political Research, Oslo.

Van Til, John. 1988. *Mapping the Third Sector: Voluntarism in a Changing Social Economy.* New York: The Foundation Center.

Van Zoonen, Liesbet. 1996. A dance of death: New social movements and mass media. Pp. 201–22 in *Political Communication in Action,* ed. D. Paletz. Cress Hill, N.J.: Hampton Press.

Verba, Sidney, and Norman H. Nie. 1972. *Participation in America.* New York: Harper and Row.

Verba, Sidney, N. H. Nie, and J.-O. Kim. 1978. *The Modes of Democratic Participation.* Beverly Hills, Calif.: Sage.

Verba, Sidney, Kay Lehman Schlozman, and Henry E. Brady. 1995. *Voice and Equality: Civic Voluntarism in American Politics.* Cambridge, Mass.: Harvard University Press.

Veugelers, J., and M. Lamont. 1991. France: Alternative locations for public debate. In *Between states and markets,* ed. R. Wuthnow. Princeton, N.J.: Princeton University Press.

Vidal, A. C. 1992. *Rebuilding Communities: A National Study of Urban Community Development Corporations.* New York: Community Development Research Center, Graduate School of Management and Urban Policy, New School for Social Research.

von Eschen, Donald, Jerome Kirk, and Maurice Pinard. 1971. The organizational substructure of disorderly politics. *Social Forces* 49: 529–44.

Walker, J. 1983. The origins and maintenance of interest groups in America. *American Political Science Review* 77:390–406.

Walker, J. L., Jr. 1991. *Mobilizing Interest Groups in America: Patrons, Professions, and Social Movements.* Ann Arbor, Mich.: University of Michigan Press.

Walker, R. B. J. 1995. Social Movements/World Politics. *Millennium* 23, no. 3: 669–700.

Wall, Ellen, Gabriele Ferrazzi, and Frans Schryer. 1998. Getting the goods on social capital, *Rural Sociology* 63, no. 2: 300–22.

Walth, B., and J. Barnett. 1996. Enron on a mission to reshape world energy business. *The Oregonian*, 8 December, A1.

Walzer, Michael. 1991. The idea of civil society: A path to social reconstruction.
Dissent 38: 293–304.

———. 1992. The civil society argument. Pp. 89–107 in *Dimensions of Radical Democracy: Pluralism, Citizenship, Community*, ed. Chantel Mouffe. New York:
Verso.

Wandersman, Abraham, Paul Florin, Robert Friedmann, and Ron Meier. 1987.
Who participates, who does not, and why? *Sociological Forum* 2 (summer):
534–55.

Wapner, P. 1995. Politics beyond the state: Environmental activism and world civic
politics. *World Politics* 47:311–40.

———. 1996. *Environmental Activism and World Civic Politics*. New York: City University of New York Press.

Warren, Mark. 1995. Social Capital and Community Empowerment: Religion and
Political Organization in the Texas Industrial Areas Foundation. Doctoral dissertation, Harvard University, Cambridge, Mass.

———. Forthcoming. *Dry Bones Rattling: Community Building to Revitalize American
Democracy*. Princeton, N.J.: Princeton University Press.

Warren, Mark R., J. Phillip Thompson, and Susan Saegert. 1999. Social capital and
poor communities: A framework for analysis. Paper presented at the conference
on Social Capital and Poor Communities: Building and Using Social Assets to
Combat Poverty, New York City, February.

Wasserman, Stanley, and Katherine Faust. 1994. *Social Network Analysis. Methods
And Applications*. Cambridge, U.K.: Cambridge University Press.

Waterman, R. H., Jr. 1994. *What America Does Right*. New York: Penguin Books.

Wattenberg, M. P. 1990. *The Decline of American Political Parties 1952–1988*. Cambridge; Mass.: Harvard University Press.

Weber, Max. 1958. The Protestant sects and the spirit of capitalism. Pp. 302–22 in
From Max Weber: Essays in Sociology, ed. H. H. Gerth and C. Wright Mills. New
York: Oxford University Press.

———. 1968. *Economy and Society*. Ed. Guenther Roth and Claus Wittich. Berkeley:
University of California Press.

Weick, K. 1979. *The Social Psychology of Organizing*. 2nd ed. New York: Random
House.

———. 1995. *Sense Making in Organizations*. Thousand Oaks, Calif., London, New
Delhi: Sage Books.

Wellman, B., and S. D. Berkowitz. 1988. *Social Structures: A Network Approach*.
Cambridge, Mass.: Cambridge University Press.

White, D. F., and T. J. Crimmins. 1980. How Atlanta grew: Cool heads, hot air,
and hard work. In *Urban Atlanta: Redefining the role of the city*, ed. Andrew M.
Hamer. Monograph 84, College of Business Administration. Georgia State University, Atlanta.

———. 1999. *Constitutional Construction: Divided Powers and Constitutional Meaning*.
Cambridge, Mass.: Harvard University Press.

Wilentz, Sean. 1988. Many democracies: On Tocqueville and Jacksonian America. Pp. 207–28 in *Reconsidering Tocqueville's* Democracy in America, ed. Stuart S. Eisenstadt. New Brunswick, N.J.: Rutgers University Press.

Willetts, P. 1996. *The Conscience of the World: The Influence of NGOs in the United Nations System.* London: C. Hurst.

Williams, Bernard. 1988. Formal structures and social reality. In *Trust: Making and Breaking Cooperative Relations*, ed. Diego Gambetta. Oxford: Blackwell.

Williams, P. J. 1994. Dual transitions from authoritarian rule: Popular and electoral democracy in Nicaragua. *Comparative Politics* 27: 169–85.

Williamson, Joel. 1984. *The Crucible of Race: Black/White Relations in the American South Since Emancipation.* New York: Oxford University Press.

Wilson, John, and Marc Musick. 1997. Who cares? Toward an integrated theory of volunteer work. *American Sociological Review* 62 (October): 694–713.

Wilson, R. H., and P. Menzies. 1997. The colonias water bill: Communities demanding change. Pp. 229–74 in *Public Policy and Community: Activism and Governance in Texas*, ed. R. H. Wilson. Austin: University of Texas Press.

Wilson, William Julius. 1987. *The Truly Disadvantaged.* Chicago: University of Chicago Press.

——. 1996. *When Work Disappears: The World of the New Urban Poor.* New York: Knopf.

Wittner, L. 1997. *Resisting the Bomb: A History of the World Nuclear Disarmament Movement, 1954–1970*, vol. 2. Stanford, Calif.: Stanford University Press.

Wolfinger, Raymond F., et al. 1964. America's radical right: Politics and ideology. In *Ideology and Discontent*, ed. David Apter. New York: Free Press.

Woliver, Laura R. 1993. *From Outrage to Action: The Politics Of Grass-Roots Dissent.* Urbana: University of Illinois Press.

Wong, P. 1997. The indigent health care package. Pp. 95–118 in *Public Policy and Community: Activism and Governance in Texas*, ed. R. H. Wilson. Austin: University of Texas Press.

Wood, Richard L. 1994. Faith in action: Religious resources for political success in three congregations. *Sociology of Religion* 55, no. 4: 381–401.

——. 1995. Faith in action: Religion, race, and the future of democracy. Doctoral dissertation, University of California, Berkeley.

Woodward, J. 1980. *Industrial Organization: Theory and Practice.* 2nd ed. Oxford: Oxford University Press.

Woolcock, Michael. 1998. Social capital and economic development: Toward a theoretical synthesis and policy framework. *Theory and Society* 27: 151–208.

World Bank, 1996. *From Plan to Market.* Washington D.C.: World Bank World Development Report.

World Values Study Group. 1994. *World Values Survey, 1981–1984 and 1990–1993.* Ann Arbor, Mich.: Inter-university Consortium for Political and Social Research.

Wuthnow, Robert. 1994. *Sharing the Journey: Support Groups and America's New Quest for Community.* New York: Free Press.

——, ed. 1991. *Between State and Markets: The Voluntary Sector in Comparative Perspective.* Princeton, N.J.: Princeton University Press.

Yamagishi, T., and M. Yamagishi. 1994. Trust and commitment in the United States and Japan. *Motivation and Emotion* 18, no. 2: 129–66.

Yates, M., and J. Youniss. 1996. Community service and political-moral identity in adolescents. *Journal of Research on Adolescence* 6: 271–84.

———. 1999. *Roots of Civic Identity: International Perspectives on Community Service and Youth Activism*. New York: Cambridge University Press.

Yearley, Steven. 1992. *The Green Case*. London and New York: Routledge.

Young, Marjorie W., ed. 1963. *Textile Leaders of the South*. Columbia, S.C.: The R. L. Bryan Company.

Young, Stephen. 1999. Participation strategies and local environmental politics: Local agenda 21. Pp. 181–97 in *The New Politics of British Local Governance*, ed. Gerry Stoker. Basingstoke: Macmillan.

Youniss, J., and M. Yates. 1997. *Community Service and Social Responsibility in Youth: Theory and Policy*. Chicago: University of Chicago Press.

Zald, Mayer N. 1996. Culture, ideology, and strategic framing. Pp. 26–74 in *Comparative perspectives on social movements*, ed. D. McAdam, J. D. McCarthy, and Mayer N. Zald. New York: Cambridge University Press.

Zingraff, Rhonda. 1991. Facing Extinction? Pp. 199–216 in *Hanging by a Thread: Social Change in Southern Textiles*, ed. Jeffery Leiter, Michael Schulman, and Rhonda Zingraff. Ithaca, N.Y.: ILR Press.

Zucker, Lynne. 1988. *Institutional Patterns and Organizations: Culture and Environment*. Cambridge, Mass.: Ballinger.

Zysman, J. 1983. *Governments, Markets, and Growth*. Ithaca, N.Y.: Cornell University Press.

Contributors

Cynthia Anderson is Assistant Professor of Sociology at Iowa State University. Her research appears in *Rural Sociology, Journal of Rural Studies, Gender and Society,* and *Work and Occupations.* She is the author of *The Social Consequences of Economic Restructuring in the Textile Industry: Change in a Southern Mill Village* (Garland Press, 2000) and co-editor of *Feminist Foundations: Towards Transforming Sociology* (Sage Publications, 1998). In addition to analyses of social capital across communities, Anderson is currently examining gender, service industry employment, and income inequality across labor market areas.

Sheri Berman is Assistant Professor of Politics at Princeton University and is the author of *The Social Democratic Moment: Ideas and Politics in the Making of Interwar Europe* (Harvard University Press, 1998), as well as articles on political parties, policy making, and the collapse of the Weimar Republic. Her research interests include comparative political economy, European politics and political development.

Jeffrey M. Berry is Professor of Political Science at Tufts University. He received his A.B. from the University of California at Berkeley and his Ph.D. from Johns Hopkins University. His publications include *The Interest Group Society* (1997), *The Rebirth of Urban Democracy* (1993, with Kent Portney and Ken Thomson), and *Lobbying for the People* (1977). His current research focuses on citizen groups in national politics.

John A. Booth is Regents Professor of Political Science at the University of North Texas. He received his Ph.D. from the University of Texas at Austin (1975). He is author of *The End and the Beginning: The Nicaraguan Revolution* and *Costa Rica: Quest for Democracy,* co-author of *Understanding Central America,* and co-editor of *Elections and Democracy in Central America, Revisited.* He has published articles and chapters on revolution, political participation and culture, civil society, social capital, and democratization in various journals and anthologies.

Mario Diani is Professor of Sociology and Head of the Department of Government at the University of Strathclyde in Glasgow. He has published extensively on social movement theory and methodology, ethnonationalist movements, and environmental politics. His most recent books include *Social Movements* (Blackwell, 1999, with D. della Porta) and *Green Networks* (Edinburgh University Press, 1995). He is the European editor of *Mobilization.*

Carla M. Eastis is a doctoral candidate in the Department of Sociology at Yale University whose research interests include organizational sociology, political institutions, and social movements. Her dissertation research examines the emergence of new issues and organizational networks in the U.S. environmental movement from 1970 to the present.

Bob Edwards is Assistant Professor and Graduate Director in the Department of Sociology at East Carolina University. His core research interests center on social movements, organizations, and contentious politics, especially in the environmental arena. His current research examines different forms of social capital and their effect on organizational behavior. His research has appeared in the *American Sociological Review, Journal of Democracy, Journal of Public Policy, Nonprofit and Voluntary Sector Quarterly,* and *Sociological Forum*.

Michael W. Foley is Associate Professor of Politics at Catholic University of America. His work on post–civil war civil society in El Salvador has been published as "Laying the Groundwork: The struggle for civil society in El Salvador," in the *Journal of Interamerican Studies and World Affairs* (spring 1996). He is co-editor with Virginia Hodgekinson of the forthcoming *Civil Society: A Reader*. He is currently completing a book on the role of peasant organizations in the recent rural conflicts in Mexico. He is director of a major study of the role of religion in the social and civic incorporation of new immigrants in the Washington, D.C., area.

Andrew Greeley is a professor at the University of Chicago and the University of Arizona. He earned his Ph.D. at the University of Chicago in 1962. He also serves on the staff of the National Opinion Research Center. His principle research interest is in the sociology of religion. His most recent books on the subject are *Religious Change in America* (Harvard University Press, 1989) and *Religion as Poetry* (Transaction, 1996).

Charles H. Heying is Assistant Professor of Urban Studies and Planning at Portland State University, Portland, Oregon. His research interests include civic elites, social networks, and urban politics. His most recent publication, co-authored with Mathew Burbank and Greg Andranovich, "Antigrowth politics or piecemeal resistance: Citizen opposition to Olympic-related economic growth," appeared in the January 2000 edition of *Urban Affairs Review*.

Lane Kenworthy is Assistant Professor of Sociology at Emory University. He is author of *In Search of National Economic Success* (Sage, 1995) and of recent articles in *American Journal of Sociology, Social Forces, Social Science Quarterly, Comparative Political Studies, European Journal of Political Research,* and *Law and Social Inquiry*. His research focuses on the causes and consequences of differing economic institutional arrangements, policy choices, and performance patterns across industrialized nations.

William Maloney is a Reader in the Department of Politics and International Relations, University of Aberdeen, Scotland. His research interests are in public policy and interest group politics. His major publications include: *Managing Policy Change in Britain* (Edinburgh University Press, 1995; with J. J. Richardson), *The Protest Business?: Mobilizing Campaign Groups* (Manchester University Press, 1997; with Grant Jordan), and *The European Automobile Industry: Multi-Level Governance, Policy and Politics* (Routledge, 1999; with A. M. McLaughlin).

Jeffrey A. McLellan is a research associate at the Life Cycle Institute at the Catholic University of America. His current work is focused on the impact of community service on the social and moral development of youth.

Debra C. Minkoff is Associate Professor of Sociology at the University of Washington. She received her Ph.D. from Harvard in 1991. She is the author of *Organizing for Equality: The Evolution of Women's and Racial-Ethnic Organizations in America, 1955–1985* (Rutgers, 1995) and a number of published articles on the organizational ecology of the feminist and civil rights movements. Her current research focuses on the development of a national social movement sector in the United States since the 1960s.

Kenneth Newton is Professor of Politics and Government at the University of Southampton and Executive Director of the European Consortium for Political Research. His research interests cover media politics, mass political opinion, and comparative politics. Recent books include *The Political Data Handbook* (Oxford, 1997; with Jan-Erik Lane and David McKay), *The Politics of the New Europe* (Addison-Wesley, 1997; with Ian Budge), and *Beliefs in Government* (Oxford, 1998; with Max Kaase), which was one of a five-volume series on beliefs in government.

Kent E. Portney is Professor of Political Science at Tufts University. He received his A.B. from Rutgers University and his Ph.D. from Florida State University. His publications include *The Rebirth of Urban Democracy* (Brookings Institute, 1993; with Jeffrey M. Berry and Ken Thomson), *Siting Hazardous Waste Treatment Facilities: The NIMBY Syndrome* (Auburn House, 1991), and *Controversial Issues in Environmental Policy* (Sage, 1992). His current research focuses on the communitarian foundations of sustainable communities.

Patricia Bayer Richard is Dean of University College and Professor of Political Science at Ohio University. She received her Ph.D. from Syracuse University in 1975. She has published scholarly articles on elections and campaigns, public opinion, gender issues, and civil society and social capital in such journals as *American Journal of Political Science, Journal of Politics, Social Science Quarterly, Women's Studies Quarterly*, and chapters in such books as *Elections and Democracy in Central America, Revisited; The Practice of Political Communication; The Politics of Abortion in the American States*.

Thomas R. Rochon is Executive Director of the Graduate Record Examination at the Educational Testing Service. He is the author of *Mobilizing for Peace* (Princeton, 1988), *Culture Moves: Ideas, Activism and Changing Values* (Princeton, 1998), *The Netherlands: Negotiating Sovereignty in an Interdependent World* (Westview, 1999), and numerous articles on European politics and political behavior.

Richard Rose is Director of the Centre for the Study of Public Policy at the University of Strathclyde in Glasgow. He has authored more than forty books in comparative politics and public policy and his works have been translated into seventeen languages. His most recent co-authored book is *Democracy and Its Alternatives: Understanding Post-Communist Societies* (Johns Hopkins, 1998).

Michael D. Schulman is Professor of Sociology at North Carolina State University and Adjunct Professor of Health Behavior and Health Education at the UNC–Chapel Hill School of Public Health. His publications on the textile industry have appeared in *Social Forces, The Sociological Quarterly, Rural Sociology,* and in *Hanging by a Thread* (ILR Press, 1991), which he co-edited. His current research includes projects on rural restructuring, sustainable community development, and occupational hazards and injuries among working youth. He was named an Alumni Foundation Distinguished Graduate Professor.

Graham Smith is Lecturer in Politics at the University of Southampton, U.K. His research interests include urban politics, innovative democratic institutions, and green politics. He is the author (with James Connelly) of *Politics and the Environment: From Theory to Practice* (Routledge, 1999) and a number of articles on citizens' juries, deliberative democracy, and social capital.

Jackie Smith is Assistant Professor of Sociology at the State University of New York at Stony Brook. She is co-editor of *Transnational Social Movements and Global Politics: Solidarity Beyond the State* (Syracuse University Press, 1997) and of numerous articles on the politics of transnational social movements. Smith's current research focuses on civil society responses to global economic institutions. She did her graduate work at the University of Notre Dame's Kroc Institute for International Peace Studies and is currently serving as a co-editor of *International Sociology*.

Gerry Stoker is Professor of Politics at the University of Manchester. His publications include *Theories of Urban Politics* (Sage, 1995), *The New Politics of British Local Governance* (St. Martin's, 2000), *Theory and Methods in Political Science* (St. Martin's, 1995), and *The New Management of British Local Governance* (St. Martin's, 1999). He was Programme Director of the ESRC Local Governance Programme.

Dietlind Stolle (Ph.D., Princeton University) is Assistant Professor in Political Science at the University of Pittsburgh. Her dissertation is titled "Communities of trust: Social capital and public action in comparative perspective." She has published on social capital in *American Behavioral Scientist* and in *Political Psychology*. She was co-director (with Marc Hooghe) of the European Consortium for Political Research Workshop on Voluntary Associations, Social Capital and Interest Mediation in 2000.

Mark R. Warren is Assistant Professor of Sociology at Fordham University in New York City. He received his Ph.D. in sociology from Harvard University in 1995. Warren is the author of a book on the Texas Industrial Areas Foundation, entitled *Dry Bones Rattling: Community Building to Revitalize American Democracy* (Princeton, 2001). He is also co-editing a volume focused on the role of social capital in combating poverty in the United States.

Keith Whittington is Assistant Professor of Politics and John Maclean, Jr., Presidential Preceptor at Princeton University. He is the author of *Constitutional Construction: Divided Powers and Constitutional Meaning* (Harvard, 1999) and *Constitutional Interpretation: Textual Meaning, Original Intent, and Judicial Review* (Kansas, 1999), as well as articles on American constitutional theory and development, federalism, and the presidency.

Richard L. Wood earned his doctoral degree in political sociology and the sociology of religion from the University of California, Berkeley, in 1995. His doctoral research was an ethnographic study of community organizing. Now on the faculty at the University of New Mexico, he continues to write on religion and social action, as well as on the political sociology of urban policing through a grant from the National Institute of Justice.

Miranda Yates is the Director of Transitional Living Programs at Covenant House California. Previously, she was a project director at the Menninger Foundation's Child and Family Center and a postdoctoral fellow at Brown University's Center for the Study of Race and Ethnicity in America. Dr. Yates received a Ph.D. in psychology (human development) from the Catholic University of America. Her research has focused on identity development and urban adolescents' participation in community activism.

James Youniss is Professor of Psychology at the Catholic University of America. He is co-author with Miranda Yates of *Community Service and Social Responsibility in Youth* (Chicago, 1997) and co-editor of *Roots of Civic Identity: International Perspectives on Community Service and Activism* (Cambridge, 1998).

Index